CROSSING THE RED LINE

CROSSING THE RED LINE

BIDEN, HIS ADVISORS, AND ISRAEL'S WAR IN GAZA

AKBAR SHAHID AHMED

W. W. NORTON & COMPANY

Independent Publishers Since 1923

Printed in the United States of America
First Edition

For information about special discounts for bulk purchases, please contact W. W. Norton Special Sales at specialsales@wwnorton.com or 800-233-4830

Manufacturing by Lakeside Book Company
Production manager: Devon Zahn

ISBN 978-1-324-11819-0

W. W. Norton & Company, Inc., 500 Fifth Avenue, New York, NY 10110
www.wwnorton.com

W. W. Norton & Company Ltd., 15 Carlisle Street, London W1D 3BS

Authorized EU representative: EAS, Mustamäe tee 50, 10621 Tallinn, Estonia

10 9 8 7 6 5 4 3 2 1

For Zaib-un-Nissa Hamidullah, a trailblazer who questioned the powerful against tremendous odds, and my Bibi June. She hoped to see her books published in America; without her, this one would not be.

And for Shahid Nazir Ahmed, whose work resonated more than he knew.

CONTENTS

AUTHOR'S NOTE

Based on interviews with more than 150 officials and others involved, as well as dozens of documents, this book examines why the Biden administration acted as it did regarding Gaza and whether it could have been more humane and less feckless about its own stated goals and values. I discussed the war and Biden's policy with nearly every key player in the policymaking process. Much of the information here comes from such conversations with my sources, many of whom I have known for years. Nearly all requested some degree of anonymity, citing fear of retaliation, often from their own former and potentially future colleagues in the U.S. government, but also from Israel or its backers. I have noted in the text where material came from personal interviews with me, identifying each source in a way with which that source was comfortable. Sometimes I also cite my own articles where they offer a more detailed discussion of a point being made. I have also verified through additional reporting most of the information and impressions that came to me from individuals who asked not to be named. I have included many individuals' specific responses to my discussion of them in the text of the work, but some responses are shown in endnotes. Joe Biden, Jacob Lew, and Lloyd Austin did not address requests for comment. Brett McGurk broadly denied certain specific allegations concerning him but otherwise declined to speak with me about the book. I have identified in the text the few specific denials he conveyed to me.

CROSSING THE RED LINE

INTRODUCTION

IN THE SPRING OF 2025, AS I WAS WRITING THIS BOOK AMID the mounting chaos of the second Trump presidency, a Biden White House official I had chased for more than a year called me. He was ready to talk. It was when I brought up Rafah, the southernmost town in the Gaza Strip, that the former official became heated and snapped, "We can have a huge argument about this."

I didn't want a fight, just an honest reflection. A year earlier, Rafah's fate had encapsulated America's enabling of staggering Israeli violence in Gaza and the hope the Biden administration might change course. President Joe Biden repeatedly said that invading the town without a plan to limit suffering among the more than 1.4 million Palestinians sheltering there would cross a red line. It was part of a consistent pattern of suggestions that U.S. support for the Israeli offensive in Gaza had some limit after Israeli attacks had already killed at least 34,725 Palestinians. Ultimately, Israel stormed Rafah in May 2024 without meeting Biden's conditions. The Biden administration never altered its policy. The episode sent the clearest signal the administration's approach amounted to impunity for Tel Aviv and complicity in Washington. And subsequently, with more brazen tactics—like implementing a plan for northern Gaza that U.S. officials privately called ethnic cleansing—and greater rigidity in U.S.-backed talks to end the war, Israel proved it got the message.

But a year later, the former Biden aide tried to present the administration's fickleness about its red line as a victory: "Our approach to Rafah was pretty heavy-handed" toward Israeli prime minister Benjamin Netanyahu. Arguing the administration made the assault less devastating than past Israeli offensives in Gaza's other cities, he claimed the rate of Israeli killing "slowed and it was not just because there was nobody left to kill." The narrative was at once chilling and clarifying: I was even more certain the moment when Israel crossed Biden's red line is at the heart of any reckoning with the ruinous thinking and choices of the president and his advisors.

This is why blurring that line has been a priority for many in the administration, one they have pursued by downplaying a period that killed at least three thousand Palestinians, pushed more than 1 million into harsher conditions, crippled Gaza's humanitarian aid network, and closed the only entry or exit point for the strip that Israel did not fully control. Throughout the sixteen months during which the Biden administration oversaw America's role in the Gaza war, U.S. officials asked journalists and the public to join them in ethical compromises and distorted reality—in a gray zone. With each deflection away from violence that bore American fingerprints, each claim it was impossible to know whether war crimes occurred, and each denial that Israeli conduct crossed plain and measurable thresholds for consequences from the United States, the administration promoted uncertainty and an acceptance of bloodshed to dodge accountability. The question officials appeared to prioritize was not whether the U.S.-Israeli campaign in Gaza was appropriate or wise but how much U.S.-enabled death and misery among civilians was the right amount.

Gaza is roughly the size of Detroit and home to more than three times as many people: around 2.2 million, nearly half of them children. After October 7, 2023, the U.S.-backed Israeli offensive displaced nearly all of them while destroying or damaging 92 percent of homes in the region. An accurate measure of the killing and the war-related nonviolent deaths from hunger and disease has been elusive. Between estimates from researchers drawing on both official figures widely understood as an undercount and an independent survey, and projecting the number of Palestinians buried under rubble, the war's toll in the Biden era appears to exceed 84,000 as of this writing. That loss represents more than 4 percent of Gaza's population.[1] At least 171,000 have been wounded, roughly a quarter sustaining life-altering injuries. Among the dead were thousands of entire families and victims such as toddlers with sniper bullets in their brains. The grim group of survivors included the highest number of child amputees anywhere in the world and thousands of children falling into a new category medical workers were forced to create during the war: Wounded Child No Surviving Family, or WCNSF.

Israel's U.S.-backed offensive and blockade of supplies for Gaza pulverized the resources Palestinians might have counted on to endure the war: 94 percent of Gaza's hospitals were attacked, with many shuttered and hundreds of health workers killed and detained; 86 percent of cropland and 97 percent of schools were damaged; and man-made shortages of basic food, clean water, medicine, and other supplies traumatized and wore away at hundreds of thousands.[2] "It's like a nuclear bomb has hit," Suhair al-Absi, a mother of seven, said upon returning to her Gaza City neighborhood in October 2025.[3] In Gaza and in Lebanon, where the Biden administration helped Israel wage a concurrent war, Israeli forces deployed complex tools enabling annihilation at a breathtaking scale, such as remote-controlled, explosive-packed armored vehicles; artificial intelligence–driven bombing procedures; and booby-trapped pagers and walkie-talkies. The post–October 7 campaigns made warfare more deadly in a way some have cheered and that will long haunt many Palestinians and Lebanese. The devastation would be impossible without American policymakers and taxpayers arming Israel and shielding it from ramifications. Hamas, the Palestinian militant group, began the war with a gruesome incursion into Israel in which Hamas fighters and fellow invaders slaughtered and kidnapped hundreds of innocents and ravaged dozens of communities; its strategies and disregard for human rights principles caused widespread pain then and for months afterward. But Washington and Tel Aviv largely determined the scale of the nightmare that followed Hamas's move, fueling the deadliest chapter in eighty years of Israeli-Palestinian conflict.

Years of reporting on the team's Gaza decisions have convinced me the administration's policy was a result of harrowing mismanagement and willful blindness; officials had some good, if often misguided, intentions, yet their policy was dominated by timidity, ambition, callousness, and staggering hubris. It was, choice by choice, a moral and strategic disaster, but not a master plan. Its effects, however, were so comprehensive as to feel deliberate, torpedoing standards for warfare that were meant to shield us all and destroying a society of millions. In charting the Biden team's moves amid the dust of their shattered red line, I became gripped by an unshakable vision of the darker future the Gaza war ensures: The next bloodbath will be easier to normalize. Its victims could include any of us.

In August 2019, Amit Gilutz of the Israeli watchdog group B'Tselem emailed me and used a delicate phrase to describe the chances I could meet my goal of reporting from Gaza: They were, he wrote, "not high, but not non-existing." Gilutz had just spoken with the Israeli Government Press Office after B'Tselem invited me on a trip for journalists to the occupied Palestinian territories, not realizing I was a Pakistani citizen and had a passport stating on page 3 that it was not valid for Israel. But a collision of unlikely factors brought me into the strip that November and kept me there longer than planned. Rushing to build ties with Muslim-majority countries (and without a settlement with the Palestinians) during the first Trump presidency, Tel Aviv gave me the first-ever Israeli press credential issued to a Pakistani. Spending a night in Gaza City, I awoke to the boom of an Israeli strike sparking a round of conflict with the militant group Palestinian Islamic Jihad (PIJ) and news the Erez Crossing was closed until further notice.

Gaza had already shown me resilience and ingenuity amid cycles of tragedy and suppression—in the pride of a nurse showing off the prosthetics her team jerry-rigged from the limited material allowed into the strip through the Israeli blockade, many for Palestinians wounded while protesting that blockade in what they called the Great March of Return, and the determination of a lawyer who refused to cover her head per Hamas's guidelines for courts. I learned through the Israel-PIJ flare-up just how much life in Gaza hinged on decisions outside the strip, which could instantly turn it into a full-on mass prison, and how Palestinians there lacked any predictability—a basic building block for progress or stability. The impression of stymied lives, of joy and ambition tempered by global forces and accidents of birth, made Gaza remind me even more of Karachi, my hometown. I had already sensed echoes in wry laughter amid absurd and tough conditions, the curves of crumbling buildings dating back to British colonial rule, and the ubiquitousness of the sea, almost mocking you with its seeming but hollow promise of freedom.

My group of visiting journalists was not equipped for war reporting. We negotiated an exit, an option available to few in Gaza as the flare-up dragged on and grew deadlier, eventually killing at least thirty-four Palestinians, including several children (Israel claimed twenty-five were militants). Once back in Israel, we were whisked to cocktails in Tel Aviv. The dissonance between that scene and my feeling of entrapment hours earlier and less than an hour's drive south left a deep impression on me and a gut feeling it was unsustainable.

Memories of Gaza returned to me often. They became inescapable and invaluable once, in October 2023, my reporting focused on the increasingly horrifying impact of U.S. policy on the strip. Profoundly grateful to have experienced the strip before Israel's brutal campaign, I felt determined to imbue my coverage with some understanding of life there and how quickly Israel could turn neighborhoods into battlefields with tacit or, after October 7, proud American support.

That conviction, combined with my decade of experience reporting on the Washington foreign policy machine, made me view the Biden administration's role in the war as one of possibility—as a restraining force or an enabler, with huge leverage as Netanyahu's chief backer.

Officials wanted to show solidarity with Israel and pressure Hamas, conscious of American citizens among its captives, but those instincts could drive a variety of policy choices, depending on whether vengeance or long-term peace guided them and how they went about making decisions. Soon, my reporting pointed to a pattern of disregarding dissent and prioritizing a full-throttle, rushed embrace of Israel. I exposed the State Department's directive to American diplomats to avoid talk of de-escalation, calm, or a ceasefire, and broke the news of turmoil over Gaza policy among U.S. national security officials—including the first of several resignations, that of Josh Paul at State. Eventually, I revealed the administration's first internal acknowledgment of famine in Gaza and a secret White House plan envisioning that Biden could claim triumph and reshape the Middle East after months of enabling mass death. Step by step, I documented how administration officials were missing opportunities to save lives, instead counting on rhetoric and moon-shot alternatives. Their posture was most egregious when they followed their most effective use of American leverage—Biden successfully threatening Israel to make it boost aid after its killing of aid workers belonging to the group World Central Kitchen in April—with the crumbling of the Rafah red line in May and June 2024. Administration officials had excuses for their failure, usually Netanyahu, Hamas, or the stubbornness of the president and American politics, but sustaining it in defiance of hundreds of government experts, most of their Democratic political base, a growing number of Democratic Party leaders, and the lessons of their own experiences throughout the war was their own choice.

What made Biden and his closest aides, particularly National Security Advisor Jake Sullivan, Middle East coordinator Brett McGurk, and Secretary of State Antony Blinken, so averse to a policy shift? I knew Israel-Palestine drove a unique dysfunction in American policy—particularly blatant abandonment of the United States' talk of equal dignity among communities when it came to Palestinian life and an inversion of the alliance between a small and a much larger country. Investigating the Biden administration during the war, I was still shocked by episodes and details revealing how deference to pro-Israel hard-liners obscured facts and analysis for officials and how they nearly all—not just the past-his-prime president—ignored changes in thinking among Democrats and outside observers about how to handle Tel Aviv. But I also saw how the Biden team's decisions were inseparable from disturbing broader trends in U.S. policymaking; that attributing the war to the U.S.-Israel relationship functioning like a blank check regardless of other concerns is both inaccurate and a way to obfuscate responsibility. Gaza's tragedy flowed from America's post-9/11 disasters in the Muslim-majority world and a refusal among policy elites to reckon with its flaws. Among U.S. foreign policy professionals, the War on Terror fostered comfort with jaw-dropping atrocities and dehumanizing of people in the region, as Washington intervened there more than ever before, and a goldfish-style inability to anticipate blowback. Within America's system of checks and balances, the era limited scrutiny of presidents and their aides, reversing progress toward transparency in the twentieth century, while holding few liable for abuses or crimes committed in the name of U.S. national security.

Natives of the global affairs establishment like Biden's advisors said they learned from the grisly recent past, but the lessons they referenced were telling. They blasted regime change and major U.S. military deployments abroad as distractions from what Sullivan called "a foreign policy for the middle class."[4] Yet officials, both Democrats and Republicans, did little about accountability, America's huge military spending and weapons exports, or higher standards for preventing harm to civilians and nuanced diplomacy with foreign communities. Instead, they often armed and supported partner governments in their own military interventions, only to produce quagmires as the United States had in Iraq and Afghanistan. It's a practice that anyone who grew up in the shadow of American-backed conflicts, as I did, knows has only deepened the visceral sense that Washington foments carnage. Many in the Biden administration claimed to have understood the folly of that approach after they, while working for President Barack Obama, enabled a vicious campaign by Saudi Arabia and the United Arab Emirates in Yemen. They had few incentives, however, to translate reflection into a systemic overhaul when they regained power. By October 7, Biden's team was poised to overwhelmingly yield to Netanyahu and subject Gaza to harsh, often self-defeating tendencies from the U.S. playbook.

The Gaza war has always been an American war. Over its excruciating duration, it has become central to America's own evolution. During Biden's presidency, the war galvanized mass protests and then the biggest wave of arrests on American campuses since the Vietnam War. Disillusionment over Biden's embrace of Netanyahu contributed to a broader sense that Democratic Party leadership was out of touch and to the disaffection among key voter groups that helped Trump regain the White House. Since then, Trump has made Palestine a defining domestic issue, conflating antiwar activism and antisemitism to justify his power grabs against colleges and the detention and attempted deportation of students and journalists. Full-throated pushback to Trump is inconceivable without establishing a real difference from him—which entails grappling with Democrats' own role in restricting questioning of the Gaza war among Americans and the link between obstinacy over troubling actions abroad and a less democratic system at home. Meanwhile, the way Biden's calamitous policy enabled even more U.S.-backed Israeli escalation under Trump, like a three-month full blockade on aid and two wars against Iran, as well as another offensive in Lebanon, offers a warning for those seeking to shape U.S. foreign policy in the future—including Republicans, whose ranks have seen a new wave of questioning of Tel Aviv.

Near the end of this book, I describe how Biden administration officials up to the president had a new concern in late 2024 about U.S. support for Israel's campaign in Gaza violating American and international law and crucially whether U.S. officials were breaking the law themselves. They chose not to change their policy and to hand it off to Trump, an open foe of any standards in warfare. The administration was never willing to hold itself to account. In reporting out this book nearly three years—in Washington, The Hague, Doha, London, Paris, Berlin, at the United Nations in New York, and at the Democratic National Convention in Chicago—I saw a broader yearning for Gaza's pain to be confronted and the architects of that pain made to answer. (Israeli restrictions kept me and other journalists from freely reporting in Gaza.) As cases about the war advance at the International Court of Justice and the International Criminal Court, and as discussions of it occur among Americans and in deliberations in Congress about renewing the United States' $3.8 billion annual aid package for Israel by 2028, understanding the Biden administration's record will be vital.

Language matters intensely when discussing Israel-Palestine; it's not only a tool but often a weapon or even a gag. I use "the war" to describe the period this book covers, October 7, 2023, to January 20, 2025. I do so without using the term "genocide" (except when citing others) and with awareness of the violent occupation of the Palestinian territories since 1967 and of other bloodshed during the Israeli-Palestinian conflict, including gut-wrenching attacks on Israelis during the Second Intifada of 2000–2005 and the mass expulsion of Palestinians during Israel's establishment (the Nakba). My intent is not to deny this period could constitute a genocide or to cast it as unique and ahistorical but to present it as the players I focus on—the Biden administration—were thinking, and to be clear the scope of my project is documenting U.S. policy choices and options. In keeping with that frame, I call those kidnapped on October 7 hostages but do not use the term to refer to the Palestinians imprisoned by Israel, many without charge and including thousands of detainees from Gaza—though I do believe it is possible they merit that term, too. Finally, I have been careful in characterizing the ideological bent of various voices. I refer to pro-Israel forces often, but I am wary of the term "pro-Palestinian," which is often applied to antiwar figures and suggests they are on one side of the conflict—the side it's easier, in America, to demonize—rather than urging peace. I generally avoid the phrase.

Gaza has been less accessible than much of the world for twenty years, but for the past three, Palestinians' broadcasts of life—and death—have deeply affected millions. The White House is available to the public in snippets, but the closed-door conversations and dynamics that determine its impact on the world are almost never accessible. This book is an effort to defy the remoteness of these contexts that will shape our collective future.

CHAPTER 1

FROM SHOCK TO SHOCK AND AWE

October 7–18, 2023

AROUND MIDNIGHT WASHINGTON TIME ON OCTOBER 7, 2023, A group of officials on the seventh floor of the State Department began hearing about an attack inside Israel. They were members of the Watch, an elite team that constantly monitors global affairs. Generally young and uniformly ambitious, the Watch is entrusted with leading the U.S. government response to sudden international crises by tracking down and briefing senior officials at a moment's notice and analyzing thousands of streams of incoming data from diplomats, intelligence agencies, and media sources. That night, as updates from Israel began filtering in, for several hours the Watch decided not to disturb the sleep of Secretary of State Antony Blinken.

Led by Hamas, Palestinian militants had first launched sweeping rocket barrages that drove many Israelis into shelters, then had overrun Israel's southern regions bordering the Gaza Strip by land, sea, and air in an unprecedented invasion. Fighters from the Al-Qassam Brigades, Hamas's armed wing, and other Gaza-based militant groups were killing hundreds of Israelis, targeting military bases and towns, shooting and lobbing grenades at those seeking shelter or escape, and rounding up hostages. The shock of the assault combined with a haphazard response from Israeli authorities to create prolonged, widespread uncertainty and pandemonium.

The Watch assessed reports from social media and statements from Hamas and the Israel Defense Forces (IDF) that suggested a new war was beginning. Personal outreach poured in too, a person present told me: requests for guidance from embassies and calls from worried Americans. One simply kept repeating he hadn't heard from his girlfriend, who was attending a music festival in southern Israel. The Nova festival was later confirmed as the site of the largest massacre that day, in which Hamas-led attackers killed almost four hundred people.

Still, the manager of the Watch wasn't sure the situation deserved an all-out alarm: The Biden administration had made clear the region was not a priority; Israel had a pattern of sudden, short wars with Palestinian militants; and the scale of the killing was unclear.

It wasn't until 6:00 a.m. that the team woke Blinken.

From the start of the Gaza war, it was apparent the real players for U.S. policy were a handful of officials at the White House surrounding President Joe Biden. National Security Advisor Jake Sullivan and Biden's Middle East coordinator Brett McGurk were tracking the Hamas-led attack starting at 2:30 a.m. Washington time, even before Israel's government made its first extensive statement to its own people.[1] The two men, each at the pinnacle of his power at roughly fifty years old, viewed themselves as national security experts with unparalleled judgment and experience—but they had also devised the Biden-era strategy of treating Israeli-Palestinian affairs as a second-tier concern, which fueled frustration among Palestinians and emboldened hard-line Israeli policies.

That morning, Sullivan, McGurk, and Blinken huddled with Biden. In an hours-long closed-door meeting, they held calls with Israeli prime minister Benjamin Netanyahu and other leaders and consulted with Biden's longtime advisors on domestic politics, Mike Donilon and Anita Dunn, who had an eye on the president's hopes for a second term in office and a certainty that it was politically unwise to question Israel.[2] The group was constantly getting new information from southern Israel and Gaza—now battlefields—but they were dealing with a constant: Biden. Older than the state of Israel, the president was a self-described Zionist who believed the United States should support Tel

Aviv for moral reasons and as a geopolitical asset and who was deeply averse to wielding American leverage over the country.

Between Biden's strong views and little appetite among his staff to question his judgment, the administration initiated a policy of support for Israel that was more far-reaching and more deadly than any in American history. The commander in chief began rolling it out in a statement at 2:45 p.m., declaring: "The United States stands with Israel. We will not ever fail to have their back." Though Israeli air strikes were hitting the Gaza Strip as he spoke, Biden did not mention growing Palestinian deaths or the U.S. and international laws that ostensibly constrained Israel as a signatory to various global standards and as a recipient of billions in American aid, including weapons. He did, however, affirm his belief in immediate retaliation, without planning or debating the wisdom of more bloodshed. "Israel has the right to defend itself and its people. Full stop," Biden said. That evening, a senior official told reporters the administration was speeding U.S. weaponry to Israel.[3] He denied seeing a statement from Netanyahu telling residents of Gaza to "leave now because we will operate forcefully everywhere"—an early indication of Israeli interest in collective punishment and potential ethnic cleansing.[4]

In just the first few hours after the Hamas attack, Biden was "pouring fuel on the fire" of Israel's response, a former senior U.S official who had worked with the president told me. That choice and a series of pivotal decisions by the administration over the following ten days set a grim course for the war that followed.

"OH MY GOD, WHAT IS ISRAEL GOING TO DO?"

Fierce Israeli retribution against Hamas and significant U.S. involvement in that campaign seemed unavoidable after the October 7 attack. The assault was the bloodiest day in Israel's history—sparking national trauma amplified by viral, chilling raw footage of the events—and drew comparisons to the Holocaust as the deadliest day for Jews since that genocide, coming amid a season of Jewish holidays. Palestinian militants captured 251 hostages, from octogenarians and infants to migrant workers, taking them back to Gaza in pickup trucks and golf carts. At least one thousand attackers, among them paragliders and, eventually, some Palestinian civilians who crossed the shattered Israeli border fence, joined the rampage, sexually assaulting some victims and executing Israelis who resisted, like sixty-seven-year-old Kinneret Gat, who had stuck out her tongue at a Palestinian fighter. Of the 1,195 killed, 815 were civilians.[5]

The sheer scale of the calamity signaled the capacity of Hamas leaders and Israeli foes such as the group's Gaza chief, Yahya Sinwar, himself free because of a prisoner swap for an Israeli hostage. And the moment seemed existential for both Israel, as the self-proclaimed safe haven for Jews, and its leader Netanyahu, who presented himself as shielding Israelis against a wide range of threats (including Sinwar, whom he had helped release in a decision his critics were now highlighting). Jeremy Ben-Ami, a foreign policy professional in close contact with the Biden administration, told me that in Washington, "lurking in the back of every conversation [was] the thought of, 'Oh my God, what is Israel going to do?'" American participation, meanwhile, was not in question. Pro-Israel sentiment, driven by both political donations and personal views, ran deep among American officials, and for many decision-makers who had spent decades working closely with Israeli counterparts, the attack felt personal. "Were there not an Israel, the United States of America would have to invent an Israel," Biden had said forty years prior, as a senator. It was a statement he would repeat after October 7.

Despite those certainties, the specifics of the Biden administration's approach to the Israeli campaign were not yet determined. Top U.S. officials were discussing ideas like some limits on military support to the IDF and whether to make demands from Netanyahu, such as requesting a battle plan that addressed ending the war and a peaceful future for Israel-Palestine. The first three days following the attack represented the administration's "one chance to constrain the response," Jon Finer, Biden's deputy national security advisor, maintained in internal deliberations, he later recalled to a friend.[6] The administration had no contingency plan for an eventuality it had never envisioned and was not immediately emphasizing a Gaza invasion. When Barbara Leaf, the top Middle East official at the State Department, briefed senior lawmakers on the evening of October 7, she said the administration still lacked key information, and its main request to Congress was to rapidly confirm Biden's proposed ambassador to Israel, Jacob "Jack" Lew, a congressional aide recalled to me. The aide remembered a separate call that day that suggested Washington should tread carefully with its ally: Speaking to congressional staff, former IDF general Amos Yadlin referred to the many statements condemning Hamas's onslaught from legislators and other power players and said Israelis felt the "battery" of legitimacy and justification for their actions had been charged. Now Israel would, he continued, deplete it.

In Israel, with fighting, damage assessments, and support for victims ongoing—in some areas, the IDF was still battling Palestinian fighters until October 9—officials had not fully turned their focus to Gaza. And with the precise nature of the U.S. green light for Israeli retaliation amorphous, the Biden administration could take time to devise a policy that was informed by the failure of their own record in the region; Netanyahu's defensiveness and the mood of vengeance among the Israeli public; and the United States' experience of mismanaging responses to attacks, spurring blowback and cycles of violence internationally while undermining America's stated values. Instead, Biden aides overlooked crucial context.

Willful blindness had already defined the administration's approach to Israeli-Palestinian matters for two and a half years. Though Biden and other top Democrats had said Trump-era shifts in U.S. positions had hurt the chances of peace between the two communities, by giving ground to Israel without pressing it to make concessions to Palestinians, the president's team kept most of those policies in place. The Biden administration continued recognizing Jerusalem as Israel's capital, treating Israeli settlements in the occupied West Bank and control of part of Syria's Golan Heights region as legal, and labeling products from the West Bank as "made in Israel"—declining to return to pre-Trump U.S. norms and standing apart from other world powers, as well as international law. Despite promising to reestablish a U.S. consulate in Jerusalem for Palestinians and to reopen the Palestinian diplomatic mission in Washington, Biden never delivered on either pledge. The general impression was that the administration did not want to spend political capital on an issue the president and advisors like Sullivan viewed as too ossified to solve. Biden notably became the first president since Richard Nixon to not even propose a road map for Israeli-Palestinian peace. His positions set him apart from much of his party, which had become more skeptical of both Netanyahu and Israel backers in U.S. politics, who were increasingly challenging progressives and bolstering far-right Republicans. And at high-level meetings led by Finer, even many of Biden's hand-picked senior staff formally but unsuccessfully recommended the reversal of the Trump-era policies on settlements and labeling of West Bank products as Israeli, a senior official told me.

The administration demonstrated its view of the region during an Israel-Hamas war in May 2021. Their policy was to back the Israelis and allow them to demonstrate dominance over Palestinian militants before privately telling Netanyahu "to knock this off," a senior State Department official recalled to me, saying it worked "to pretty good effect." The perception of achieving success by embracing Israel became "part of the DNA of some members of the administration," Rob Malley, who served as special envoy for Iran for the first half of Biden's presidency, told me. Yet it was a disheartening depiction of triumph. With Biden's support, that Israeli offensive killed at least 266 Palestinians, including 66 children. Rockets from Palestinian militants during the period killed 13 Israelis. Human rights groups said Israel's U.S.-backed campaign involved multiple war crimes, and even the IDF conceded that five Israeli military personnel violated its targeting standards in launching air strikes on Gaza. In keeping with their long-standing pattern of little punishment for violence against Palestinians, Israeli officials did not prosecute the accused soldiers.

The consequences of continued impunity and a lack of progress toward peace became clearer when an Israeli soldier killed Shireen Abu Akleh, a high-profile reporter, in the West Bank on May 11, 2022. The Biden administration deemed the U.S. citizen's death an accident despite American officials concluding in a preliminary investigation that the shooter targeted a clearly identified journalist, one of the officials, Colonel Steve Gabavics, later revealed.[7] "Once we identified it was not a Palestinian, we were going to say it was a combat-related mistake," Gabavics told me, noting that was the conclusion of an internal State Department report—which did, however, recommend reforming Israeli military practices, and which the Biden administration never published, despite calls to do so.

Overall, Biden's approach echoed Trump-era logic: allaying Palestinian frustration with Israel's violent occupation by suggesting they focus on economics, not sovereignty. Some justified the limited ambition by saying anything stronger would endanger the 2021–22 Israeli rule of Naftali Bennett and Yair Lapid, the country's first non-Netanyahu government in twelve years. "In the history of U.S.-Israel relations, there's always an excuse . . . a reason not to do the thing that you later wish you had done," Malley, a veteran Middle East expert, later quipped to me. U.S. officials got Israel to offer more work permits to Palestinians: Day laborers inside Israel could make up to ten times the daily wage in the Palestinian territories, Mike Casey, an official at the U.S. embassy in Jerusalem at the time, told me. But once Netanyahu finagled a return to power in December 2022, forming the most right-wing government in Israeli history, those ad hoc measures were easy to stymie.

Indications of a new all-out conflict grew, as income into Gaza plummeted and Israel and Palestinian Islamic Jihad—one of the strip's armed groups—clashed the following May. The flare-up killed eleven Palestinian and two Israeli civilians.[8] The year 2023 also saw far more Israeli settler attacks on Palestinians in the West Bank, and Hamas claiming responsibility for Palestinian attacks inside Israel, fueling suspicions that Netanyahu would launch an offensive in both Gaza and the

West Bank, and that Hamas might try to preempt him, Casey said. He described the Biden administration as "in denial" about how U.S. support for Israel enabled carnage. "Come on, the IDF doesn't participate in settler violence!" Barbara Leaf from the State Department protested to diplomats on a visit, he recalled. In fact, analysts had for years agreed the Israeli military enabled attacks by West Bank settlers. Biden had granted greater autonomy to the office of Palestinian affairs at the U.S. embassy in Jerusalem rather than establish an American consulate to the Palestinians, but as officials in that office issued warnings that Palestinian desperation would boil over, "we heard crickets from Washington," Casey said. His team issued a report days before October 7 describing Gaza's "unsustainable" economic situation. "This place is going to go off a cliff," the memo effectively argued. Gabavics, also based in Jerusalem, told me he saw five American intelligence reports sent to Washington in the three months before the Hamas invasion that warned of a rising threat but were seemingly ignored.

In U.S. national security circles, it was clear the administration saw Israel-Palestine as "a managed conflict" that was unlikely to erupt in unpredictable ways, according to Harrison Mann, a former Defense Intelligence Agency analyst. When top Biden aides did consider Israeli-Palestinian peace, it was in the context of a moon-shot plan for an alliance between the United States, Israel, and Saudi Arabia—which involved throwing a bone to Palestinians for the sake of demonstrating Arab solidarity, and which they felt would earn them a place in history. McGurk and Blinken were finalizing a draft U.S.-Saudi agreement with minimal concessions on Palestine in the days leading up to October 7.[9] And days before the Hamas attack, Sullivan had publicly stated that under Biden, "the Middle East region is quieter today than it has been for two decades," publishing an essay in *Foreign Affairs* magazine with the same claim.[10] The assertion was not only inaccurate; it angered Biden administration critics from pro-Palestinian progressives to national security hawks, who noted that Sullivan and his team had done little to stem the power of Iran, a U.S. foe that armed Hamas.

The Biden team's vision of relative stability in Israel-Palestine without a political settlement, involving horrifying bouts of bloodshed that officials described as limited and hence acceptable, partly mirrored the thinking of Netanyahu. Crafting policy after October 7, administration officials had a chance to acknowledge that they and the Israeli leader had misjudged the danger of such logic. Further, their decision-making could tap their new understanding of the limits of Israel's capabilities and their awareness that Netanyahu's analysis and policy preferences were often shaped by personal political motivations and fixations. Both those factors suggested American guidance and guardrails would be key to preventing the response from becoming a tremendously destructive debacle.

At age seventy-three, Netanyahu wanted to cement his legacy, concentrate influence among fellow right-wing Israelis, and avoid jail time as Israeli prosecutors tried him on corruption charges. His hold on power—which helped him challenge those overseeing his cases—depended on ultranationalist politicians, who demonized Palestinians and could at any time shatter Netanyahu's coalition in Israel's parliament, the Knesset. In January 2023, Netanyahu demonstrated how closely aligned he had become with those extremist figures by proposing a plan to weaken Israeli judges' independence and ability to restrict far-right policy changes. Sparking huge protests from Israelis, Netanyahu's trajectory drew public critique even from the intrinsically pro-Israel Biden administration: The president said Netanyahu was threatening Israel's democratic credentials and delayed meeting with him for months after Netanyahu had reentered office.

That meant Biden's aides knew he had a wariness of Netanyahu and willingness to prod him toward different choices. They also recognized the Israeli leader's ability to manipulate the U.S.-Israel relationship for his own interests, honed since Netanyahu's formative years as a diplomat in Washington and New York, and his cynicism, exemplified by his tacit support of Hamas's rule in Gaza and split from the Palestinian Authority, which controls part of the West Bank. "If anyone is most responsible for the empowerment of Hamas . . . it's not Sinwar, it's not [Hamas political chief Ismail] Haniyeh, it is Bibi," a senior State Department official told me, using a nickname for Netanyahu. "Over the course of his twenty-five years in and out of office, it is the by-product of a strategy predicating on seeing to it that there was no united Palestinian governance [but] dueling power centers."

More generally, U.S. officials were developing a better understanding of Israel's military and intelligence capabilities—long assumed to be exemplary, and central to any retaliatory campaign against Hamas. "We were all surprised by the ineffectiveness of the Israeli defenses and by the unpreparedness on the part of Israeli intelligence," the senior State official told me. Israeli officials obtained and reviewed Hamas's battle plan for October 7 more than a year before the assault but doubted it was feasible and ignored advice to prepare, a *New York Times* investigation found.[11] And just weeks before the attack, the chief of intelligence for the IDF, Aharon Haliva, told his U.S. counterparts that Hamas had been "domesticated," a top Biden aide told me. In a major U.S.-backed Israeli offensive, such miscalculations could hinder choices in Washington and Tel Aviv, with harsh consequences for innocent people, particularly because American intelligence agencies were unlikely to pick up the slack. Focusing on Al Qaeda and its offshoots since the 9/11 attacks, the official said the United States had "outsourced" information-gathering about Palestinian militants to the Shin Bet and Mossad, Israel's chief security agencies, and Gabavics separately told me that U.S. reliance on Israeli intelligence meant the CIA was "horrible" in analysis on Gaza. Well before October 7, Washington had clues Israel's capacity was exaggerated, a former U.S. intelligence official argued to me, saying Israeli counterparts were evasive in giving American spies access to their raw intelligence and techniques.

With the United States and Israel effectively beginning a joint mission together, top Biden administration officials had good reasons—and a proven appetite—for more forcefully directing its course. Choosing to do so was a different matter.

A DUBIOUS PLAYBOOK

For Israelis and Arabs, the Hamas-led offensive had particular resonance because it came amid the fiftieth anniversary of the 1973 surprise attacks on Israel by its neighbors. For most in the Biden administration, the more salient historical comparison was to the September 11, 2001, attacks in the United States and their aftermath. Harmful patterns from that period, from selective American regard for international law to reductive approaches toward foreign populations, deeply influenced U.S. officials as they settled on their role in the nascent Gaza war.

Biden's foreign policy advisors cut their teeth amid the so-called War on Terror, during which American officials rejected accountability or transparency around their actions in the name of national security, even when their decisions involved massacres of civilians and practices like torture. All the while, U.S. troops invaded Afghanistan and Iraq and extensively bombed Pakistan, Yemen, and other nations, then struggled to deal with the ramifications. Presidents Barack Obama, Donald Trump, and Biden wound down parts of the policy, acknowledging the unpopularity of missions that skeptics called "forever wars." But each sustained much of the War on Terror infrastructure, like denying limits on presidential decisions about war and assassinations, high military spending, and far-flung U.S. troop deployments.

Described by many Israelis as their nation's 9/11, the Hamas-led assault triggered deep-rooted instincts among Biden and his aides. Sympathy toward Israel overshadowed any pre–October 7 context on Israel-Palestine, Malley later told me, and Tess McEnery, a former Biden and Trump administration official, recalled that she quickly predicted her former colleagues would fuel "another forever war" in Gaza because "the War on Terror framework for how we do foreign policy in the Middle East . . . was just immediately available." That approach would echo the Bush-era proclivity for identifying enemies and battling them, asking questions about their motivations and possible nonmilitary solutions later—often too late, once the United States had inspired dangerous retaliation, to which America would in turn respond. Some players even had extensive experience in implementing that framework, such as the White House Middle East coordinator. Brett McGurk began his career on the Bush administration team tasked with stabilizing Iraq after the 2003 U.S. invasion and overthrow of Saddam Hussein's regime. The team largely failed, as demonstrated by the subsequent insurgencies by Al Qaeda in Iraq and its eventual progeny, ISIS, but subsequent presidents nevertheless tapped McGurk to direct the U.S. responses to those dilemmas. "Do you learn from your mistakes if you keep being employed because of your mistakes?" McEnery asked.

Evidence of War on Terror habits quickly emerged. At the Pentagon, officials posted huge maps of Gaza in their offices that a Defense Department staffer described to me as delusional, because the images provided a sense of scale that downplayed how tightly packed the enclave's population was, with fourteen thousand people per square mile, and how devastating air strikes and a ground invasion would be.[12] In discussions with Israeli counterparts, Biden aides encouraged the idea that an offensive in Gaza could end support for Hamas among Palestinians, Gabavics, still at the embassy in Jerusalem at the time, told me. "It's the same thing as Iraq. . . . We literally took the idea from 2003–6 and put it into Israel's hands, saying, 'There's not going to be an insurgency, they're going to love you,'" he said. Biden was a significant Democratic booster of Bush's Iraq invasion, a position he later called a mistake.

As with past foreign misadventures, top U.S. officials were permitting little room for absorbing criticism. The Gaza policy circle was small and insular—comprising the president and his chief foreign policy aides, a group of white, Ivy League–educated men mostly of the same age and with lengthy government experience. "No policy I have ever worked on has been so controlled by the White House," said one White House official who worked with Biden administration colleagues on other crises, such as Ukraine, as well as during the Obama administration. This official told me the Biden team's handling of the issue was less inclusive even than the "very small team" of U.S. officials who covered Israel-Palestine under other presidents. "The process was not what it is on virtually any other issue," a senior State official separately told me. Groupthink and other risks were inevitable. "The problem with running a very small process is that you don't necessarily have someone to check you when you make mistakes," the White House official said. Already, the president had run what Thanassis Cambanis, a well-connected national security analyst, described to me as "a personalistic, loyalistic administration, maybe the most that way since Nixon." Fixating on fealty, Biden "only seeks advice from people he knows and has known for a long time, in the kind of relationship that probably precludes you from telling hard truths," Cambanis continued, saying the pattern had potentially catastrophic implications: "When he's wrong, he's wrong with conviction."

Biden's inner circle on Gaza also lacked voices who could dissent with the clout of figures in previous administrations. Past presidents' policymaking often included officials with stature of their own, which gave them greater confidence in dealing with a commander in chief, from secretaries of state Hillary Clinton and John Kerry for Obama to the retired military leaders Jim Mattis and Colin Powell for Trump and George W. Bush, respectively. The men with whom Biden discussed the October 7 response were best known as staff to him and other politicians.

With power concentrated in the president's hands, his diminished capacity at nearly eighty years of age mattered immensely, too. Over the two days after the Hamas-led attack, Biden was interviewed by Robert Hur, a Justice Department special counsel. Hur ultimately deemed Biden an "elderly man with poor memory," and the transcript of the conversation on October 9 shows the president forgot dates and wandered off on tangents.

Flaws in the Israeli and U.S. approach to Israel-Palestine were obvious as post–October 7 policy took shape. Still, even as American officials debated their options, Washington's inclinations were clear: From the day of attack, Biden administration officials were rushing American weapons to Israel's military, issuing approvals that would normally take months in a matter of hours, officials told me.

LIVES IN THE BALANCE

As the Biden administration tried to settle on a strategy, Israel was already bombing Gaza with increasing intensity and U.S. support. Palestinian civilians, as well as American citizens, were paying a growing price. On just the day of the attack, Israeli strikes killed at least 230 Palestinians, according to Gaza's health ministry.[13] By the following day, more than 73,500 Palestinians fled their homes and sought shelter in United Nations schools. In a hint of the assault on civilian infrastructure that was to come, an Israeli attack badly damaged one UN school, hosting 225 people.[14] Still, Palestinians had little hope of safer alternatives: Nearly all of Gaza's borders were controlled and blocked by Israel, except the Rafah Crossing, which led into Egypt. Although Egypt had no interest in accepting an influx of refugees, the IDF repeatedly bombed the crossing.

As Israeli bombs hit neighborhoods, hospitals, and mosques, Gaza-based journalist Ghada Kord said life began to feel like a nightmare.[15] She had no electricity; spotty communications networks meant she couldn't contact relatives to check if they were safe; and a fuel shortage left ambulances and other emergency workers struggling amid a constantly growing number of wounded people and bombing victims trapped under pulverized buildings. "Two million people live in Gaza—not all of them belong to [armed] factions," Kord said, but she described little optimism about an end to the attacks. "We are going to face a huge disaster."

She shared those impressions with Rowaida Abdelaziz, my colleague at *HuffPost*, on October 10, by which point the Palestinian death toll was approaching eight hundred—including at least ninety children—and one in ten Gaza residents had fled their homes. The day before, Israeli authorities had halted the flow of water into Gaza from Israel, the source of more than half the region's drinking water.[16] The day after, IDF spokesman Daniel Hagari said the Israeli military had already dropped "thousands of tons of munitions" on Gaza. "While balancing accuracy with the scope of damage, right now we're focused on what causes maximum damage," Hagari told journalists. Netanyahu had mobilized 4 percent of Israel's population as reserve troops and had begun to gather forces along Gaza's borders in preparation for a ground invasion of the strip.

International pressure was widely understood as the only factor that might rein in Israel, and the only outside player with meaningful leverage over Netanyahu was the Biden administration. Those counseling restraint believed that even if moral or humanitarian reasons could not move the president, concerns about the United States' own standing might; some State Department officials privately began urging senior colleagues to show they were not ignoring Palestinian anguish.[17]

The presence of hundreds of Palestinian Americans and U.S. permanent residents in Gaza—as well as thousands of relatives of Americans—posed a simple test for the United States: For their sake, would it try to stem the crisis? The group of hundreds included Abood Okal, his wife, Wafaa Abuzayda, and their one-year-old son, Yousef. The Massachusetts family had traveled to Gaza to introduce Yousef to his cousins and grandparents; now, Okal was sheltering apart from his parents, who were stuck in a house whose windows and doors had been blown out, and he was running low on both water and tricks to distract the baby from the bombs, he reported.[18]

Okal wanted to go home. Across Israel-Palestine, so did hundreds of other Americans—but those on Israeli soil, where fighting had ended, got markedly better treatment than those trapped amid the daily risk of death in Gaza. With a two-hundred-person team established at the State Department to support U.S. citizens, officials organized flights and cruise ships to help Americans leave Israel; one Pentagon official recalled to me that they evacuated a dog belonging to U.S. citizens. But Biden administration staff told me they experienced severe limitations in helping Palestinian Americans, largely because of political calculations in Washington. Early in the war, indications the administration had a double standard—treating Palestinian life as cheap—were already strong.

The initial advice was that the United States would help people if they could leave Gaza for Israel, a State Department official told me. That was impossible. As Palestinian Americans called the department in hysterics, staff improvised, putting the names they were given on the manifests of departing flights and ships regardless of whether they could embark. That had the benefit of highlighting vulnerable individuals and granting the coveted title of "U.S. person" to relatives of Americans even if they held only Palestinian nationality. Even as they bent the rules, their efforts often fell short: The official recalled, his voice shaking, that several people he was advising via WhatsApp "stopped talking." He assumed they were killed by U.S.-backed air strikes.

Trying to help Okal's family, the official was confounded. On one occasion, American officials secured a spot for them on the daily lists of select people whom Israel, Egypt, and Palestinian officials agreed to allow through the Rafah Crossing, but when they traveled through active bombing and waited for hours in the sun before the gate, Egyptian officials would not let them pass. Cairo said it would not operate the crossing without guarantees it would also be used for aid and protected from Israeli strikes. The official was stunned Washington did not retort that relief for people in Gaza—its own citizens—was nonnegotiable. "There was not an interest in pushing the Egyptians," the State Department official said, even though they were among the biggest recipients of U.S. aid after Israel, largely because of their willingness to work with Tel Aviv. When the official and others pressed their bosses about using American influence to open alternative routes for evacuations from Gaza—for example, by asking Israel to allow ships to access the territory's coast—the leaders offered "no follow-up . . . effort or creativity."

Meanwhile, at the American embassy in Jerusalem, Mike Casey and other officials wrote twice-daily reports on evacuations from Israel. Casey tried to highlight the disparity in the treatment of those Americans and Palestinian Americans, he told me, by regularly inserting a sentence into the updates: "Zero left Gaza." He said senior officials consistently deleted the reminder. Beyond U.S. citizens, others connected to America were already suffering because of the war: Some Israeli staff of the U.S. diplomatic mission lived in areas attacked by Hamas, Casey recalled, and he was deeply worried about five Palestinian employees who lived in Gaza. One night, an Israeli air strike hit a coworker's home as she was sheltering there with her children and extended family; the U.S. had flagged the location for the IDF.

She was injured, but Egyptian officials did not let her through the Rafah Crossing for weeks. The process for getting people safely out was becoming a microcosm of the cynicism and short-sightedness of key players in the war. Hamas, which had partial control of the Rafah Crossing, "realized they were also holding seven hundred American hostages" beyond the October 7 victims, Casey told me; the group used that to wield influence in negotiations with the Israelis, Americans, and Egyptians over supplies for Gaza and to pursue its broader goals such as surviving beyond the war. Hala, an Egyptian company, began charging exorbitant rates from Palestinians for passage.

Beyond IDF attacks, American officials were receiving bigger indications that Israel would create a humanitarian crisis and ignore the core principle of the laws of war and the Geneva Conventions—protecting civilians during wartime—which Israel said it was respecting. Netanyahu and his officials repeatedly indicated they were pursuing collective punishment for Palestinians, to punish Hamas and, some analysts later claimed, as a strategy to inspire backlash to the group and militancy.

On October 7, Netanyahu said he would turn Gaza into a "deserted island," and two days later, Israeli defense minister Yoav Gallant announced: "I have ordered a complete siege on the Gaza Strip: There will be no electricity, no food, no fuel, everything is closed." His statement blatantly disregarded international law, which mandates that innocent people receive essential supplies during conflicts. Gallant's stunning declaration reflected the way a preexisting dehumanization of Palestinians—already common in Israel and, to a degree, in the United States—provided a foundation for extreme methods in the war against Hamas and an abandonment of human rights standards. Speaking about the militant group, Gallant said: "We are fighting human animals, and we are acting accordingly." On October 12, Israeli president Isaac Herzog, whom the Biden administration treated as a voice of moderation, said: "It's an entire nation out there that is responsible. It's not true, this rhetoric about civilians not aware, not involved." Though Herzog said at the same appearance that there were innocent people in Gaza, it was clear the more aggressive part of his comment resonated: Graffiti near West Bank settlements and statements among IDF soldiers came to include the phrase "there are no uninvolved."[19] Israeli officials and their allies in the United States later said it was unfair to treat the statements from Gallant and Herzog as a threat to all Palestinians. These same statements were later widely cited by lawyers, watchdog groups, and other governments as evidence of Israel's genocidal intent.

Still, some in the Biden administration doubted the Israelis would go as far as all signs suggested. On October 11, Netanyahu formed an emergency war cabinet to oversee the anti-Hamas offensive, bringing in voices beyond his far-right government—then Gallant said the body agreed to wipe Hamas "off the face of the earth."[20] Almost certainly impossible, that maximalist goal seemingly justified unimaginably broad attacks on Gaza. Still, the senior State Department official recalled thinking: "This is Bibi. Is this bluster or is this something real?" Speaking to me nearly a year later, the official added: "It turns out it was more real than we might have imagined." The misinterpretation was an early example of the administration misreading Israeli patterns of behavior by tying them to Netanyahu, a crass figure who was easy to demonize, instead of acknowledging dark systemic realities. It was already clear much of Israel—across the ideological spectrum, and beyond the boasts of politicians—wanted to be ruthless in Gaza, and that bloodthirsty remarks amplified and legitimized that sentiment in a self-reinforcing loop. Netanyahu's war cabinet included the centrist politician Benny Gantz, long seen in Washington as an ideal alternative Israeli leader, while outside the cabinet, the more moderate politician Yair Lapid, Netanyahu's strongest opponent, endorsed both Gallant's siege policy and the cabinet's idea of "no Hamas." On the political right, which was likely to helm any alternative government, Netanyahu's rival was Naftali Bennett, the former prime minister with whom the Biden administration worked closely in 2021 and 2022. "These are animals. . . . We have to deal with this as though they are Nazis," Bennett said on October 9, invoking a unique historic right for Israel to deploy extraordinary force.[21] And the Israeli hate speech monitor Fake Reporter found that in the five weeks after October 7, Hebrew posts on X included eighteen thousand calls to flatten, erase, or destroy Gaza, compared with only sixteen mentions of those phrases on the website in the six weeks before the Hamas-led attack.[22]

As portents of an Israeli rampage grew, U.S. officials began not ignoring but challenging inconvenient information. For the first time in Casey's three years at the embassy in Jerusalem, "everybody was interested in Gaza," he told me—but that often meant fellow U.S. officials would doubt the reported death count and deprivation. "They didn't want to believe anything: They were saying these are from Hamas," Casey said, foreshadowing assertions that Biden and the Israeli government would eventually deploy against criticism of the U.S.-Israeli offensive. Amid a man-made, swelling disaster, American officials who could have limited it "were fighting about the actual conditions . . . as we were saying people are thirsty in the streets," Casey said.

"THE TRAIN IS LEAVING THE STATION"

By October 9, a firm internal direction for the Biden administration began to seem overdue. Soon, the president and top advisors—Sullivan, McGurk, and Blinken—made a "fundamental" decision, the senior State Department official told me: The administration would heavily back Israel's offensive with no expectation or timeline for quietly encouraging a ceasefire, and officials would prioritize the decades-old principle of "no daylight," or no public disagreements, between Washington and Tel Aviv. Effectively, Biden was issuing Netanyahu a blank check—which U.S. officials quietly, foolishly, and wrongly believed would buy them private influence over his choices.

Choosing that approach meant Biden and his aides were choosing to treat stronger sources of American leverage as untouchable. Israel needed the United States to continue arms shipments to resupply its military and to stave off international criticism if it wanted to sustain the anti-Hamas offensive beyond a few weeks. Even with Israel's post–October 7 status as a righteously indignant victim—as well as its U.S. allies in Congress, the American Jewish community, Christian Zionist groups, and beyond—Netanyahu might struggle if he had to spend time and political capital seeking such support or pushing back if it appeared in question. The Biden administration's position let him take for granted the resources to wage war and showed him they were reluctant to play all their cards, creating a dynamic in which restraining destructive Israeli impulses became hard for Washington for months, guaranteeing horrors for Palestinians.

The policy the president and his aides settled on was not inevitable, but it was predictable. Though they said it was a strategic, calibrated plan, idiosyncrasies of the Biden administration, timing, and outside factors all shaped it significantly—which made their refusal to adapt later especially dumbfounding.

Biden's intense pro-Israel sentiment was central. Dennis Ross, a retired diplomat known for pro-Israel tendencies, said the president had stronger ties to Israel than any commander in chief for the past fifty years, and Aaron David Miller, a more centrist former State Department official, told me: "I watched [President Bill] Clinton mourn the death of [assassinated Israeli prime minister Yitzhak] Rabin in a way he'd mourn a father. . . . But not even Clinton was Joe Biden."[23] In Miller's view, "Biden considered himself part of the Israeli story." Tied to those tendencies was Biden's trademark stubbornness. "He thinks he knows it all," Shibley Telhami, a critic of traditional U.S. Israel-Palestine policy who discussed it directly with Biden over decades, told me. "He listens but then he wants to prove you wrong rather than take it in."

The president also saw himself as an expert on people. In his estimation of Netanyahu, his obstinacy on Israel and on judging world leaders combined: This was someone he had known for four decades, from when the then–U.S. senator and the Israeli diplomat—just seven years apart in age—met in Washington in the 1980s when each was a young man seeking to make his name. Their relationship deepened despite disagreements over matters like U.S. diplomacy with Iran in the Obama era, which Biden supported and Netanyahu tried to scuttle. In that period, the then–vice president said he autographed a picture for his Israeli "buddy," writing: 'Bibi, I don't agree with a damn thing you say but I love you.' "[24] Even as others noted that the Israeli leader had become more conservative and inflexible, particularly on Palestinians, and more vicious toward critics, including U.S. officials, calling them disloyal and antisemitic, it was not until months into the war that the president began reevaluating Netanyahu.

Biden's intractability and fierce temper made his advisors careful in discussing shifts in U.S.-Israel policy with him. But even within the bounds the president's ideas placed on the administration, officials from the start of the war saw reasons and ways to limit Israel. Israeli officials spent the days after October 7 bringing their American counterparts wish lists of arms they said they needed, multiple U.S. officials serving at the time told me. Among them was a package of thousands of rifles for civilian defense teams, many of which had been outgunned during the Hamas-led attack—in part because the IDF had taken weapons from them because it underestimated the possible threat from the strip.[25] The military had meanwhile given thousands of weapons to Israelis in the occupied West Bank, in settlements and outposts that are illegal under both Israel's own laws and international law. American officials feared more rifles would help Israeli settlers, close to Netanyahu's far-right ministers, run amok; they refused to license the arms deal until Israel promised the guns would be controlled by the police, which does not arm Israelis in the West Bank.[26] Still, in handling the vast majority of other Israeli requests, Biden's staff stated no conditions, a choice with severe implications. When arming countries at war, the United States often demands written, detailed assurances about how they will use American weapons; a State Department lawyer described the practice to me as both appropriate and self-interested, helping combat future charges that American officials intended to aid and abet war crimes.

The Biden administration never proactively sought such guarantees for the Gaza campaign, the lawyer continued, saying government attorneys "could have and should have been more forceful" to prevent the outcome the U.S. was hurtling towards: deep complicity.

The administration's priority was unity with Tel Aviv. On October 10, Biden delivered his first extensive speech about the Hamas-led attack and described supporting Israel as a personal and national imperative.[27] He harked back fifty years, saying he knew the "black hole in your chest" among Israelis who lost family—Biden lost a wife and child in a 1972 car crash—and, in a comment that would later seem depressingly ironic, characterized Israel as a bulwark against repeating "the atrocities of the past." While suggesting a unique status for Tel Aviv, Biden also drew a parallel to the United States, saying that in a just-concluded call with Netanyahu, his third in four days, he told him Washington would in a similar situation provide a "swift, decisive, and overwhelming" response, and noting that Hamas's victims included American citizens. (He did not mention possible U.S. victims of Israel's Gaza offensive.) The war against Hamas was, Biden said, "about the security of our world, the security of the United States of America."

Biden hinted at calibrating Israel's retaliation: Respecting the law of war made the country "stronger and more secure," differentiating it from Hamas, he said, and he drew a line between the militant group and "the Palestinian people's right to dignity and self-determination." After describing steps to prevent any post–October 7 violence against Jews within the United States, the president noted he did not want to see hate against Muslims either—a line he added at the urging of Vice President Kamala Harris.[28] The dominant message, however, was clear: "full-throated identification [with Israel] to the point of almost making it our struggle," Rob Malley, Biden's special envoy for Iran, later told me. That influenced U.S. officials' behavior while diminishing the prospect of a future course correction. In Washington, "the longer you adhere to a policy, the higher the cost of shifting it. You don't have to justify why you stuck to it as long as you did, but you do have to justify any change," Malley said.

A shower of praise further strengthened the administration's commitment to its plan. Many of the voices the administration saw as most relevant vindicated Biden's posture, like pro-Israel groups and donors with influence in policy circles and, crucially, the election. Among them were Jewish American organizations, many of them members of the Conference of Presidents group, which the administration often treated as bellwethers on Israel policy even as many American Jews often disagreed with their positions.[29] The administration felt like "big heroes," Ben Rhodes, an Obama-era colleague of many Biden aides, told me. The White House sent reporters roundups of thankful comments from Israeli officials, and foreign policy hard-liners, including those in Congress, cheered the idea of a major U.S. role in fighting Hamas.[30]

Along with the public embrace, U.S. officials were beginning to try to wield the influence they assumed it would grant them. The administration dispatched Blinken and Defense Secretary Lloyd Austin to Israel for consultations, knowing that could delay Netanyahu's promised invasion of Gaza. Blinken arrived on October 12, by which point the Palestinian death toll exceeded that of Israelis on October 7, hitting fifteen hundred. At a Tel Aviv press conference, Blinken expressed sympathy with Israel but noted: "For democracies like the United States, like Israel, it's vitally important that we respect and follow international law, humanitarian law, the law of war, as applicable."[31]

Austin landed in the city the next day. A retired general with urban warfare experience, Austin privately told Israeli military leaders their bombing and rallying of troops was excessive, and it would be best not to pour forces into crowded Gaza but to strike Hamas targets by air and prepare special operations squads for raids based on intelligence tips.[32] Both men asked Israeli officials to consider how excessive violence might hurt their country in the long run, seeding resentment, and recommended allowing aid into the strip.[33] Traveling from Israel to Arab capitals, Blinken issued more calls to shield Palestinian civilians, and once back in the United States, Austin began a series of direct calls with Gallant that included discussions of the laws of war and the humanitarian needs of Palestinians.[34] The substance of the conversations with the Israelis was making the Biden administration increasingly nervous, as their counterparts spoke of killing many civilians and cited sweeping U.S. bombing during World War II as a justification—a repudiation of norms established afterward, which aimed to make the world more peaceful, and a reminder of the cost of rarely seeking accountability for excessive bloodshed.[35]

Top U.S. officials might have, at this point, sensed they alone could stop an Israeli offensive of unprecedented brutality and pushed for moderation. Instead, the Biden administration's early cautions to the Israelis consistently included loopholes, tacit green lights, and hints that solidarity would dominate U.S. Gaza policy.

During his Tel Aviv visit, Blinken described Israel's suffering as even greater than what the United States had previously endured—calling October 7 "the equivalent of ten 9/11s"—and said that "as a Jew . . . I understand on a personal level the harrowing echoes that Hamas's massacres carry," echoing Israeli officials' references to the Holocaust.[36] The secretary also repeated Israel's narrative that Hamas treated Palestinians "as human shields," giving a U.S. blessing to the line the IDF would use to justify thousands of attacks on civilian infrastructure. Under international law, the presence of Hamas fighters or equipment did not erase the need for Israel to avoid disproportionately killing innocents.

Contradictions also muddied Austin's message. The Pentagon chief's calls with Gallant about the laws of war tracked with his conviction that restraint in warfare was morally and strategically necessary. Austin had instituted a new Defense Department policy to limit civilian casualties from U.S. military operations and empowered officials who were skeptical of War on Terror tactics, and he repeatedly urged Israel to protect Palestinian civilians. But his dialogue with Gallant still emphasized Israeli-U.S. unity and so arguably conveyed a sense of license for significant violence. An American official recalled to me that in one of their early conversations after October 7, Austin read out talking points on protecting civilians prepared by his staff, then switched to a more personal, casual tone—and ended the call by telling his Israeli counterpart: "Happy hunting."

Even the Biden administration's nudge to Israel over the rifles amounted to little real limit on misusing American weapons and did not prevent a rapid spiral of settler violence in the West Bank. "There was no enforcement" of Israel's promise to safeguard the rifles, Gabavics told me. And the Israeli police, who were treated as responsible custodians of the weapons, had their own record of human rights violations, while sending them more arms freed up guns that Israeli officials could redistribute, including to extremist settlers.

The low likelihood of the administration's chosen policy course producing Israeli moderation became clear amid some of the most chilling news yet about Tel Aviv's war plans. Hours after Blinken left Israel on October 13, the IDF ordered a mass displacement from northern Gaza, giving 1.1 million Palestinians, more than half the region's population, just twenty-four hours to leave. The demand covered hundreds of thousands of people who had already fled their homes once, directed aid groups to leave behind supplies, and made no accommodation for staff and patients in twenty-three medical facilities, some of whom could not be safely moved. It suggested an Israeli attack of unimaginable proportions was imminent, and UN secretary-general António Guterres called the order "the language of genocide."[37] The move was so brazen that the International Committee of the Red Cross—which championed neutrality and was seen as the gold standard among humanitarian groups—publicly condemned it and privately alerted U.S. officials. They provided an assessment of expected Israeli war crimes that Dana Stroul, a senior Pentagon official, told colleagues in an email left her "chilled to the bone."[38] That same day, however, the Biden administration was making clear it had little interest in talk of U.S. constraints on Israel's offensive. Hours after the Israeli evacuation order became public knowledge, I obtained and published internal guidance from the Middle East bureau at the State Department to thousands of staff. In discussing the Gaza war, certain phrases were out of bounds for American officials, the email stated: No mention could be made of "ceasefire," "de-escalation," or "restoring calm." The death toll in Gaza was approaching two thousand.

By this point, the Biden administration was fully embroiled in an Israeli offensive that officials knew might evolve in terrifying ways. Still, staff perceived that stance as wise and careful, even if some came to regret it. "There was a calculation made that the freight train was leaving the station. We could have climbed aboard and helped to guide it and help them navigate. Or we could say, 'Godspeed and you're on your own,' and we would have no leverage whatsoever over it," the senior State Department official argued to me. Speaking ten months and tens of thousands of deaths later, the official added some reflection. "One can question whether we chose to use the leverage: Whether we were trying to grab the wheel or just providing charcoal to the engine," the official continued. "Reasonable people can debate that."

"MAKING RATIONAL DECISIONS"

As the war took shape, U.S. national security leaders came to see their responsibility as bigger than the lives of Israelis and Palestinians—becoming convinced that Washington alone could prevent huge strife across the Middle East, between Israel and the United States on one side and Israel's neighborhood foes, tied to Iran, on the other. That assessment would have major ramifications for the war. Their confidence in it was cemented by their handling of an early intense episode regarding Lebanon.

Hezbollah, the Lebanese militia aligned with Hamas and Iran, began attacking Israel on October 8, arguing it was acting in solidarity with Palestinians. Israel fired back with increasing intensity. Many of its security officials saw Hezbollah as a threat they could no longer tolerate and hoped American sympathy for Israel would create support for a fatal blow to the militia, while Israelis living in areas bordering Lebanon feared an October 7–style invasion. Biden and those nearest him, however, believed an Israeli offensive against the Lebanese group would overstretch the IDF and spark Iranian blowback, including potentially against U.S. troops; Hezbollah's ability to pummel Israel was widely understood as a deterrent against an Israeli strike on Iran. (The humanitarian toll of a war in already-struggling Lebanon concerned some senior officials, but it never drove the president.)

On October 11, the American and Israeli preferences over Lebanon collided. That morning Washington time, Netanyahu advisor Ron Dermer called Jake Sullivan to say Israel was preparing to bomb the Lebanese capital, Beirut—arguing it had to because Hezbollah was about to overrun the Israel-Lebanon border, and that it would kill Esmail Qaani, the leader of Iran's Quds Force military branch, and Hezbollah's leader Hassan Nasrallah, per a then–White House official. With Israeli fighter jets already in the air, Tel Aviv wanted U.S. approval to strike, intelligence support, and American attacks on additional targets in the country.

When Sullivan gathered other senior officials on a conference call to strategize at 8:45 a.m., Biden's team was terrified. They unanimously rejected the Israeli idea, and Biden agreed Washington should push back. He initiated a call with Netanyahu and his team in which, the White House official recalled, "the president just led in immediately with how crazy this is." The U.S. officials could sense competing impulses among their Israeli counterparts: trauma and fear of another invasion, but also fear of what might follow. "Clearly, Bibi had major hesitations: He is risk-averse even though he's a nightmare," the then-official told me. With Biden offering to help deter any Hezbollah assault and advising caution, the official continued, "you could hear [Netanyahu] immediately almost taking the lifeline the president threw him." But the decision lay with Israel's far-right cabinet—and Dermer called Sullivan back shortly afterward to claim Hezbollah had sent paragliders into Israel just as Hamas had on October 7, while within Israel, the IDF and local media also suggested an attack had begun, sparking mass panic.[39]

American officials probed their own intelligence and found little basis for the claim; in a rare message to the United States, meanwhile, Iran said it did not want to expand the Israel-Hamas war. Told that Dermer could not speak because he was in an Israeli cabinet meeting, Sullivan sent him a note saying he was acting irrationally based on poor intelligence, according to a report in *The Atlantic*.[40] Dermer called within forty-five minutes: The cabinet had voted against the strike on Hezbollah.

The Biden team's rationality appeared to have prevailed. For months afterward, White House staff cited the moment as evidence of the effectiveness of working closely with the Israelis and persuading them not to make harmful choices—rather than threatening them with consequences like cutting off U.S. weapons—and to counter the argument that the administration did too little to wield American leverage over Netanyahu.

Sullivan's message to Dermer underscored that the administration now saw itself as the sensible part of a joint U.S.-Israeli front. But that self-assured narrative was a poor foundation on which to base further policymaking. U.S. officials had known for years that, in the words of the then–White House official, "Bibi's caution is the one thing that can be useful about him sometimes," and Israel's own intelligence officials had, before the cabinet made its decision, agreed with the United States that there was no Hezbollah incursion. To credit the lack of a strike to Washington's savvy was to ignore those realities.

Separately, there were growing indications of a lack of rationality in the administration as well. Some American officials had such a strong reaction to October 7 that their response to Hamas was less about strategy than revulsion and a War on Terror–style image of the group as an unfathomable evil that could be met only with extreme force. In Biden's October 10 speech, he said the Palestinian group had beheaded babies, despite his aides telling him that claim was unverified.[41] The line was later proved to be untrue; Biden never apologized. In a press conference after that speech, Sullivan described Hamas as responsible for "the same evil and barbarity that we've seen from ISIS."[42] Three days later, McGurk posted on X a video from the Israeli government—which was by now running a social media campaign promoting its anti-Hamas offensive—that included footage of the 9/11 attack and excerpts from Biden's speech.[43] The White House advisor, who was rarely active on the platform, highlighted one quote from the address: "There are moments in this life when unadulterated pure evil is unleashed on this world. . . ." Rejecting the brutality of the Hamas-led attack was understandable, but some U.S. officials worried that a simplistic narrative of incomprehensible violence reflected a continued misunderstanding of Israeli-Palestinian tensions and tacitly justified impunity in Israel's response to October 7. One former U.S. official who had worked with McGurk and highlighted the video felt it both drew "false analogies" and bolstered "anti-Muslim, anti-Arab bigotry," this official told me. By shifting the focus away from decades of Palestinian frustration rooted in documented violations of international law, and the reality that many Palestinians saw Hamas as their only champion, the Biden administration was "categorizing it as some insane, hate-filled, ISIS-esque situation . . . [which] produces wrongheaded policies."

Just a few days after McGurk's post, it became clear that misconceptions and blind spots about the region were hindering U.S. policy, just as they had in the War on Terror. Iran-linked fighters in Iraq and Syria had been targeting American bases since October 7—then suddenly on October 19, the Houthi militia in Yemen joined in, launching missiles at targets tied to Israel. The United States had long discounted the Houthis as regional players even as American-backed policies such as a vicious Saudi-led military campaign against them helped them entrench their power. Now, their willingness and capacity to act over their stated concern for Palestinians shocked the Biden team.

Yet generally, top Biden aides' confidence in their ability to chart the right course on Gaza—without applying heavy U.S. pressure on Israel—was growing, increasing their resistance to those questioning their policy. Tangible demonstrations of American power bolstered that sense: Biden ordered major Navy deployments to the Mediterranean Sea, saying he was shielding Israel, and quashed a UN Security Council resolution urging a ceasefire in Gaza.[44] Additionally, the White House began to think it could use its role in Israel's offensive, seen in Washington as just, to advance its overall foreign policy goals, particularly U.S. support for Ukraine, which had become less popular as Republicans increasingly questioned it; officials began crafting a joint package of $95 billion in military aid for Kyiv, Tel Aviv, and Taipei that they planned to sell as evidence of Biden's global commitment to allies and a major win for his record. Increasingly dire reports from Gaza had little hope of tempering the administration's growing self-assurance. "There's something about those jobs where you just don't see the Palestinian kids," Ben Rhodes told me. "It's the antiseptic intelligence reports, it's Israel saying Hamas is behind every rock, and it's twenty years of dehumanization of people in that region as civilian casualties or collateral damage."

BEAR HUG

In the days after October 7, Israeli officials started talking about Biden visiting their country. The president was immediately enthusiastic.[45] A high-profile image of U.S.-Israeli solidarity appealed to both governments. For Biden, it reflected his sympathy for Israelis and his political brand. Earlier in 2023, the Biden administration promoted a visit by the president to wartime Kyiv as proof of his vigor and commitment to American partners. For Netanyahu, meanwhile, hosting his old friend could boost his long-standing argument to Israelis that he was uniquely positioned to handle global affairs and distract from domestic criticism of his government failing to halt the Hamas invasion and international criticism of rising Palestinian pain.

For U.S. officials, a trip made sense for their plan of keeping Israel close. The administration was privately exploring hostage negotiations with Hamas and wanted to "slow things down" in Gaza, altering Israel's original plan and an invasion that was so intense prisoner releases became impossible, McGurk said in a later interview.[46] The president's presence would likely force Israel to hold off on expanding its offensive into the strip.

Netanyahu formally invited Biden in an October 14 call, leaking the invitation to reporters to make rejecting it hard, and Biden finalized his travel plan after lengthy deliberations on October 16. His aides concluded that Biden should go beyond meeting Netanyahu to see the leaders of the Palestinian Authority, Egypt, and Jordan. They also deemed a trip to Israel as necessary for pushing Tel Aviv on the issue of aid: Israel was still refusing to allow supplies into Gaza, contrary to the law of war and U.S. demands. Blinken, who had already visited Israel twice, was close to a deal but was told it could be clinched only by his boss. To Biden's aides, that showed their persuasion method was bearing fruit and simply needed to be deployed by the right person—an analysis that ignored how they were treating Israeli compliance with international law as a bargaining chip rather than a necessity, which would become a corrosive habit.

Then came the news of October 17. A huge explosion killed hundreds of people, many of them children, at Al-Ahli Hospital in Gaza City. Hamas blamed Israel; Israel blamed Palestinian militant groups. Later investigations by Human Rights Watch and the research group Forensic Architecture found, respectively, that a rocket like those used by Palestinian fighters may have been responsible and that Israel spread false information to pin the blame on Palestinians. In a press conference at nearby Al-Shifa Hospital, a group of doctors surrounded by corpses told the world every part of Gaza was at risk. Ghassan Abu Sittah, a British Palestinian doctor present at the scene, later said that moment was when the U.S.-backed Israeli offensive "stopped being a war, and became a genocide."[47]

Amid public horror and heightened fears that any option other than an immediate truce would ensure more mass casualty events, Arab leaders said they could not meet with Biden. The president gathered advisors to consider whether he should still go; they discussed disturbing possibilities such as Air Force One facing fire from Gaza. Biden was adamant, however: "I've got to see these guys face to face."[48]

The president's trip made American entanglement in the escalating Israeli offensive clearer than any shipment of bombs or White House address could have. On the tarmac, he and Netanyahu embraced, in an image that became widely referred to as the bear hug. "You are not alone," the president told Israelis, and he underscored that he was uniquely committed to their country—noting he was the first U.S. president to visit Israel during a time of war—and that he saw the war through the lens of America's decades-long battles after 9/11. Biden used the parallel to say the United States had made "mistakes," the anti-Hamas fight should be "deliberate," and to speak of shielding civilians, but he also once again cast the Palestinian faction as irredeemably evil, speaking of beheadings, and echoed—without offering evidence—Israel's claim that a Palestinian group caused the October 17 hospital blast. In Israel afterward, "many people here were heard to say they wished he were their Prime Minister," *The New Yorker* reported.[49]

In the State Department, the term "desk officer" refers to an official with a specific focus on one international subject—not someone making big decisions, but a middle manager who jealously guards their limited influence. Given Biden's obvious predilection and White House control of almost anything relating to Gaza, bypassing normal deliberations, one American humanitarian official told me that when it came to the war, "the big joke was that the president was the desk officer."

Biden's visit to Tel Aviv shed more light. In his view, he was an officer, and he was at war.

CHAPTER 2

DISSENT, THEN DEFLECTION

Mid-October 2023–Mid-December 2023

JUST A WEEK INTO THE WAR, SERIOUS CHALLENGES TO THE Biden administration's Gaza policy began growing among the president's own allies, including Democratic members of Congress and crucial voter blocs, and among nonpartisan government experts. Dissent mushroomed as Israel's U.S.-backed campaign expanded. After the ground invasion of the strip, it appeared the administration's emphasis on unity and delicate persuasion was having little effect on Israel, and Washington saw a burgeoning, unprecedented discussion of using American leverage over Netanyahu. "By mid-November, it became very clear to me and an increasing number of people that there was no fucking plan whatsoever," a White House official later told me.

Critics of the U.S.-Israeli war strategy increasingly doubted it would kneecap Hamas, free the Israeli hostages, or promote Israeli-Palestinian peace—in short, that it could achieve any of its stated goals. Biden aides pursued and secured a truce-and-hostage-release deal among Hamas, Israel, and the United States, bringing the only pause in fighting in Gaza between October 7, 2023, and the end of Biden's presidency in January 2025, but then recommitted to their "bear-hug" approach, which enabled more killing of Palestinians, deepened tensions over the war in American society, and alienated

Biden supporters. Ignoring possible off-ramps, Biden's decision-making circle prolonged a war the president himself began to describe as too bloody.

CRACKS EMERGE

Over several evenings and several stiff whiskies, Josh Paul inched toward the decision that would change his life. At age forty-five, he had worked at the State Department's arms-deals office for nearly twelve years and in the Western foreign policy establishment for twelve years prior, but in working on Biden's post–October 7 policy, he felt uniquely disturbed. When Paul emailed dozens of colleagues on October 8 suggesting Netanyahu might go too far in retaliating, not one wrote back. Two called, one to say the dissent was meaningless and the other to ask whether he was about to be fired. As Paul processed expedited U.S. weapons shipments to Israel in the subsequent days, he saw no deliberation over shipping bombs and ammunition to a government that was speaking of collective punishment for Palestinians. He drafted a resignation letter but, like the career bureaucrat he was, he tried one last time to trust the system: On October 17, Paul headed to a secure room in the State Department to examine classified intelligence, seeking evidence that Biden was privately restraining Israel or that media coverage of Israeli attacks was exaggerating their viciousness. He found none. That afternoon, he told me, he handed in his resignation.

Some other U.S. officials were already alarmed by Israel's sweeping bombing of Gaza, coupled with the sense that there was little room for disagreement within the administration. "It feels like post-9/11 . . . you're really afraid of being seen as anti-American or an antisemite," one official told me that week.[1] Another felt silenced even as evolving U.S. policy seemed to directly conflict with a personal motivation for working in national security and said: "I don't want us dragged back into another Middle East war."

On October 18, Paul announced his resignation on LinkedIn. A top State Department official saw it as a bellwether, telling me: "There's basically a mutiny brewing within State at all levels." I knew Paul from conversations in which he defended U.S. arms deals to Saudi Arabia and the United Arab Emirates during their vicious war in Yemen, and I was shocked he would quit over human rights. I chanced a call to him and secured his first post-resignation interview. In past government discussions over weapons sales, there had been real debate, he said, but with Israel after October 7, "it was clear there's no arguing." For Paul to be the first government official to resign over Gaza, sparking headlines globally, demonstrated how Biden's policy was becoming understood as a strategic calamity. Paul was a proponent of U.S. global power, and his resignation showed how Washington's foreign policy apparatus, home to few bleeding hearts, was abuzz with anxiety about the United States being implicated in Israel's campaign. Officials at several national security agencies passed around an essay from the Israeli American scholar Raz Segal describing the offensive as "A Textbook Case of Genocide," as, per one senior official, government personnel felt "a clear signal from the top . . . other pathways weren't possible."[2]

High-ranking Biden aides treated discomfort in the administration as a matter of managing emotions and showing that with "the most diverse presidential administration in history," per a common talking point, they would face some frustration as a result of different identities on their team—rather than acknowledging that divergent views were grounded in officials' expertise and judgment. Such thinking led to surreal decisions such as organizing two separate gatherings at the White House, an hour apart, for political appointees who were Jewish and for those from Muslim and Arab backgrounds.

Amid the focus on identity, particular concern for Jewish vulnerability was clear. The first message to Biden's personnel from White House chief of staff Jeff Zients on October 7 referenced staff linked to Israel without mentioning danger to Palestinians, and in the administration's early discussions about how a new Israel-Hamas war might affect American society, senior staff spoke of fears about Jewish students' safety on college campuses and a federal role in responding.

The approach seemed inseparable to many officials from the frequent contact between the White House and Jewish American community leaders and political donors; both groups are often more deferential to Israel than are American Jews as a whole. While attention to Jewish safety made sense, a more careful, balanced strategy could have avoided worsening rifts among Americans. Washington struggled to address predictable anti-Palestinian sentiment and Islamophobia amid the war. On October 14, an Illinois man claiming fear of "jihad" attacked a Palestinian American mother and child, stabbing both repeatedly in the home the family rented from him. Six-year-old Wadea al-Fayoume died on the spot.[3] The highest-ranking Biden staffer to meet with the family was a Small Business Administration official, Dilawar Syed.

"The administration's policy decisions show stunning disregard for innocent Palestinians—and that same dehumanization is also reflected in how staff are being treated," a person in the administration told me during this period.[4] When top Biden aides like Zients tried to address the imbalance—by, for instance, arranging listening sessions with Muslim and Arab officials—it was clear those forums had little influence on policy. Diversity in staff is not just about checking boxes, the administration source argued: "You want to benefit from the more informed decision-making that happens from a broader set of experiences having a seat at the table. The inner, inner circle on these issues is not at all diverse. Does that completely explain the monstrous disregard for innocent Palestinian lives? No, but it's hard to think these things are entirely disconnected."

Fear that Biden was disregarding expertise and inconvenient feedback grew especially strong among foreign policy personnel. The White House National Security Council rejected requests for an emergency meeting of a government task force on atrocities, a U.S. official on the task force told me, only holding its first session based on its normal schedule, on October 20, by which point the Israeli offensive in Gaza had killed more than 1,500 Palestinian children. At the State Department, leaders in the Civilian Security, Democracy, and Human Rights branch told their employees in an October 26 town hall that it was unclear they could affect Gaza policy in any way and recommended that officials try to make a positive impact elsewhere. The department established a task force on the war that lacked dedicated slots for humanitarian and human rights officials, even as teams from the Europe bureau to Diplomatic Security had such seats.

Outside dissent rose too. On October 7 and soon afterward, Rashida Tlaib—the sole Palestinian American in Congress—and fellow Democratic congresswomen Cori Bush, Alexandria Ocasio-Cortez, and Ilhan Omar issued statements highlighting U.S. support for Israeli repression; all but Tlaib demanded a ceasefire. White House press secretary Karine Jean-Pierre called the statements "repugnant" and "disgraceful" on October 10—amplifying a right-wing narrative that Democrats were tacitly endorsing Hamas. The condemnation from their own party was especially upsetting, a congressional aide told me, given several of those lawmakers had faced death threats and pledges to end their careers from pro-Israel hard-liners. Still, by October 17, seven more Democratic legislators—including big names like antiwar icon Barbara Lee—issued a ceasefire call too, and State Department staff were finalizing formal objections, or dissent cables, to send to Blinken.[5] The moves demonstrated there was a strategic case for a policy other than embracing Netanyahu; even if the signal could not sway Biden, it encouraged rising antiwar advocacy around the country and debate in official circles.

To a degree, the administration was already altering the war policy. On October 15, Biden appointed a humanitarian envoy for the Middle East, veteran diplomat David Satterfield. The administration's limited ambition in making the situation more humane was already clear, however. The trickle of supplies into Gaza after Biden's negotiation with Netanyahu and Egyptian president Abdel Fattah El-Sisi was a "drop in the ocean," humanitarian officials said, and in one of his earliest high-level meetings, Satterfield shocked other officials by suggesting moving Palestinians into Egypt, a U.S. official present told me.[6] (Satterfield denied to me that he ever supported a transfer.) The idea—sparking memories of what Palestinians call the Nakba ("catastrophe"), the permanent displacement of more than 700,000 Palestinians in

1948—risked a major violation of international law. Still, it was backed by some Israelis, from officials to extremists who envisioned annexing both Gaza and the occupied West Bank.[7]

"A GRAVEYARD FOR THOUSANDS OF CHILDREN"

An overhaul of Biden's war strategy could hardly come soon enough for Gaza's 2.2 million people, nearly half of whom were already living in makeshift shelters by mid-October. Before the war, two-thirds of the food consumed in the strip came from outside Gaza, with twelve thousand trucks entering in August 2023; now, Biden's negotiation with Israel and Egypt allowed twenty trucks of water, food, and medicine to enter initially, then fourteen the following day.[8]

Meanwhile, the intensity of Israeli strikes was almost inconceivable. One attack, on October 10, showed how the approach seemed, to Amnesty International, "indiscriminate."[9] An afternoon strike on a six-story building in Sheikh Radwan killed at least forty civilians—Palestinians like Iman, who had traveled there with her four children to stay with her father because the neighborhood had been spared in earlier barrages. "I couldn't protect them," Iman's father, Mahmoud Ashour, wailed as he dug through the rubble. His eldest grandchild, Rihab, had been eight; the youngest, Hamza, was just six months old. A Hamas member who had lived in the building was not there when it was attacked. Days later, an Israeli strike hit Saint Porphyrios Greek Orthodox Church, where many of Gaza's Christians were sheltering, and killed eighteen civilians. Ramez al-Sury, who lost three children, told Amnesty International his heart died with them, and he wished he was killed too. Israel never provided evidence for its surreal claim there was a Hamas control center in the church compound.[10]

While the IDF professed to follow international law, which permits some collateral damage, its interpretation of "proportional" attacks allowed far more violence than even its own past offensives. The Israeli news outlets *Local Call* and *+972* broke the news that an artificial intelligence system named Lavender was central to the bombing.[11] Lavender created kill lists of individuals linked to Hamas and other armed groups. The IDF did not require troops to probe how the system identified targets; one source personally spent just twenty seconds before each strike to ensure the target was male, the source said. By mid-October, the IDF told troops Lavender was effectively issuing marching orders, saying it was 90 percent guaranteed to correctly identify a target as linked to Hamas—basing that on a random sample and leaving open a large possibility of deadly mistakes. Lavender's targets were fed into a separate AI-powered system called "Where's Daddy?" that flagged when targets returned to their houses, meaning the IDF deliberately targeted them alongside family members, killing many women and children. Yet another AI system, called "the Gospel," identified "power targets" Israeli forces focused on immediately after October 7, like residential towers or government buildings with symbolic importance for Palestinians, per a separate *+972* and *Local Call* report.

Simultaneously, Israel loosened its limits on how many civilians were allowed to be killed in any single strike and created an expectation one Israeli intelligence officer summed up as: "Whatever you can, you bomb."[12] That made the IDF more dependent on rapid AI-generated targeting, abandoning past practices such as discussing each target with legal advisors. In hitting even junior militants, the IDF approved killing up to twenty civilians per strike.[13] Collateral damage had previously been barred—at least formally—in assassinating such low-level fighters.[14] (The permitted ratio fell and rose later in the war.) With attacks so frequent, the IDF often deployed "dumb" bombs, which cause more damage than precision munitions but are cheaper and more easily available. "That meant literally dropping the whole house on its occupants . . . [then] you immediately move on to the next target. Because of the system, the targets never end," one Israeli officer reported.

The IDF responded to the revelations by saying Lavender was "not a list of confirmed military operatives eligible to attack." AI systems were merely "tools" for analysts, and the IDF deployed dumb bombs as "standard weaponry [with] a high level of precision." The impact of Israeli attacks was clear, however, and swelled once Israeli tanks and troops entered the strip by October 28.[15] Invading amid a communications blackout that terrified Palestinians, the IDF began fighting at close quarters, focusing on northern Gaza, particularly Gaza City.[16] (Hamas fired back, killing Israeli soldiers in Gaza and launching rockets into Israel itself, which were mostly intercepted.)[17] On October 31, a single Israeli strike using two-thousand-pound American-made bombs killed at least 126 civilians, including 23 children, in the Jabalia refugee camp. "Gaza has become a graveyard for thousands of children. It's a living hell for everyone else," James Elder, a UNICEF spokesperson, reported that day, citing an estimated death toll of 3,450 children.[18] Assessing the period later, the research group Airwars called the first month of Israeli aerial attacks on Gaza "incomparable with any 21st-century air campaign."[19] By nearly all metrics, the campaign exceeded past standards for a month of bombing by the United States, Russia, Turkey, and Israel itself: almost seven times as many children killed and three times as many "high-fatality incidents" massacring twenty civilians or more.

SELECTIVE SYMPATHY

Abood Okal, his wife, and their baby spent most of October crammed into a house in the southern Gaza town of Rafah with dozens of other people. Still hoping their American passports could help them flee, they wanted to be near the crossing to Egypt. But as they waited, they faced the same miseries as most others in the strip. "Drinking water remains our biggest challenge," Okal told me in an October 23 voice note, saying the family had already once resorted to drinking nonpotable water. He added that they were short on food and milk for their one-year-old baby, Yousef, which he described as a priority because it was "his main source of nutrition as well as his comfort food." The roar of Israeli bombings made the house shake, making it hard for the Palestinian American family to sleep. When Yousef did doze off, he often woke up screaming. Lying on the floor each night, his parents kept him in between them so that if they were hit by an air strike, they would die together.

As the Okals unsuccessfully tried to leave Rafah for Egypt three times—only to be turned away amid Egyptian, Israeli, and Palestinian wrangling—their situation became a microcosm of U.S. fecklessness despite its deep ties to the parties involved. To a Washington outsider like Sammy Nabulsi, a thirty-four-year-old real estate lawyer based in Boston, the situation made no sense. Nabulsi had become fixated on the Okals since a mutual friend told him about their plight, reaching out to journalists and talking to Abood as much as Gaza's spotty internet permitted. Privately, he also cold-emailed officials across the Biden administration, only to be shocked by their responses. One U.S. official asked Nabulsi to ask his personal contacts to open the crossing.[20] Another confirmed the State Department had at one point told Americans to go to the gate—which had been repeatedly bombed—without being sure it would open. "Both the secretary [of state] and the president are clearly prioritizing military aid to a foreign government, the destruction of a foreign territory, and frankly the killing of foreign civilians over the safety of American citizens," Nabulsi argued to me. As U.S. officials emphasized the complexity of negotiations over the crossing, Nabulsi felt they were ignoring simpler matters: Couldn't Washington at least ask Israel not to bomb the parts of Gaza where Americans were located? His Biden administration contacts never responded to that point.

On November 1, the Rafah Crossing published a list of several hundred foreign nationals permitted to pass. But the group didn't include any Americans. As he waited, Okal got a message from the U.S. embassy in Cairo saying there was no timeline for when U.S. citizens would be included; he spent the night hearing air strikes land half a mile away. Still, he expressed hope, not bitterness. "We trust our State Department is doing its best to get us out of Gaza—before it's too late," he told me. Then, the next day, Palestinian officials released another list of people approved to use the crossing; Nabulsi stumbled on it through his obsessive internet searches, and found it included the Okals, as well as one of Abood's sisters and her family. He texted me, both excited and afraid: He couldn't initially reach them because of disruptions to communications in Gaza. It could have been too late.

Finally, Abood texted. The Okals had an exhausting twenty-four-hour journey to Cairo, but by November 6, they were home in Massachusetts. Still, over the following months, Okal kept thinking about his sisters and their children in Gaza; on the increasingly rare occasions when he could reach them, they described even more crowding and rampant disease.[21] The arbitrariness seemed clear: U.S. government paperwork represented the chief difference between them, while his tax dollars were driving their suffering.

But within the administration, a clear, though unspoken, grading of humanity was embedded and important to how the war was understood. Even before October 7, U.S. officials across agencies and levels had often spoken to Israeli counterparts, yet the State Department had "fewer than five" people in regular contact with Palestinians, a senior official told me. This official felt that few Biden aides were "completely dismissive or indifferent" to Palestinian life, but that the president, Middle East advisor Brett McGurk, and John Kirby, the White House spokesman for national security, had a view of Palestinians they summarized as: "This is awful, but they did it to themselves." It was hard to imagine that top administration figures would ever feel that way about Israelis. Enthusiastic support for Israel was, in fact, common. In discussions of IDF horrors like the Jabalia strike, the senior official recalled, McGurk almost seemed to be acting "as Israel's lawyer," repeating, for example, Israel's claims that it didn't mean to hit civilians. Another Biden appointee told me the chorus of staff—including those who did not work on foreign policy—loudly expressing pro-Israel views and attempting to shape policy left officials who wanted to discuss Palestinian suffering censoring themselves, doubting their instincts, and feeling outnumbered. A third official, who identifies as Jewish, described frustration with the influence of "very vocal senior Jewish staff across the administration who are openly Zionist" and were perceived as representing Jewish leadership even if other Jews on Biden's team and in the United States felt differently. Some of those senior staff said they felt their families in Washington, D.C., were in danger, communicating a sense of trauma that, the official said, made it harder for others to share divergent views about the war. Okal's citizenship made him one of the fortunate few in Gaza when fighting began; the contours of the administration meant most others had little luck.

AN "EXCEPTIONAL" PRESIDENT

As darkening news from Gaza strengthened calls for a U.S. policy shift, critics of Biden's approach pinned their hopes on history: Many of his predecessors put American support for Israel in question to discourage Israeli policies they felt risked U.S. interests.

In 1948, President Harry Truman became the first world leader to recognize Israel, rejecting advice to show concern for Palestinians and defending Israel even as he privately made antisemitic comments.[22] But his successor, Dwight Eisenhower, repeatedly used leverage over Israel to change its behavior, just as the United States might challenge other friends. In 1953, Eisenhower halted $26 million in American economic aid until Tel Aviv agreed to stop building a canal opposed by the United Nations.[23] Three years later, when Israel, France, and Britain attacked Egypt after it nationalized the Suez Canal, the Eisenhower administration was enraged over a step it saw as threatening U.S. influence in the Arab world and aiding the Soviet Union. Eisenhower de-escalated the war, but Israeli forces stayed in the Sinai Peninsula—upsetting Cairo. To secure their withdrawal, Eisenhower considered embracing a UN resolution against foreign support for Israel, including its $100 million in annual donations from, and bond sales to, Americans.[24] Citing fear of American and international sanctions, Israel left the Sinai.[25]

In 1967, Israel captured huge swaths of land, including the Sinai once more, in the Six-Day War, saying attacks by Palestinian militants from neighboring Arab states meant it had to act preemptively. Lyndon B. Johnson played an "ambiguous" role, experts at the Washington Institute for Near East Policy later wrote, noting his preoccupation with Vietnam.[26] Still, even after the war invigorated support for Zionism among American Jews, U.S. officials again sought to force Israel out of the Sinai under President Gerald Ford. Henry Kissinger, Ford's secretary of state, described backing Israel as "sentimental" but unnecessary and stopped some arms sales to the country for six months.[27] Criticism from Congress and his rival Jimmy Carter eventually drove Ford to abandon the effort.[28] When Carter became president, however, he secured Israel's withdrawal from the Sinai in exchange for peace with Egypt through the 1978 Camp David Accords; though Carter did not apply tangible pressure on Tel Aviv, his mediation also did not position the United States as reflexively pro-Israel.

Ronald Reagan, Carter's successor, returned to deploying American leverage over Israel—and like other presidents saw value in distancing Washington from controversial Israeli decisions. In 1981, the Reagan administration voted for a UN Security Council resolution critical of Israel and briefly paused fighter jet transfers to the IDF over Israeli bombing of Iraq and Lebanon.[29] The following year, as Israel battered Beirut, Reagan called then–Israeli prime minister Menachem Begin to say the entire U.S.-Israel relationship was in question, deploying language pro-Israel forces would today deem unacceptable. "I used the word holocaust deliberately," Reagan wrote in his diary, "and said the symbol of [Begin's] war was becoming a picture of a seven-month-old baby with its arms blown off." Within twenty minutes, Begin called back saying the bombing had stopped. Reagan repeatedly withheld or delayed weapons for Israel, including cluster munitions and warplanes.[30] His successor, George H. W. Bush, escalated U.S. breaks with Israel. In 1990 during a congressional hearing, his secretary of state, James Baker, blasted Tel Aviv for complicating potential talks with the Palestinians, read out the White House number, and said: "When you're serious about peace, call us." The administration then withheld $10 billion in loan guarantees for Israel until Israeli prime minister Yitzhak Shamir agreed to halt settlement-building and join an international conference on Israel-Palestine in Madrid in 1991, which helped produce the Oslo Accords, establishing some Palestinian self-rule in the West Bank and Gaza—albeit a system still dominated by Israel.

The fall of the Soviet Union reduced fears the United States would lose influence among Arabs to a rival, over Palestine or other matters, but the domestic political imperative to support Israel remained; presidents became far more cautious toward Tel Aviv. President Bill Clinton knew he had leverage over Netanyahu—"Who's the fucking superpower here?" he raged after a difficult meeting with the Israeli leader—but rarely deployed it.[31] Rooted in pro-Israel evangelical Christian thinking and militaristic policies, particularly against groups rooted in Islamist ideology like Hamas, President George W. Bush told his National Security Council to "tilt back toward Israel."[32] The Bush administration endorsed Israel's punishing 2006 offensive in Lebanon and Israel's beginning a blockade on Gaza intended to, per a U.S. diplomatic cable, keep the economy of 1.5 million Palestinians "on the brink of collapse."[33] Succeeding Bush, Barack Obama questioned U.S. foreign policy and pursued a signature achievement in opposition to Netanyahu—a nuclear deal with Iran—but did not press Israel over Palestinian rights. Trump subsequently instituted overwhelmingly pro-Israel policies, then cursed out Netanyahu for a perceived lack of loyalty.

Through all those presidencies, the United States remained Israel's chief military and diplomatic backer. Pressure came in "one-offs," Aaron David Miller, a negotiator for Republican and Democratic secretaries of state for twenty-five years, told me: "The notion that, 'Other presidents had pressured Israel, why couldn't this one?' just flies in the face of reality." Yet he also described steps Biden could have taken to restrain Netanyahu while remaining in the tradition of supporting Israel: restricting U.S. weapons or enforcing conditions on their use, backing UN ceasefire resolutions or recognizing Palestinian statehood, or talks with Hamas on specific issues like freeing the October 7 hostages.

Only a president could approve and champion such measures. Biden had a "disinclination" to do so because he was "exceptional" in his closeness to Israel, Miller argued, growing up with a father who, per Biden, "had a preoccupation with the Holocaust," then spending decades in Congress wooed by pro-Israel lobbyists.[34] And from early in the war, his advisors avoided recommending steps he might see as drastic, even if they could be effective—partly because of their own disinclination for examining how their past policy choices fueled the crisis. Key policymakers did not consider any responsibility for October 7 for "several months," a senior Biden aide told me, and officials spoke of a call for a ceasefire as a card they could play only once and which would have little impact if deployed too early.

The administration chose myopia about U.S.-Israel history, including on its watch, when a reckoning could have prevented months of carnage. As Tel Aviv began its retaliation, U.S. officials knew their "flailing" ally lacked a goal and would "lash out indiscriminately," the senior aide told me. "We had the advantage of distance: We could take a breath and say, 'Alright, where is this going?'" Delaying the Gaza invasion and discouraging civilian casualties were two early moves in that vein, but as the war expanded, U.S. officials only became more convinced there was no alternative to their obviously failing strategy.

DEALING WITH HAMAS

For Hamas, the history of U.S. involvement in Israel-Palestine was inescapable, driving its thinking about October 7 and what would follow. Hamas likely expected Washington could make Israel compromise, first on swapping jailed Palestinians for kidnapped Israelis, then perhaps in political negotiations. Hamas leaders seemingly did not, however, account for how committed the Biden administration would become to Netanyahu's narrative of decimating the group. The scale of the war arguably made it more important than ever to engage with Hamas's motivations and logic, rather than treating it as irrationally extreme. Designating the organization a terror group and highlighting its history of horrors like suicide bombings, Israel and the United States spoke with Hamas only indirectly, through mediators, usually U.S. allies Egypt and Qatar.

Hamas emerged in 1987 when Palestinian members of the Muslim Brotherhood, the cross-border movement for Islam to define governance and society, decided Palestine could escape Israeli subjugation only through intense resistance. Its founders reached that conclusion amid the First Intifada—in which Israel responded with overwhelming, disproportionate force to a movement rooted in throwing stones at tanks—and steps by the historically dominant Palestinian nationalist group, the Palestine Liberation Organization (PLO), to abandon military tactics after Israeli and other regional forces had badly weakened it. Ironically, as it sought to undermine the PLO, Israel had clandestinely supported the Islamists.[35] "Hamas, to my great regret, is Israel's creation," Avner Cohen, a former Israeli religious affairs official in Gaza, later argued.[36]

Hamas leaders loathed the idea of partitioning historic Palestine, the presumed outcome of the diplomacy the PLO had begun pursuing with Israel and world powers toward a two-state solution, and distrusted their secular counterparts, particularly the central party in the PLO, Fatah.[37] They used attacks to derail the talks, forming a military wing, Al-Qassam Brigades, in 1991. That past, the violence of the 2000–2005 Second Intifada, and Hamas's takeover of Gaza—first by winning elections across the Palestinian territories in 2006, then through a bloody 2007 civil war against Fatah, fueled in part by U.S. efforts to keep Hamas out of government—boosted critics of engaging with the Palestinian group, who said talks would empower it.[38] Throughout its history, however, Hamas had made "various concessions . . . the movement is aware of the need for a political settlement," Tareq Baconi, the president of the board of Al-Shabaka: The Palestinian Policy Network, argued in 2023.[39] He noted that Hamas was evolving toward accepting a Palestinian state limited to territories outside Israeli control in 1967, and that the PLO had also previously deployed extreme violence and been treated by Israel and the United States as irredeemable terrorists. Separately, Baconi disputed the perception that "Hamas is engaging in armed resistance or violence for the sake of violence," saying the "terrorist" framing helped U.S. and allied officials deflect from "their responsibility" to address Palestinian disenfranchisement and ensured danger for Israeli Jews. Talking to Hamas was a tough sell in Washington, however, even after the United States asked Qatar to host the group's political leadership starting in 2012.[40]

Through complex negotiations, I secured hours-long, in-person interviews in the Qatari capital of Doha with two top Hamas figures: Mousa Abu Marzouk, a founding member of the group, and Basem Naim, a former Hamas health minister in Gaza. Far-ranging and sometimes confounding as they were, our conversations at their safe houses revolved around a central axle: the role of America, as Israel's top backer and the key player in developments after October 7.

"We didn't expect this brutality of America," said Abu Marzouk, who had lived in the United States and been jailed there for nearly two years, saying he had presumed Washington would "allow for a partial aggression against Gaza." Flanked by several aides and a poster of the Dome of the Rock, the seventy-three-year-old spoke in measured tones through a translator but projected quiet authority and sometimes unnerving intensity. Biden chose "to support Israel regardless of the Israeli policies and this is against the American policies through history," he argued. Naim and I spoke one-on-one a day earlier; younger, animated, and eager for anything I would share about American views of the war, he emphasized Hamas's perspective on sparking a new round of violence. "We consider [October 7] an act of defense," Naim said, pointing to the sixteen-year blockade of Gaza by Israel and Egypt and Israeli moves in recent years to annex the West Bank and undercut Palestinian claims to Jerusalem. Echoing a statement common among critics of Israel's U.S.-backed offensive, Naim told me: "History didn't start on October 7. . . . We were squeezed." He claimed Hamas only aimed at military targets, citing a prisoner exchange with Israel as a top goal, and said violence in the Middle East keeps arising because "the Americans and the Israelis . . . have failed to tackle the root of all the turmoil in the region, which is the Palestinian cause."

The Hamas leaders' narrative had holes and obfuscations. "There was no intention to harm or to attack any of the civilians," Naim told me, blaming civilian deaths on "chaos"—but Human Rights Watch proved some Hamas fighters targeted civilians, while some Palestinian attackers in civilian clothes coordinated with Hamas. (A Hamas statement about the attack acknowledged "some faults" while highlighting Israeli conscription to fuzzy the category of who should count as a civilian.)[41] Abu Marzouk claimed Israelis "have a lot of options" because most hold dual citizenship. The statement was both untrue and hard to reconcile with Hamas's talk of Palestinian sovereignty alongside an Israeli state on pre-1967 borders, as he was hinting at hopes that as Palestinians felt empowered, Israelis would feel uncomfortable and flee. Strikingly, Abu Marzouk's comments echoed Israeli policies to reduce the number of Palestinians living between the Jordan River and the Mediterranean Sea, encouraging them to live in other Arab countries.

Still, the leaders distinguished between Tel Aviv and Washington—suggesting antipathy toward the former had not fully soured them on the latter—and made arguments that might appeal to American ears. Both said their group was committed to a statement in 2017 that tacitly accepted a division of historic Palestine and avoided the antisemitism of Hamas's original charter, saying the group's dispute was not with Jews overall. Rather than wonder whether the group was lying and committed to militancy whatever happened, Abu Marzouk told me the United States should "at least put Hamas to the test by allowing the Palestinians to create a state—the ones who are preventing that are the Israelis." He said Israeli actions hurt America's interests in the Middle East by fueling anti-U.S. sentiment and creating an opportunity for China and Russia to gain influence and by risking conflict between Iran and the United States. Similarly, Naim suggested a blank check for Netanyahu would hurt Biden politically, entangle the United States in a regional war, and hurt Israel's security and stability in the long run.

Washington had, Naim said, "all the cards to end this aggression." Acknowledging the United States' leverage did not mean ignoring its record and its overwhelming support for Israel, however. To Abu Marzouk, America seemed "the most lying country on earth," because it claimed to be seeking a two-state solution for Israelis and Palestinians while "supporting the weak Palestinian side," namely those in the Palestinian Authority who cooperated with Israel, and helping weaken other Palestinians. Hamas's sense it must advocate for Palestinians from a place of strength is core to its identity, and the two leaders blasted talk from U.S. and Israeli officials of eliminating their group or wiping out its support, noting the popularity of armed struggle among Palestinians over many years. Naim specifically condemned Biden for likening Hamas to the Islamic State (ISIS). "What is very sad and painful for us was that a big country, a superpower like the U.S. with a big president, [would] take all these idiot allegations and accusations and repeat it as a puppet . . . this was very naïve and very silly," he said. "I don't believe that America is our best friend but at least they have to respect their own intelligence. They know that we are not ISIS."

"NO NOTION THE PALESTINIANS ARE TELLING THE TRUTH"

Even as the IDF clobbered it like never before, Hamas had proved through its October 7 assault that Israel was not invulnerable and that Palestinian dispossession remained a major international concern, while gaining bargaining chips through the war crime of taking hostages. It felt, to a degree, vindicated, and well positioned to negotiate. U.S.-backed mediation by Qatar and Egypt led to Hamas releasing an American mother and daughter, Judith and Natalie Raanan, on October 20, and two elderly Israeli women, Nurit Cooper and Yocheved Lifshitz, on October 23. On October 25, Hamas told the United States it was willing to release all the captured women and children if Israel delayed its ground invasion of Gaza.[42] But amid tentative—and successful—diplomacy, most American officials still deeply distrusted Hamas, with one telling me they gave no credence to the Palestinian militants' claim the October 7 attack was bigger than intended. Israel challenged Hamas's hostage release offer, arguing the group had yet to prove the hostages were still alive; the prospect withered.

And the most important players in U.S.-Israeli policy were unlikely to seek engagement. Back in 2018, Netanyahu summed up his thinking as: "The weak crumble, are slaughtered, and are erased from history while the strong, for good or for ill, survive . . . and in the end, peace is made with the strong."[43] Determined to prove he could eliminate Hamas's strength, the Israeli leader was far from conciliatory.

Biden showed his commitment to a "bear hug" for one side of the conflict during an October 25 press conference. The president repeated that Israel should protect civilians and that Hamas did not represent most Palestinians, by now understood as rote comments without real-world impact—then he went off script. A reporter asked whether the Palestinian death toll showed Netanyahu was ignoring U.S. exhortations about civilians. Not once but twice, without halting or garbling his words as he often did, Biden responded to the question by attacking the victims of the bombs he was sending. "I have no notion that the Palestinians are telling the truth about how many people are killed," the president said. "I'm sure innocents have been killed, and it's the price of waging a war." Saying civilian deaths were not in Israel's interest, Biden concluded where he started: "I have no confidence in the number that the Palestinians are using."

The moment became defining. It resonated globally as proof the United States was callous and hypocritical for all its statements of concern for innocent Palestinians. In policy circles, it affirmed that despite Biden's reputation for empathy and efforts by some of his advisors to offer a more balanced U.S. view on the war, he was still guided by overwhelming support for Israel. The president's fixation made him break with even the U.S. government's own standards: I soon obtained nearly twenty internal State Department cables discussing the Palestinian death toll that quoted Gaza's health ministry with few caveats, including one sent just hours before Biden's remarks. Biden's comment reaffirmed the boundaries of his thinking, with implications for how officials discussed Gaza with him; this was a boss whose pro-Israel stubbornness and disdain for Palestinians often made him out of touch with reality. The moment seemed inseparable from his repeated, baseless claims months after October 7 that infants had been beheaded.

The death toll remark, which occurred despite weeks of pushback, hinted that Biden might never be able to develop a less damaging policy on Gaza. "Not only was it an aberration from past U.S. practice . . . that set him on a course that was irreversible," Shibley Telhami, the longtime Middle East analyst who advised several U.S. presidents, told me. The day after the comment, a group of Muslim American leaders met with Biden privately for a previously scheduled meeting, where attendees said he was risking Islamophobic violence in the United States and a second Trump presidency. As the session ran past its scheduled thirty minutes to more than an hour, Biden teared up, apologized, and promised to do better.[44]

The president did not, however, indicate any openness to his guests' call for a Gaza ceasefire. On October 27, White House spokesperson John Kirby told reporters in a call: "We're not drawing red lines for Israel." In a private meeting the same day, some of Kirby's more senior colleagues told current and former foreign policy officials that they knew Israel was consistently dropping bombs in Gaza without confirming it was hitting legitimate military targets.[45] For the Biden team, it was easier and simpler to permit questionable force for unclear ends—in keeping with U.S. foreign policy habits—than to engage in meaningful dialogue with Israel or with Hamas. The administration was becoming used to a vagueness about Israeli violence and American responsibility that would become one of the most egregious hallmarks of its war policy. Government personnel who were supplying a new level of American intelligence to Israel, per a secret Biden memo issued after October 7, developed guidelines for its use—but any decision to say Israel violated those directions was left to Biden's highest-ranking advisors.[46] As intelligence staff sent updates about Gaza around the administration every few weeks, those reports mentioned incidents that could represent Israeli war crimes without making legal determinations about the allegations, a senior intelligence official told me. That meant Sullivan, Blinken, and other officials could say they were aware of those incidents but were free of any requirement to act.

Administration figures with strong influence on White House decisions were already demonstrating the low chances that Biden's team would proactively challenge Tel Aviv. Confirmed as the U.S. ambassador to Israel on October 31, Jack Lew was by November recommending American shipments of thousands of massive bombs, tank shells, and missiles and dozens of bulldozers to the Israelis, with his staff conducting "incredibly pro forma" assessments of the dangers of doing so, a State Department official told me. The official said the evaluations, required by government procedure and coming amid extensive allegations those items were used in war crimes, were so perfunctory they could be swapped for one another with only the specific weapon replaced. For the fifteen months that followed, the Biden administration never made a single confirmation of Israeli misconduct. Granting plausible deniability to powerful Americans, the pattern put millions of Palestinians and Lebanese at unprecedented risk.

HELP US HELP YOU

The choice to send U.S. weapons to foreign countries is made by a president and his team. But it implicates Congress, which approves government spending and can block arms deals, like the package of U.S. military aid Biden sought for Israel and Ukraine. By the end of October, some legislators, nearly all Democrats, became more determined to use their leverage to politely but firmly encourage a different U.S. policy. The shift reflected how dire the situation had become—disturbing even established politicians who were reflexively pro-Israel—and diminished faith among Biden's allies in both his judgment and his ability to win reelection.

Popular outrage against U.S. Gaza policy had become inescapable. Students at campuses nationwide blasted their institutions' ties to Israel—spurring backlash, including doxxing, the rescinding of job offers, and threats from donors. Arab American voters, many of whom live in swing states such as Michigan and Virginia, reported a 42 percent drop in support for Biden.[47] As antiwar advocates held sit-ins and marches, some of the most high-profile were led by Jewish Americans and organized by the anti-Zionist group Jewish Voice for Peace (JVP).

Simultaneously, Netanyahu was tying Israel's offensive to Jewish history, saying in an October 28 speech that the invasion of Gaza would enable retribution akin to the biblical Israelites wiping out the nation of Amalek.[48] The link hinted at massive bloodshed and cast a contested policy as fundamental to a religion, threatening animosity toward Jews globally. On November 2, as Biden campaigned in Minneapolis, a rabbi and JVP member named Jessica Rosenberg interrupted him, saying: "If you care about Jewish people . . . I need you to call for a ceasefire."[49]

Dismissing activists as too left-wing and politically irrelevant is standard fare for the Democratic Party. But the Biden administration's approach to the war by now seemed unacceptable to a different kind of figure: Chris Van Hollen, a mild-mannered Democratic senator from Maryland, who was set to become the most significant opponent of the president's Gaza policy. At age sixty-four, he had spent twenty-one years in Congress. Unlike most of his peers, however, Van Hollen often decried the United States ignoring its stated values to shield unsavory partners, pushing both Biden and Trump to pursue justice for the journalists Shireen Abu Akleh and Jamal Khashoggi, killed respectively by an Israeli soldier and Saudi Arabian officials. The administration's handling of the Gaza war increasingly perturbed him: When Kirby said Netanyahu faced no red lines, Van Hollen texted Jake Sullivan to call the comment "outrageous."[50] Openly challenging a U.S. policy of support for Israel would require a different level of determination, however. Most Democrats had little experience doing so because, according to the former Obama advisor Ben Rhodes, the pro-Israel lobby group "AIPAC [American Israel Public Affairs Committee] and other organizations exist to make sure that the views of the Israeli government are effectively disseminated and opposing views discredited in Washington."[51] Meanwhile, as criticism of the war had grown, Israel's Embassy had begun urging government officials, congressional staffers, and journalists to attend screenings of a film depicting firsthand footage of some of the worst atrocities of October 7. Christopher Le Mon, a senior official in the State Department's human rights bureau, told me he discouraged colleagues from going, viewing the effort as likely risking trauma among staff, which State was unprepared to handle, and offering no policy benefit to experts steeped in details of violence in the region.

Some Democrats had also for years enabled an effort by AIPAC and Republicans to treat parts of their party, particularly Muslims, as suspect and potentially antisemitic for comments about Israel—and amid the war, that pattern intensified, as some intensely pro-Israel Democrats blasted colleagues such as Rashida Tlaib. On November 7, 22 Democratic legislators joined 212 Republicans to pass a House of Representatives resolution claiming Tlaib "defended" violence by accusing Israel of apartheid—as several human rights groups, including prominent Israeli organizations, had—and by using the common pro-Palestinian slogan, "From the river to the sea."[52] Visibly shaken, Tlaib responded with a speech describing Israeli and Palestinian children as equal and highlighting the movement against the war: "You can't silence their voices."

The following day, Van Hollen unveiled a letter to Biden from twenty-six senators, including more than half the Democrats in the body, which commended support for Israel but said it should not be unconditional. "It is in America's interest to ensure that any military plans to fight Hamas do not produce the same strategic mistakes as many U.S. military operations over the past few decades," read the message. The letter asked about Israel's long-term strategy for Gaza, mechanisms for ensuring the IDF respected international and American law, and U.S. plans to "insist" Israel take steps it never did over the remaining fifteen months of Biden's presidency, like fully restoring water and electricity for Gaza. The message propelled congressional action in the months that followed and confirmed that others in the party beyond Biden saw the yearslong shift in Democratic circles toward a more balanced U.S. policy in Israel-Palestine. A week later, the independent Vermont senator Bernie Sanders, a Jewish progressive whose run for the Democratic presidential nomination in 2016 catalyzed that shift, organized a private Senate lunch discussion on Gaza, where several Democrats spoke of demanding a ceasefire and placing conditions on aid to Israel, a person present told me. The surging scrutiny of Israel was "a conversation I never heard significantly before," one senator reported.[53] Both Republican and Democratic administrations had largely treated support for Israel as sacrosanct, even creating a unique process for addressing allegations of human rights abuses that could risk that aid. Named the Israel Leahy Vetting Forum, for the Leahy law addressing serious rights concerns among foreign troops receiving U.S. support, the procedure was different from investigations of any other country, requiring high-level consultations and Israeli cooperation that slowed down processes of identifying violations—and it had so far never resulted in a single Leahy sanction on Israeli forces.[54]

Most Washington critics of Biden's Gaza approach still saw themselves as working with Biden to strengthen his hand relative to Netanyahu, and the administration partially boosted that impression, sustaining an assumption of good faith. The president endorsed a "pause" in Israel's offensive on November 2; U.S. officials promoted the idea even after the Israeli leader compared it to telling the United States to halt retaliation for 9/11.

In addressing pushback, however, the Biden administration ensured Tel Aviv did not feel a need for a major change in course. Instead, U.S. and Israeli officials developed a united front against war skeptics. Heading to Israel on November 3, Blinken told reporters: "When I see a Palestinian child, a boy or a girl pulled from the rubble of a collapsed building, that hits me in the gut as much as seeing a child in Israel or anywhere else."[55] Upon arriving, he privately told Netanyahu's counterparts it was important to defuse criticism of the war, in a message that American and Israeli officials summarized as: "We don't want to stop you, but help us help you get more time."[56] Two days later, Israeli minister Amichai Eliyahu suggested dropping a nuclear bomb on Gaza. Netanyahu suspended but later reinstated him; by 2025, Eliyahu was saying Palestinians "need to starve."[57]

In a November 8 speech from Tokyo, where he had arrived for a summit, Blinken said a ceasefire would invite continued Hamas rule and attacks. The argument echoed Israel's narrative, but he also suggested moderation by saying the United States sought "durable peace" involving conditions like no reoccupation or blockade of Gaza. Netanyahu soon agreed he did not envision Israel governing the strip—as the White House announced a U.S.-Israeli deal for humanitarian pauses in the fighting.[58] Still, the administration's continued deference to Israel's plan for a punishing offensive was clear: The agreement provided four-hour breaks rather than the three-day pauses Biden had spoken of, and as it was announced, the IDF began one of the darkest periods of the war by escalating attacks on Gaza's hospitals, particularly the largest, Al-Shifa.[59]

A NEW LOW

Israel claimed Hamas used Al-Shifa to plan attacks despite denials from hospital staff and Hamas; Netanyahu widely promoted a later debunked propaganda video purporting to depict a command center.[60] By November 11, as the IDF bombed and besieged the area, Mohammed Obeid, a surgeon there, reported incubators and ventilators shutting down, killing babies and the most vulnerable patients, while shots from outside hit others.[61] The IDF said that it did not fire on hospitals and that attacks by Palestinian militants were damaging Al-Shifa—then, after the White House's Kirby told reporters that the United States agreed with Israel that the hospital was a Hamas hub, Israeli troops entered the hospital on November 15.[62] "The targeting by a U.S. ally of a compound housing hundreds of sick and dying patients and thousands of displaced people has no precedent in recent decades," *The Washington Post* noted.[63]

New gruesome patterns established at Al-Shifa with tacit U.S. blessing spread: Israeli forces soon besieged then invaded the Indonesian Hospital, and the IDF began detaining hundreds of Palestinian medical workers, many of whom later said they were tortured and some of whom died in Israeli custody. Israeli authorities denied mistreatment.

The military value of the raid—the basis of Israeli claims it did not violate international law—remained doubtful. The *Post* later highlighted that IDF photographs showing rooms at Al-Shifa linked to tunnels did not include proof fighters were there recently; that neither wards nor buildings highlighted by the IDF were linked to Hamas's tunnel network; and that footage showing hostages at Al-Shifa on October 7 did not indicate military activity there at the time of the raid. The Biden administration continued to assert U.S. intelligence backed up Israel while never declassifying such analysis. Still, by setting a new standard, the Al-Shifa moment had a major impact: Netanyahu now knew even a major hospital attack once seen as unimaginable would not cost him U.S. support. Subsequent Israeli attacks put Gaza's entire health-care system "on death row," aid groups said, and a UN commission said the pattern represented war crimes and the crime against humanity of extermination.[64]

The Biden team tied continued obstinacy in its Gaza policy to even greater efforts to downplay questions about it. Administration staff became increasingly aggressive to critics, seemingly in part because they knew how dubious their position had become. In private messages to a friend, that were shared with me, one White House spokesperson called Netanyahu "genocidal," and wrote: "People should protests [*sic*] what Israel is doing! We're speaking out too."

By November, the call for a ceasefire was endorsed by French president Emmanuel Macron—the first major Western leader to endorse the idea—and dozens of Democratic National Committee staff working on Biden's presidential campaign.[65] More than five hundred government officials across forty agencies signed a pro-ceasefire letter they sent the president, and a poll released on November 19 showed both that 70 percent of voters under the age of thirty-five disapproved of U.S. Gaza policy and that Biden was trailing Trump in a potential election scenario for the first time.[66]

On the day the five-hundred-signatory letter was sent, Andrew Bates—another White House spokesman—promoted a different letter from more than one hundred former officials under Biden and Obama, praising the president's backing for Tel Aviv. On X, Bates highlighted a sentence from the *Times of Israel* article about it: "The on-record letter follows a series of anonymous letters and memos . . . criticizing Biden's policy." Left unmentioned was the reality that it's far less risky to praise a sitting president and the U.S.-Israel relationship than to challenge them. Dissenting voices were growing stronger, but the administration was practicing selective hearing.

BRING THEM HOME NOW

Palestinian pain and domestic upheaval could not convince the Biden administration to seek a halt to killing in Gaza, but by mid-November, rising outrage over the war's impact on Israelis and Americans did spur Washington to craft a truce. It was one designed to allow for ongoing, unprecedented fighting.

After the trauma of the Hamas invasion, the attack felt never-ending to many Israelis so long as there was no resolution to the question of the hostages. Thousands had some link to one of the two hundred fifty-one captives—people like Ditza Heiman, an eighty-four-year-old who had lived alone in Kibbutz Nir Oz, dependent on a cane and daily medications.[67] Saving some October 7 victims seemed too important to be secondary to any other concern, for both humanitarian and symbolic reasons, and Netanyahu presented that as government policy, saying freeing hostages was a top IDF goal beside pulverizing Hamas.[68] As Israel expanded its offensive in Gaza, however, its troops failed to locate captives—whom Palestinian militants had carefully hidden as high-value leverage—beyond one on October 30, while Israeli officials seemed fixated on battlefield damage. "Every time someone [from the government] talks, he says, 'First destroy Hamas, destroy Gaza,' and maybe the third sentence he'll say, 'Bring them home,'" Neta Heiman, Ditza's daughter, told me in early November. "I don't think it's the first priority."[69] Relatives of hostages began camping out in Tel Aviv, in a plaza near the IDF headquarters that became known as Hostages Square, and organized rallies that quickly swelled due to general disdain for Netanyahu among many Israelis, who blamed him for the Hamas attack and had previously organized historic protests against his power grabs.

With diplomacy understood as the best hope for freeing the hostages before conflict or rough conditions cost them their lives, the Biden administration could enable or hurt hopes of an urgent deal with Hamas. The United States is "the determinant factor," Gili Roman, whose sister Yarden had been kidnapped and separated from her three-year-old daughter, told me. Biden could push Netanyahu to make concessions, a congressional staffer separately noted to me, saying the Israeli leader appeared to have "written off the hostages."[70] There was reason to believe the administration's own commitment to the hostages could lead to a different American approach. Biden had held lengthy conversations with families of U.S. hostages in both October and November and met relatives of captives and October 7 survivors when he visited Israel, shooing away aides when they told him to move on to his next appointment. Sullivan, McGurk, and their staff met with hostage families in person once or twice a month and "we got to know everyone very, very well," White House official Samantha Sutton later recalled.[71] Notably, administration decision-makers had no such regular, personal, and humanizing contact with Palestinians affected by the war.

Still, McGurk's deep involvement in a possible hostage release deal made it unlikely any compromise would involve moderating U.S.-backed Israeli tactics in Gaza. In other matters of Middle East policy, McGurk had consistently discouraged fellow officials from raising human rights issues with foreign partners such as the Saudis. Now, in internal discussions about Gaza, he repeatedly and favorably compared Israel's offensive to brutal past U.S. campaigns.[72] CIA director Bill Burns, a former diplomat with less hard-line views, managed the work of identifying language acceptable to both Israel and Hamas; Burns worked alongside the top Israeli negotiator, Mossad spy agency chief David Barnea, and Qatari officials, who spoke to the Palestinian group's leaders in Doha, who then liaised with its leadership in Gaza.

Hamas's initial proposal to swap women and children for Palestinian prisoners provided a basis for the emerging accord, as did a growing understanding among American and Israeli officials that Israel was using up munitions more quickly than they could be replaced. But the war and calculations by Biden, who was far closer to McGurk than to Burns, could still scuttle a deal. The president first pushed Hamas, through Qatar's ruler, and the group finally provided details about those it was willing to free. But then amid the U.S.-approved IDF raid on Al-Shifa Hospital, Hamas went quiet, and U.S. officials suspected the whole effort had collapsed.

By November 14, Hamas had returned to the table, and Biden called Netanyahu and persuaded him to accept an initial agreement rather than demand more. As ever, the Israeli leader's domestic political fate loomed large in his thinking. The hostage families had that day begun a multiday procession, and McGurk was visiting Israel. "We need this deal," Netanyahu told him, visibly shaken.[73] McGurk shuttled to Doha, then Cairo, where officials discussed the proposed deal text—but he made another stop that offered a troubling view of the emerging agreement. Speaking at a conference in Bahrain, McGurk said, "The onus here is on Hamas. . . . The surge in humanitarian relief, the surge in fuel, the pause in fighting, will come when hostages are released. . . . The hostages are released, [then] you will see a significant, significant change." These remarks caused considerable consternation, because under international law, aid for civilians cannot be conditioned on the behavior of one warring party. When the top State Department official for Israel-Palestine, Andrew Miller, heard the statements, he called a government lawyer and said: "That's a war crime, right?" The response, which was consistent with the opinion voiced publicly by several international law experts: yes.[74] The comments about conditioning aid on the release of the hostages were peppered throughout McGurk's remarks. Biden's Middle East confidant was offering a window into his thinking: Even amid diplomacy with Hamas and evidence of devastation already being caused by Israel's withholding of aid, McGurk was sure of U.S. and Israeli righteousness, and dismissive of international legal standards.

McGurk traveled to Israel the following day and confirmed its acceptance of the terms Hamas green-lit. Both sides signed the deal on November 21—once Netanyahu convinced his cabinet the United States "improved" the terms for Israel. Over a four-day pause in fighting, Hamas would free 50 women and children (including three

Americans), and Israel would release 150 imprisoned Palestinian women and children, as well as allow fuel and more aid trucks into Gaza; the two sides would continue talks to potentially swap more prisoners and extend their accord.[75]

On November 24, the start of the truce produced remarkable images of families being reunited. "It's vindication," a Biden administration official bragged to *Politico*.[76] On November 28, in a wheelchair and a pink cardigan, Ditza Heiman returned home.[77]

DIFFERENT TACTIC, SAME STRATEGY

Washington and Tel Aviv had not abandoned their vision of a military defeat for Hamas. During the truce, both prepared for future fighting. The Biden administration—more sensitive to antiwar critics given their prevalence in the United States versus in Israel—worked to reduce dissent over the conflict and to redirect criticism by framing the predictable collapse of the deal as driven by Hamas.

The brief quiet in Gaza made the lack of a road map for its future beyond conflict even more jarring to U.S. officials working on Israel-Palestine policy. Netanyahu continued to reject the Palestinian Authority taking over the strip and to insist Israel would retain "security control" of Gaza, undercutting hopes of moving toward the two-state solution, which remained Biden's stated goal.[78] A White House official told me that while it "felt great" to free hostages, the administration now seemed unmoored even to some who had previously believed in its strategy: "If we're supporting the military campaign because we plan to replace Hamas with something different and we can achieve that while pressing Israel as hard as we can on providing humanitarian aid, that would be something I would be okay with." Reflecting the official's Washington mindset, the comments ignored Palestinians' autonomy in choosing their future. "But to let [Israel] do what they're doing in Gaza with an open hand without pressing them harder is for nothing, because they have no plan," the official said. Visiting Israel on

November 30, Blinken made clear the administration was not getting tougher on Netanyahu; in a press conference, he spoke of Israel resuming its offensive with greater regard for civilians but did not describe any new commitments by the Israelis.[79] "Intent matters, but so does the result," Blinken said—and there were clear results of the United States continuing to arm Israel while hoping words alone would encourage IDF temperance. The pace of the killing in Gaza had exceeded "even the deadliest moments of U.S.-led attacks in Iraq, Syria and Afghanistan," a review by *The New York Times* found.[80] Amid new fighting, likely designed to extend the IDF's control into southern Gaza, the "marginal uptick" in aid during the truce would make little difference given the devastation of infrastructure across the strip, the International Rescue Committee warned.[81] And to the extent Israeli officials had a new strategy for civilians, it was nightmarish: cramming more than a million Palestinians into a so-called humanitarian zone in a tiny bare stretch of Gaza's southern coast called al-Mawasi.[82] Aid groups warned the proposal could hasten Palestinian deaths by forcing people into a particularly underresourced region, making them targets, and boosting false Israeli claims that civilians who stayed elsewhere no longer had special protections.[83]

Still, the biggest shift in war policy Biden aides were attempting came in the form of the CIA's Burns pushing Israel to consider a longer truce than the ten-day limit Netanyahu had set, so that more hostages, including Americans, could walk free.[84] Top officials continued to stonewall calls for a bigger change, even from ostensibly influential critics. At a meeting of Biden administration staff unhappy about Gaza policy in mid-November, Finer, the deputy national security advisor, offered an assessment of the situation so insipid in its insistence that a ceasefire wasn't possible and that Israel was doing its best to minimize casualties that an official told him it amounted to reciting pro-Israeli talking points, a person present told me.[85] When twenty Democratic senators met with Jake Sullivan on November 28 to discuss their concerns about how Israel was using American weapons, Sullivan said Biden was adamant about shipping billions more in bombs and equipment to Netanyahu. Amid the inflexibility, the domestic toll of the war rose: On November 25, in Vermont, a man shot at three students of Palestinian descent as they walked down the street chatting in Arabic and English and wearing keffiyehs, leaving one, Hisham Awartani, paralyzed.

The truce was always shaky. Israel had agreed to extend it for each day that Hamas provided ten hostages, freeing thirty jailed Palestinians in return, but Hamas said it was running low on captives it would swap at that ratio, as some had been killed, many of the women and children had been released, and it viewed most of those remaining as combatants and so expected more Palestinian releases in exchange. On December 1, after 105 hostages had been swapped for 240 prisoners over seven days, the final extension expired; Hamas launched rockets into Israel and the IDF resumed bombing Gaza. The Palestinian death toll began to soar once again.

The Biden administration tried to revive negotiations, but it chiefly approached the moment as a PR problem—its usual response to uncomfortable developments in the war. Washington pushed a story about the collapse of the truce that was rooted in tropes about Muslim men that policymakers had long used to justify aggressive treatment of them: that they were deeply, almost uncontrollably violent and a particular threat to women linked to the Western world. The day the deal collapsed, White House officials started telling reporters it was because of how Hamas had treated young Israeli women, asking them to imagine what might be happening. The narrative quickly became more explicit—with no evidence offered. Hamas didn't "want these women to be able to talk about what happened to them during their time in custody," State Department spokesman Matt Miller said in a press conference on December 4, and two days later, the news outlet *Puck* quoted a senior Biden administration official saying Hamas was keeping women in order to keep raping them.[86] *Puck*'s American sources said they lacked proof but were operating off the thinking of the Israelis, and two senior Israeli officials provided an assessment resembling Miller's comment to *Axios*.[87] Yet those views were contested, not least because of the anxiety they could cause hostage families: After Miller's comments, the IDF issued a statement calling the discussion of remaining captives in Gaza "irresponsible [and] inaccurate."[88]

Discussions of sexual violence in the war were extremely charged and often intermingled several issues: its occurrence on October 7, whether it occurred afterward, and whether global officials and human rights groups were appropriately concerned about it. A UN investigation found "reasonable grounds" to believe Palestinian fighters committed rapes and "clear and convincing information" hostages in Gaza experienced rape and other sexual violence.[89] UN experts have also highlighted Israeli officials subjecting Palestinian detainees to rape and sexual violence, underscoring the dehumanizing effects across the lines of the ongoing conflict.[90]

When it came to war strategy, however, it would be uncharacteristic for Hamas—violent but disciplined and fixated on Palestinian nationalism—to let sexual motivations drive major choices like abandoning a truce the group had sought for months. Still, it suited the Biden administration to shift attention to a different, increasingly high-profile debate. On December 4, the day of Miller's comments, Israeli officials hosted Hillary Clinton, Sheryl Sandberg, and the Democratic senator Kirsten Gillibrand at an event at the United Nations to criticize how rights advocates were addressing claims of sexual violence by Hamas. The back-and-forth over the allegations soon obscured any discussion about whether the truce could have been handled differently, and more bloodshed in Gaza avoided; speaking to me several weeks later, a Qatari official said the U.S. approach made Hamas warier and harder to mediate with.

FULL SPEED AHEAD

Israel's U.S.-backed offensive was resuming as if the truce had never happened. The IDF ordered hundreds of thousands of Palestinians to leave their homes—this time from the biggest city in southern Gaza, Khan Younis—and resumed major air strikes, like a December 2 attack in Gaza City involving a shocking nine two-thousand-pound bombs provided by the United States, which destroyed fifteen buildings and killed at least sixty people.[91] Israeli forces destroyed an IVF clinic housing four thousand Palestinian embryos, boosting fears the war would cripple the community's long-term survival. Still, the Biden administration tried to suggest that even as it was not acceding to its critics' demands, it was more sensitive to their voices.

On December 2, Vice President Kamala Harris told a conference in Dubai: "Too many Palestinians have been killed." Harris met with Arab leaders critical of the U.S.-Israeli war policy, the first time she or Biden had done so since October 7; notably, the leader of the United Arab Emirates, the Persian Gulf monarchy closest to Israel, expressed new wariness of Netanyahu to her, a White House official told me. That official said Harris sought to differentiate herself from Biden. Though administration officials denied that at the time, the claim tracked with Harris's internal lobbying for U.S. officials to show more concern for humanitarian conditions in Gaza, as well as her sensitivity to antiwar sentiment among Democrats, given her ambitions for higher office.[92] At a forum in Los Angeles the following day, Defense Secretary Lloyd Austin said Israel risked "a strategic defeat" through excessive civilian killings and permitting bloodshed in the West Bank, remarks a Pentagon official emphasized to me Austin chose to make public rather than keep private.

Rhetoric from officials was not enough to overcome huge doubts about their judgment: Soon afterward, Chris Van Hollen proposed legislation backed by several fellow influential Democratic senators to put new conditions on Biden's proposed military aid for Israel. And even as the administration hoped more forthright rhetoric would nudge Netanyahu and demonstrate its savvy, its own stubbornness about its policy undercut its effort to suggest reflection and change had occurred. On December 7, a reporter at a White House press conference asked Kirby whether the international community had failed Gaza. The spokesman lashed out as defensive Biden aides often did, deflecting from a question of justice to a matter of credit: "Name me one more nation, any other nation, that's doing as much as the United States to alleviate the pain and suffering of the people of Gaza," Kirby shot back. "You just can't."[93]

At a December 12 campaign event, Biden added to the confusion by saying Israel was carrying out "indiscriminate bombing." If the administration knew that to be true, its claims of improved Israeli behavior would be outright lies—and the U.S. policy of continued bomb shipments to Netanyahu would be even more appalling than if, as American and Israeli officials claimed, precautions were taken before strikes and civilians were mistakenly killed. Officials scrambled to say the president's comment was not a formal U.S. government assessment. But the implication was hard to bury. "The definition of a gaffe in Washington is when someone speaks the truth," quipped former ambassador Gordon Gray.[94] Privately, State Department lawyers began telling Blinken in December that they believed Israel was likely breaking international law, and Avril Haines, Biden's director of national intelligence, had become so concerned weeks earlier that she sought Israeli assurances intelligence shared by the United States would not be used in major human rights violations.[95]

For Sullivan, arguably the most powerful U.S. foreign policy official after Biden himself, the Gaza war now risked becoming a major challenge to his career plans. He had struggled to move past criticism of his role in the U.S. withdrawal from Afghanistan in 2021, and was deeply sensitive to the appearance of being implicated in bloody chaos. As the administration struggled to prove it had matters under control, Sullivan made his own mid-December trip to Israel, widely publicizing the expectation he would deliver a clear change benefiting Palestinians, of whom at least 18,897 had now been killed.[96]

"There will be a transition to another phase of this war, one that is focused in more precise ways," Sullivan pledged at a press conference on his first day in Tel Aviv. No such change or major drop in civilian casualties occurred in the following months, as the Israelis repeatedly said they had to launch new offensives across Gaza to deal with Hamas regrouping.

Sullivan's trip did, however, bear fruit in a way that deeply affected how the administration talked about its policy afterward: by playing up its work on aid. With more than 90 percent of Gaza's population now deemed to be in "crisis or worse" in terms of access to food, the Rafah Crossing remained the only route for supplies to enter the strip. It had limited capacity even in an ideal scenario, and it was deeply inefficient under the system devised by the United States, Israel, and Egypt. For trucks to be inspected, as required by Israel, they had to make lengthy trips to far-off Israeli checkpoints and then return, because Netanyahu would not allow supplies for Palestinians to travel through Israeli territory.[97] Another crossing could be opened: Kerem Shalom, at the point where Egypt, Gaza, and Israel meet.

Amid his talks with Netanyahu, Sullivan gave the Israeli leader an ultimatum: I will not leave Israel until that gate is opened. Ultimately, the Israelis approved the step just before his departure, and he proudly recalled the later episode to a group of outside White House advisors. But one expert present found the moment less laudatory than revelatory. "Jake seemed to think this was a good story about the administration's efforts," Matt Duss later told me. "But to me it was actually a story about how fucked up this policy is: that the national security advisor of the most powerful country on the planet is forced to do a sit-in."

Still, Sullivan's visit cemented the centrality of aid in the administration's thinking going forward. U.S. officials' handling of humanitarian matters would soon dominate their conversations as the core question of the war, American military support for Israel, got far less airtime. The outcome was an alarming system for aid that was governed by Israel's preferences, offered little real support to Palestinians even as their needs swelled, and fueled breaking points in the administration's policy in April and May.

CHAPTER 3

ENABLING MAN-MADE MISERY

December 2023–February 2024

BY ALLOWING ISRAEL TO RESUME ITS OFFENSIVE, THE BIDEN administration ensured Gaza's humanitarian crisis would swell into a catastrophe. U.S. fingerprints were already on the sources of the suffering: massive bombing runs and Israeli policies that prevented aid agencies from operating as they would in other war zones. It was hard to miss the irony in America helping create a man-made, avoidable disaster—one that eventually grew so dire that polio reemerged in the strip—under a president who prided himself on his reputation for compassion and his moves to restore U.S. funding for global humanitarian groups.

Over the course of December and January, the administration became increasingly involved in trying to get food, medicine, and fuel to those in need. The choice deeply implicated Washington in one of the fundamental questions about the war: Did Israel's restrictions on essential supplies for Palestinians prove it was carrying out a genocide? Some Biden staff sought greater U.S. involvement in the aid process because of revulsion at the effects of their administration's policy and a yearning to use American influence to alleviate them. Others saw the choice in less altruistic terms: If it lacked even a veneer of moderation, Israel's U.S.-backed military campaign would likely face overwhelming disapproval from both the international community and Americans themselves. Whatever their motivations, the approach they developed to humanitarian relief never came close to meeting Palestinians' needs. The administration developed a system of negotiation with Israeli authorities—from ministers to the coordinator of government activities in the territories (COGAT), the Israeli military unit controlling logistics for Palestine—that largely depended on the constantly shifting attention of White House officials and tacit deference to the never-proven Israeli claim that standard aid operations were infiltrated by Hamas. Those choices enabled an ever-expanding Israeli assault on the humanitarian system in Gaza, including an unprecedented number of attacks on aid workers themselves, which later culminated in U.S.-Israeli efforts to abandon traditional aid infrastructure altogether and instead rely on the military to distribute supplies, echoing deadly U.S. practices during the War on Terror.

High-ranking Biden aides like Sullivan and McGurk personally tracked aid deliveries down to the specific shipment in this period. While they presented this and renewed talk of Israeli-Palestinian peace as evidence of how much the administration cared, both another truce and an effective humanitarian system eluded the Biden administration until its dying days.[1] Still, U.S. officials said they were "relentlessly" focusing on aid.[2] In an interview days before he left office, Blinken boasted that the administration worked to surge humanitarian assistance.[3] Courtney Blake, a veteran U.S. humanitarian official who worked on Gaza, told me she was appalled by the comment, saying of the American approach to aid: "How it played out on a day-to-day basis was a nightmare."

AN INTERNATIONAL FIG LEAF

By mid-December, frustration within the Biden team over the humanitarian toll of the U.S.-backed military campaign in Gaza was reaching new heights. When Sullivan organized a rare meeting on the war for the Principals Committee, a high-level panel focused on various national security concerns, two attendees blasted the policy: Samantha Power, who ran the U.S. Agency for International Development and had worked closely with other top Biden aides during the Obama administration, and Linda Thomas-Greenfield, Biden's ambassador to the United Nations. While private, the dispute demonstrated the growing internal desire for a public shift, particularly among officials who were most attuned to the human and diplomatic cost of the U.S.'s carte blanche for Israel. In subsequent months, Sullivan rarely convened meetings of the committee to discuss Gaza, and when he did, often arranged a "small group" format without Thomas-Greenfield and Power, fueling the impression that the two women were being excluded. Even when they were included, a White House official told me he witnessed the two—who were both political players anxious for access—repeatedly "pulling their punches" by limiting critique of the administration's policy. Thomas-Greenfield ignored multiple requests to speak with me for this book; Power told me she would not criticize specific colleagues and did not answer my request for a general statement of any regrets she had or mistakes the administration made. (Sullivan's spokesperson, meanwhile, told me that Sullivan "oversaw significant interagency dialogue" on Gaza and "was in frequent and direct touch with" both Power and Thomas-Greenfield.)

One key venue for a policy shift on the war was squarely in Thomas-Greenfield's purview: the UN Security Council, the organization's most powerful body. The United States often used its veto power as a permanent member of the council to defend Israel from critique at the United Nations, and American and Israeli diplomats, as well as some independent experts, said parts of the institution, notably the General Assembly and the Human Rights Council, subjected Israel to hypocritical and disproportionate attacks. Washington had also occasionally refused to deploy the veto to demonstrate displeasure with Israel and pressure its leaders, allowing Security Council resolutions skeptical of Israel to pass.

Between October 7 and early December, the United States vetoed three resolutions seeking to limit Israel's offensive in Gaza. One urged an immediate ceasefire, and two targeted specific alarming

Israeli tactics: its order for civilians to leave northern Gaza and its aid blockade.[4] Thomas-Greenfield said the proposals overlooked Hamas atrocities—but in challenging the aid-related resolution, she demonstrated how the Biden administration was extending its questionable broader logic that skeptics should trust their choices to benefit both Israelis and Palestinians, saying the resolution would hurt the president's own diplomacy with Netanyahu for a truce, hostage release, and more supplies for Gaza.[5]

Becoming known worldwide for defending a U.S.-Israeli policy decried by UN experts and a growing proportion of the world's nations was not the trajectory Thomas-Greenfield expected. At age seventy-one, the career diplomat's job was the pinnacle of her career; she had quit the Foreign Service under the first Trump presidency but returned to government at Biden's request, echoing his rhetoric of restoring responsible U.S. global leadership. Thomas-Greenfield told reporters she was "a humanitarian at heart"[6] and often discussed her journey from growing up in the Jim Crow South to being one of the handful of Black women in U.S. history to secure a cabinet-level job, calling that evidence of America's promise.[7] She had, along the way, worked with refugees from the Rwandan genocide and the Afghanistan war. Now Thomas-Greenfield was the face of Biden's resistance to a ceasefire. Fellow State Department officials who had once seen her as an inspiration began comparing her to Colin Powell, America's first Black secretary of state, whom the Bush administration dispatched to the United Nations with a dishonest case for the 2003 invasion of Iraq. Beyond her personal discomfort with the administration's Gaza policy, which people close to her described to me, it was hurting Thomas-Greenfield's legacy. She had championed Ukraine, but her staff began halting plans for Security Council resolutions condemning Russia because they judged other countries would not see them as credible amid American support for Israeli devastation in Gaza and would vote against Kyiv to appear "anti-U.S.," an official told me, adding: "It wasn't just resolutions. . . . What meetings do we call? Do you really want to go into the Security Council talking about Russian attacks on the health-care system?" Palestinian pain was being highlighted by governments in the Global South, like South Africa, to whom Thomas-Greenfield sought closer U.S. ties; those nations compared Israeli practices to tragedies from their own past and accused Washington of a double standard after condemning other governments for similar apparent war crimes. Even governments such as Costa Rica and Botswana that usually helped the United States win support for its UN positions among their respective neighbors became harder to court, a senior State Department official told me.

As the war progressed, the ambassador sought compromises that could satisfy the White House and foreign counterparts. Her back-channeling first bore fruit in November, when the United States let the Security Council pass a resolution from Malta demanding "urgent and extended humanitarian pauses" in Gaza but condemning neither Israel nor Hamas specifically.[8] The Biden administration had now shown some flexibility in its backing for Israel at the United Nations—notably while blessing a position Biden had already adopted, rather than letting the body direct a change in the course of the war. "The closer a resolution got to our policy, the closer we got to abstaining" and so letting it pass, a senior official later told me, underscoring the administration's rigidity and disdain for serious consultation at the United Nations. Could such actions help save lives? Israeli attacks had by this point killed more than eleven thousand Palestinians.

The Biden team provided an answer the following month, choosing to keep enabling bloodshed, isolating America, and undermining international moral standards. On December 6, UN secretary-general António Guterres rang the most powerful alarm bell at his disposal, citing Article 99 of the UN Charter to make an emergency appeal over Gaza to the Security Council because of "a severe risk of collapse of the humanitarian system."[9] Only the fifth time in the charter's seventy-eight-year history that Article 99 had been triggered, the move coincided with the final month of a temporary term on the council for the United Arab Emirates (UAE), an Arab government close to the United States and to Israel. The UAE submitted a resolution for an immediate Gaza ceasefire—and the United States vetoed it alone, with nearly all other countries voting yes and even its closest ally, Britain, abstaining. "I don't see any contradiction between the right to fight against terrorists, including Hamas, and the absolute necessity to stop attacks against civilians," Nicolas de Rivière, the French ambassador to the United Nations, told me at the time.[10]

Thomas-Greenfield skipped the session, so America's veto was deployed by her deputy Robert Wood, who cast it with a chilling smile that went viral. But while her spokesperson told me she had previously scheduled travel, UN watchers noted it was the second Gaza-related veto she avoided. By the time she returned to New York, there was a growing sense of unstoppable pressure for a U.S. concession at the Security Council. More than 80 percent of the UN General Assembly voted for an immediate ceasefire on December 12, and UAE and U.S. officials began intense private discussions about a resolution that could satisfy both Biden and those seeking a change in Gaza.[11] At the Americans' behest, the focus of the resolution changed from a call for halting fighting to developing a new system for delivering aid, and I revealed that Thomas-Greenfield had used a trip to D.C. to personally lobby the president against vetoing it. Diplomats told me Biden remained willing to issue one regardless of how out of touch the United States would seem.

The core of the resolution—the reason it had huge long-term ramifications for the war—was Israel's handling of supplies for Gaza. Aid workers said the crisis there was man-made, caused by Israeli practices like subjecting shipments to several rounds of inspection and denials for unclear reasons, preventing private businesses in Gaza from importing food, and dispatching inspectors to border crossings for only a few hours, thus creating bottlenecks though supplies were ready and waiting to be checked.[12] Meanwhile, U.S.-backed Israeli attacks had pulverized much of Gaza's farmland and food infrastructure, from bakeries and warehouses to water facilities. In other war zones, the United States and other world powers regularly tapped the United Nations to control aid inspection, even when there were fears that weapons might slip through—as Tel Aviv claimed might happen if it did not fully control the checking process. As rumors swirled that Biden had decided no middle ground was possible, diplomats felt pressure from both the calendar and the darkening evidence about the toll of the status quo. On December 21, the gold-standard global forum of experts on hunger—known as the Integrated Food Security Phase Classification (IPC)—reported that Gaza was seeing the highest share of residents at serious risk of starvation that its tracker had ever recorded in any part of the world, with Palestinians in most households going whole days and nights without eating.[13]

Eventually, diplomats voted for a proposal to establish a new UN role focused on supplies for Gaza—while leaving tangible control of those goods in Israel's hands. When the resolution passed on December 23, Thomas-Greenfield celebrated the outcome, though Biden only let her abstain, not even vote in favor. The United States had managed to "extract a lot of concessions," Richard Gowan, a UN watcher at the International Crisis Group, told me, while the mechanism it established predictably did little to improve Palestinians' conditions.

The new job went to Sigrid Kaag, a Dutch politician who had worked in the UN system for years. Given the framework the Security Council ultimately approved, "I don't think she was ever set up for success," a U.S. aid official told me. Thomas-Greenfield had dodged another embarrassing veto and Kaag gained a credential, but the chief effect of the Biden administration's December moves was to enshrine damaging Israeli control of the aid system and defuse pressure for stronger action. At the same time, they provided apparent progress that could be cited by defenders of the U.S.-Israeli approach to the war. Later, at the end of Biden's presidency and in a period when Israeli officials were blocking more than 60 percent of aid missions that humanitarian workers sought in Gaza, another American humanitarian official spoke of Kaag's appointment as a fig leaf.[14] "You can't get anyone to say she's done anything other than get meetings with the Israelis that other people in the UN system can't," this official told me. "But to what end and at what cost?"[15]

OBFUSCATION AND AMBITION

By the waning weeks of 2023, evidence about the toll of Israeli attacks and aid policies had swelled, through testimony from Palestinians themselves, the handful of foreigners permitted into Gaza (whose ranks still excluded international journalists), and experts' remote analysis of social media and satellite imagery. The pause in fighting in November allowed a fuller accounting of the suffering among civilians. The cost of Israel's willingness to attack hospitals was put in sharp relief, for instance, when Palestinian journalist Mohammed Balousha accessed a hospital in Gaza City from which staff were forced to flee weeks earlier—leaving behind infants on life support who could not be safely moved. Balousha showed the world their corpses, abandoned and decomposing.[16] (He was shot shortly afterward in what he believed was an attack by an Israeli sniper; a year later, an Israeli drone strike killed him.)[17] A couple of weeks later, American intelligence officials concluded that nearly half of the bombs Israel had dropped since October 7 were unguided and had a high likelihood of killing innocent people.[18]

Amid the increasingly horrifying revelations, members of Biden's own party pressed the administration to reflect and share more of what it knew. Six Democratic lawmakers who had previously worked in national security wrote to Biden on December 18 arguing a change in the U.S.-Israeli strategy for the war was needed because they "know from personal and often painful experience that you can't destroy a terror ideology with military force alone."[19] Legislators reported that they had yet to see a list of the U.S. weapons Biden had sent to Israel or receive detailed data on Israel's use of American arms and intelligence, even in classified briefings, and a group of senators noted in another letter to the president that Biden was requesting even more "limits" on transparency in his proposed military aid package for Israel and Ukraine.[20] There was a growing sense among U.S. government officials that Israel's sweeping operation might not only implicate Israelis in war crimes but also bring into question the appropriateness of certain actions taken by Biden administration officials. On Capitol Hill, staffers for Chris

Van Hollen dug up an overlooked statute known as Section 620I of the Foreign Assistance Act, which banned the provision of U.S. weapons to countries that blocked the delivery of U.S.-funded humanitarian assistance. As John Kirby regularly argued, the United States was the top humanitarian donor to Palestinians—yet the agencies that were trying to get American-funded supplies to desperate families uniformly said U.S.-backed Israeli actions were preventing them from doing so.

The Biden administration was clear in its disdain for the pushback from fellow Democrats. Twice in December, Blinken invoked emergency powers to ignore the standard procedures for U.S. arms deals—which involve consultation with Congress—so that Washington could rush equipment to the Israelis. In a blistering LinkedIn post, Josh Paul detailed the ramifications of the move: It meant Netanyahu could pummel Gaza while preparing for a possible war in Lebanon; it redirected ammunition that was desperately needed by Ukraine; and it meant "more children will die."[21]

Privately, McGurk was finalizing a proposal that would treat the war as an opportunity for positive headlines. Since early in the war, Biden aides had held discussions about what they referred to as "the day after," envisioning that Hamas would collapse and they would help organize reconstruction, aiming to use the moment to deliver on the United States' long-standing promise of a two-state solution. Though Netanyahu publicly decried the idea of Palestinian self-governance, uniting Gaza and the occupied West Bank, Israeli officials joined the planning, a former U.S. official involved in the talks told me, noting that many Israelis in military and intelligence positions saw "separation" from Palestinians as vital even if it would be politically difficult to sell because Israeli hard-liners referred to such sovereignty as a "prize" for the October 7 attack.

In December, McGurk took over the conversation. He cut out many officials who had been involved, and refocused it onto his long-standing priority, the U.S.-Israel–Saudi Arabia deal. Such an agreement was widely referred to as "normalization" because the Israelis and Saudis had never had normal diplomatic relations. "Normalization remained

[McGurk's] primary objective, and this was the first opportunity he saw to put it back on the agenda," Andrew Miller, then the top official for Israel-Palestine at the State Department, told me. Taking shape prior to October 7, that idea had always involved an American treaty commitment to protect Saudi Arabia, U.S. nuclear technology for the Saudis, and some Israeli concessions to Palestinians in exchange for Saudi recognition of Israel; by giving all sides something they wanted, the arrangement theoretically enshrined a regional alliance network friendly to Washington. Now McGurk tacked on a commitment for the Saudis and other wealthy Arab states to pay for the rebuilding of Gaza in return for Israel accepting a joint government across the two Palestinian territories—and all within ninety days from when Israel declared victory over Hamas. The plan was classic Washington: a cover-all-bases solution perfect for a conference room or simulation but with little prospect in the real world or consideration for the views of the people whose lives would be affected. "There was an excessively rosy expectation of how quickly they could move from a ceasefire to a normalization agreement, in part because they were looking at the electoral timetable. . . . That's in part why they were thinking it was a matter of months rather than it being a longer period of time," Miller told me. Another senior official who recalled the McGurk bid told me the Biden team sought to clinch the deal before the election as part of their cooperation with Republican lawmakers who also liked the idea and worried about the chances of the Senate ratifying the U.S.-Saudi treaty involved in the bargain. "That was the whole Lindsey Graham thing—you had to get it done while there was a Democratic president because that way you'd get Democratic senators on board. . . . There was a time limit," that official said.[22] But the idea that it could all happen in three months, or that Israel was about to agree to a ceasefire at all, was implausible.

That McGurk felt he could establish a new Middle Eastern order, suddenly solving an eighty-year dispute, was both unsurprising and a warning sign the new pitch could mirror old missteps. He had extensive experience and relationships from twenty years of American policy in the region. But he had shepherded moves that created more instability, such as encouraging the rise of the autocratic Iraqi leader Nouri al-Maliki, and he rarely prioritized democratic representation for those living there. He was known among fellow officials for opposing efforts by other officials to pressure autocrats like Syria's Bashar Assad and Egypt's Abdel-Fattah el-Sisi. Perhaps most important, he had never spent significant time in Israel/Palestine or previously directed policy choices for that especially complex region.

Still, his influence kept swelling. "If a nuclear bomb was dropped on D.C., two forms of life would survive: cockroaches and Brett McGurk," a former U.S. official told me for an article I published in December 2023. Another official in the Biden administration argued: "He's an unstoppable force of failing up. . . . He's always my example of why it's great to be a white guy."[23]

McGurk grew especially close to Biden during the war, often outgunning other advisors in shaping major choices. Some foreign policy professionals began comparing McGurk to Jared Kushner, who as Trump's son-in-law had wielded significant influence in global affairs during his first presidency despite doubts about his judgment.[24] The relationship was "a son in need of a father and a father who had just lost his oldest son," a senior Biden aide argued to me: McGurk had written about struggling with his own father, and Beau Biden's death in 2015 was a defining agony for Biden.

Beyond him, however, other top administration officials also upheld reductive views of communities in the Middle East that had become entrenched in U.S. policymaking circles. When one outside analyst suggested to Sullivan at a meeting that U.S.-Saudi-Israel negotiations were not feasible after October 7, the analyst said Sullivan snapped back: "Are you seriously telling me the Arabs are not going to accept a Palestinian state?!" Another Biden aide added that several Arab regimes had cut deals with Israel that their populations disliked, and those deals had lasted for years. While true, that argument both blessed undemocratic policymaking and ignored the fact that Anwar Sadat, who had signed Egypt's 1979 treaty with Israel, had been assassinated over it;

Saudi Arabia's de facto ruler, crown prince Muhammed bin Salman, privately spoke of fearing the same fate should he be seen as short-changing Palestinians.[25]

For the administration, McGurk's gambit offered a chance of triumph rather than confronting American responsibility for the mounting death toll in Gaza. U.S. officials began speaking of a "Jeddah-Jerusalem Pact," several Biden aides told me—a phrase hinting at the PR framing of the plan, focusing on alliteration rather than accuracy (the Saudi capital is Riyadh, not Jeddah)—and the plan envisioned Biden visiting the Middle East as an iconic peacemaker, bolstering his standing just before the U.S. presidential election.

Other officials were skeptical. It was hard to ignore the fact that the plan would result in McGurk's "saving face," said one U.S. official at the time, who saw that as a key motivator given that the region he was supposed to be managing was in chaos and that his years of work on a U.S.-Saudi-Israel deal were at risk of being for naught.

As I reported at the time, one government expert called the idea "delusionally optimistic" because a host of forces would likely try to derail any attempted deal, from anti-U.S. militias linked to Iran to anti-Arab extremists in Israel, and another official commented, "This is what happens when you put people at the top who lack a lot of historical and cultural context in the region."[26] The official was referring to the fact that not only was Israel still rejecting the idea of a Palestinian state, but even though U.S.-friendly leaders remained open to growing closer to Israel, extensive coverage of atrocities in Gaza had made their populations far more resistant to such a move: A poll published in late December showed nearly 96 percent of Saudis wanted all Arab states to cut ties with Israel over its behavior in Gaza.[27] And it was clear the United States was already struggling to deal with possible obstacles. The Iran-backed Houthis had since November attacked ships in the Red Sea and were expanding their attacks, which they cast as a show of solidarity with Palestinians. Washington and its allies had failed to stop the disruptions of a vital global trade route—so on January 11, Biden approved a plan for the United States and Britain to start bombing

Houthi military facilities, even though previous U.S.-backed bombing of the country had only helped the militants consolidate their power.

I broke the news of Biden's decision thanks to a well-placed source who told me the air strikes belied the lack of a "cohesive strategy," which soon even the president acknowledged.[28] When a reporter asked him whether the expensive American strikes were working, Biden responded: "When you say working, are they stopping the Houthis? No. Are they going to continue? Yes." Brian Finucane, a former State Department lawyer, told me the policy amounted to the United States "playing the role of arsonist and firefighter simultaneously in the Middle East because of the White House's unconditional support for Israel."

Even amid changing circumstances and skepticism from foreign policy professionals, McGurk remained staunchly committed to his plan. Twenty-four hours after I broke the news of his proposed "Jeddah-Jerusalem Pact," White House spokeswoman Adrienne Watson, whose team had declined to comment for my story even after I repeatedly extended my deadline at their request, abruptly sent me a statement claiming my story was false and I had made up the quotes in it. Watson had issued the most serious possible charge against a journalist, without evidence or any indication she knew who my sources were, and after I had already faced smears from ardent Israel supporters. The move stank of the scorn for the press that was part of the undemocratic tendencies among Trump's circle that Biden's team said they were trying to keep away from the White House. (Not long thereafter, White House spokespeople walked back Watson's accusations, first asserting that she had only meant that certain quotes in my article were not from any document—which was not something I had claimed, since the quotes came from unnamed live sources—and then saying that they had not intended "to question the journalism." They still maintained that no document detailing McGurk's plan existed.)[29]

More than a year later, when I spotted and approached McGurk at a gala, he became enraged, quoting the article back to me and claiming he was never foolish enough to believe he could solve the war and deliver regional peace within ninety days and denying using the term "Jeddah-Jerusalem Pact." Yet from mid-January 2024 onward, administration officials continued to unveil parts of the plan, for example at Sullivan's appearance at the World Economic Forum in Davos, Switzerland, that month, and at various public appearances by Blinken.[30] A person familiar with McGurk who is himself a Middle East expert was not surprised that McGurk persisted in his thinking despite the predictable hostility from constituencies in both Israel and Saudi Arabia and the slim chances that the plan could actually address long-running Palestinian frustration. "He truly doesn't believe the Palestinian stuff matters . . . and he's always been a self-defined realist who thinks public opinion doesn't matter that much" in the Arab world, the person said, recalling that on occasions when he brought up to McGurk wariness in Arab societies about various American policy preferences, McGurk's usual response was that Arab dictators could "take care of it." With most of McGurk's interactions with people in the region occurring at elite levels in elite settings, "he doesn't have a good grasp of what people outside palaces think," the person said. Over more than twenty years of working on the Middle East, McGurk had notably maintained that he never had time to learn Arabic.[31]

But even if he thought that a U.S.-Saudi-Israel deal was the right policy to confront Iran and other American foes, and that his contacts wanted to get it done, it was striking that the Biden advisor refused to acknowledge the war had scrambled regional dynamics and potentially required a new set of ideas that took into account the fact that Saudi thinking had shifted. "Kissinger would have adapted—even Dennis Ross would have adapted," the person said, referencing chief aides to past presidents. "Brett just didn't seem capable of adjusting."

The Biden administration continued to push the "Jeddah-Jerusalem" idea as their top goal in the region through the end of his presidency. McGurk was "extremely skillful at keeping balls in the air," the person familiar with him noted. Still, this person added, "eventually, the bill comes due." Netanyahu categorically ruled out the idea of accepting any Palestinian sovereignty between the Jordan River and the Mediterranean Sea.[32] And Saudi Arabia hardened its position on what it expected from Israel in any possible deal, stiffening its language to say it had to see an irreversible path to Palestinian statehood.[33] The proposal—involving months of work among senior officials amid crises in Gaza and beyond—never became reality. As evidence bearing out my story revealing and questioning the McGurk plan kept mounting, the Biden administration never provided the apology I requested or proof for its potentially career-ending lie. Upon leaving office, Sullivan hired Watson as his personal spokeswoman.

TAKING THE REINS

Even as the administration envisioned sweeping regional diplomacy and McGurk remained focused on his moon-shot plan, top Biden aides spent much of early 2024 focused on the nitty-gritty of humanitarian needs in Gaza. Officials felt the Israeli concessions in permitting greater aid deliveries after entreaties from Biden and Sullivan, in October and December, respectively, proved high-level involvement was essential to progress. They were "desperate to see a win," noted a U.S. humanitarian official who worked directly with the White House in this period; while critical of the administration's approach, the official added: "They wanted to get help in. . . . They're not heartless, unfeeling people." Another senior official noted to me that the humanitarian situation was, for the White House, "a place you could more easily measure whether you had succeeded in achieving anything on a given day than you could on . . . dealing with the Hamas threat. There was very rarely good news on that front: All the statistics we saw internally showed a very, very heavy civilian toll and very modest militant toll of this war." The process the Biden administration developed, however, left it constantly dissatisfied and Palestinians increasingly desperate. Because of U.S. backing, the Israeli government still controlled access into the strip. American officials struggled to negotiate with their Israeli counterparts because their tactics were rooted in Washington's deference to Israel: They avoided inconvenient information and analysis; they ignored the humanitarian playbook that worked in other contexts; and they sought small-bore accomplishments rather than big shifts toward a reliable flow of supplies.

The U.S. government had tackled international calamities for decades, often as the largest donor to step in. So even as American-backed policies pushed Gaza into a quicker descent into mass suffering than experts had tracked elsewhere, some U.S. officials knew what steps could help. But Biden himself had set a tone of doubt about Palestinians' reporting of their conditions and his team established a precedent that even basic steps to help civilians that Israel was obligated to take under the law of war depended on getting the attention of someone at or near the top of the U.S. government. "The president was a kind of desk officer for humanitarian access . . . in the early phase," Samantha Power recalled to me. Meanwhile, a key route for internal warnings and recommendations ran through the American embassy in Jerusalem, controlled by the American ambassador to Israel, Jack Lew. A former Treasury secretary close to pro-Israel Jewish groups in the United States, Lew was seen by many fellow Biden aides as "captured" by his host country—a common condition in which envoys become deeply sympathetic to the perspective of the nations where they are posted. Asked about Israeli behavior after leaving office, Lew claimed the media exaggerated. Palestinian children killed by the IDF were often the children of Hamas fighters, he alleged, without providing proof or explaining why that should make observers less distressed that young lives were destroyed.[34]

Led from Jerusalem, an American government disaster-response team began working on Gaza days into the war. Their attempts to convey humanitarian data to Biden's policy team through the embassy faced "pushback, censorship, and delays," a U.S. humanitarian official told me. According to this official, it took eight weeks for Lew's team to approve a diplomatic cable about the December 2023 finding from the global famine tracker on mass hunger among Palestinians, as embassy staff argued the assessment "isn't fair to all the efforts being made by the Israelis"—even though the yardsticks in question were not measuring attempts but verifiable outcomes like the rate of malnutrition.

In other crisis contexts where the official had worked, U.S. embassies issued multiple cables on humanitarian matters weekly. In this case, the official said, embassy staff echoed Israeli government claims that relief groups, including the United Nations, were exaggerating the scale of the suffering. Meanwhile, academics close to Netanyahu were sending top U.S. officials their own milder analyses of Palestinians' conditions that David Satterfield, Biden's humanitarian envoy, and staff at the White House regularly referenced, the official said.

Without extensive humanitarian cables from Jerusalem, aid officials "didn't have the grist" in discussions with other administration staff over how to help Gaza—and, tacitly, whether to deploy U.S. leverage over Israel—the U.S. humanitarian official told me. Officials tried other routes to share information, such as updates sent via the U.S. Agency for International Development. But such an update "doesn't carry the same weight" among policymakers as an official diplomatic cable, the humanitarian official explained. Another U.S. official working on humanitarian issues tried a route that was less sensitive and so less carefully monitored by the Jerusalem embassy: unclassified cables. Crafted to avoid any hint of opinion, their assessments on food scarcity and health problems among Palestinians were widely circulated inside the government around the start of 2024, and the official heard they had reached Sullivan and Finer, members of the innermost circle of Biden administration discussions on the war.

But the news came with a chilling indicator of the lack of awareness about Palestinians' conditions among those who could help. The official was told the two men actually were surprised that hunger had become so intense. Throughout the war, senior Biden aides disputed assessments of Palestinian deprivation from both humanitarian and intelligence officials, prompting even their own colleagues to suggest the administration had a double standard shielding Israel. Such assessments "would've been taken as gospel in any other context," a senior State Department official told me. In December, after the first truce collapsed, McGurk took a meeting with representatives from aid groups in which he surprised them by denying that conditions would worsen, suggesting he would be able to secure another Israel-Hamas deal, and articulating an overly optimistic view of humanitarian prospects in Gaza, two people present recalled to me, with one saying those became "standard talking points" from McGurk.

Even when hearing gritty details of Palestinian vulnerability, top administration staff often deflected. Also in December, Blinken gathered dozens of State Department staff to discuss humanitarian needs in Gaza and heard stark assessments, including from an official with former combat experience who detailed in technical terms why the 2,000-pound bombs that Washington kept sending Israel would inevitably endanger many civilians. The secretary responded by emphasizing emotional trauma among Israelis over October 7 and strategic reasons for arming Israel, including an American law requiring presidents to sustain a Qualitative Military Edge (or QME) for Tel Aviv relative to its neighbors, a person in the meeting told me. Around the same time, several officials told Blinken's chief of staff Suzy George that if the secretary was serious about his statements urging Israeli compliance with international law, he should ask the U.S. intelligence community for its assessments of potential war crimes, demonstrating high-level interest to spur deeper investigations. Four senior State Department officials told me that, to their knowledge, the secretary never formally made such a request; another senior State official said Blinken's team requested assessments but intelligence personnel claimed they lacked sufficient information.

Meanwhile, extreme sensitivity about expressing skepticism of Israel—for fear of angering the president or long-term career consequences—led to officials feeling silenced across key parts of the Biden administration. At the State Department, the chief official overseeing human rights work, the veteran diplomat Uzra Zeya, regularly discouraged other staff under her purview—members of the teams most likely to question Israel given their expertise—from internal critiques of the U.S.-Israeli approach to the war, five State Department officials told me. Four State officials recalled Zeya discouraging "split memos," in which some State Department offices formally oppose a policy move that others endorse, such as a specific weapons shipment for Israel. A split memo required Blinken to be on record making a final decision between the two positions. One senior official said Zeya repeatedly argued for watering down certain criticism to avoid its rising to the level that would require a split memo. By contrast, "consensus memos," which did not register any formal objections, allowed arms transfers to be approved automatically at a lower level, creating what the official Christopher Le Mon described to me as "herd impunity," since "if everyone is responsible for the decision, then no one is responsible for the decision." (A senior State Department official disputed that portrayal to me, saying that multiple split memos did advance through the department, and that Zeya advocated shifts in U.S. policy toward Israel in internal debates among Blinken's advisors but did not prevail.) And at USAID, senior official Sonali Korde personally edited fact sheets, meeting notes, and other documents related to Gaza that would normally never rise to the level of someone in her job, Karin Huster, a colleague, told me. Huster recalled Korde removing the word "Palestinian" from one document, even when junior staff pointed out it was in the title of a document from an organization outside the U.S. government.[35] Months later, when the Famine Early Warning Systems Network, a U.S.-backed monitor, was preparing to suggest famine was occurring in Gaza, Korde "strongly" urged the body to insert caveats.[36] Korde developed significant power and especially close relationships with Israeli counterparts throughout the war, as she first worked for Satterfield and then was promoted to run USAID's Bureau for Humanitarian Assistance. At her swearing-in ceremony, colleagues were stunned to see she had invited the Israeli ambassador in Washington.

Korde's position and contacts could be valuable for aid groups, a senior administration official told me. She became a "one-woman red phone" for humanitarian staff, the official said, repeatedly receiving calls in the middle of the night and persuading Israeli Southern Command "to get the guns to go quiet" amid attacks on aid workers.

The setup potentially saved lives, and Korde's deep immersion in humanitarian discussions was undisputed. But her record mirrored the administration's disturbing broader style of ad hoc fixes—as patterns of Israeli violence persisted—and extreme intimacy with Tel Aviv that could distort policymaking.

Eventually, USAID personnel prepared formal complaints alleging that Korde's conduct with her Israeli counterparts was inappropriate and was hurting her stated mission, two staffers told me. For example, one reported, Korde told USAID colleagues to alter an internal U.S. government infographic depicting Israeli actions because she "got a howler" about it from Israeli colonel Elad Goren. The reference to letters in the Harry Potter universe that scream at their recipients suggested Goren had strongly objected to the document. In any case, as the USAID official told me, "That is not stuff we share, certainly not with a belligerent to a conflict that we're covering." (Korde told me she did not share any internal infographics with the government of Israel.) Even the senior administration official raised the question, "By virtue of having all this access, does it skew one's perspective?"

Korde's role also reflected a self-defeating tendency in the Biden administration's handling of aid for Gaza: tightly limiting the circle involved, often to people without relevant experience. Negotiations over aid deliveries in war zones, for instance, are usually run directly between warring parties and the chief UN humanitarian office that handles crisis situations, known as the Office for the Coordination of Humanitarian Affairs (OCHA), or by experts at aid groups themselves, one U.S. humanitarian official told me. But in Gaza, with the Biden administration casting itself as the mediator between relief groups and Israeli authorities, "you had three people negotiating humanitarian access who have little history in humanitarian access," the official continued. The group comprised Satterfield, Korde—whose experience was largely in combating infectious disease—and a low-profile State Department official named Scott Turner.

The administration's humanitarian dialogue with its Israeli counterparts was "very, very guarded," the U.S. aid official told me. Supporters of the approach cast it as key to handling a still-traumatized American partner, given opposition among many Israelis to any aid for Palestinians, but the closeness between Tel Aviv and Washington risked coloring the Biden administration's approach to aid in ways that worsened the crisis. Neutrality is a core principle for humanitarians, not just for building trust with aid recipients but for ensuring their strategy is guided by human concern rather than political preferences. With the United States shaping aid operations as it worked closely with the Israeli government, armed Israel daily, and blessed its war goals, would the humanitarian system for Gaza always rank below other priorities, and would the Israelis really feel pressure to improve the process? Evidence for that trajectory was already emerging: On January 31, Martin Griffiths, the UN OCHA chief, said aid workers' ability to function in Gaza "remains grossly inadequate," citing the continued lack of security for humanitarian personnel—dozens of whom had been killed in Israeli attacks—and "frequent rejection for entry of much needed items . . . by Israel, for unclear, inconsistent and often unspecified reasons."[37]

Aid groups said there was no consistent resolution to any of those problems throughout Biden's time in office. And in high-level administration discussions, the camaraderie between Washington and Tel Aviv combined with Israeli policies limiting information about the war—problematic in their own right—to fuel persistent doubts about how serious conditions were in Gaza. "The fact that the movement inside Gaza is so circumscribed by our partners meant that USAID was kind of two or three steps removed," Power recalled to me. "People [in the administration] felt, 'Well, we're doing all we can, we're raising all these issues,' and when we were trying to say, 'Yes, but conditions are deteriorating in these ways, these are going to be the consequences of Israel closing checkpoints or pulling supplies off of convoys,' we were not able to say, 'Our USAID staff saw with our own eyes this and that.'" In her view, "that shouldn't have mattered: We knew how to fact-check, and we had worked with most of our partners in war zones for decades." But the administration's approach represented one more instance of the United States handling Israel-Palestine differently than other crises, with deadly consequences. "In Syria, nobody was motivated to question the information we were getting and passing along," Power told me.

The centralization of the U.S. aid operation in early 2024 undercut its efficacy from the onset, some officials felt. The key figures' inexperience in negotiating on aid access meant they failed to maximize the amount of supplies entering Gaza. One U.S. humanitarian official observed Satterfield repeatedly make requests for a daily target number of aid trucks that was too low: "If he starts asking for 250 trucks, Israel will get it down to 100. You ask for 1,000 if you want 500."

Empowered by Biden, and often deferred to by Sullivan, Blinken, and Power, Satterfield exercised influence that made it harder to know if Israelis faced accountability for hurting Palestinians, or to achieve lasting humanitarian improvements, several officials told me, describing how the envoy set up a new and opaque system for dealing with alleged Israeli misconduct. Satterfield tasked USAID staff with added responsibilities beyond their remit, the humanitarian official said, by asking them to compile and send back to him regular reports of attacks on civilians, which would normally be assessed by other officials with expertise in human rights violations and international law. Documents I reviewed showed that incidents on the ever-growing list were then marked as "resolved" or "addressed" after responses about them from Israeli officials were included, or even without such answers, without any indication of whether those answers were credible or whether Satterfield's ad hoc process was producing accountability or changes in Israeli behavior. (The savage course of the war eventually answered the second question in the negative.) Among the examples I reviewed, a January 27 case of IDF firing on Palestinian repair workers and a February 7 IDF attack on a Palestinian Red Crescent ambulance were marked "addressed" and "resolved," respectively, without any Israeli answer included, and several attacks, including a deadly January 30 assault on Al Amal Hospital, were tagged similarly despite notes that Israeli investigations were pending. A March 13 Israeli strike on an UNRWA facility that killed five Palestinians and injured twenty-two was marked "resolved," following an Israeli explanation that a Hamas commander had been present diverting aid—without any discussion of whether that was a proportionate attack or Satterfield's own public comment that he had not seen evidence for Israel's claims of Hamas stealing aid. And the January 29 killing of Hind Rajab (who was not named) was marked "pending."[38] After an incident on Satterfield's list was marked as addressed, even without details of how thorough the response was and whether information about it might affect overall U.S. policy, other officials were often told they could not raise that event with the Israelis again, a State Department lawyer told me.

Satterfield communicated constantly with McGurk, boosting the impression that the aid operation was secondary to the Biden administration's bigger strategic Middle East goals coordinated by McGurk. Along with Sullivan and a handful of other senior officials, they participated in nightly calls during this period to discuss aid access and received daily reports that narrowly focused on minor daily problems, while humanitarian experts urged them to use their influence to enact bigger changes in Israeli conduct. They would, for instance, track a specific truck hour by hour to ensure it reached its destination, U.S. humanitarian officials told me. The micromanagement swallowed hours and attention that could have been better deployed to meet the administration's professed goal of helping Palestinians. On one such call, one staffer recalled being asked to detail the differences between a Palestinian box truck and one from Jordan to a group of leading White House aides that included Sullivan's chief of staff, Curtis Reid. "This is not where [Reid] needs to put time," the humanitarian staffer said. The fact that McGurk, Satterfield, and other busy, distracted, and nonexpert top officials were tracking individual truck deliveries signaled throughout the humanitarian system that those same top officials had to be consulted on even minor decisions relating to aid delivery. This created delays amid life-or-death conditions because "things that a State Department desk officer [ordinarily] would give permission for were things we [now] would [have to] go to the top of our government to ask for," the same staffer told me. Speaking with me later, Satterfield said he worked "in direct coordination with the president" and fellow high-ranking officials, including Blinken and his advisor Derek Chollet, and argued: "This required very senior political engagement and progress was not simple. We did as much as was possible given the nature of the conflict and political realities both in Israel and Washington."

Simultaneously, suggestions for more comprehensive solutions got little attention, from Israel resuming electricity supplies to Gaza—easing fuel shortages that crippled hospitals, bakeries, and homes—to allowing in de-mining equipment to tackle thousands of unexploded Israeli bombs, many of them American-made, which added a new layer of danger to daily life for Palestinians. And the concentration of decision-making among officials unfamiliar with standard humanitarian processes courted huge sudden risks that could quickly heighten Palestinians' despair. In January 2024, the UN felt its foreign staff in Gaza were at such risk that it nearly withdrew all of them, removing from the crisis hundreds of aid personnel with irreplaceable skills, the U.S. humanitarian official recalled to me. She said Biden administration decision-makers struggled to understand that that withdrawal might occur and be a result of their own actions, such as limiting "deconfliction" conversations about Israeli targeting to American and Israeli officials. (Washington was ultimately convinced to fund more UN security personnel.)[39]

The administration's hamstrung aid plan was never likely to produce more than minimal improvement in Gaza—but between the limited expertise of those who laid the foundation for Biden's humanitarian policy and the administration's resistance to the step aid groups called vital, a ceasefire, recognition of that reality was a challenge. In one meeting, the U.S. humanitarian official recalled telling a group of White House staff about more than a dozen Palestinians dying of malnutrition—a preventable condition. "Will it get worse?" one of them said in response. The aid expert was flabbergasted but direct: "You pay me for my expertise. Yes, you will see more dead children in the news. . . . One truckload will not stop famine," she recalled responding.

KNEECAPPING UNRWA

As U.S. officials attempted to direct a new aid system for Gaza, the Biden administration faced a major revelation about the organization that historically had the strongest humanitarian capacity in the Gaza Strip:

the United Nations Relief and Works Agency for Palestine Refugees in the Near East, commonly referred to by its acronym, UNRWA. Washington responded by turbocharging the already-expanding humanitarian crisis.

Established in 1949, UNRWA swelled into a quasi-government as Palestinians remained stateless decade after decade. It was particularly critical in Gaza as the strip's institutions crumbled from 2007 on because of the enmity between Hamas and the Palestinian Authority (which still ran some government functions) and the blockade by Israel and Egypt. Prior to October 7, UNRWA had thirteen thousand employees in Gaza and operated more than three hundred facilities in the region, from health centers to fuel depots. Amid the war, its importance grew. With its infrastructure, including a trained and extensive local staff at a time when Israel was often blocking the entry of foreign aid workers, UNRWA became the backbone of the humanitarian operation upon which nearly all aid work—including by other groups—relied. For Palestinians, the agency provided not just food and medical care but shelter for hundreds of thousands seeking safety or rendered homeless by Israeli attacks. By early January, nearly 1.4 million people were living in UNRWA buildings. Still, as humanitarian workers constantly said, nowhere in the strip was safe: Israeli strikes hit UNRWA buildings at least sixty-three times by early January, killing 319 Palestinians, including 146 UNRWA employees—the highest number of UN staff ever killed in conflict.

On January 18, an Israeli diplomat told UNRWA chief Philippe Lazzarini his government had evidence that at least a dozen of Lazzarini's employees took part in the October 7 attack. Right-wing Israelis and their allies in the United States had long criticized the UN agency, saying it promoted extremism and an unnecessary special status for Palestinians compared with other refugees. UNRWA's defenders believed the real reason for the opposition was that it "represents [Palestinians'] right to a fair and lasting political settlement," in the words of a UN official, by sustaining a unique status for those displaced amid the creation of Israel and their descendants.

The claim that employees of UNRWA—which counted the United States as its chief donor—participated in murder, kidnapping, and other crimes under Hamas's direction was astonishing. UNRWA gave Israel lists of its staff for vetting and approval each year, a reflection of Israel's influence even within Hamas-controlled Gaza, the scrutiny of any support for Palestinians, and the fact that, like any UN agency, it did not have an intelligence arm. It was immediately clear the situation represented an unprecedented threat; what UNRWA didn't expect was that the Biden administration's response would produce even greater danger.

The agency dispatched the names provided by Israel to a single human resources staffer in hopes of preventing a leak, asking the staffer to comb through its list of thousands of employees in Gaza. Nine names matched those of UNRWA staff; two were dead. Lazzarini fired the others, then traveled to UN headquarters in New York and, on January 24, Washington, where he spent two days discussing UNRWA's future with U.S. officials. Concern had already spread within the American government: A U.S. humanitarian official in the region received calls that week from Washington asking what was afoot at UNRWA, this official told me. Lazzarini, returning to his base in Amman, Jordan, thought his team had a solid plan in motion. Beyond the dismissals, they had agreed to launch an investigation and participate in a separate UN probe, and they planned to issue a statement about the situation that Friday to be public about prioritizing accountability, the UN official told me. The timing happened to coincide with a major moment in the global debate about the war—the UN's International Court of Justice (ICJ) was set to issue its first ruling in a case accusing Israel of a genocide in Gaza—and UNRWA wanted to ensure that whatever the outcome, it had taken ownership of the alleged problem before Israel put out its own narrative about the claim.

Almost immediately after Lazzarini issued his statement, the Biden administration announced it had "temporarily paused additional funding for UNRWA."[40] The move set in motion consequences that U.S. officials did not anticipate by boosting skepticism toward the essential

UN agency among foreign governments and U.S. lawmakers—both of whom had power over UNRWA's budget, and interpreted the pause as a signal to cut off the agency. Over the following weeks, the agency faced a $430 million financial crunch due to halted funds from the United States and allies like Canada and Japan and scrambled to simultaneously serve Palestinians and plead for money that had already been pledged to the agency and accounted for in internal planning. The dilemma came without verification of the Israeli claims; U.S. intelligence officials soon reported they did not believe Hamas had infiltrated the agency and noted in their assessment that Israel's historic dislike of UNRWA might bias its analysis.[41]

Pro-Palestinian commentators linked the rollout to the ICJ ruling, claiming it was a U.S.-Israeli distraction. Speaking with me soon after the events, the UN official doubted the domino effect of U.S. allies rapidly halting UNRWA funding was spontaneous. Biden staffers privately began echoing talking points from the agency's opponents, saying other aid organizations might replace it—an idea deemed impossible by humanitarian experts but popular among anti-UNRWA voices, many of whom opposed Palestinian rights broadly.

Still, a State Department official denied Washington asked others to follow its example and told me: "We see the suspension of funding as a means to . . . do all we can to preserve" UNRWA. Many in the Biden administration knew no alternative could replace the agency, according to a senior U.S. official I interviewed later. The second official found it "indisputable" a handful of UNRWA employees were involved in the attack—in which analysts said many everyday Palestinians took part after Hamas breached Israel's border defenses—but also indicated awareness of the broader push to kill the agency: "What is it about the organization that would make it persona non grata if all the problematic people were removed?"

Reflecting nearly a year later, the senior Biden aide suggested the administration should have stated conditions under which it would restore UNRWA funding or taken a different move to demonstrate it was serious about concerns with the agency, such as seeking another chief instead of Lazzarini, who had made a habit of social media fights with Israel. "The suspension in isolation simply egged on Congress to do more," the aide said. Privately—but wrongly—the administration had thought Lazzarini would resign of his own accord, a U.S. humanitarian official told me.

Staunchly pro-Israel lawmakers began to pursue legislation barring American funding for the agency. A handful of U.S. officials lobbied Capitol Hill, arguing a legal ban would be disastrous; one humanitarian official had "never seen people fight so hard to keep money in place," the official told me, and recalled sleepless nights of preparing backup plans for UNRWA's collapse. Government experts were "doing their best," the senior Biden official told me, but they were "speaking a language that just doesn't matter" compared with the narrative the Israeli government and its supporters were spreading among legislators. The moment stands as a telling instance of when the Biden administration was willing to challenge Congress over Gaza. In this situation, taking serious action would have meant lining up against hard-line pro-Israel voices—and that route was not chosen. In instances when top Biden staff did pressure legislators, they did so in concert with Israel backers and against critics of their policy who invoked Palestinian rights—usually in seeking more weapons for the Israelis.

In March, Congress passed the UNRWA funding ban. Reacting to the news, Israel Katz, the Israeli foreign minister, underscored that opposition to the agency's very existence drove the push against it, writing on X: "UNRWA will not be a part of Gaza's landscape in the aftermath of Hamas."[42] Katz invited other countries to follow the American example. But the Biden administration increasingly stood alone, as one by one, other nations restored donations to UNRWA, citing Palestinians' suffering and the fact that independent investigations did not evince a fundamental rot at the agency. Nearly a year later, after multiple probes, one of the biggest data points indicating militant infiltration in UNRWA was a set of internal Hamas documents that Israel shared with *The New York Times*, which suggested just twenty-four of thousands of staff at UNRWA schools were members of armed Palestinian groups.

(Another outside probe, by the UN's internal oversight office, was never released, but a copy seen by the *Times* said it did not review Israeli-provided material alleging nine UNRWA staffers were also militants.)[43]

Washington, however, had not been driven by facts as much as political calculations and an unwillingness to confront Netanyahu and his allies. By July, the United States was the only major UNRWA donor that had not resumed its contributions. In defending its lack of engagement with Palestinians, the Biden administration regularly highlighted its decision to resume funding to UNRWA after Trump had pulled the plug in 2018. But its own actions meant UNRWA struggled when it was most needed—with the loss of a quarter of its funding ensuring a persistent shortfall into 2025—and that a U.S. ban on support for it was established bipartisan practice by the time Trump returned to power, and hence easier to prolong.[44]

"WE ARE WORKING IT VERY, VERY HARD"

As each passing week showed the Biden administration failing to achieve its stated goals—a deal to free Hamas hostages and pause the fighting in Gaza, and getting more aid to Palestinians—officials faced a growing belief in Washington that they had mired the United States in a morally and strategically costly morass. The spiraling toll of their policy was undeniable, painful, and, perhaps most important in the circles the administration most cared about, embarrassing. The Biden team responded with a firm message: Trust us. Their strategy hinged on amplifying their credentials, deflecting responsibility away from Americans toward both Israelis and Palestinians, and trying to carefully manage investigations of their choices.

In mid-January, Bernie Sanders brought the most serious challenge yet to the administration's appeal for faith in its approach. Sanders, the independent senator from Vermont, forced a Senate vote on Israeli conduct by citing a law that permits Congress to request a human rights report from the State Department about any country receiving U.S. aid. His bill seeking such a report put legislators on the spot—particularly

Democrats who cheer liberal values and some of whose voters were firmly antiwar—and denied them the easy excuse of wanting to defend an ally because, as Sanders noted, demanding an inquiry would not cut "a nickel" of America's military aid to Israel. Biden administration officials lobbied against the bill, and shortly before the vote, the Israeli ambassador to the United States, Michael Herzog, met with top senators.

Yet ten Democratic senators—one-fifth of the caucus—endorsed the Sanders idea, and Kentucky senator Rand Paul even provided a Republican vote for it.[45] The episode showed the devastation in Gaza was striking enough for a big chunk of Biden's own party to vote against him, risking pushback from pro-Israel voices—while also demonstrating the administration firmly opposed scrutiny of the strategy, even as its officials regularly declared that it needed serious improvement. It was a signal of a growing double game.

Led by Jake Sullivan, administration officials had been privately negotiating a compromise with critics on Capitol Hill since December, through discussions with Van Hollen. The Maryland senator had crafted his own bill, stating that U.S. partners must respect international and American law, including in their treatment of humanitarian aid. The language did not explicitly mention Israel, but Van Hollen's focus was clear, and the combination of his careful approach and his moderate reputation helped him gather nearly half the Democrats in the Senate to endorse the idea.[46] Still, neither he nor the administration wanted a vote; the White House feared further proof of a divide over Gaza within Biden's party, and Van Hollen knew the proposal would fail, perhaps embarrassingly. "We didn't know whether it would get nine votes or twice that number," Tim Rieser, a longtime congressional staffer close to Van Hollen, told me, noting that lawmakers commonly question pro-Israel policies in private and then panic about doing so publicly.

On February 8, Van Hollen announced a deal: Biden would issue a presidential directive modeled on his bill, to be known as "National Security Memorandum 20" and—crucially—to include a requirement for a report to Congress within ninety days on foreign countries' compliance with the memo. The agreement was rooted in the faith many foreign policy watchers still had in top Biden aides and in past practice: U.S. administrations often push difficult foreign counterparts by saying they need to demonstrate changes to Congress. The memorandum could have been used as leverage relative to Israel, Rieser said. But the administration quickly defused any impression of new pressure on Netanyahu. "There are no new standards in this memo," Biden's press secretary, Karine Jean-Pierre, said, and an unnamed official told reporters the administration did not believe Israel had violated U.S. and international law in either its attacks or its treatment of humanitarian aid.[47] John Kirby, who was increasingly supplanting Jean-Pierre as the face of the White House on Gaza, had said the month prior that the U.S. government was not even investigating possible Israeli war crimes, which it was required by various regulations to do if there was credible evidence of them. This statement was untrue: The White House, State Department, and Pentagon were all privately assessing apparent Israeli violations of international humanitarian law, as well as possible breaches of its agreements with the United States, three officials and another source familiar with the discussions told me, and I reported, in February 2024.[48]

Amid the mounting humanitarian crisis within Gaza, a new timeline had been set up for Washington to test the administration's "trust us" narrative. Officials continued to suggest they deserved confidence; pressed on aid shipments, Kirby urged reporters to give the Biden administration credit: "We are working it very, very hard."[49] Van Hollen was quietly preparing a potentially serious challenge to that message. In the 1990s, a fellow Maryland politician had said Van Hollen "plays poker the way he plays politics—friendly, aggressive, and you never know exactly what his hand is."[50] Soon after he unveiled his compromise with Jake Sullivan, Van Hollen called one of Sullivan's best-known critics: Josh Paul. The senator asked Paul to assemble an outside panel of experts to produce their own report on the U.S.-backed Israeli offensive as a benchmark against which to compare the Biden administration's claims. "Let's hold their feet to the fire," was the message Paul told me he received.

For many Palestinians, the idea that U.S. policy was taking human lives into account had already proven hollow, and Biden's approach seemed almost deliberately cruel. A couple of weeks after Van Hollen's announcement, I traveled to a dusty apartment complex on the outskirts of Doha, Qatar, to visit some of the few Palestinians who had secured Israeli permission to leave Gaza for medical treatment. Watfah, a thirty-year-old mother who accompanied her severely wounded thirteen-year-old son, told me she was constantly thinking of her other children still trapped in the war zone, with her daughter being forced at age nine to become "a parent" to younger siblings.[51] She had seen television coverage of Biden at a New York ice-cream shop discussing with reporters the prospect of an end to the fighting. The footage offered a dark twist on his old brand: Uncle Joe was now a widely criticized wartime commander in chief. Sugar cone in hand, Biden licked at his mint chip scoop and claimed a ceasefire was days away. "He's doing it while eating ice cream—mocking us," Watfah told me, visibly anguished.

In the United States, however, the Biden administration's messaging still had traction, thanks to many observers' tendency to offer the benefit of the doubt to political elites. Journalists' willingness to adapt simplistic narratives about complex foreign policy problems also helped the administration. And so a specific belief began to dominate Washington conversations and media coverage of the administration's approach to the war in early 2024: that Biden was failing to resolve the Gaza crisis because of other forces, not ineptitude or callousness. The chief villain in the narrative was Netanyahu. While the administration publicly affirmed U.S.-Israeli cooperation, people close to Biden were willing to share anecdotes for news articles about the president's frustration with the Israeli leader every few weeks. His patience with Netanyahu was running out, read a January 14 story, and on February 12, Biden was reported to have told people the Israeli was an "asshole" who was "giving him hell."[52]

Reporters, myself included, have always risked giving undue credence to Washington power players, but the problem seemed especially bad in the Biden era, after many in the press had grown close to Democratic operatives during Trump's first presidency, as they shared information and alarm about Trump's assault on long-standing U.S. principles. The coziness that persisted—with figures who the press was more comfortable having back in power—shaped how the war was depicted to the American public, bolstering the idea the Biden administration strove to improve conditions even as it chose daily to enable air strikes and aid restrictions in Gaza.

An incident at the end of January showed me how the assumption of good faith on the part of U.S. officials led some covering the war to bizarre, callous impressions of the situation, creating a broader environment of coverage obscuring American culpability and Palestinian humanity. The heads of several aid groups—who had jointly described seeing "nothing like the siege of Gaza" before—invited a few reporters to a private briefing.[53] They spoke of Palestinian colleagues who were killed or starving and Israeli officials turning away truckloads of aid over one banned item in the shipment, without providing a prior list of what would be allowed. Then a fellow correspondent posed a question. She said Biden administration officials often raised a good point: The aid groups kept demanding changes from the Israelis and Americans, but why not press Hamas?

U.S. law bars American-funded organizations from engaging with U.S.-designated terror groups—Hamas among them—and the Palestinian group was not operating the blockade, the attacks, or the cutoff of water and power that relief groups identified as their chief concerns. Meanwhile, though Israel accused Hamas of stealing aid, the Biden administration had said there was no evidence for the claim, and analysts saw the risk of theft as chiefly a result of Israel's attacks on Gaza's police force.[54] Through terse smiles, the aid officials shared that information. Twenty minutes later, the same reporter raised another question. Israel and the United States said the Gaza operation must continue to ensure Hamas was destroyed, yet aid groups had demanded a ceasefire for months. So, she asked the aid workers, do you want Hamas to win?

The six-word question carried so much. It was a snapshot into how mass violence can be tacitly justified even by those ostensibly concerned about it. That it was posed by a respected, experienced professional in a matter-of-fact way reflected how deep acceptance of the war's logic ran in Washington. And it echoed dangerous ideas that long predated October 7, like George W. Bush's "you're with us or against us" thinking—showing how tolerance for developments in Gaza was making global affairs far more brutal. It felt like the logic justifying killing aid workers in the strip was taking hold on K Street.

The man-made humanitarian crisis was by now inseparable from every part of the war, including actual bloodshed, even as the Biden administration sought to dodge blame for it. On February 29, one of the deadliest incidents since the fighting began occurred in what became known as the "flour massacre." Rumors of an aid delivery in northern Gaza, where Israel had allowed no supplies to enter for over a month, drew hundreds of Palestinians to a spot the convoy was supposed to pass. Instead of getting essentials, at least 118 Palestinians were killed and 760 wounded by Israeli troops, tanks, and aircraft; some were so desperate they tried to reach for supplies even after the firing began.[55] Israel first denied involvement, alleging there was a stampede and only warning shots. A CNN analysis of dozens of videos found the firing began earlier than the IDF had claimed and included shots within close range of crowds, killing people trying to flee. An image emerged of a blood-soaked aid package. "We must die in Gaza," said one man present, "and feel humiliated for a bag of flour."[56]

In Washington's telling, the incident was one in a spate of seemingly uncontrollable tragedies. "Far too many innocent Palestinians have been killed over the course of this conflict, not just today, but over the past nearly five months," State Department spokesperson Matt Miller said. Yet choices by Miller's colleagues were a big reason for that trajectory, and in the subsequent weeks, administration officials appeared to at least partly reconsider their deference to Israel, in part to appease critics. Still, the Biden administration almost never offered tangible reasons to take its talk of concern for Palestinian life seriously.

CHAPTER 4

SOMETHING HAS TO GIVE

Early February–End of March 2024

AFTER MONTHS OF CLAIMING WITHOUT EVIDENCE THAT nudges of, never threats toward, Netanyahu could shield civilians and prevent a man-made famine, Biden had to try a different approach. The pressure for the president to alter his policy grew overwhelmingly throughout February and March 2024, particularly from critics within his own political camp, from Democratic primary voters to legislators and some of Biden's own officials.

The administration in this period provided its own growing acknowledgments of how dire the war had become. For the first time, Biden drew a red line for Israel, saying it could not pursue a catastrophic invasion of the Gaza town of Rafah without risking American support—establishing what would eventually be the biggest test of his war policy. The U.S. government began directly providing supplies to Palestinians, even as Washington still provided the weapons killing them and supported Israel's undermining of the chief aid agency focused on them, UNRWA. Those efforts, through airdrops and a floating pier along Gaza's coastline, were launched despite objections from humanitarian experts and made no meaningful dent in Palestinian suffering or public outrage. Neither did new U.S. policies toward the West Bank, including sanctions on a handful of settlers. Ironically, the Biden team was strengthening the case of its opponents: By the administration's own stated standards of upholding U.S. and international law, minimizing civilian deaths, and fostering long-term Israeli-Palestinian peace, its Gaza policy was a failure.

Administration officials began passing the buck: They slammed Netanyahu as a unique problem while dodging reflection on how their war policy had strengthened hard-line political trends and an assumption of impunity in Israel, and they suggested that tweaks to Palestinian politics could lower tensions. Those arguments got little traction, but they indicated Biden's aides were struggling to justify their stubbornness on questions like using U.S. military aid to Israel as leverage. By the end of March, the stage was set for the most significant moment of U.S.-enforced restraint in Israel's offensive throughout Biden's presidency.

LISTEN TO MICHIGAN

Biden's Gaza policy was by now a major political factor, nine months from Election Day. The president's campaign advisors continued to prioritize overwhelming support for Israel and some distance from the pro-Palestinian movement. In December, the administration disavowed the largest Muslim civil rights group in the United States, the Council on American-Islamic Relations (CAIR), after its executive director linked the October 7 attack to Palestinian self-defense.[1] Though the CAIR chief specified he did not endorse targeting civilians, the administration decided no engagement with the group or its independent chapters across the country was acceptable.[2] The perception that Biden's aide Anita Dunn—who was both working in the White House and advising his reelection campaign—was committed to that position spread through "whisper networks" in the administration, which made those officials and Democratic Party personnel wary of engaging even with CAIR's chapters and so increased alienation between the president and American Muslims, a Biden staffer later told me.

Regardless of political aides' feelings, the facts showed that impressions of Biden as either weak or bloodthirsty for his role in the carnage in Gaza were aggravating young people and voters of color who drove his 2020 win and giving Trump an opportunity to peel off voters just as he was solidifying support among Republicans. Frustration over Gaza was mounting at the same time that questions about Biden's age and viability as a candidate gained traction. Some officials and Democratic operatives had for months urged the administration to acknowledge it was bleeding support, particularly among Muslim Americans and Arab Americans. By February, Biden advisors began to respond, but the steps they took did nothing to stop the daily killing in Gaza and so did not stem domestic disenchantment.

On the campaign trail, as Trump argued Biden was unfit to be president, he pointed to the war as evidence. When he won the first contest of the GOP presidential primary, in Iowa on January 15, he promised to "straighten out the world," citing "death and destruction" and saying the conflicts in Gaza and Ukraine would not have occurred if he were president.[3] Trump offered no detail on how he would handle the warring parties—he had criticized Israel for failing to anticipate October 7, then blasted Hamas and its backer Iran, pledging to free Israeli hostages—but his message of a quick resolution was easy to understand. Meanwhile, it was becoming clear that Trump's election denialism, convictions, and chaotic first term would not end his grip on the GOP or his political career. With his second primary win, in New Hampshire on January 24, Trump had all-but-officially vanquished Republican rivals to become the party's presidential nominee, and with his unique capacity to be vague about his positions, unlike a standard-issue GOP foreign policy hawk, Trump could use Biden's Gaza policy against him among both antiwar voters and pro-Israel hard-liners.

As Biden campaigned, anger toward him about Gaza was ubiquitous. More than one thousand faith leaders in the Black community, the Democratic Party's strongest voting base, were demanding a ceasefire.[4] On January 23, when Biden held his first joint election rally with Kamala Harris in Virginia, protesters interrupted his speech a dozen times. Some Democratic operatives griped that antiwar voices should target Republicans, who almost uniformly remained indifferent or outright hateful toward Palestinians, and rejected even Biden's mild rebukes of Israel. But it was Biden, of course, who was allowing U.S.-provided weapons and U.S.-enabled aid restrictions to kill Palestinians, and he had preserved many Israel-Palestine policies instituted by Trump and Republicans. The president did not dismiss demonstrators, privately telling allies at his Virginia stop that they should acknowledge the protests as important, but his staff's preferences were clear.[5] On February 1, Biden visited Michigan, the swing state with the highest proportion of Arab Americans, but the trip saw him "studiously avoiding" them, *The Washington Post* reported, and his team was more secretive than it normally was about campaign appearances. Still, at one stop, Biden faced the chant "How many kids did you kill today?" It was a slogan that had originated in the uproar against President Lyndon B. Johnson's Vietnam policy and showed how protesters aimed to similarly galvanize American society against Biden's choices over Gaza. Biden, for his part, said he "wore sport coats," unlike his activist peers in the 1960s.[6] The similarities to LBJ and the Vietnam War would only grow.

Before Biden visited Michigan, his campaign manager, Julie Chávez Rodriguez, traveled to the Arab-majority city of Dearborn on January 26 and sought to meet with Arab American and Muslim American leaders—only for several of them to refuse to see her, including Dearborn's charismatic young mayor, Abdullah Hammoud. "Conversations must be had with policymakers, not campaign staff. I will not entertain conversations about elections while we watch a live-streamed genocide backed by our government," Hammoud wrote on X.[7] On the day Biden traveled to Michigan, the White House said it would soon dispatch administration officials to the state. The same period brought reports that people in northern Gaza were so desperate they were eating animal feed—and even that fodder was running low.[8]

The meeting between Arab American community leaders and policy officials was set for February 8. When the Michiganders got on a call to strategize, Abbas Alawieh—a local who had built ties across the Democratic political world, returning to Dearborn in 2023 after four years working on Capitol Hill—urged his peers to "light them up," he later told me, saying Biden "needs to know how bad it is" in a community where many had lost dozens of family members to the war.

The administration's delegation was led by two officials who had told friends they disliked their boss's course of action: USAID chief Samantha Power and Jon Finer, the deputy to Jake Sullivan. Both were former journalists who sought greater influence over foreign policy by working in government. They were not as defined by working in the U.S. national security establishment as colleagues like Brett McGurk—but both were also cautious about ideas Biden might dislike or angering others in the administration and being excluded.

When Power, Finer, and other White House aides met with Alawieh and others, attendee Osama Siblani of the *Arab American News* said the result was "a hot, hot conversation."[9] Alawieh described living in Lebanon as a child in the 1980s and hearing the IDF drop U.S.-made bombs; raising his voice, he asked each delegate if they had advised Biden to seek a ceasefire, he later told me. Steve Benjamin, the White House public engagement chief, retorted: "You're not going to get that answer."[10] The administration was offering limited introspection, not policy change. Acknowledging "missteps," Finer said: "We have left a very damaging impression based on what has been a wholly inadequate public accounting for how much the president, the administration, and the country values the lives of Palestinians."[11] He added that the administration should have condemned dehumanizing Israeli rhetoric and spoke of ending the war through its U.S.–Israel–Saudi Arabia deal involving "meaningful" gains for Palestinians. Finer and Power both expressed sympathy to Alawieh after the meeting concluded; Power said she had been in war zones as a reporter and understood their intensity.

Alawieh thanked her but left determined to make a stronger statement to Biden's circle. He and other Michigan activists—including Layla Elabed, sister of the Palestinian American congresswoman Rashida Tlaib—had on February 6 launched a campaign called "Listen to Michigan." They sought to prove a link between Gaza and Biden's reelection hopes by rallying voters in their state to mark themselves as "uncommitted" in its Democratic primary. The move would not hurt Biden immediately, because the party's presidential nomination was not in question, but could convey the risk of losing votes come November if the war continued.

Michigan's primary—the first of the 2024 election in a battleground state—was scheduled for February 28. In the run-up, the Biden administration unveiled several policies suggesting the United States was getting tougher on Netanyahu but offering little for Gaza. The most significant were sanctions on violent Israeli settlers in the occupied West Bank, who used support from the Israeli government and U.S. donors to try to displace Palestinians from the region. Biden aides started considering the step in 2022, judging that while it would be unprecedented, it might not be politically impossible: The West Bank was the heart of America's promise of a Palestinian state; settler violence was opposed by some Israelis and pro-Israel voices in the United States, including Biden, who felt it hurt Israel's own stability; and dealing with the region did not, unlike addressing Gaza, involve dealing with Hamas. When a reporter pressed McGurk during the Gaza war on whether his plan for an Israel-Saudi-U.S. deal could really provide relief for Palestinians, he snapped back: "The focus was on the West Bank, okay?"[12] In November 2023, Biden directed officials to speed up proposals for financial sanctions against the assets of settlers and their backers, which would also bar Americans from doing business with them. The work reflected the delicacy of U.S.-Israel ties: The threat of litigation over Israel-related sanctions "is higher than for any other country," a senior official told me, and a White House staffer noted that the United States lacked intelligence on Israelis, even those known to be undermining American goals.

In December, the administration said it would deny visas to some settlers. (Earlier, Biden had controversially added Israel to the U.S. Visa Waiver Program.) Sanctions went further, because they could spur even Israeli banks to cut off targeted settlers, for fear of losing access to the U.S. financial system. As U.S. officials deliberated, both the significance of addressing settler violence and the limited value of doing so amid an

Israeli culture of impunity became clear. In attacks in the West Bank between October 7 and January, Israelis killed at least 368 Palestinians, including 94 children. Eight were killed by settlers and 360 by Israeli troops. The United States already had a process for sanctioning foreign military forces for human rights abuses, under the Leahy Law—but it had never been used against Israelis, and while a State Department panel did in December recommend such sanctions on parts of the IDF, top Biden aides were not yet considering that step.[13]

By early 2024, officials sent Biden options ranging from targeting minor settlers to punishing pro-settler officials in Netanyahu's government, such as the national security minister, Itamar Ben-Gvir. The tension between Biden's sense he had to do something, both politically and strategically, and his instincts was immediately clear. The case against Ben-Gvir—which a senior U.S official described to me as a "slam dunk" given his convictions and arrests by Israeli authorities—drew a "very strong" rebuke from Biden, who said the United States should not sanction allied officials, per a separate White House staffer. The sanctions "sat there" despite "general support for them," that official recalled—until Biden planned his Michigan trip. Just before heading to Detroit, the president chose one of the most modest proposals he was sent: sanctioning four individual settlers. The administration statement announcing the move made no mention of Gaza, and administration spokespeople—falsely—told the press there was no internal discussion about sanctioning Ben-Gvir or another hard-right minister, Bezalel Smotrich. (The administration reached "legal sufficiency" for sanctioning Smotrich, the senior official told me.) Publicized as a big shift, Biden's step was actually within the Democratic mainstream—reflected by, for instance, the ardently pro-Israel Maryland senator Ben Cardin urging more aggressive action, like sanctioning U.S. citizens—and easy for Netanyahu to defy. An assessment by the International Crisis Group and Century Foundation think tanks on Biden's sanctions a year later (after Trump reversed them) called their impact "comparatively marginal" because Tel Aviv continued huge support for settlers. "Sanctions cannot be truly effective as long as they are a surrogate for a broader policy on Israel's settlements," the report argued.[14] When Biden officials played up the sanctions at their meeting in Dearborn, Alawieh told me: "Given that the extreme pain point was Gaza, it felt like them deflecting."

Also in February, Biden called Israel's offensive "over the top," the White House agreed to Chris Van Hollen's idea of the National Security Memorandum 20 (NSM-20) report to Congress on Israeli conduct, and Tony Blinken announced that the United States would revert to its pre-Trump norm of calling Jewish settlements in the West Bank illegal—a move that could have happened years earlier and simply mirrored nearly one hundred thirty other governments. Biden's team saw a yearning for a firmer U.S. position toward Israel, but the milquetoast remedies it offered were deeply insufficient for those tracking Gaza's pain. On February 25, twenty-five-year-old U.S. Air Force serviceman Aaron Bushnell set himself on fire in front of the Israeli embassy in Washington. "I'm about to engage in an extreme act of protest but compared to what people have been experiencing in Palestine at the hands of their colonizers, it's not extreme at all," Bushnell said as he live-streamed his death.[15]

On February 28, Michigan voters gave their verdict on Biden's handling of the war. More than one hundred thousand people voted "Uncommitted" rather than vote for Biden, shocking the Democratic establishment and making headlines internationally. Alawieh and his allies had dialed up pressure on the president, and a knock-on effect on Biden's ties to Netanyahu seemed unavoidable.

"BEING PLAYED"

As criticism of its Gaza policy grew, the administration hoped America's involvement in aid flows into the territory would provide some cover. U.S officials played up Biden negotiating the reopening of the Rafah Crossing into Egypt in October, Sullivan pushing Netanyahu to open the Kerem Shalom Crossing into Israel in December, and senior White House aides haggling over the movement of trucks across Gaza in early

2024. In addition to seeking credit for measures most legal and humanitarian experts viewed as the bare minimum—not a matter of largesse but of norms and standards in war—the framing suggested a surreal U.S.-Israel relationship. Beyond being Israel's military patron, the United States was taking on Israel's legal responsibility, as an occupying power and combatant, to prevent the starvation of civilians or barriers on food, water, and medicine, all while effectively operating as Israel's junior partner, pleading for concessions. (Israel denies occupying Gaza, noting its 2005 withdrawal, but the International Court of Justice says it is doing so.) With humanitarian conditions worsening in March, Biden aides doubled down on the convoluted U.S. government role in providing aid. They decided to launch airdrops and build a maritime pier for aid—distracting from proven, effective, and straightforward plans, and, given the impression that the United States was effectively a combatant in the war alongside Israel, undermining the principle of neutrality in aid deliveries. In the long run, that laid the groundwork for Trump and Netanyahu to, by 2025, fully take over the distribution of supplies, driving hundreds of deaths among Palestinians.

Israel's slow and arbitrary process of inspecting aid had been a problem throughout the war. Miles-long queues of fully loaded trucks waited to be reviewed as Israeli facilities observed standard eight-hour days and closed for holidays, showing no urgency despite Palestinian starvation; inspectors turned back whole shipments by flagging items in them as "dual use," or potentially helping Hamas fight, from croissants to oxygen cylinders, while never releasing a list of what was and wasn't permitted.[16] "It is perfectly engineered chaos," a person involved in relief told CNN. The supplies making it in faced additional challenges as the IDF ramped up operations against personnel involved in distributing aid. In early February, an Israeli ship fired at an UNRWA food convoy heading to northern Gaza, where more than a half a million Palestinians were "a step away from famine," and Israel killed several Palestinian police officers, who had been providing security for aid trucks. The police stopped escorting the shipments or deploying to the Gaza side of the Kerem Shalom Crossing, enabling attacks on trucks by desperate civilians and gangs even in the holding area.[17] Meanwhile, right-wing Israeli protesters repeatedly shut down the other side of the crossing, further reducing the flow. By February 21, the United Nations said sixty-two trucks had entered Gaza each day for the past two weeks, compared with the two hundred daily that Israel pledged and the five hundred that aid groups saw as necessary.[18] Hamas, while still battling the IDF, was "a nonfactor" in the supply crunch, a veteran aid worker told me.

U.S. officials who pressed Israel to either justify or loosen its policy to let more help into Gaza found that Israeli counterparts would do neither. Israeli officials at the government body COGAT and beyond were "rarely persuasive on humanitarian matters because they started by slamming the UN and NGOs and almost never took responsibility for [Israel's] obstruction of food or for the Israeli army's attacks on civilians. We could never start our conversations with a shared understanding of facts," Samantha Power, the USAID chief, told me. "As they denied visas to some of the most capable humanitarian operators in the world, they kept putting forward the ludicrous idea that there was some other humanitarian cavalry out there that could reach civilians at scale."

Palestinians reported that they were eating food scraps left by rats.[19] In Washington, however, the Biden administration continued to claim humanitarian credentials: The United States was "at the forefront of advocating" for more aid and remained "the largest humanitarian donor to the Palestinian people," State Department spokesperson Matt Miller said on February 26. Biden had indeed approved millions in additional U.S. funding, but he had said it could no longer flow to UNRWA—the chief humanitarian agency in Palestine—and the problem was not money to buy supplies but getting them to those in need.

Power already oversaw most of America's aid grants to groups operating in Gaza, like the UN's World Food Programme and Catholic Relief Services. Now, the self-described "idealist" joined other top administration officials in pushing for the United States to directly deliver supplies—ironically echoing the approach of Sullivan and McGurk in defying humanitarian experts within the government, and arguably legitimizing Israel's preference for tailor-made aid efforts in line with its wariness of the UN and other aid operators. What the seemingly different officials shared was a narrow vision of how much Israel and the United States might alter their policies, and a belief they knew best.

Power had privately expressed doubts about Tel Aviv. When a USAID employee pressed her directly during a Zoom conversation about Israeli aid restrictions, Power put her phone up, showing a number she said belonged to an Israeli general, and said she could call, and he would say yes to anything she requested, then "nothing will happen," the employee, Karin Huster, recalled to me. As the Biden team in February began its report to Congress about the war, Power wanted to be frank about Israeli responsibility for aid blockages even if that was not "popular" in the administration, "not just for policy purposes but for the historical record," a senior humanitarian official told me. Yet the administrator was mostly absent from the nitty-gritty of USAID conversations about Gaza, according to three USAID officials—declining to apply what one called "the Sam Power hammer" to surge aid as she had elsewhere, like Ukraine. Her staff was increasingly demoralized; in November, more than one thousand USAID personnel signed a letter calling American aid "moot" without a ceasefire, and one resigned in January, then interrupted a public speech by Power to contrast the administrator's participation in Biden's Gaza policy with the Pulitzer Prize–winning book she published in 2003 condemning the United States for permitting genocide.[20]

Those seeking a different approach from Power urged both a public resignation that would embarrass Biden—an idea she quietly considered, sources told me (although she declined to confirm or deny it)—and increased influence in the administration's policymaking. Yet her instincts about aid could not necessarily provide what Gaza needed. Power began privately supporting airdrops in the spring of 2024, believing that they would provide some aid at least and that regardless of whether the United States tried them, it would not affect Israel's refusal to open more land routes for assistance or Biden's resistance to pressuring Tel Aviv. Other humanitarian officials and aid groups continued to oppose the idea, saying it distracted senior officials from other tactics and noting airdrops provide far fewer supplies than land shipments at a far higher cost and risked further chaos, because they involved no plan for distribution. "It's a known poor delivery system that has killed people in other contexts," one USAID official told me; the United States mostly used airdrops as a last resort for helping in remote areas, and prior aid dropped by Jordan had already landed in the Mediterranean.[21]

Power, however, often endorsed unconventional but dubious humanitarian practices, per another USAID staffer. The same staffer opined that Power had "a blatant disregard for existing systems" and that even as she advocated for traditional approaches to aid, she was easily swayed by well-placed contacts, like counterparts in other governments who were urging controversial ideas. In late February 2024, Power traveled to Jordan, where King Abdullah made a case to her for joint U.S.-Jordanian airdrops. Subsequently, the USAID staffer said, Power told fellow Biden aides that Jordan had agreed to provide the food, weakening the argument from other U.S. officials that the airdrops were too expensive. After the "flour massacre" of February 29, Biden approved the idea. Announcing it on March 1, the president presented the shortage of food in Gaza as a U.S. responsibility: "We won't stand by until we get more aid in there."[22] Airdrops would not close the gap, however, and to the USAID staffer, the instance was a prime example of Washington focusing on workarounds rather than how it was "being played" by Israel. Operating as though America could not force a change in Israeli policies, U.S. decision-makers "kept having 'good ideas' and we kept telling them we know this will not work." Oxfam America issued a statement arguing the airdrops would "mostly serve to relieve the guilty consciences of senior U.S. officials," and a Biden official noted to me that the plan also helped Jordan's King Abdullah, who faced skepticism among Arabs for his closeness to the United States and Israel, "to claim credit for U.S.-enabled humanitarian aid."[23]

The first U.S.-Jordanian airdrop occurred on March 2 and provided roughly the same amount of aid as six trucks, nothing near the hundreds of additional daily truckloads that Palestinians needed.[24] Subsequent drops, most providing similar quantities of aid, continued throughout March and April, then waned in May before the effort ended.[25] Inevitably, the airdrops provided only minimal, ad hoc improvement for Palestinians—and repeatedly led to aid falling into the sea.[26] USAID staff began drafting an internal memo documenting the airdrops as a deviation from best practice, anticipating future investigations, and as other countries followed the United States' lead with their own airdrops, the chilling link between purported humanitarian efforts for Gaza and Palestinian deaths deepened: Pallets killed people on the ground, and Gazans drowned as they swam out for supplies.[27]

"Gaza is a space for all bad ideas to come to fruition," one USAID official later told me of this period. A week after the airdrop announcement, Biden used his State of the Union address to unveil another effort that became emblematic of the administration's failure on aid: a $230 million U.S. military operation to ferry a maritime pier to Gaza's coast, anchor it there, and deploy American troops and contractors to transfer aid from Cyprus to ships, to a floating platform, to the pier, and then to Palestinians. For the administration, the combination of the pier and the airdrops helped counter the impression of powerlessness. But in addition to failing Palestinians, the efforts sucked up resources and redirected attention away from Israel's throttling of land routes for supplies, including by implicitly promoting alternatives.

Biden's March 7 announcement of the so-called maritime corridor surprised even many of the Pentagon officials who had been tasked with running it. Like many administration choices on Gaza, the idea had become policy through insular discussions among top officials and discounting inconvenient opinions, even if they were well informed.

Officials began considering a pier in January, a Pentagon staffer told me, as deepening suffering in Gaza led them to consider outlandish options to "work around man-made restrictions . . . under a president who won't do the easiest thing," namely lean on Israel. The administration had developed a scarcity mindset about its influence, which made staff hesitate about even basic acknowledgments of Palestinian humanity. In this period, a UN official asked American officials to help gain

Israeli approvals for missions to secure human remains and organize dignified burials, this official told me, and summed up the response as: "We're not interested in using our political capital to pick up dead bodies." The UN worker shot back: "Since you're not going to keep them alive, do this." It was clear American nudges would be the only way to shift Tel Aviv's hard-line thinking. As ideas about Gaza's coast were discussed, the Pentagon staffer recalled a meeting with Israeli counterparts in February where an American official suggested encouraging Palestinians to fish. An Israeli immediately retorted that it was IDF policy to shoot anyone fishing. "It was just blanket no—no discussion," the Pentagon source told me, adding: "They don't think of Palestinians as human." When we spoke, I thought back to meeting a fisherman in Gaza in 2019 who had, like dozens of others even before the war, been shot by Israeli ships while seeking his daily catch.[28] He had lost his livelihood and his love for the sea, he said, but he carefully kept the bullets extracted from him in little brown pouches in a chipped, heart-shaped porcelain dish.

In internal meetings, military experts argued against the pier idea, a senior Biden aide told me, and USAID staff warned the administration should focus on "more efficient and proven" aid routes, specifically the land crossings Israel was choking. Satterfield, Biden's humanitarian envoy, told colleagues the original conceptualization of a pier from a private contractor resembled "a work of science fiction." Though the United States had deployed joint logistics over-the-shore (JLOTS) programs elsewhere, it had never done so during a war.[29] Their success hinged on bringing the pier extremely close to land, which Israel would not permit in Gaza, the Pentagon staffer told me; predictably, the pier was eventually disrupted by rough seas and weather. But Biden's decision-making around the war involved little consultation outside his inner circle, and Netanyahu was enthusiastic about the pier—so the proposal advanced, like other ideas that were "not submitted to the same level of fact-checking or reality-checking" that big policy moves normally faced, the former Biden aide said. They linked that pattern to the president and Jake Sullivan having placed Brett McGurk, who was known for operating independently and often overruling or bypassing fellow officials, in the role of "Middle East coordinator," which was meant to mesh expertise from across the government. In other words, at least some responsibility for whatever McGurk did or didn't do lay with Sullivan. "If you leave a steak out unprotected and a dog eats it, you don't blame the dog," McGurk's former colleague told me.

In his announcement, Biden said the pier would drive "a massive increase" in aid for Gaza and emphasized he was not deploying American troops into the battlefield, as the IDF would provide security and the United Nations would distribute supplies. The carefully designed rollout mostly ignored the fact that the crisis measure was a depressing reflection of U.S.-Israel relations five months into the war.

Notably, Washington's entry into the aid delivery business dovetailed with Israel's own evolving strategy. Israeli officials were making new moves to suggest they were moderating their campaign and respecting international law, largely to respond to outside scrutiny, without tying those actions to halting the war. After the UN's International Court of Justice (ICJ) in January rejected an Israeli request to dismiss a case from South Africa accusing Israel of genocide in Gaza, Tel Aviv ramped up probes of alleged war crimes by Israeli troops and sent the ICJ a report on steps taken in response to an order by the court to let aid flow to Palestinians.[30] The war crimes investigations could also bolster Israel's case as Biden aides prepared their report to Congress on Israeli adherence to U.S. and international law, and as outside prosecutors, such as those at the International Criminal Court, mooted arrest warrants for alleged crimes in Gaza. Israeli officials highlighted the principle of "complementarity"—under which international indictments occur only if a country's own legal system does not address suspected violations.

Biden's involvement in aid epitomized how the administration still had competing impulses to be rigid about U.S.-Israeli cooperation and responsive to the mountain of evidence it was creating mass suffering. The former was always stronger. A year later, Satterfield told me the administration rolled out the pier both to "show we were willing to do literally anything to get assistance in, even knowing the cost [and] the likelihood of interdiction by weather and by the sea" and to encourage Israel's own actions to boost aid, like opening more border crossings and letting supplies for Palestinians move through the Israeli Port of Ashdod near northern Gaza. The humanitarian envoy spoke of "getting political support within the cabinet," a nod to the influence far-right Israeli ministers had over Netanyahu's decision-making, which Biden had allowed to become a limiting factor for the United States. The approach to Tel Aviv remained persuasion, not ultimatums.

DRAWING A RED LINE

Though Biden's decisions on aid did not subject Israel to a threat or rebuke to change its behavior, the prospect of him doing so was growing. The president was regularly disparaging Netanyahu in private[31] and the Israeli leader was increasingly talking about invading Rafah, the southern Gaza town sheltering 1.4 million Palestinians, which could be the most destructive part of the U.S.-Israeli offensive yet. By early March, Biden made a public pledge. The United States had a red line for Israel: no invasion of Rafah without a plan for preventing a humanitarian disaster and causing less damage than past offensives. His choice put the administration on a course to demonstrating, in April, that U.S. power could prevent deaths and hunger among Palestinians and then confirming, in May and June, that even their own word was not enough to make Biden and his advisors use that power consistently.

Back in October, Israel's order for Palestinians to leave northern Gaza had sent hundreds of thousands south, but the IDF then spent December and January pounding much of what it had called a safe zone around the southern town of Khan Younis. Israeli bombings and attacks were so heavy they reshaped the area's topography, the UN official told me, and spurred more displacement—to Rafah, the last section of the strip that Israel had not invaded. With more than twenty-two thousand people sheltering per square kilometer, disease spread throughout UN facilities, crowded homes and tents, and the streets. The ailments were those of overcrowding and contaminated food and water: lice, smallpox, diarrhea, and hepatitis A. The thin silver lining was that because Rafah was on Gaza's border with Egypt, a direct route for humanitarian aid and staff persisted, though Israel still tightly limited their entry. Even though the IDF regularly bombed the town, relief groups had established systems for storing and distributing supplies that became the foundation for the wartime aid apparatus across Gaza. An assault on Rafah seemed certain to subject the two-thirds of Gaza's population sheltering there to more deaths and chaos than past phases of the war, which had already killed at least twenty-eight thousand Palestinians, while severely worsening the man-made humanitarian crisis in the region.

Yet Israel's goal of a military triumph over Hamas, enabled by the United States even though officials knew it was extremely unlikely, appeared to necessitate an offensive in Rafah. The militant group had a big presence there, likely including multiple battalions and some remaining hostages. Washington and Tel Aviv needed at least a semblance of moderation. Biden administration officials began creating expectations for steps Israel had to take in its treatment of the town—all while the president became more forthright about his sense that Netanyahu needed to face a new level of American pressure. On March 8, Biden told a senator he planned a "come to Jesus" chat with the Israeli leader. Interviewed by MSNBC the next day, Biden was asked about the comment, which had been caught on a hot mic; after he said it referred to "a serious meeting," the host asked whether he was setting limits, particularly over Rafah. "It is a red line," Biden responded. "I'm never going to leave Israel," the president continued, saying he would not cut off its U.S.-funded Iron Dome missile defense system—but also repeating the idea of a breaking point with Netanyahu. "There's red lines that if he crosses . . . " Biden said, trailing off and then saying: "Cannot have thirty thousand more Palestinians dead." Sullivan's claim at a press briefing shortly thereafter that the president actually hadn't made "any declarations or pronouncements" drawing a red line convinced few within or beyond the administration. In his own private conversations with Netanyahu, Sullivan repeatedly said that casualties among Palestinians—including the proportion among civilians—were enormous and there was little basis for doubting the numbers reported by authorities in Gaza, which Israel and its backers often called overblown, Sullivan told his colleagues. "The way that Bibi sought refuge in the 'Hamas-run ministry of health' was a red herring," a senior official argued to me, saying: "Israel itself—and their definition of combatant was way too expansive—[had a] tally overall [with which there] wasn't that much daylight."

Beyond Israel's own data fueling doubts about the war, some administration officials grew warier because of what Israel would not share. U.S. officials had by now made potentially hundreds of inquiries to Tel Aviv about specific attacks and tactics. On the rare occasions when the Israelis responded, a senior intelligence official told me there was a worrying pattern: Israel never provided raw substantiating intelligence that U.S. officials could themselves analyze to, for instance, evaluate if a certain strike was proportionate or appropriate. (Biden's deference helped enable that approach, and his aides let it endure throughout his presidency, the official said.)

Separately, a new factor was threatening Israel's unlimited American support and making it easier for Biden to be tough on Tel Aviv. Liberal Jewish groups had long been essential to enabling criticism of Israel in Washington; they countered claims from AIPAC and pro-Israel hard-liners that questioning the Jewish state was antisemitic and highlighted that most American Jews (overwhelmingly Democratic voters) opposed Netanyahu and the occupation, unlike the more conservative leaders of most establishment Jewish American groups. Left-leaning Zionist groups had struggled to take a position on the war after the shock of October 7, but on March 5, a coalition of ten such groups jointly endorsed a "bilateral ceasefire" in Gaza. Some had already made that call, but for others, like the political heavyweight J Street, it was a shift. "As American Jews . . . we firmly believe that there is no military solution to this conflict; the only future for Israelis and Palestinians is a shared future; and we must raise up, not shut down, our shared humanity in this moment," read their letter.[32] The moment proved skepticism about the U.S.-Israeli offensive now extended beyond the vocal but small minority of Jewish Americans who were anti-Zionists, and suggested J Street and other well-connected organizations could help the administration and Congress change Biden's policy.

Signs of restraint in the Gaza war, particularly on aid for Palestinians, now increasingly mattered for both Tel Aviv and Washington. Israel welcomed Biden's pier announcement and days later gave its first approval for aid deliveries into northern Gaza from Israeli territory and via the Gaza coastline.[33] Still, with killing ongoing and Biden hinting at a bigger change, critics of the war used the moment to amplify calls for overhauling the U.S.-Israeli dynamic. Bernie Sanders, the prominent Vermont senator, issued a statement praising the pier but urging Biden to show that U.S. help for Tel Aviv was not unconditional. "It's time we stop *asking* Israel to do the right thing and start *telling* Israel what *must* happen if they want the support of the United States," Sanders argued.

Soon afterward, Sanders, Chris Van Hollen, and six other senators, as well as a separate set of human rights and humanitarian groups, sent Biden letters with an even more striking argument: that Netanyahu and, implicitly, the president himself had triggered a U.S. law barring American military aid for countries that interfere with the delivery of U.S.-funded humanitarian aid.[34] Tacitly, they were presenting a route for tougher U.S. policy choices that did not appear to single out or disrespect Israel, simply demanding respect for America's own statutes. Opposition to Biden's Gaza policy was both broadening and fine-tuning its case, as the president slowly appeared more receptive.

PICKING PRIME MINISTERS

With a U.S. policy shift expected but still theoretical, and any possible humanitarian impact from their new policies months away, Biden administration officials tried to assuage critics through new rhetoric and quixotic interventions in Israeli and Palestinian politics.

The administration had avoided the word "ceasefire" since the State Department directive I obtained at the start of the war, and continued to do so into 2024, with White House spokesperson John Kirby saying on January 22 that Biden wanted "pauses," not an "end to the conflict," and the U.S. vetoing yet another UN Security Council ceasefire resolution on February 20. The president publicly used the word on February 26, however, surprising Israel. Biden and aides regularly mentioned the term afterward; though they were referring to a temporary Israel-Hamas truce focused on exchanging detainees, not a permanent ceasefire, co-opting the term was another bid to narrow the gap between the administration and war skeptics.

For Kamala Harris, the rhetorical evolution represented an opportunity. Less enamored with a vision of left-leaning, besieged, twentieth-century Israel than Biden, and closer to groups critical of U.S. Gaza policy such as Black church leaders and younger women, including her stepdaughter, Ella Emhoff, who raised funds for UNRWA, the vice president internally argued against deference to Netanyahu. For months, a senior White House official told me that the two had different views, characterizing them as, "She was, 'Let's end this shit,' and [Biden] was, 'Let's give the Israelis space.' " Harris publicly sympathized with Palestinians more than her running mate, but the White House aide noted she hinted at their different views "very carefully." After Biden spoke of a ceasefire, Harris decided to include a section on Gaza in a speech she was scheduled to deliver in Selma, Alabama, on March 3.[35] She and her team drafted a criticism of Israel's responsibility for the humanitarian crisis in the strip, selecting language that was "strong but not controversial," a U.S. official told NBC News. White House aides balked at the draft, watering it down and editing it up to moments before Harris spoke, effectively censoring her, a senior Biden aide told me. Still, her delivery had its own strength: The vice president uttered the phrase "immediate ceasefire," then took a breath and paused, nodding as huge applause broke out. She went on to describe the six-week time frame approved by the administration, but a lasting image stuck with political observers, journalists, and antiwar activists, and the Biden administration's embrace of a ceasefire became more firmly associated with Harris than the president or others who had been using the term for days.

The ceasefire talk was a product of the administration's attempt to secure another Israel-Hamas truce in Gaza, covering Ramadan. Amid that push, conducted via American talking points and diplomacy by U.S. allies Qatar and Egypt, Washington projected the impression it could succeed if only Israeli politics shifted, weakening Netanyahu—or even tapping a new Israeli prime minister. U.S. officials were deciding to treat long-shot political gambles as easier than applying American clout.

On March 4 and 5, the Biden team held high-profile meetings in Washington with the Israeli opposition politician Benny Gantz. U.S. officials and liberal Zionist groups in the United States who disliked Netanyahu had long viewed the former general as a reasonable, politically viable alternative, noting that Gantz's military credentials were hard for right-wing Israelis to challenge—even as Palestinians highlighted that the record included Gantz directing the devastating Israeli military offensive in Gaza in 2014 and then in 2021, when he formed a coalition government that excluded Netanyahu, leading another punishing Gaza war and a crackdown on Palestinian NGOs. After October 7, Gantz formed an emergency unity government with Netanyahu, entering his war cabinet. But he now felt that left him with far less influence than the prime minister's far-right political allies, and with Gantz rising in Israeli polls, some believed he might be able to replace Netanyahu. Ahead of his rival's Washington trip, the Israeli leader was seemingly anxious, calling Gantz to emphasize that the country had only one prime minister and directing Israel's embassy not to support the visit.[36]

The Biden administration hosted Gantz to signal that as it remained fundamentally pro-Israel, alternative leadership was preferable, two officials told me. Harris, Sullivan, and Blinken met with Gantz and discussed easing Israeli aid restrictions, establishing Palestinian Authority control of Gaza, and the Biden team's vision of a U.S.-Saudi-Israel deal. Decision-making power on all those matters still rested with Netanyahu, who—free of real U.S. pressure—remained stubborn. Yet the administration hoped he might use votes from Gantz and other opposition politicians to win Israeli parliament approval for another ceasefire–hostage release deal despite objections from his ultraconservative allies, the White House official told me. He immediately offered a caveat: Netanyahu had "a twenty-year track record on these things—he always sticks with his base."

A week after Gantz's trip, the anti-Netanyahu push got a boost from Chuck Schumer, the top Democrat in the Senate, a bulwark against criticism of Israel within his party and arguably the most powerful Jewish American in U.S. politics.[37] Schumer gave a speech in which he said Israelis had to elect a new leader because Netanyahu prioritized his ultranationalist political alliance over a deal to free Israeli hostages and risked making Israel a "pariah." The administration clarified it did not suggest the move, though Schumer gave the White House a heads-up. Asked about the speech, Biden said Schumer's "serious concern [is] shared not only by him but by many Americans."[38] Though Netanyahu rallied Republicans to condemn Schumer—with Trump seizing the moment to argue Democrats "hate Israel"—the senator told *The New York Times*: "You can still love Israel . . . and totally disagree with Bibi Netanyahu."[39] The growing talk of a better Israel neatly avoided reflection on how Israeli conduct had been shaped by U.S. choices.

Schumer had also spoken of Palestinian Authority (PA) president Mahmoud Abbas stepping down. And in conjunction with picturing a different Israel, the Biden administration was seeking an overhaul in Palestine. In November 2022, the administration had suggested greater interest in America's relationship with Palestinians by appointing the first-ever U.S. special representative for Palestinian affairs: Hady Amr, a fixture in Democratic foreign policy circles, and one of Biden's highest-ranking Arab American aides.[40] Though Amr was well liked by fellow officials across the region and helped shape U.S. policy after the 2021 Gaza war as the State Department's top Israel-Palestine official, his new appointment came with no policy changes. The title was soon seen as a demotion because he no longer dealt with the Israelis—always Biden's focus—and another official, Andrew Miller, took his old, more influential job. After October 7, Amr privately worked on narrow efforts, like efforts to evacuate sick children from Gaza, but abruptly stopped doing public and media appearances.

Amr was sidelined to the degree that even most critics of U.S. Gaza policy pitied rather than blasted him—but by the spring of 2024, as Biden tried to show he could both continue overwhelming support for Israel and answer critics of his war policy, engaging with Palestinians suddenly became vital for the administration. Amr and other U.S. officials, from Blinken to Harris's advisors, had for months been meeting with officials in the PA, the U.S.-backed body that ruled parts of the occupied West Bank and coordinated closely with Israel.[41] According to a White House official, the hope was that the United States could bolster the PA's political and military capabilities and prove that the United States did not envision endless war or Israeli occupation of the strip, restoring the United States' image among Arab nations in hopes that those nations would eventually pay for the rebuilding of the strip and grow closer to Israel. American officials pushed Abbas, the authority's eighty-seven-year-old president, to appoint a new government to demonstrate reform was underway, saying the U.S. would in exchange bolster funding for the Palestinian body, the White House official told me. Abbas was elected in 2005 and his term expired in 2009, but he had refused to call new elections for Palestine's presidency and parliament, citing Israeli restrictions but also, in the view of many Palestinians, from Hamas to leftists, as well as outside observers, seeking to preserve power for himself and his party, Fatah.[42] A December 2023 poll of Palestinians showed 92 percent of West Bank residents and 81 percent of Gazans wanted Abbas to resign.[43] With the U.S. suggestion unlikely to shake Abbas's power, he was willing to heed Washington's advice: PA prime minister Mohammed Shtayyeh resigned on February 26, and Abbas soon replaced him with his advisor of twenty years, Mohammed Mustafa. Chuffed, the White House issued a statement anticipating "credible and far-reaching reforms . . . establishing the conditions for stability in both the West Bank and Gaza."[44] José Vericat, a well-connected analyst, told me Mustafa's appointment represented "the opposite" of the ambitions among Palestinians seeking to reconstruct leadership in their community. Neither Palestinians nor even the U.S. envoy focused on them were suddenly empowered, but the administration had a new, upbeat talking point about U.S.-Palestinian relations.

The administration's political machinations and rhetorical tweaks had little tangible impact, suggesting Biden staffers were either clueless about or willfully ignoring realities that could undercut any policy they chose.

Focusing on Netanyahu as the source of Israeli obstinacy, for instance, misread his country's politics and the effect of decades-old norms in U.S.-Israel relations, such as little accountability for Israeli violations of American and international law. In Gantz's meetings with Biden's deputies, the Israeli opposition politician was surprised to hear aid for Palestinians discussed as a major concern, a White House official told me, describing his reaction as: "Holy shit." That showed how little attention the issue got among Israelis and how U.S. statements on the matter had been mostly brushed off amid the lack of any consequences. Reflecting long-standing trends in Israel, "Gantz's politics, like those of the wider Israeli 'center,' mimic many of [Netanyahu's] right-wing policies in all but name," the analyst Amjad Iraqi wrote in 2022, and his assessment proved still relevant as, amid Gantz's Washington visit, the other leading Israeli opposition politician, Yair Lapid, called for a two-state solution with "a power advantage in [Israel's favor.]"[45] The Biden administration's misreading of Gantz showed it was still overestimating the ease of a U.S.–Saudi Arabia–Israel deal with some progress for Palestinians; while Washington saw the idea as a win-win-win worth domestic criticism for all parties involved, it increasingly seemed the war had widened the gap between the vision of Palestinian sovereignty acceptable to Tel Aviv and that acceptable to Riyadh. In February, the Saudi foreign ministry published an uncharacteristically direct statement describing "its firm position to the U.S. administration that there will be no diplomatic relations with Israel unless an independent Palestinian state is recognized" and the war is ended.

With no policy change secured, Gantz flew back to Israel, and on the same day, the number of Palestinian children who had starved to death hit at least sixteen.[46] CNN reached one mother as she sat clutching the fingers of her dead, starved three-year-old. "She used to eat eggs every day. . . . Now nothing," Anwar Abdul Nabi said, sobbing.[47]

The hollowness of Washington's push against Netanyahu was also clear from the fact that a champion for the message was Schumer—who had shown no openness to limiting U.S. aid to Israel, and who had previously broken with a Democratic president in favor of Netanyahu, pro-Israel hard-liners, and the GOP, by voting against Barack Obama's Iran nuclear deal. Tel Aviv could reasonably assume Schumer's speech was a trial balloon, not a fixed position, and the senator soon proved that was the case. That summer, Schumer joined the Republican speaker of the House of Representatives, Mike Johnson, in inviting Netanyahu to Congress, then attended his speech and repeatedly applauded, while many Democrats boycotted it; and a year later, when Netanyahu made another Washington trip while facing an International Criminal Court arrest warrant and embracing Trump, Schumer posed for photographs with him, smiling.

The U.S gambit with the PA did little to change the damaging status quo in Israel-Palestine either. It was already clear the Biden administration would not use U.S. influence to address the fundamental questions about peace. In January, Amr privately gathered dozens of foreign diplomats for a meeting at the State Department and told them the United States did not see a state for Palestinians as viable anytime soon, a person present told me. Speaking with me later, a former senior official described Biden's team as less willing to challenge Israel than even its Democratic predecessor, saying he had seen Obama's Secretary of State John Kerry become visibly furious with Netanyahu over his surprise plan to give a speech in Congress opposing the Iran deal in 2015. Among Biden's advisors, "I rarely heard that emotion," the official told me, saying: "I don't know if I'll ever know if Brett [McGurk] and Tony [Blinken] and Jake [Sullivan] were directed by the president to follow his instinct to be deferential toward Israel, and did it for that reason, or believed it themselves, or they spun it to the president. None of the three are good."

With the administration's ambitions limited, it took a predictable view of reforming the PA. Because the body's inefficiency and unpopularity were indisputable, the idea was often mentioned as vital, but it could mean different things: Advocates for Palestinian self-determination highlighted the body's corruption and entanglement with the occupation, while Israeli officials and pro-Israel voices said the PA made Palestinians intransigent. The latter interpretation—which didn't involve exploring Israeli culpability—was always more appealing to Washington. Mike Casey, the American diplomat in Jerusalem, recalled discussing PA reform with other U.S. officials who fixated on matters like Israeli objections to Palestinian textbooks. "No one gets radicalized by their math textbook—you get radicalized by the fact that the occupation comes to your house and murders your brother," Casey told me. Meanwhile, Casey said, there was talk but little real pressure over PA policies that could win the body greater credibility with the United States and Israel, like payments for the families of Palestinians killed or imprisoned by Israel (which Israel said encouraged militancy) or budget tightening. "We don't want them to reform because the Israelis don't want them to either: They want them to remain this weak, corrupt entity," Casey said.

The reform the United States did encourage and celebrate—a new prime minister and cabinet—had little practical significance. Mousa Abu Marzouk, the Hamas leader, told me Mustafa's appointment lacked legitimacy among Palestinians, and Khaled Elgindy, a former advisor to the Palestinian leadership, described the step as Abbas strengthening his grip on the PA. After the Biden administration deprioritized Palestine and helped pummel Gaza, Elgindy doubted the administration understood how its actions seemed to Palestinians, and told me the U.S. effort echoed the Bush administration's self-defeating promotion of Abbas twenty years earlier. Once again, Washington seemed unable to learn from its past mistakes of seeking favored players rather than understanding whole societies.

Chiefly, American outreach to Palestinians remained shaped by Israeli concerns. As the Biden administration held talks with the PA about Mustafa's circle, they directed officials like Casey to confirm the new Palestinian appointees had not criticized Tel Aviv or been linked to Hamas, he said: "It was not, 'Are any of these people good?' . . . They were concerned about a government of militants. We said it's a government of losers." Eventually, even the administration acknowledged the effort had failed, a White House official told me. Israel continued objecting to the PA. After October 7, Israel had begun withholding tax revenues it collected from Palestinians and was supposed to send to the PA, saying money earmarked for Gaza could aid Hamas. It continued to do so. Abbas felt the United States "didn't deliver," the official said, as the PA never received its full budget for the remainder of Biden's presidency—further diminishing its authority and hurting the broader Palestinian economy, as tens of thousands of PA employees went without their salaries for months.

By the end of March, Biden's Gaza policy was largely repeating itself in bloody, depressing ways. Blinken made his sixth official trip to the Middle East since the start of the war. Speaking to reporters on March 22 after meeting with Netanyahu's cabinet, he gave comments that could have been from any point over the past six months: Aid getting into Gaza was "not enough," a ceasefire–hostage release deal was close but still out of reach, and the Biden administration was working toward both Israel's self-defense and long-term regional peace.[48] His visit came amid another IDF raid on Al-Shifa, the sprawling hospital complex in northern Gaza that Israel had already invaded in November and where three thousand Palestinians were sheltering. Israeli defense minister Yoav Gallant said Al-Shifa was infiltrated by Hamas, yet Gallant had in January said the IDF had completed its major anti-Hamas operations in the north of the strip. Amid air strikes and diminishing supplies inside the hospital, up to six people lived on one shared bottle of water per day,[49] while Israeli forces detained, stripped, and beat Palestinian health workers and journalists.[50] Militants had recently entered Al-Shifa, one eyewitness told CNN, giving some weight to Israel's claim it was justified in once again breaking the international law against targeting hospitals. But a bigger question remained: What was the U.S.-backed offensive really for by this point? "Between November and April, if we had taken a harder line, we could have saved thousands of Palestinian lives and prevented terrible carnage," one White House official told me. With the administration's attempts to justify its Gaza policy now almost fully discredited, a harder line from Biden finally emerged in early April—and vindicated those who said he should have heeded his critics far sooner.

CHAPTER 5

WHAT MIGHT HAVE BEEN

April 2024

APRIL 2024 BROUGHT THE WAR TO ITS SIX-MONTH MARK. Palestinians faced mass starvation and a badly weakened medical system as Israeli forces drew closer to Rafah, the southernmost district in Gaza and the final refuge for more than 1 million displaced people. The death toll crossed thirty thousand, with women and children representing the majority of those killed, and Israel remained far from achieving its stated goals. The freedom of Israeli hostages still depended on concessions to Hamas that Netanyahu was loath to make, and the continued decimation of Gaza fueled desperation, helping the militant group recruit replacements for fallen fighters and proving an Israeli military triumph was likely impossible, all while giving pro-war voices an argument for more IDF attacks. It was hard to envision a change to the bloody, largely static dynamic. Near-daily mass killings of Palestinians drew international condemnation and were quickly forgotten. But then an unexpected Israeli attack shook the Biden administration like no other moment since October 7, setting off a chain of choices and events that answered a question that had been asked throughout the war: What would happen if the United States actually threatened to cut support for Israel? The answer, it turned out, was tremendous, lifesaving change—improvements that administration officials quietly acknowledged they could have secured months earlier, limiting bloodshed the way they had been claiming they wanted to.

On the afternoon of April 1, the Israeli ambassador in Washington, Michael Herzog, called the White House. Appointed by Netanyahu's predecessor in 2021, Herzog was close to the Biden administration, even as—and in part because—the U.S. grew frustrated with Israel's leader. His message this time, however, was deeply unwelcome: Israeli drones had attacked an aid convoy belonging to the World Central Kitchen (WCK), an American nonprofit founded by celebrity chef José Andrés. The strike killed seven aid workers, including a U.S.-Canadian dual citizen, nationals of Poland, Australia, and Britain, and a Palestinian, hitting each of three clearly marked armored cars that coordinated their route with Israeli forces.[1] "This is unforgivable," WCK said in a statement, accusing the IDF of "a targeted attack."[2]

Israeli officials said they had made a mistake and would investigate.[3] But it was clear the United States would need its own response. The war had already killed at least 196 aid workers, nearly all Palestinians hit by the IDF—almost triple the death toll among humanitarians the United Nations had ever recorded in one year of conflict.[4] For that pattern to extend to WCK meant it hit Biden's team personally. Andrés had been publicly celebrated by the president; one slaughtered WCK worker, Lalzawmi "Zomi" Frankcom, had been among a group of humanitarians handpicked to meet with the U.S. ambassador to the United Nations, Linda Thomas-Greenfield, to discuss Ukrainian refugees; and Andrés's Washington restaurants often hosted American policymakers. The moment was unique: "When Israel is killing Palestinian aid workers, it doesn't get the president's attention," a well-connected source quipped to former official Jeremy Konyndyk at the time. Unlike those frequently overlooked deaths, Andrés and his multinational group could drive headlines and sympathy globally.

The impact of the WCK killings on the administration first became clear as the United States began saying Israel was deliberately enabling a humanitarian crisis, in a shift from its talking points blaming Hamas or suggesting problems were unintentional and inevitable in war. At a press conference on March 27, State Department spokesperson Matt Miller denied that recent new U.S. efforts to boost aid were because of Israeli conduct, saying: "It's not a question of pressuring Israel more."[5] By April 2, Biden issued a statement saying he was "outraged and heartbroken" on WCK's behalf, describing the attack as "not a stand-alone incident" and continuing: "This is a major reason why distributing humanitarian aid in Gaza has been so difficult—because Israel has not done enough to protect aid workers trying to deliver desperately needed help to civilians."[6] Officials began preparing for a call between Biden and Netanyahu, drafting what one senior State Department staffer described to me as "demands" for the Israelis to respond to "on an accelerated time frame"—the first-ever U.S. directive throughout the war that would come with an "or else."

A combination of factors altered the Biden administration's calculus in a way one alone could not have. Months of Israeli disregard for U.S. requests to change targeting procedures and end aid restrictions had fostered bitterness in the White House, with Jake Sullivan disputing the claims of Netanyahu aide Ron Dermer that Israel was doing all it could. Meanwhile, the WCK incident exacerbated a sense of embarrassment and wounded ego among America's political and policy establishment, who all but begged Biden to punish Netanyahu in a way they had not during six months of Palestinian deaths. On *Morning Joe*, the MSNBC show the president watched daily, former Council on Foreign Relations president Richard Haass spoke of American sanctions on Israel, carefully noting: "I'm sorry it's come to this."[7] Anyone familiar with the situation understood it would only change because of steps by the United States. Though they publicly promoted Israel's justice system and promises to respect the laws of war, American officials knew that, as one White House advisor said before the Biden-Netanyahu call, "Israel investigating itself is not going to result in any meaningful consequences."[8]

Meanwhile, WCK was harder to ignore than, say, UNRWA, which

was still being regularly demonized in Washington even as Israel killed scores of its staff. Referred to in Biden's statement as "my friend," Andrés had broad connections and respect for his philanthropy, as well as experience rallying outrage and credibility among Democrats from years spent battling Trump. He combined a humanitarian's grasp of aid delivery with a brand unique in the sector. In his initial response, Andrés emphasized the pain of the loss and Palestinians' continuing needs, but once the Israelis put out their standard arguments—with Netanyahu calling the strike the kind of mistake that "happens in war"[9]—Andrés got combative. In high-profile interviews, he said the convoy was targeted "systematically, car by car"; produced a paper trail of Israeli approvals for the mission; and accused Tel Aviv of a "war against humanity itself."[10] It was difficult for staunch Israel supporters to criticize Andrés by suggesting wrongdoing or Hamas links as they did about other aid workers, because he was close to the IDF, worked outside the UN system, cooperated with Israel and the United Arab Emirates on coastal deliveries of aid to Gaza in March,[11] and only endorsed a ceasefire months after other humanitarian leaders.

The WCK strike "was a shock to the Israelis, up to [Netanyahu], because this was a group Israel wanted to be able to show as a success," David Satterfield, Biden's humanitarian envoy for Gaza, later told me. WCK was indisputably effective, with a USAID official telling me the organization had almost unparalleled access to help the neediest Palestinians, in northern Gaza, and a "fast track" for inspections of its trucks by Israeli and Egyptian officials. But its arrangement with Israel arguably also helped Israeli officials resist calls for a full overhaul of the humanitarian system and undercut other organizations they saw as too sympathetic to Palestinians, chiefly UNRWA. Samantha Power told staff she was "dismissed very quickly" by Israeli counterparts when she said they had to do more to allow aid distribution because they countered by speaking of WCK's work, the USAID official recalled. Now, however, Andrés was making it hard for Israeli or American officials to attribute Palestinians' struggles to differences among humanitarian groups; with fulsome U.S. support, the IDF had clearly become used to behavior that endangered them all, rendering effective aid work impossible without changes. WCK halted its Gaza operations.

Netanyahu's playbook of denial and deflection about aid had worked for months; directly pressed by Democratic senators in February, he claimed that he thought the safety concerns among aid workers had been addressed.[12] But Israel's war policy was facing a stronger challenge just as the consequences of failing to permit an effective humanitarian system were becoming clearer too. The day after the WCK attack, USAID experts privately made their most serious assessment yet of Palestinian suffering: "Even in the best-case scenario," famine was likely occurring in Gaza, the humanitarian analysts wrote in a message sent to the White House and U.S. diplomats globally. The rapid spread of hunger was "unprecedented in modern history," and American proposals like airdrops and the pier "are insufficient to address Famine at the scale required," they concluded.[13] I obtained that cable and published its findings. A week later, Democratic congressman Joaquin Castro pressed Power about my story during a congressional hearing. She admitted famine was underway in Gaza—that the nightmare situation the Biden administration promised to avoid had come to pass, and its deadly ramifications were likely to worsen and accelerate.[14]

Evidence kept mounting that Biden's thinking had changed significantly. Meeting with Muslim American leaders on April 2, the president said the First Lady, Jill Biden—one of his most influential advisors—had been saying of the Israeli campaign: "Stop it, stop it now."[15] The following day, Biden told Univision, the Spanish-language television network, that Israel should agree to a ceasefire immediately and that he saw Netanyahu's strategy as "a mistake."[16] The administration's pro-Israel slant had not disappeared: There was no talk of stopping a transfer to the IDF of American bombs and jets that Biden had unveiled the week prior; an attendee of the April 2 session said they were "told to manage our expectations" about an evolution in U.S. policy; and John Kirby, the White House spokesman, claimed the IDF would run "a thorough, comprehensive and transparent" investigation, emphasizing there was no deadline.[17] But the president's new willingness to suggest something must change was taken seriously.

On April 4, Biden held his long-awaited phone call with Netanyahu. The session was a short, pointed thirty minutes: The purpose was not to recall October 7 or express solidarity in opposition to Hamas but to demand new Israeli steps to boost aid, confirming that American policy was at a potential hinge point and would, per the White House's readout, "be determined by our assessment of Israel's immediate action."[18] In other words, Israel could no longer take America's unflinching support for granted. Reflecting how senior officials often treated Gaza policy as a matter of the president's mood, Biden's new forcefulness made his aides more proactive about advice from experts they had discounted for months. In discussing protections for aid deliveries, for instance, the administration's humanitarian envoy David Satterfield had regularly referenced talks with the Israeli government body COGAT—even though it could not issue orders to the Israelis responsible for launching air strikes or shooting bullets. After the WCK killings, Washington finally began pushing Israel to connect humanitarian groups to its operational commanders, a senior U.S. official later recalled to me, shaking his head and saying: "The knowledge existed within the government, but it wasn't utilized." (Satterfield told me he had also engaged with others, including the IDF chief of staff.) Israel could be more precise in a territory it largely controlled: The same day as the WCK strike, the IDF located and hit sensitive Iranian targets in unfriendly territory, Syria, former Israeli diplomat Alon Pinkas noted in the Israeli newspaper *Haaretz*.[19] More than ever before, the administration was acknowledging systematic problems of accountability and Israeli intentions. Sullivan privately told an aid agency representative he now agreed with their assessment the United States had been letting Israel "drive drunk," the representative recalled to me.[20] When hearing reports of the IDF killing aid workers, Satterfield told me he thought of "the scared young people out on those [Israeli] checkpoints" in Gaza and limited communications resources among humanitarian groups. The United States tried to investigate the incidents, he said, and "in most cases got Israel to acknowledge, 'It was our error.' Then the question was, 'What are you doing to prevent it happening again?'" Another senior U.S. humanitarian official said some in the administration knew by now that real change could only occur if Washington stopped giving Tel Aviv the benefit of the doubt. "For every [Israeli] commitment on paper, there was implementation, which was a different story, and our belief was this wasn't just kids on the ground who didn't get a memo. This was an active policy," that official told me.

Aid workers did not see the matter as simply one of communicating: A month before the WCK attack, an Israeli air strike killed a Palestinian nurse named Mohammed Hamed Mansour Madi of the nonprofit Project Hope. When the organization asked Madi's surviving colleagues whether they wanted to start sleeping in a location that would be shared with Israel, they said that would put them in greater danger.[21] Four days after the strike on WCK, the IDF said it had concluded its investigation, dismissed two officers and reprimanded three, and expressed "deep sorrow" and willingness "to learn the lessons from the incident," but still treated the attack as a mistake, the result of errors "contrary to the standard operating procedures."[22] WCK responded with its own statement, saying "systemic change" and an independent commission remained necessary.[23]

As Andrés and Biden made clear the moment would not simply fade away, Democratic lawmakers pressured Israel in new ways, ensuring the incident was treated as a major domestic political moment, not just a far-off tragedy. They felt ready: The president's tacit admission of U.S.-Israeli failure made it less likely the notoriously touchy Biden would see allies as disloyal for more firmly demanding change, while months of consistent advocacy for various policy changes by Chris Van Hollen and Democratic-linked activists helped show Congress there was a range of options for wielding influence, and that pushback from pro-Israel groups could be weathered. Shocking even longtime political observers, Nancy Pelosi—the former Speaker of the House of Representatives and still one of the most powerful Democrats—endorsed a call to stop sending American offensive weapons to Israel.[24] On April 9, the top

Democrat on the House Foreign Affairs Committee, Gregory Meeks, suggested he was unwilling to approve F-15 fighter jets for Israel—tacitly halting Biden's plan.[25] It was previously unimaginable for a lawmaker to use that post to stop a weapons shipment to Israel, and the administration notably did not publicly or privately challenge Meeks over the matter, per a congressional source. That person described the general mood among Democrats: "It was cool to push back a little bit."

Rather than simply being a matter of politicians suddenly becoming more assertive or empathetic toward Palestinians, the developments reflected antiwar sentiment and organizing among the Democratic Party base, who polls now showed were more skeptical of Israel's Gaza campaign than were their elected representatives. Among Americans broadly, support for the U.S.-backed offensive had dropped to 36 percent, according to a Gallup poll in March, even before the WCK attack.[26] The same survey showed 75 percent of Democrats disapproved of Israeli actions, with most independents sharing that view too, and in ongoing Democratic primary voting, organizers tied to the "Uncommitted" movement, who sought to deny Biden support without a shift on Gaza, exceeded their expectations in Wisconsin's vote on April 2. Uncommitted had sought twenty thousand votes, mirroring Biden's margin of victory in the swing state in the 2020 presidential election to show that its supporters could be a decisive factor in the president's reelection; ultimately, fifty thousand voted "uninstructed."[27] In the weeks prior, protesters in Arizona, Wisconsin, Vermont, and California had targeted Biden's wife, donors, and party offices with calls for a ceasefire. Even cautious allies of the president took note. Chris Coons, who had succeeded Biden as a senator from Delaware, went on CNN and said he was more open to conditions on aid for Israel than ever before, then received a call from the commander in chief directly afterward, a source familiar with the matter told me.[28] Biden said he was shocked. Coons responded that his thinking had evolved. The administration was realizing how distant they were on U.S.-Israel relations from even moderates in their party; now they had to decide whether their Gaza policymaking would stop being limited by the sense among

Biden and his hidebound advisors that it was political suicide to question Israel and account for Americans' clear desire not to be implicated in preventable Palestinian deaths.

Over the six months between October 7, 2023, and the WCK attack, defenders of Biden's policy often argued there was no guarantee that a threat of withholding American support would sway Netanyahu. Those voices often redirected responsibility away from the United States toward Israel's body politic, saying hard-right politicians and the traumatized nation generally could not abide huge aid flows into Gaza. Inside the White House, that narrative sometimes veered into straw-man arguments, with Sullivan, for instance, asking fellow officials whether they thought it was appropriate to leave Israel without U.S. defensive support in case of an attack by Iran, per a source familiar with the conversations, even though most advocates for a change were talking about offensive weapons. Hamas was regularly mentioned too: Because the group was "not quiescent" but still battling and killing Israelis, "making the argument [was] harder" for U.S. officials asking Israelis to allow in more aid, Satterfield told me. Under the laws of war, however—which Israel and the United States professed to respect—the actions of one combatant do not eradicate all sides' responsibility to shield civilians and permit essential supplies.

After debates and theorizing, the WCK moment presented a real-world test. Those vindicated were not the skeptics of applying pressure but those who had urged Biden to at least attempt it. Shortly after the president's call with Netanyahu, Israel announced that it would open two new routes for supplies to enter Gaza, via the Erez Crossing in the north of the strip and the Port of Ashdod, and permit more Jordanian aid shipments through the southern Kerem Shalom Crossing. As talk of either Biden or Congress restricting weapons continued further into April, more changes in Israel's behavior followed. Suddenly, Israeli authorities were approving far more truckloads, of both aid and commercial imports, and Israeli military officials began direct discussions with aid groups, rather than liaising through COGAT. Each step indirectly acknowledged that with American backing, Israel had previously been choosing not to ease the humanitarian situation, regardless of orders from the International Court of Justice and requests from the Biden administration. The sudden changes were hard for aid groups to adapt to logistically, a then–USAID official told me, reflecting how a mostly arbitrary system ensured both preventable Palestinian suffering and greater Israeli stubbornness, as Israeli officials amplified their claims that shortages were not because of them but because of sloppiness by the United Nations and other relief groups. But by the end of April, even northern Gaza was receiving far more aid, with one hundred trucks arriving daily compared with three hundred fifty during all of March.[29] "We saw one phone call essentially double the amount of assistance going in," a senior U.S. humanitarian official later told me.

Fear for Palestinians persisted, a former U.S. official told me, noting widespread, deep-seated malnutrition that could not be reversed simply by rushing in food. Still, they agreed the post-WCK period was the peak of aid during Biden's presidency. Satterfield recalled discussions at the end of April among U.S. officials, UN agencies, and nonprofits about the scale of relief into Gaza, which by then included the first stretches since October 7 when more than five hundred trucks entered daily, akin to the prewar norm. Instead of counting trucks and prioritizing basics, he said, aid workers felt ready to start focusing on specialized assistance for vulnerable populations like pregnant mothers, newborns, those with preexisting conditions, and the chronically malnourished. It was "a signal moment," he said. The United States would, of course, "have been happier with those outcomes sooner," yet "in the real world," he continued, the nudge to the Israelis had to happen at Biden's level and when he was ready for it.

But if that choice by the president deserved credit for April's gains, so too did his choices for all the days prior. In the middle of the month, Van Hollen spoke with Nick Kristof of *The New York Times* about the president's actions. "When he did exercise some leverage," the senator noted, "he got more results in one hour than he's gotten in six months."[30]

For many administration officials working on Gaza, the aftermath of the WCK attack was hugely significant as a sign of what their policy could have been, instead of what it was. One White House official described measuring the "shift in the Israeli approach" after Biden "ripped into Bibi" in the decline in reports of civilian casualties among Palestinians throughout April. "The biggest mistake we made is that the president should have had that conversation in late November or early December," the official told me.

Old habits in the administration's thinking had already been withering away, per another senior official. First to die was the Israeli line after October 7 that the fighting would be over by the end of 2023, which Biden's inner circle, in the words of one official, "chose to believe" though many were doubtful, including senior staff. A widespread sense on Biden's team that Israel was "playing us" only set in by February, the official continued, and by early April, the WCK strike ushered in "a willingness to do something about it." Like the delays in Biden's choices, that slow realization had a clear human cost. Second, the administration gained proof of the straightforward and common nature of a dilemma it had been presenting as singularly beguiling. The period showed, a senior State Department official said, "this relationship isn't all that different from other relationships, in that the Israelis respond to pressure." The administration could have learned that "when you use pressure in a strategic way, you do see results," but the president chose not to do that "consistently," and the administration "sort of moved on" after highlighting some Israeli concessions, the official continued.

The outcome for Gaza was predictable, though the sense of possibility made it even more maddening. Within the IDF's investigation system, the incident "simply disappeared," an officer told *Haaretz*.[31] Israel torpedoed humanitarian operations in the strip a month after the strike by attacking Rafah, closing the entry point there for supplies, and destroying the infrastructure aid groups had developed in the town, while displacing more than 1 million Palestinians into worse conditions. The number of Israeli-approved trucks for Gaza per month never again under Biden reached the level permitted in April, regularly dipping to half that number or fewer.[32] And Biden never again seriously used American leverage to shield humanitarian aid work—by, for instance, enforcing his own red line against a cataclysmic Rafah assault.

Briefly, Washington had a visceral sense of the horrors it was fueling. Van Hollen told me he was among many who attended a packed memorial at the National Cathedral for the WCK workers. But the senator then added: "The other tragedy is, you had Palestinian workers being killed in big numbers both before and since and there was no public outrage here." In November 2024, after WCK had resumed work in Gaza, another Israeli air strike killed three more of its workers; the humanitarian crisis had by then grown far deeper.

One senior Biden official drew a parallel that helped explain the administration's behavior despite the progress in April. "We said . . . we're tired of your bullshit," the official recalled, and Israeli moves occurred because "the U.S. put its foot down." Then he suggested Netanyahu's crossing of Biden's red line over Rafah was similar because the Israelis partly altered their battle plan for the town, again demonstrating U.S. arm-twisting could work. That moment was brazen and ruinous for Palestinians, but some U.S. officials long remained keen to spin it as a partial success. The administration had briefly showed the Gaza war could go differently, but its inconsistency, its internalized limits on what it might do to moderate Israeli behavior, and its ever-shifting consideration of Palestinian humanity ensured the U.S.-backed campaign would grow more gruesome.

CHAPTER 6

THE ROAD TO RAFAH

January–April 2024

WITH THE WORLD CENTRAL KITCHEN KILLINGS, APRIL 1 HAD ushered in the Biden administration's strongest pressure on Netanyahu throughout the war. But the same day set off a chain of events epitomizing the administration's abiding deference to Israel, which soon defined its Gaza policy once more—ensuring the United States continued to fuel killings and apparent crimes such as enforced starvation in Palestine, Lebanon, and beyond. The period that saw Biden most alter his approach was inseparable from his reversal to that strategy by the end of April. By May, any hope he might champion human rights and hold his red line over Rafah collapsed.

Hours before Israeli officials told U.S. counterparts they had killed the aid workers, they informed Jake Sullivan of a separate strike that killed Iranian officials in Iran's embassy complex in the Syrian capital of Damascus. Where the WCK attack violated a standard the Biden administration showed inconsistent concern about, the prohibition on killing humanitarian personnel, Israel's April 1 move in Syria breached the United States' only consistent limit on Netanyahu: avoiding a regional war with Iran and its network that would embroil the United States. Israel had now struck Iranian sovereign soil, an embassy, showing that Netanyahu felt he was "playing with house money," as Lloyd Austin at the Pentagon put it, by taking big gambles while confident the cost would be incurred by others.[1] Even the Mossad had called the strike too risky.[2] As Tehran vowed vengeance, anxious American officials conducted back-channel diplomacy with Iran and deployed more U.S. aircraft and destroyers to shield Israel.[3] One told me the president became almost exclusively focused on the chance of a major war; when the official raised critiques of the Gaza policy to him in this period, Biden argued back: "Do people not realize how much work I'm doing keeping this from growing into something broader?"

On April 13, Iran launched more than three hundred missiles and drones at Israel—the first-ever such attack from Iranian soil, targeting multiple cities and supplemented by strikes from Iran-aligned fighters in Iraq, Yemen, and Syria. Nearly all the projectiles were intercepted, with the United States rallying a defensive coalition that included Britain, France, and three Arab states: Jordan, Saudi Arabia, and the United Arab Emirates.[4] Rather than intimidating Israel, the moment affirmed Netanyahu could still count on U.S. help in deepening Israeli ties with other countries—including those officially advocating for Palestinians—and avoiding consequences for escalations. Soon, Iran said it saw the incident as concluded, and even Israeli experts deemed its attack was designed for minimum damage.[5] Netanyahu, leery of a spiral that could panic war-weary Israelis, for once defied hard-liners by responding to Iran with a minor strike.

With two more historic precedents on direct Israel-Iran fighting shattered, the conflagration Washington feared was more likely. Yet the Biden administration found deep satisfaction in the moment. Arab leaders' willingness to help Israel despite Gaza's pain bolstered the long-standing argument from Brett McGurk (and his former colleagues in the first Trump administration) that the United States could unite America's Middle Eastern partners against Iran while treating Palestinian concerns as a side issue. Subsequently, the president repeatedly sought credit for the U.S. role in defending Israel against the Iranian barrage. That rosy depiction allowed both Washington and Tel Aviv to distract from questions like whether it was appropriate or wise for the United States to back another Israeli violation of international law and more tension with Tehran. Sabrina Singh, a Pentagon spokeswoman, had said the administration did not support attacks on diplomatic facilities, but after the U.S.-Israeli victory lap over the conclusion of the kerfuffle, such statements seemed hollow—a bad omen for those hoping the administration would prevent further Israeli steps that could spur broader war, like an invasion of Lebanon.

Biden and his aides were well positioned to resume close cooperation with Netanyahu after the WCK strike. Even as their frustrations with him grew throughout 2024, culminating in their April ultimatum, they had also from the start of the year taken steps that solidified their deference to Israel. Several decisions from January onward—a pattern that was overlooked amid the evidence of Biden-Bibi clashes that emerged in the same period—encouraged Netanyahu to treat the administration's talk of enforcing Israeli restraint as unserious and its Rafah red line as malleable, cementing Gaza's grisly fate.

"WHAT CAN WE GET AWAY WITH?"

U.S. officials began 2024 by repeatedly indicating a break with Tel Aviv remained deeply unlikely, despite evidence that it might be strategically, legally, and politically necessary. On January 2, an Israeli drone strike hit a multistory building in Beirut—sending body parts and shrapnel spraying into a residential street. Killing senior Hamas official Saleh al-Arouri and six others, Israel had begun the wave of assassinations it had been promising, even though history suggested such targeting could not eradicate Hamas's dispersed leadership and might only inspire more enemies and violence.[6] More broadly, Netanyahu showed he saw all of Lebanon as fair game, not just border areas where Israeli forces had for months been exchanging fire with Hezbollah, the Lebanese militia allied with Hamas.

It was a clear violation of the Biden administration's unspoken expectation that retaliation for October 7 should be limited to Gaza, the constant, chilling corollary to U.S. officials treating most Palestinian bloodshed as tolerable. Given the alliance between Hezbollah and Iran,

American officials and most experts believed an Israeli war in Lebanon against the group would prompt widespread vengeance, endangering U.S. troops and destabilizing a nation of 6 million that was already fragile after decades of interventions by neighboring Israel and Syria, hosted the most refugees per capita of any country in the world, and experienced a devastating blast in the port of Beirut in 2020.[7] Israel did not give Washington advance notice of the al-Arouri strike, but American and Israeli officials confirmed its responsibility, and U.S. officials had for months believed Netanyahu was stockpiling American weapons to use in Lebanon.[8] "What we are doing in Gaza, we can do in Beirut," Israeli defense minister Yoav Gallant said two weeks before the al-Arouri assassination, and Israeli attacks into Lebanese territory had already included apparent war crimes, such as a strike killing and wounding journalists, including U.S. citizen Dylan Collins, and the firing of U.S.-provided white phosphorus munitions at civilians.[9] As in those instances, Israel faced no repercussions for the Beirut escalation from the administration.

Biden aides instead soon demonstrated that their perspective on the region remained alarmingly narrow, through a statement on January 14, the one-hundred-day anniversary of Hamas's assault.[10] "I will never forget the grief and the suffering I have heard in my meetings with the families of the American hostages," the president said, continuing: "No one should have to endure even one day of what they have gone through, much less one hundred." Though he mentioned fighting in Gaza and even the aid increase during the brief November truce, the message did not reference the nearly twenty-five thousand deaths among Palestinians since October 7. "This may be the most shameful statement I have ever seen from an American president," Barnett Rubin, a longtime foreign policy expert who worked with Biden in the Obama administration, wrote on X.[11] Among officials, some felt that months of arguing internally for moderation, while avoiding public controversy, had been for naught: "It's harder day by day to justify working for this cruel and almost bloodthirsty administration," one State Department official told me, and a separate U.S. official noted administration leaders from Tony Blinken to White House chief of staff Jeff Zients had by now heard repeated pleas to be more balanced in speaking of Israelis and Palestinians. There could have been "no ignorance on the choices there," the official said.

An administration spokesperson later defended the message as coming at hostage families' request and not being intended to address the entire war.[12] Still, the episode confirmed Biden aides, particularly those controlling messaging, still prioritized demonstrations of support for Israel and were wary of seeming pro-Palestinian. The group included senior staff like Anita Dunn, whose former firm SKDK was simultaneously working on behalf of pro-Israel groups to discredit critics of Tel Aviv outside the administration, and Andrew Bates, who privately berated reporters, insisting that their asking tough questions about Biden's Gaza policy was helping Hamas, thereby deflecting the discussion at hand from the question of whether the United States could do more to save Palestinian lives.[13] (Bates denied doing this.) When the Biden Interior Department appointee Lily Greenberg Call aggressively questioned U.S. Gaza policy at an internal listening session, she saw Dunn "spit out her water," and her boss later said she was making top staff uncomfortable, implying she was endangering her career, she told me. (Greenberg Call eventually became the first Jewish resignee from the administration.)

By the end of January, the Biden team made its stubbornness about the war clearest internationally, including to Israel, through their handling of the case about Gaza at the International Court of Justice, the body in The Hague that adjudicates disputes between UN member states. On December 29, South Africa—which had long highlighted similarities between its history of apartheid and Palestinians enduring similar conditions—had filed a suit at the court, alleging Israel was violating the international Genocide Convention, to which both nations are signatories. South Africa's lawyers highlighted dismal incidents and trends in Gaza and said incitement to mass killing was underway, quoting Israeli officials, while Israel's representatives emphasized self-defense, accused South Africa of procedural mistakes, and downplayed

Israeli responsibility for Palestinian deaths. In Washington, the Biden administration derided the proceedings; White House spokesperson John Kirby called South Africa's case "meritless, counterproductive, and completely without any basis in fact whatsoever."[14] Quietly, however, American officials prepared a surreal effort to portray the court's most likely determination as a vote of confidence in their choices.

On January 26, the ICJ unveiled its landmark ruling, affirming a "plausible" right of Palestinians to be shielded from genocide and a risk of "irreparable harm" to that right.[15] Though a determination of genocide had not yet been made, it remained under consideration, and the court imposed provisional measures on Israel, with fifteen of its seventeen judges from different nations ordering an end to policies that might constitute genocide, and sixteen, including a specially invited Israeli jurist, directing Tel Aviv to end potentially genocidal statements and speed aid to Palestinians. Israel had wanted the case dismissed. Instead, a country that itself emerged from genocide and, by extension, its American patron—which frequently said it championed international law—were being treated as potentially genocidal.

The court clearly deemed Gaza's status quo unacceptable. Yet Kirby told reporters the ICJ ruling was "consistent with many of our positions" about Israel's needing to change its practices, even though one reason the ICJ handed down its order in the first place was that Biden's statements about Israel's having to provide more aid and having to shield civilians in fact were not moderating Israeli conduct. Washington had avoided what it saw as the "nightmare" scenario, a U.S. official working on Middle East policy told me: a court order for a ceasefire. So, the Biden administration sought to co-opt the actual order, by claiming that the United States had been pushing Israel all along to do what the court was ordering now, thereby dodging both a fight with the court, and the reality that as the only party with leverage to ensure Israeli compliance with the ICJ ruling, the United States needed to change its policy too, if it was to be seen as respecting the court. This was not the only example of startling spin by Kirby during televised press conferences. Comments that presented Israel as so judicious in waging war that it was morally superior to the United States angered observers outside and in the administration. In December 2023, the White House spokesman said Israel's announcements of areas to evacuate—which often came with little notice and no certainty other areas were safe—amounted to "telegraphing your punches. . . . I don't know that we would do that." And in February 2024, he highlighted the practice again, saying: "We have seen them take actions, sometimes actions that even I'm not sure our own military would take, in terms of informing civilian populations ahead of operations where to go, where not to go."[16] A senior Biden aide told me that with his rhetorical gymnastics, Kirby "almost seemed like a Trump spokesperson who's performing for the boss." The approach paid off: Two weeks after the ICJ ruling, Kirby was promoted.

The administration's cynical treatment of international law reflected the influence of Yale Law School graduate Jake Sullivan. Though he publicly spoke of prioritizing the international system, including just days before the ICJ ruling, he was privately more "America First."[17] During a high-level meeting in the fall, colleagues had told Sullivan the U.S. position on Gaza was alienating influential countries, including South Africa. According to someone briefed on the discussion, Sullivan had responded: "Fuck South Africa," specifically criticizing its opposition to the Western military intervention in Libya in 2012. The moment encapsulated the U.S. foreign policy establishment's preference for empowering the same people and choosing navel-gazing over humility or introspection. Amid the Libyan campaign, Sullivan advised one of its chief proponents, then–Secretary of State Hillary Clinton; eventually, the Libya gambit came to exemplify unpopular overreach abroad that even Sullivan himself began condemning. South Africa's position was, to a degree, vindicated. (Sullivan's spokesperson denied to me that he made the comment.)

Not long after the ICJ order, Sullivan met with a group of experts outside the administration and, according to a person present, when asked about Israeli behavior amounting to war crimes, suggested that was impossible since Israel had said it did not intend to break international law. This statement was inconsistent with applicable law: While intent is a key legal element of genocide, proving intent is not an element of many other international law violations, including war crimes and crimes against humanity. Perpetrators need only have knowledge of the attacks or other crimes, and even those responsible for mistakes can be criminally culpable, including for failing to prevent them.[18] For Sullivan to claim that lack of proven intent to violate international law precluded Israel's having committed war crimes suggested that the administration could never acknowledge that that occurred. Sullivan's claim also seemed to contradict Biden's own policy even before October 7 that specified no country should receive U.S. weapons if it seemed "more likely than not" the arms would be used in human rights violations.[19]

U.S. officials had gotten used to twisting or conveniently misinterpreting human rights safeguards in international affairs, particularly after 9/11. Simultaneously, the branches of government that are meant to balance the power of the executive branch—Congress and the courts—often let administrations cite national security concerns to evade transparency. Brian Finucane, a former State Department attorney, told me the upshot was that government lawyers began not seeking the best analysis but asking: "What can we get away with?" The answer could often be assumed to be limitless. Few Americans faced prosecution or pariah status for breaches of domestic or international law during the so-called War on Terror, from torture to the invasion of Iraq; many who supported those policies gained more power, like Clinton and Biden. "The general lack of accountability did contribute to what we're seeing in Gaza. . . . People feel free to help Israel bomb people," Finucane told me at the tail end of the Biden presidency. "We've not only seen this movie before, but we've been participants in this movie before."

Given structural resistance in the government to applying international legal standards on war and peace, Finucane said, "who sits in the Oval Office really matters, their judgment [and] their willingness to course-correct." Biden's stubbornness was one of his trademarks; Sullivan and others closest to him began to behave similarly, such as by questioning the Palestinian casualty counts, even as they received more and more information from intelligence and humanitarian officials that showed how their policy had failed to ensure that aid reached Gazans. Sullivan and Finer "don't want to be spending hours a day talking about how much water is going to get through" into Gaza given their other priorities, a person familiar with them told me. And senior officials, many of them with government experience and aspirations to higher office, had reputations to consider, externally and for their own sense of self: Sullivan had "an unshakable faith in his own excellence," a Biden appointee told me. Often described by peers as one of the most intelligent people they had ever known, Sullivan partly treated Gaza as one more problem to outsmart; multiple officials told me he became obsessive about details of aid and nutrition.

He and his colleagues were, however, in a mental prison of their own making that they constantly reinforced. They were simultaneously treating Gaza's humanitarian crisis as a priority while casting doubt on its severity and providing legitimacy to ideas that helped prolong its cause: Israel's campaign. Amid widespread warnings of famine in early 2024, for example, McGurk and his deputy Terry Wolff echoed the then-common claim of many Israel supporters that people in photographs from Gaza did not look skinny, two sources told me. Sullivan repeatedly expressed the same view, per multiple sources. Sullivan presented his questions about a lack of photographic evidence of starving Palestinians as checking what he had heard from Israel, according to one source. But fellow officials got the strong impression that the policymaker closest to the president had little faith in the facts of Palestinian pain.[20] Such signals of Sullivan's thinking that spread across the administration were especially important because of how rarely even senior officials, including Cabinet members, directly discussed Gaza with Biden. (Sullivan's spokeswoman denied to me that he commented on Palestinians' bodies.)

January closed with the first U.S. military casualties linked to the war, when a drone attack by an Iran-backed militia hit an American base in Jordan, killing three soldiers. "We were saddened—but not surprised," Harrison Mann, a Pentagon intelligence analyst who quit the Biden administration, later wrote, noting near-daily "close calls" at bases across the Middle East, which militias said were driven by anger over Gaza, and "no real plan" other than continuously deploying more forces to the region.[21] The president was on the tarmac when the bodies came home, but his policy did not change; U.S. support for Israeli attacks continued, and so did reprisals against Americans risking further deaths. Yet another form of human loss proved insufficient to overcome the administration's rigidity.

A RED LINE AS AN OPPORTUNITY

For Netanyahu, fixated on retaining power to undercut investigations into his alleged corruption and responsibility for the October 7 attack, early 2024 was a dicey period. With more than one hundred Israeli hostages still in Gaza, two forces in Israel pulled Netanyahu in countervailing directions. Advocates for the captives increasingly said Israel should cut a deal with Hamas even if the militants maintained significant power. Adina Moshe, a seventy-two-year-old former hostage, addressed Netanyahu directly at a February 7 press conference, saying: "I'm really afraid that if you continue the way you do, the destruction of Hamas, there won't be any hostages to release."[22] Yet Netanyahu's far-right political allies, who could end his rule by abandoning his coalition government, deplored diplomacy with Hamas and spoke of Israelis settling in Gaza, which would entail even bigger military operations and the forced removal of hundreds of thousands of Palestinians. The Israeli leader's instinct was to stay close to those ideologues, which meant prolonging the war. Increasingly, he used disputes with the United States over the fate of Rafah to sustain that position and attract additional support, frustrating Biden administration officials as they had given him license to do.

Visiting Israel on February 7, Blinken declared optimism for another truce-and-hostage-release deal after Hamas had offered fresh terms, and back in Washington, his spokesperson Vedant Patel said the alternative was Israel attacking Rafah, which "would be a disaster" because there was "no planning."[23] But Netanyahu immediately pushed back—with messaging targeting pro-Israel Americans. Amid Blinken's visit, Netanyahu released an English-language video again promising "total victory over Hamas" and saying Israeli troops would "soon go into Rafah."[24] He then announced he had told the IDF to devise a plan for "evacuation" of Palestinians to allow "a massive operation,"[25] and used an interview on ABC News to suggest the Biden administration was aligning with Israel's critics. Asked about U.S. warnings of the ramifications of a major assault on Rafah, Netanyahu suggested there was no difference between that position and saying no offensive there was acceptable, arguing the line amounted to Biden saying, "Lose the war. Keep Hamas there."[26] The administration had helped create an all-or-nothing understanding of U.S. support for Israel, which Netanyahu could exploit; that made it hard to have a nuanced conversation about the relationship and different ways to use American leverage and further undercut Biden's "bear-hug" logic of overwhelming support guaranteeing U.S. influence over Israeli decisions.

The prime minister's statements echoed claims from Republican lawmakers and pro-Israel conservatives that Biden was tying Israel's hands merely by mentioning moderation in Gaza. In reality, nearly each day brought reports suggesting little Israeli restraint: The day after Netanyahu's ABC News interview, the latest round of Israeli air strikes and shelling in Rafah killed more than one hundred Palestinians—including children—amid an IDF raid that freed two of Hamas's hostages.[27]

Still, Netanyahu benefited from an impression he was doing dirty but essential work for Israel, which matched his long-standing narrative that he was uniquely qualified to lead; it helped him to have not just Hamas as a foe but, surreally, the United States, which gave at least $3 billion in annual aid to Israel and had approved roughly one hundred more arms deals with the country since October 7. By mid-February, several polls showed Israeli voters expressing more support for Netanyahu while also mostly supporting hard-line policies toward Palestinians he and other conservatives championed but the United

States opposed.[28] The Israeli leader was by then boasting of securing "unprecedented freedom of military action," unlike Israel's past experience of ending wars amid international backlash, and abandoning an idea to let displaced Palestinians return to northern Gaza.[29] For months, skeptics of Netanyahu had hoped Biden could use the goodwill from his post–October 7 embrace of Israel to rally Israelis for a different approach to Hamas. That became less feasible as Netanyahu exaggerated differences with Biden to weaken the president's standing among Israelis, a White House official told me.

As the political machinations became more obvious, so did the importance of the administration's position on Rafah for the war and the region's future. "We just need a few more weeks," Tel Aviv had repeatedly told Washington as its campaign stretched beyond 2023, when senior Biden aides thought it would end, per another top administration official; by the spring of 2024, Netanyahu's fixation on a Rafah attack was, for the White House, "the critical moment [of realizing] there will always be another objective . . . now we understood 'total victory' means every last Hamas fighter." The loss of faith in Israeli moderation was long overdue: Credulousness in Washington about Israeli narratives was, in addition to being lethal, unlike how the United States handled messages from almost any other country. The difference was jarring, including to some Biden aides who were used to handling other parts of the world. One staffer told me: "Surely our job here is to see through the message and try to figure out what the angle is—that is not the way a lot of people operate who work on the Israel account." They recalled that Ron Dermer, Netanyahu's longtime aide, could easily sway U.S. counterparts, using detailed Israeli briefings to challenge American assessments of the war and parrying American requests for policy changes from Tel Aviv, pushing U.S. officials to settle for minimal improvements. "The U.S. says do the following ten things to buy a little more time—the Israelis do three of them," the official said, saying that pattern largely continued throughout the Biden era.

The administration's internalizing of Israeli narratives was reflected in constant doubts about the extent of Palestinian loss. Recalling internal tussles over that question, USAID chief Samantha Power told me she tried to cite expertise to quell some of the skepticism, albeit gingerly: "When I was engaging with the inter-agency, I had to have humility about precise casualty numbers—I knew it was hard to pinpoint them. But we knew the order of magnitude of civilians who were being killed, and we knew from UN agencies and trusted NGO partners about the large death toll in specific incidents."

Still, candor about Israeli tendencies had grown, driving more public talk of a red line and making the administration more determined to prove its influence on Rafah. There was little interest in suggestions from some officials, including Linda Thomas-Greenfield and several military advisors, to stay out of the prospective battle altogether because the Israelis had not heeded past U.S. advice and because of its humanitarian risks, a U.S. official told me.

In February and March, developing a framework for a battle for Rafah became an obsession at the highest levels of the administration. That intensified a debate over Gaza that was already roiling Biden aides: whether to see Israel's conduct as acceptable by U.S. military standards—particularly those set during the 2016–17 fight by American-backed forces against the so-called Islamic State in the northern Iraqi city of Mosul, a battle that many within and outside the government compared to fighting Hamas in the strip. The comparison mattered for both the specifics of what the administration might demand from the IDF and for arguably the bigger dilemma of defending such demands against Netanyahu and his supporters, who relished accusing critics of hypocrisy and selectively scrutinizing the Jewish state. It resonated personally too: Leading Biden national security figures had worked on Mosul under Obama and even Trump.

The comparison rested on the similar population in the two contexts and both ISIS and Hamas weaving fighters and facilities throughout civilian infrastructure. McGurk cited the example to claim mass bloodshed was unavoidable, pointing to an American military evaluation that said Israeli targeting standards resembled those of the United States. "What standard are you holding these Israelis to?" McGurk often asked colleagues.[30] Into 2025, pro-Israel voices, like *The New York Times* columnist Bret Stephens, continued highlighting the huge civilian toll of the Mosul offensive, inaccurately claiming it had not sparked outrage or produced lingering problems.[31] But Biden advisors with more specific expertise than McGurk, who was disliked in Iraq, were wary of suggesting a parallel to bless Israel's preferences. Defense Secretary Austin, who had helped craft the battle plan for Mosul, told Israeli officials the situation was different; he "could see through" Israeli claims they followed the IDF's stated standards, a top Biden aide told me. Israel's antipathy toward Palestinians made it unwilling to help hundreds of thousands of fleeing civilians alongside the UN and other aid groups, as Iraq had, while Netanyahu was offering no postwar vision for Rafah or Gaza as a whole.[32]

Back in October, Biden had cautioned Israel to learn from U.S. "mistakes" and be deliberate in pursuing Hamas.[33] Discussing Rafah with David Satterfield—the U.S. humanitarian envoy for Gaza—showed me the administration struggled to be consistent with that advice. Satterfield said he told Israeli officials not to compare Gaza to Mosul but also believed the Israelis had to attack Rafah, so he saw his role as emphasizing hard truths such as the likelihood of pandemonium among Palestinians even if the IDF said they did not have to flee. Still, he signaled how policymakers often dodge responsibility: "The devastation wrought upon Mosul is what it is," Satterfield told me. "But I can assure you, having watched this campaign, it was not because we chose to destroy that building, that historic site, that mosque, but because ISIS embedded itself within them. It was a cruel necessity." The responsibility to be proportional in attacks and shield civilians does not hinge on the other side's behavior, of course. Israeli and American impunity remained symbiotic.

Whatever their conclusions about Mosul, U.S.-Israeli discussions about a Rafah attack were unlikely to produce an outcome that could be relied on by humanitarian groups and the Palestinians forced to depend on them. "Every time the Israelis have said they aren't going to do something, they do it, so why would we be caught flat-footed?"

one American aid official recalled to me of this period, describing how she prepared a diplomatic cable projecting the dark impact of a Rafah attack. She said the U.S. Embassy in Jerusalem refused to send it to Washington, arguing that a leak might destabilize U.S.-Israeli negotiations. Lew and Stephanie Hallett, his deputy at the embassy, reportedly blocked several cables, arguing they lacked balance, including one describing "catastrophic humanitarian needs" witnessed by aid personnel who visited northern Gaza, reporting they saw human femurs and other bones along the roads.[34] U.S. government spokespeople were already publicly doubting Israel, however,[35] and the humanitarian official felt this was an emergency, so she sent a milder draft of the cable through the U.S. Office of Palestinian Affairs, and it was quickly leaked. Humanitarian officials were used to what one senior USAID staffer referred to as "getting McGurk'd": The advisor regularly overruling aid experts' advice on Gaza. Still, there was a chance that their warnings might reach and influence Biden before it was too late. On February 13, Martin Griffiths, the UN's top humanitarian official, said in a statement: "The scenario we have long dreaded is unraveling at alarming speed."[36] Those in Rafah, "like the entire population of Gaza, are the victims of an assault that is unparalleled in its intensity, brutality and scope," continued Griffiths, who had worked on crises worldwide for fifty years. "History will not be kind." By the end of the month, Samantha Power confirmed in a speech that the United States had still "seen no credible plan" addressing its demands for an IDF operation in the town.

Israel's obstinacy was becoming a matter of Biden's personal credibility and of his will contra Netanyahu's. The president repeatedly spoke of limiting Israel's actions in Rafah in March. His aides tried to restore the vagueness they preferred and hoped they could use to justify a range of possible future actions, with Sullivan telling reporters, "The red line issue . . . [is] something that is posed in your questions; it's not stated as a declaration of our policy."[37] But multiple officials told me the sense of a boundary had become clear inside the administration: A red line, and major expectations, had finally been established.

Netanyahu responded with even more disdain for the United States and suggestions Biden was ignoring Israeli security—the issue the administration had regularly treated as more important than international law or even U.S. interests. "I have a red line," he said in a March 10 interview with Axel Springer, a German media conglomerate whose constitution binds it to support Israel's existence.[38] "You know what the red line is? That October 7 doesn't happen again." The IDF soon claimed it was developing "humanitarian islands" where Palestinians in Rafah could go. That never happened, while by March 21, Israel was bombing the city almost daily.[39] "Our life has become a nightmare," said resident Hadeel Abu Sharek, age twenty-four, who was sheltering in a closed-down restaurant with relatives, including her three-year-old.[40] Amid "terrifying" bombing, her family was living on one meal a day and water that seemed to be making them sick.

On March 22, Blinken again arrived in Israel. He privately told Netanyahu's war cabinet their Rafah plan meant they would be "stuck in Gaza" and suggested international opposition to Israel could become untenable and "you might not realize it until it's too late."[41] This was a reframing of the red line to appeal to the Israelis' own interests—notably still suggesting consequences. The State Department downplayed division, issuing a statement endorsing "the lasting defeat of Hamas, including in Rafah." But Netanyahu issued his own statement reemphasizing an Israeli-American split on the looming battle, saying: "I told [Blinken] I hope we will do it with the support of the U.S., but if we have to, we will do it alone."[42]

American administrations had long wanted to avoid international institutions intervening in Israeli-Palestinian matters, instead encouraging bilateral negotiations with heavy U.S. mediation, usually to Israel's advantage.[43] Now, the Biden administration's failure to address concern over Rafah's future prompted the International Court of Justice to issue another order on the war just two months after its first one. Despite its binding order in January for Israel to avoid potential genocide, "the catastrophic living conditions of the Palestinians in the Gaza Strip have deteriorated further," the court declared, noting at least thirty-one people, including twenty-seven children, had already died of malnutrition and dehydration, presaging a bleak future.[44] Affirming that international law required a shift, the court specified that its directions to Israel to boost aid and shield innocent Palestinians applied to Rafah, where UNICEF had recently said people, six hundred thousand of them children, were on average living on less than a liter of water per day (compared with the recommended minimum of three) and sharing toilets with eight hundred fifty others.[45] Even the lone judge to fully reject the last ICJ order on Gaza, Julia Sebutinde of Uganda, now endorsed most of its recommendations.[46] The Rafah red line, variably a negotiating tactic and a political cudgel, was now a standard watched by the world.

THE PENDULUM SWINGS BACK

The red line discussions were growing in the spring as Biden was pledging a tougher approach to Israel. Concurrently, however, his administration undercut two of its clearest steps in that direction—a UN vote and sanctions on West Bank settlers—in March, and then in April doubled down on U.S.-Israeli military collaboration through actions in Congress.

Linda Thomas-Greenfield, the U.S. ambassador to the United Nations, had for months privately questioned unconditional backing for Tel Aviv while publicly shielding the policy by quashing Security Council resolutions for a ceasefire in Gaza. After one more veto, in February, the diplomat redoubled her efforts to avoid another, telling colleagues she might leave her job if she could not. The United States on March 25 allowed the Security Council to pass its first call since October 7 for "an immediate ceasefire" in Gaza, including the release of Hamas hostages. (Thomas-Greenfield praised the resolution but said she did not vote for it because it did not condemn the Palestinian group or emphasize its hostages.)[47]

Though the resolution described a halt for Ramadan rather than a permanent ceasefire, the moment had symbolic significance—at least, until the Biden administration emphasized it was limited to symbolism.

An aide to Thomas-Greenfield had inserted the word "nonbinding" into her statement about the resolution, anticipating other countries would argue that it gave Israel an obligation to halt its offensive, and the ambassador read it out loud. Immediately, the White House highlighted the caveat: "There's no impact at all on Israel," spokesman John Kirby argued. That framing "took all the attention. . . . It was like a gift to the Israelis and that's not how it was intended," a State Department official later argued to me. The emphasis was additionally jarring in terms of both international law and diplomacy; legal experts, as well as countries that supported the resolution by compromising with Thomas-Greenfield to remove its reference to a permanent ceasefire, challenged the American interpretation.[48] The administration's narrative instantly undercut a very similar resolution calling for a ceasefire in the worsening war in Sudan which the United States had encouraged just two weeks earlier, Aditi Gorur, a senior advisor at the American mission to the UN, later told me. Most important for the lives hanging in the balance in Israel-Palestine, if the resolution had no implications, Netanyahu's obstinacy, IDF attacks on Palestinians, and Hamas's detention of captives could continue, despite the United States' claim it was moving closer to a truce-and-hostage-release deal.

For suggestions of a shifting U.S. Gaza policy, the episode was a dark portent. Washington had again set closeness with Israel as its north star, and Thomas-Greenfield's acquiescence confirmed she would not resign or act assertively as a Cabinet member to alter Biden's course; the path of least resistance tracked with her past as a foreign service officer, but it also handily sustained her position and relationships. Biden aides from the White House down continued treating pressure on the Israelis at the UN as objectionable, and though some of Thomas-Greenfield's staff prepared memos arguing the Gaza policy undermined U.S. diplomacy on other matters, several officials told me that a top advisor to the ambassador, Sean Misko, pushed colleagues to comply with the administration's line. Misko heavily edited American statements at the world body, emphasizing Israeli pain and Tel Aviv's perspective, two State Department officials recalled. Both said Misko strongly argued in discussions among officials—including a WhatsApp group chat focused on Gaza—for prioritizing U.S.-Israeli dialogue over international involvement in the conflict, dismissing colleagues and casting his positions as Washington's view. (Misko disputed this portrayal and said he supported Thomas-Greenfield in UN efforts to reduce human suffering caused by the war and secure a ceasefire–hostage release deal.)

Predictably, Netanyahu seized the moment. The United States "teed it up for him," an American official told me, to turn a possible caution into both a green light for his war and an opportunity to, on a surface level, boost the administration's fear of being seen as anti-Israel, bolstering his heft relative to Washington. He called the abstention "a retreat" by the United States and canceled a planned Israeli delegation to Washington to discuss Rafah.

The next day, the Treasury Department weakened Biden's measures against Israeli violence toward Palestinians in the occupied West Bank through a letter saying settlers under American sanctions could still withdraw money from Israeli banks to buy various goods without those banks facing U.S. punishment. The statement came after Netanyahu's finance minister, Bezalel Smotrich, a settler and extremist himself, threatened to throttle the economy of the Palestinian Authority.[49] Biden aides denied they had given in, but a long-serving career U.S. official had never seen such a letter in other sanctions programs, this official told me, and a later analysis by the Century Foundation found such "detailed, public clarifications" were unprecedented.[50] Sixteen months later, one sanctioned settler who got relief—Yinon Levi—allegedly shot and killed Palestinian activist and teacher Awdah Hathaleen; Hathaleen had worked on the Academy Award–winning documentary *No Other Land*, about Israelis pushing Palestinians out of the West Bank, and Levi had been damaging property in a Palestinian village.[51] (Levi claimed the fatal bullets came from elsewhere. Trump had already lifted the sanctions on him the day he succeeded Biden.)

The flip-flopping on sanctions and the UN statement reflected continued caution on Israel across the administration despite senior officials' complaints about Netanyahu, horror over the war, and evidence their Gaza policy was, in addition to driving a catastrophe, hurting American policy efforts broadly. Like Thomas-Greenfield, other prominent officials unhappy with the Gaza policy, such as Jon Finer, Samantha Power, and Hady Amr, expressed despair and discontent in private yet continued arguing it was wisest for them to avoid public disagreement and retain access to high-level conversations. Blinken, meanwhile, received direct warnings about the backlash over Gaza from aides like Desirée Cormier Smith, whom he had appointed as the first-ever U.S. special representative for racial equity and justice at the State Department. Foreign counterparts refused to meet with her or be photographed if they did, Cormier Smith told me, saying U.S. officials tried to exclude that information from diplomatic cables, but she repeatedly expressed concerns directly to Blinken, arguing: "It wasn't just a 'Middle East' or 'Arab' issue. Indigenous peoples, people of African descent, and (in Sri Lanka) Hill Country Tamils, basically anyone who was oppressed . . . questioned how the United States could say we cared about their human rights when we were complicit in the obvious violation of Palestinians' human rights." Cormier Smith felt the secretary's response was limited to being "polite" and "diplomatic." And even as April brought the WCK killings and Biden's reaction, the president's core instincts persisted: Someone in the administration who attended a White House event early in the month told me that they told Biden details about massacred Palestinian children, only to have him respond that the stories of October 7 victims in Israel had stuck with him.

Broadly, the Israel-Iran back-and-forth drove the administration to recommit to its pro-Israel and hawkish norms. Concern over the Iranian missile barrage "took the wind out of the sails" of conversations among U.S. officials about holding Tel Aviv accountable for the WCK attack, one State Department official argued to me. The UAE's involvement in defending Israel, meanwhile, strengthened the tendency among Biden personnel to disregard the vicious Emirati role in the worsening civil war in Sudan; "everybody knew who the bad actor was," a senior State Department official told me, but understood the administration would not call out its Arab partner. (U.S. officials and defenders of Biden and Israel often cited Sudan's mounting suffering when trying to downplay concerns about Gaza, ignoring that both dilemmas were fueled by the myopia among American policymakers their critics were highlighting.)

Biden's foreign policy team turned back to domestic concerns. After the Iranian missile barrage, U.S. politicians' instinct to demonstrate support for Israel after an attack made Republicans who controlled the House of Representatives say that after months of stonewalling, they would vote by late April on the package of weapons for Israel, Ukraine, and Taiwan that Biden had proposed after October 7. That the proposal would pass Congress was certain—but frustration over Gaza could lead a notable number of Democratic lawmakers to oppose the Israel portion, rebuking Biden and strengthening the antiwar movement.

Growing questions about U.S.-backed Israeli excesses from legislators, mostly Democrats, frustrated Biden staff; they sought to turn down the volume, not reflect on the reason for the complaints. Sullivan's February deal with Chris Van Hollen to develop a report on Israeli conduct blocked a vote that could have recorded Democratic disaffection over Gaza, then work on the report was treated by senior officials as "an exercise in placation," not a genuine effort, one told me. And to stop Bernie Sanders from forcing a vote on legislation blocking weapons to Israel, Biden personally called the independent Vermont senator, to whom he was close; the president told Sanders he would take a dramatic step his staff had thought was inconceivable for him, by placing sanctions on an Israeli minister, Itamar Ben-Gvir, a senior aide told me. Sanders upheld his part of the bargain. Biden did not, but Sanders never publicly criticized him for it.

Ahead of the late-April vote on the weapons package, Mira Resnick, a Biden appointee in the State Department's arms-deals bureau who previously worked on Capitol Hill, began to run what one antiwar activist described to me as "a White House scare campaign" to convince Democratic lawmakers it would be politically damaging to reject the administration's proposal. Like McGurk, Resnick regularly battled administration colleagues who doubted American weapons for Israel, multiple officials told me. One recalled that Resnick's office at State featured awards from the Israeli military on the walls. Once Washington began pressing Tel Aviv to investigate war crimes allegations, the Israelis often said they would discuss their investigations only with Resnick and McGurk, a State Department official recalled. "They're only giving information to people who they think are not going to make things problematic for them," the official continued. Tolerated by the administration, the Israeli practice helped McGurk and Resnick say their views should carry more weight in debates among officials over Gaza.

Resnick intensely lobbied Democrats in the House of Representatives, where the Israel aid was in its own bill, which meant lawmakers could reject it without concurrently opposing aid to Ukraine. Conversely, Congressman Joaquin Castro and other progressive legislators were organizing votes against the Israel bill, expecting to rally up to sixty Democrats and send a significant rebuke to the Biden administration, a congressional aide told me. At an April 18 meeting, several lawmakers compared the significance of the vote to the widely condemned 2002 vote supporting the invasion of Iraq, and Congresswoman Alexandria Ocasio-Cortez told her colleagues that the vote represented their best chance to stop Israel attacking Rafah—or represent those Democrats enabling that assault.

The administration's lobbying ensured history would record the latter. Resnick's work—including a last-minute briefing exclusively for legislators, who are more cautious and focused on political matters such as relations with donors than their younger, subject matter–focused staff—meant only thirty-seven House Democrats opposed an additional $14 billion in arms for Israel. Twenty Democrats who had just days earlier signed a letter opposing offensive weapons for Israel ended up voting for the package; at least one, Congresswoman Veronica Escobar, changed positions directly after Resnick's briefing, the aide said.[52] Blinken gave Resnick a promotion four months later. Upon leaving office, she publicly described her pride in helping create "a 134 percent increase" in arms deals globally under Biden.[53]

When the package reached Congress's upper chamber, only Sanders, an independent, and two Democratic senators rejected it. One of them, Jeff Merkley from Oregon, later told me he had tired of the narrative that Biden was privately haranguing Netanyahu to allow more aid for Palestinians. "The leverage isn't how loud your voice is on the phone," Merkley said. He found it "very, very hard" to vote against aid for Ukraine but felt he had to say no "with our weapons being used for such mass casualties." Just weeks earlier, other Washington power players were similarly moved to defy convention and act over Gaza—a development Biden could have used to rally support for his Rafah red line. Instead, the administration had suppressed allies' appetite for challenging Tel Aviv.

For advocates of unchecked U.S. backing for Israel, the votes represented a clear victory, suggesting their view retained bipartisan support among America's political elites regardless of months of massacres in Gaza and objections from foreign policy, legal, and humanitarian experts. The bill even included a ban on TikTok, the social media platform that many pro-Israel voices blamed for Americans' growing opposition to Israel's offensive; some still treated controlling information about the war as more important than conditions on the ground.[54] As Israeli officials celebrated the outcome, Senate Democratic leader Chuck Schumer took credit for shepherding the package in cooperation with congressional Republicans like Mike Johnson, the House Speaker, who was close to Christian Zionists and to whom Schumer, a Jewish American, recalled saying: "God wants us to do the right thing."[55] Though he had weeks earlier called Netanyahu reckless and self-defeating, Schumer was now arming him; in spite of the strategic arguments often cited to justify U.S.-Israel ties, religious and political connections continued to define them. Amid the congressional moves, the Biden administration issued yet another pro-Israel veto at the United Nations, barring recognition of Palestinian statehood.

The package headed to the president's desk on April 23, hours after the UN's human rights office highlighted that Palestinians were finding mass graves containing hundreds of bodies, some stripped naked and with their hands tied, at Gaza hospitals raided by the IDF.[56] The following day, Biden signed the legislation, ensuring more American weapons for Israel.

BIDEN'S VIETNAM

The gambit in Congress showed U.S. officials were restoring their deference to Tel Aviv not only by creating loopholes in international and U.S. standards but also by quelling domestic dissent against the war. In late April, the administration took on student antiwar protesters, arguably the most prominent coalition of critics of the U.S.-Israeli approach. Biden and his aides aligned themselves with the long-running campaign against students, largely a Democratic voting bloc, by uncompromising defenders of Israel, many of them Trump allies. For their policy on Gaza, the choice had a similar effect as the decision to rally Democrats behind more weapons for Tel Aviv: The administration was strong-arming its own political partners to sustain an image of U.S.-Israel amity and so weakening itself relative to Netanyahu for the coming battle over the red line. Additionally, U.S. officials' involvement in the battle over campuses legitimized the actors and ideas that would later, under Trump, drive a crackdown on fundamental freedoms and universities' independence.

Immediately after October 7, Republicans in Congress and wealthy Israel backers began suggesting students expressing concern for Gaza were driven by hatred of Jews. Though bolstered by new testimony from Jewish students that they felt unsafe at universities, the effort was years-old, an acceleration of a quest to limit discussion of the U.S. role in Israeli human rights abuses and in Palestinian suffering. The campaign was from the start heavy-handed and silent about Jewish activism against Israel's offensive or the intertwined vulnerabilities of minority groups: By the fourth week of the war, professors at the University of Pennsylvania said that donors there, led by investor

Marc Rowan, and university officials were trampling on academic freedom and fueling threats and harassment toward faculty and students, endangering Jews, Palestinians, Arabs, and Muslims.[57] Still, lawmakers led by Elise Stefanik—a GOP congresswoman from New York who herself promoted antisemitic tropes like the "Great Replacement" theory, which suggested wealthy Jews were importing nonwhite immigrants to reshape American society—kept exacerbating the tensions.[58]

Meanwhile, in Biden administration discussions about antisemitism and the relationship between the war and American Jewish life, officials often deferred to groups that were extremely wary of any critique of Israel, one administration official recalled to me, citing the Anti-Defamation League (ADL). The group "had the White House under their thumb," to the point where the ADL successfully convinced the White House to alter other government agencies' plans to engage with Jewish groups, the appointee recalled, continuing: "Is this about Jewish voices or not? It's about very specific Jewish voices." By December, Stefanik was organizing a Capitol Hill hearing with the presidents of Penn, Harvard, and MIT. Congressional staff approached the universities with a presumption of guilt and little flexibility, a person involved later told me, telling each president they had two hours to agree to testify or they would face a subpoena and setting a different deadline for each school so they could not coordinate. Before the hearing, Stefanik called for ending government funding for various universities. During the hearing, she conflated students' talk of an "intifada," an Arabic term for "uprising" that many Israel supporters associate with the violent Second Intifada period of Palestinian militancy, with calls for a genocide of Jews, then asked whether such calls represented harassment under the schools' codes of conduct.[59] The presidents fumbled their responses, and within weeks, the presidents of Penn and Harvard resigned—the outcome sought by alumni who promoted claims of campus antisemitism, like Rowan and fellow pro-Trump billionaire Bill Ackman. Emboldened, House Republicans scheduled a roundtable for March; there, Jewish students chosen by a congressional committee blasted their schools.[60] Alarm among Jewish Americans about rhetoric from some activists, such as endorsements of Hamas, had indisputably grown, but Republicans selected "the most extreme" pro-Israel voices on campuses, said the person familiar with the process. Motivations beyond a sudden surge of antisemitism were clearly driving both protesters and their opponents. Six months since October 7, more Americans, and a growing number of Jewish groups, opposed Israel's U.S.-backed Gaza offensive, while the solutions endorsed by critics of universities included controversial ideas long promoted by ardent Israel supporters, like officially equating antisemitism with anti-Zionism. Meanwhile, the spring brought Stefanik her best fundraising quarter ever and a "Defender of Israel" award from the foundation of Israeli American billionaire Miriam Adelson, a recipient of a Presidential Medal of Freedom award from Trump, as well as rumors she was under consideration for the Republican vice-presidential slot.[61]

In mid-April, Stefanik's campaign against universities became arguably the biggest news story in the country thanks to hapless leadership at Columbia University and the White House. Columbia had unique significance as the site in 1968 of activism by students against the U.S. war in Vietnam that fueled demonstrations nationally, the movement to which protests over Gaza were often compared. It was also run by Minouche Shafik, Columbia's first woman and first Arab president. On April 17, the day Shafik had agreed to appear before Stefanik's committee, hundreds of Columbia students began an encampment in the heart of campus over their monthslong demands for the university to divest from Israeli institutions and end a collaboration with Tel Aviv University. Both Shafik and the Biden administration largely endorsed Stefanik's narrative that repression was the best answer (rather than, say, reaching deals with students to end disruptions, as Brown and Northwestern had). Advised by a group including aides to Biden, Barack Obama, and Hillary Clinton, Shafik used her Capitol Hill appearance to suggest she would be tougher than other university presidents.[62] The following day, she asked the New York Police Department to break up the encampment, in an echo of its role suppressing the Vietnam protests; more than one hundred students were arrested, even as Columbia acknowledged the "vast majority" had never previously broken college rules.[63] At the same time, she imposed suspensions on the protesters—which for some meant they immediately lost university housing.[64] Campuses got even more tense, and politicians, smelling blood in the water, got more aggressive: Hundreds of Columbia faculty condemned Shafik, decrying an "unprecedented assault on student rights"; fresh demonstrations began while nonstudent activists—some openly hateful—gathered at the campus; and encampments grew at dozens of other colleges, with administrators at Yale and New York University following Shafik's model by ordering arrests. Lawmakers and campus officials played up the sense of pandemonium, which suited their ends: USC's president canceled the main graduation ceremony, thus avoiding a planned speech by pro-Palestinian valedictorian Asna Tabassum; multiple lawmakers traveled to Columbia, from GOP Speaker Johnson to pro-Israel Democrats like Josh Gottheimer and Dan Goldman, all saying antiwar activism was akin to antisemitism and could only be addressed through extreme steps, including Shafik's resignation. The campaign was hard to dismiss as an effort to embarrass Biden by suggesting he had let chaos grow because it represented a bipartisan effort to counter questioning of Israel in parallel to the bipartisan endorsement, through the just-concluded congressional votes, of more U.S. military aid for the country. Less than a month after the uproar over the WCK killings, Tel Aviv's sacred cow status in U.S. politics was being restored.

Some, like Beth Miller of the group Jewish Voice for Peace Action, urged politicians to take a more nuanced view of the protest movement, highlighting Jewish participation and students' specific demands and rights. But Miller—a veteran activist largely focused on Congress—later told me that was hard because of "the media story about these students, which was amplified by Biden administration smears."

Most White House officials had little understanding of, or patience for, the campus demonstrations. Many seemed influenced by cable news coverage emphasizing alleged antisemitism, an aide later told me, recalling a conversation with a National Security Council staffer "at the top of the pyramid" who had no clue about the protesters' demands but called them "pro-Hamas." The impression dovetailed with an idea common among Biden aides, up to Sullivan and Blinken and including some of those unhappy with the president's Gaza policy: that the administration's critics were unfair and failed to condemn Hamas for Palestinians' pain. They complained about protests outside government offices and the homes of senior officials and felt, one White House official told me, that such demonstrations rarely acknowledged the rights of all groups, including Jews and Israelis, or complexity in Israel-Palestine. "You didn't see that from any of the campus activism," claimed the official, calling the movement "actively counterproductive" for efforts to make the United States press Israel on human rights because "for the Israelis and for some of my colleagues it fed this narrative that all of the carping on the outside is just one-sided, on an anti-Israel basis."

Responding with stubbornness rather than considering the antiwar movement's perspective was questionable, but defensiveness was habitual to many Biden staffers after six months of their policy failing to change as the administration promised it would and hearing fierce criticism. "There was a lot of 'We're the good guys here,'" Hadar Susskind of New Jewish Narrative, another activist, told me. He noted the administration chose not to emphasize students' freedom of speech. White House officials often heard from pro-Israel bigwigs in the Democratic Party, a U.S. official told me, like businesswoman Sheryl Sandberg and actress Debra Messing, and another official noted that high-ranking Biden aides had echoed fears that Jews were becoming unsafe in the United States; the instinct to address those concerns helped "silence" internal reflection on the Gaza policy, said the official, who is Jewish. Simultaneously, Biden advisors argued to reporters there was little chance the war could cost the president reelection, even as the College Democrats of America warned of disillusionment among young voters.[65]

The administration's private sentiments translated to public remarks that boosted alarm over campuses. On April 26, the White House issued its first statement about Columbia, as spokesperson Andrew Bates—who was known for suggesting antiwar activists were pro-Hamas, a person familiar with Bates told me—weighed in on a video promoted by the right-wing media outlet Daily Wire, which showed a student saying, months earlier, "Zionists don't deserve to live." The remark "should serve as a wake-up call," Bates said, though the student and Columbia's protest movement had disavowed the comment.[66] Other Democrats were speaking of temperance and returning attention to Gaza. "Ninety-five percent of the young people who are on these campuses are there because they believe there is a fundamental injustice being perpetrated," Chris Murphy, a senator from Connecticut, told Fox News on April 28.[67] Decision-makers helped guarantee more mayhem, however. On April 29, Columbia said its deadline for negotiating with students had expired and they had to disperse; in response, some protesters took over the university's Hamilton Hall. They began calling it "Hind's Hall," for six-year-old Palestinian Hind Rajab, who in January had slowly died among dead relatives, trapped in a car hit by an Israeli tank and pleading for help via phone as the IDF killed a medical crew trying to reach her.

The following morning, the White House issued another statement presenting the takeover as criminal, again suggesting hate was motivating students, and tacitly blessing a crackdown by saying "protests must be peaceful and lawful." Messing shared the message to her more than 1 million Instagram followers, tagging the FBI and using the hashtag "if you hate America leave."[68] Shafik soon requested another NYPD response. Between raids on Columbia and the nearby City College of New York, the police arrested nearly three hundred people, as students reported being body-slammed, bloodied, and thrown down flights of stairs.[69] The same day, law enforcement in California did nothing for hours as opponents of student protesters at UCLA viciously attacked their encampment. The day showed that powerful Americans would not only tolerate but encourage suppressing speech over Gaza—creating a more permissive environment for later power grabs by Trump, who called the NYPD roundups "a beautiful thing to watch."[70]

When Biden made his own comments on the protests two days later, he sealed the impression the administration had botched another key moment, diminishing faith he would demonstrate leadership either domestically or on Gaza. "We are not an authoritarian nation," the president said, "but neither are we a lawless country . . . and order must prevail." Biden's conservative critics could seize on his admission of disorder on his watch, while those in the mostly Democratic-aligned movement against the war felt even more alienated. "Joe Biden chose to support the Israeli government over Jewish safety," said Beth Miller.

A little over a year later, I interviewed Mahmoud Khalil. In 2024, he mediated between Columbia and student demonstrators; in 2025, he became the best-known target of the Trump administration's crackdown on pro-Palestinian activism, facing arrest and possible deportation over alleged antisemitism (which he repeatedly denied). "The Biden administration laid the groundwork to my detention," he told me. "To me, it's a no-brainer that Biden was as bad as Trump is." Both presidents' policies repeatedly treated Israel as exempt from standards the U.S. government professed to champion, from the right to free speech to Biden's red line.

Both Netanyahu and Biden were by mid-2024 presenting a battle in Rafah as defining their role in the war: the president with his red line, the prime minister by proclaiming that Israel was "a step from victory." Whether the town remained a shelter and lifeline for Palestinian civilians would now determine whether the Biden administration's word on Gaza meant anything. Through a string of choices from January on, culminating in his mistreatment of the student protesters in April, the president shored up a view of U.S.-Israeli relations that had little tolerance for criticism or meaningful American pressure on Tel Aviv. Predictably, the weeks that followed saw Netanyahu embarrassingly and devastatingly cross Biden's red line.

CHAPTER 7

THE RED LINE IS CROSSED

May–June 2024

ISRAEL INVADED RAFAH IN EARLY MAY 2024. HEAVY FIGHTING continued into June and included an escalation of U.S.-backed air strikes that killed dozens of civilians.[1] The IDF assault forcibly displaced 1 million Palestinians—most of them already displaced, weakened by the war, and traveling on foot—to previously pulverized areas or a remote coastal zone where there was little food, water, or medicine; soon, Israel said 86 percent of Gaza was off-limits for civilians, worsening crowding and disease.[2] The attack closed the only entry point to the region that was not fully controlled by Israel and destroyed Gaza's humanitarian hub, cutting off a route for food aid for seven hundred thousand Palestinians, shuttering nearly thirty of the few remaining health-care facilities and the route for medical evacuations for fourteen thousand critical patients, and accelerating mass starvation and avoidable deaths. And the operation epitomized the Biden administration's complicity in a moral and strategic disaster—as well as its abandonment of its own promises. What the offensive failed to do was fulfill Netanyahu's promise of wiping out Hamas, as the Palestinian faction continued holding more than one hundred hostages and battling Israeli troops.

Israel never developed the plan for humane treatment of civilians in Rafah that the Biden administration had repeatedly demanded. Right up to the president, American officials continuously said they were serious about a policy shift over Rafah, even, for the first time in Biden's presidency, limiting bombs for Israel. Then they retreated to their pattern of sending more U.S. weapons to Israel as it committed apparent war crimes, and claiming Netanyahu would accept an American-brokered ceasefire—though his defiance of Biden and disregard for Palestinian survival were at their peak. While the administration tried to gaslight those who noted the United States' backtracking, its failure was blatant; even its multimillion-dollar aid pier for Gaza, unveiled in this period, broke apart. To Biden aides, the episode affirmed their part in impotence and chilling enablement. Rafah was "one of the most upsetting moments" in a twenty-year career in American foreign policy, a White House official later told me, and a State Department official said the moment fueled "real depression" among those still hoping U.S. influence might save Palestinian lives. The administration knew how it got here: Figures like Vice President Kamala Harris had internally said enforcing a red line was essential to avoid Israel pursuing "salami slicing," a senior official later recalled to me, referring to a strategy of crossing a boundary through a seemingly minor escalation, seeing whether others fail to react, and if not, becoming more aggressive. Those who feared Netanyahu would violate Biden's red line step by step were vindicated, the official told me; another U.S. official who separately used the term noted it was usually applied to Chinese pressure to take over Taiwan and told me: "I can't believe we use it now for how an ally tests our will." Rafah had symbolized the lingering possibility that Israel's response to October 7 would not simply amount to U.S.-funded collective punishment for Palestinians. As Israel crossed Biden's red line, his administration's Gaza policy crossed from controversial to unconscionable.

"FOLDED LIKE A TENT"

Over several weeks prior to the invasion of Rafah, the Biden administration undercut the credibility of its red line—starting with its mishandling, from late April onward, of its pause on a shipment of American bombs for Israel.

Israel had been dropping bunker-buster bombs—whose blasts can kill people nearly four hundred yards away—on crowded Gaza neighborhoods from the beginning of the war. Calling the attacks indiscriminate and likely violations of both U.S. and international law, human rights groups urged the administration to stop providing huge munitions. More broadly, activists and some U.S. officials wanted Washington to bar some weapons for Tel Aviv, saying that might spur Netanyahu to meet Biden's demands for fewer civilian casualties and a strategy for Israeli-Palestinian peace. Jake Sullivan and Brett McGurk, the president's chief advisors, resisted suggestions to suspend weapons shipments. (Sullivan "encouraged debate and discussion of" suspending arms to Israel, a spokesperson later told me, saying he presented the option to Biden "on multiple occasions"; she did not specify whether he framed it as serious or worthwhile.)

But two-thousand-pound bombs leave forty-foot craters that can be spotted by satellites, and December brought investigations into their use by *The New York Times* and CNN. Feeling greater scrutiny, the administration began discussing a cutoff. The IDF had by then already dropped nearly six hundred of the bombs; Biden had sent five thousand to Israel after October 7, despite objections from several State Department offices that they were, a senior State official told me, "fundamentally incompatible with an urban battle space."[3]

The administration's shift on the bombs was inseparable from Biden's red line talk and insular decision-making process. As Washington and Tel Aviv sparred in the spring, the president inched toward accepting a limit on equipment for Israel, two senior officials told me, and the idea was approved at the Deputies Committee, a forum of top national security aides. Then by mid-April, with Netanyahu calling a Rafah attack imminent, the president and the tiny circle closest to him discussed arguments for and against stopping some bomb shipments, with McGurk opposing the idea while officials including Jon Finer, Sullivan's deputy, argued for it. Biden agreed to pause a shipment of two-thousand-pound bombs and five-hundred-pound bombs that was already en route to Israel. Yet even as the administration took its first tangible step to restrain Tel Aviv, the move had inherent flaws. The idea was to highlight some equipment as inappropriate in Rafah, not to use U.S. leverage to prevent an IDF campaign there, another White House aide recalled—a mixed message when the administration was simultaneously arguing against an Israeli ground invasion. Senior officials remained extremely cautious in questioning Israel, a person in the administration told me, recalling Finer treating Democratic critics of the war as "basically disloyal," Sullivan being "very cold" in discussing Palestinian suffering, and both obsessing over criticism, or the potential for it, from pro-Israel forces. And like other botched plans, the hold on bombs did not involve deliberations and counsel from government experts working on Gaza, many of whom only learned about the decision from the press, two senior officials told me; one, who was eventually tasked with explaining the plan to Congress, did not learn until months later even which type of two-thousand-pound bombs was affected.

The move was ad hoc, secretive, and temporary by design: It was envisioned as a private inducement to Israel to change its Rafah calculus and spare Biden from having to enforce his red line. As an added nudge, Tony Blinken privately told Netanyahu the day the hold went into effect that a big assault on Rafah would prompt open condemnation from Washington; it was clear by then that even after months of prodding, the Israelis were far from developing a plan matching Biden's demands, another senior State Department official told me.[4] For Biden's inner circle to still count on delicate persuasion showed they continued to misread the dynamic they had created. "The assumption was the Israelis would keep it quiet," a senior U.S. official told me, describing his colleagues' assessment as "crazy." Israeli officials—shocked after months of unchecked U.S. backing—leaked the news about the bombs to Barak Ravid, an Israeli reporter working in Washington for the digital news outlet *Axios*. An IDF reservist until six months before the war, Ravid became known for scoops on U.S.-Israel relations, winning fame but also reflecting a distorted dialogue between Washington and Tel Aviv.[5] Though governments regularly use leaks to communicate, the frequency of Ravid's exclusives indicated a unique breakdown in discussing Gaza, fueled in part by the two nations' failure to be candid about problems and disagreements. Prickly Biden aides especially liked the tactic because they felt Ravid reported what he was told, without much unflattering context, one U.S. official who heard this from a colleague told me. Beaming, the president had presented Ravid with an award from the White House Correspondents' Association just days earlier. Now, however, the White House was enraged: Netanyahu said evidence of U.S.-Israeli differences aided their shared enemies, an idea American officials echoed, and "we did not put out a press release for exactly this reason," a high-ranking official told me, calling the leak "hypocrisy on the part of Bibi." The official did not comment on the administration's responsibility for enabling such behavior.

Ravid's story revealed what looked like the biggest American policy shift in seven months of war, creating an impression of Biden challenging Israel. Hamas had hours earlier killed four Israeli soldiers in an apparent attempt to stymie the Rafah invasion; now the group announced it would accept ceasefire terms. Hours later, the IDF began its offensive, ordering one hundred ten thousand Palestinians to flee, increasing air strikes, and capturing the crossing into Egypt; Netanyahu seemingly felt he had no time to waste. With Biden's word on Rafah clearly in question, the administration confirmed it was withholding the bombs—but instead of explaining the move, it sought to downplay it. There was no "final decision" on whether to send Israel the shipment, Defense Secretary Lloyd Austin told a Senate hearing on May 8, and that evening, Biden created greater confusion in a CNN interview, saying he would not supply weapons the IDF had used in other Gaza cities and mentioning artillery, which was not affected by his hold. Both men stressed their commitment to defending Israel, and the president reiterated his red line while showing it was flexible, and easy to eventually misrepresent: "They haven't gone in Rafah yet," Biden said. Yet Israeli bombing and forced displacement was echoing the IDF's past process of leveling Palestinian cities, and a UN worker who was on the ground at the time told me the spiraling Israeli assault meant "we lost access to everything overnight" in Rafah warehouses that were the basis of aid work across Gaza. Getting those supplies in had already been arduous, and Israeli and U.S. officials had told humanitarian groups they would be able to transfer them elsewhere; they were informed that would require at least three days' notice, the aid worker said. In the days before its attack, however, Israel tightened restrictions on supplies, which meant UN trucks could not be loaded before the disruption of the main route for aid.

In the United States, the administration's fumbling over the bombs shifted its focus from Israeli strikes in Gaza that destroyed packed apartment buildings to a debate over Biden's pro-Israel credentials; once again, U.S. officials were in a defensive crouch, and Netanyahu was in the driver's seat. Israeli officials and allies abroad had already worked "to rile up Congress" in April, before the Rafah attack, by suggesting the International Criminal Court would imminently issue arrest warrants over Gaza, one senior State Department official told me, noting the U.S. government's sources said such warrants remained far off. News of the bomb hold further galvanized Israel backers: Senate Republican leader Mitch McConnell called Sullivan to complain while the Democratic mega-donor Haim Saban urged the president to reconsider what he characterized as an appeal to "Muslim voters that care about Hamas."[6] The pushback jibed with Biden advisors' continued view that questioning Israel was politically toxic. Though leading Democrats and polls were signaling otherwise, old-school caution consistently shaped choices on Gaza even among figures ostensibly focused on global affairs. Sullivan, for instance, "came out of politics so sees this issue through that lens first and foremost," a White House official close to him told me. Despite his professional focus on foreign policy, it also would have been hard for him to ignore the fact that his wife, Maggie Goodlander, was running for Congress, having raised more than $100,000 from hard-line pro-Israel donors.[7] The administration saw some antiwar appetite among voters, which boosted the case for halting bombs, one Biden staffer told antiwar activist Abbas Alawieh, but amid the fallout, officials tallied up the organizations attacking the pause and deemed the list longer and more influential than the list of groups in support. Within weeks, the administration moved toward releasing some of the bombs, and never again stopped weapons for Israel. “Biden folded like a tent and . . . I never sensed them think twice about their policy after that one shipment,” Ben Rhodes, who worked with Biden, Sullivan, and other administration figures in the Obama presidency, told me.

THE WHITEWASH

Biden’s gamble on bombs partly failed because it was purely political: The step did not emerge from investigations into whether Israel was violating international laws or breaching its agreements with the United States that governed war tactics and the use of American weapons, so when it was challenged, officials lacked research and arguments to justify the action. Ironically, around the same time as the pause and through a separate process, the administration issued a report considering those questions—choosing to clear Israel, even though many government experts concluded its actions were illegal. The report released on May 10, known as NSM-20 for the National Security Memorandum initiating it, encapsulated how Biden’s team dodged plain evidence and frank discussion about Israel’s attacks and blockade of aid at the Gaza war’s most important juncture, instead continuing to trust their own judgment even after it had proven calamitous for the Palestinians.

The administration could not have known NSM-20 would coincide with its Rafah dilemma; officials devised the process months earlier not because they wanted to probe Israel but because they were struggling to quell criticism on Capitol Hill. There, the administration “conceptualized their role as being on the Israeli side,” a congressional aide later argued to me: “They didn’t even think in terms of, ‘How can we achieve a better outcome for U.S. interests?’ ” That framing and the administration’s caginess defined NSM-20, which emerged from discussions starting in late 2023 between Sullivan and Chris Van Hollen, the Maryland senator leading legislators in challenging Biden’s Gaza policy. Van

Hollen was rallying support for legislation emphasizing that U.S. weapons must be used in compliance with American and international law, and eventually he told chief Senate Democrat Chuck Schumer—a firm ally of Israel and the White House—he wanted a vote, noting he had backing from enough senators to stymie the passage of Biden's proposed Israel-Ukraine-Taiwan aid package. Still, judging his bill would never pass while executive action might produce results, Van Hollen decided he might instead support a new policy from the Biden administration requiring assurances from partner countries about such compliance and the U.S. evaluating the credibility of those assurances itself. Sullivan and his staff negotiated hard. "Their goal was to minimize the commitments they were undertaking," Van Hollen told me. Sullivan and National Security Council legal advisor Joshua Geltzer sought to only provide an oral briefing, not a written report, which Van Hollen wanted. (A senior administration official told me the White House had conveyed concerns from State Department and Defense Department staff about taking on an added task.) Eventually, on February 8, Biden signed the memorandum, directing the State Department and Pentagon to report within ninety days on whether Israel (and other countries fighting wars with American weapons) were committing war crimes and restricting U.S.-funded humanitarian aid. Either conclusion could legally require the administration to stop sending weapons.

Working on the report bedeviled many administration officials from the start, from those wary of questioning Israel to those who felt accountability for it was overdue. The United States had an established procedure for evaluating atrocities abroad, which was to be initiated by the secretary of state. Blinken never triggered it for Gaza, however, so the new order meant experts were analyzing the war through a process without legal and strategic precedent, per a senior State Department official. "If it were any other country, we would absolutely have an atrocity determination," the official told me. Separately, two other State officials questioned NSM-20 to me by repeating old narratives U.S. policymakers used to avoid reflecting on choices in the Middle East. One called the process an overreaction that would inevitably embarrass the administration, and the other described a "prevalent" view that the report could hinder diplomacy with Tel Aviv and that withholding weapons could cause unintended consequences.

As the investigation proceeded, the administration's choice of who to empower and involve hurt faith in the report. The State Department's weapons-sales bureau was put in charge—though it had little experience verifying countries' compliance with U.S. and international law and its overarching priority was to avoid any disruption in weapons sales and military aid. Its leader, Jessica Lewis, dodged debates on Gaza, which gave her staunchly pro-Israel deputy Mira Resnick outsize influence. Lewis sought an unusual intervention from higher-ranking officials Derek Chollet and Victoria Nuland when her colleagues in the Middle East and human rights bureaus challenged a particularly controversial emergency shipment of shells to Israel, according to one State official. Others told me she often left her name off arms-sales approvals and sent Resnick to meetings as her proxy.

Resnick was subsequently a key player in the preparation of the NSM-20 report and in other procedures that could produce reprimands for Tel Aviv, such as investigations of compliance with the Leahy Law—a domestic statute barring U.S. military support for foreign units credibly accused of major rights abuses—and probes of possible Israeli war crimes that were taking place through the State Department's Civilian Harm Incident Response Guidance (CHIRG) process. The way Lewis and Resnick operated slowed down those investigations, three State officials told me—and ultimately, none of the inquiries led to consequences for Israel throughout the Biden presidency. Resnick challenged research from Amnesty International, a frequent source the government normally treated as reliable, and pushed arguments other officials found dubious, such as that when Palestinian civilians were killed in a collapsed tunnel, it was because the tunnel had crumbled—only for others to respond that the collapse had been caused by Israel's dropping U.S.-provided bombs. (A State official argued to me Resnick was not disputing Israeli responsibility but was probing if the tunnel collapse was the result of secondary explosions.) Resnick also highlighted fears of backlash from influential pro-Israel forces. In one instance that a senior official recalled to me, she was worried about how Capitol Hill would respond to a finding that Israel had breached its commitments to the United States; repeatedly, she pushed for the United States to wait on details from Israel about its actions. The bureau's investigative processes "assumed Israeli cooperation . . . [but] it almost never came and when it did come it was only after extensive pushing and prodding," the senior official continued, noting that Netanyahu "micromanaged" how Israeli defense officials interacted with U.S. counterparts and knew that confirmations of Israeli misdeeds would anger his ultranationalist allies. As the bureau under Lewis and Resnick effectively prolonged the process of landing on firm conclusions for months—notwithstanding alarming patterns of Israeli behavior—further atrocities occurred in Gaza, so even more investigations were opened while the existing ones remained in limbo. That created a situation of "process constipation," another State official told me.

The uncertainty worked symbiotically with a stubbornly sunny view of Israel among officials, sustaining the administration's calamitous course. A State Department lawyer described counterparts consistently arguing the Israelis were "good actors with good processes." The depiction had nothing to do with whether accusations of misconduct were credible, the lawyer continued, while ignoring both the consistent lack of Israeli government accountability for violations of Palestinian rights and the reality that "with no other country would we go out of our way to wait a year for them to respond to us." Separately, a senior intelligence official recalled to me a discussion in late 2023 where some officials suggested seeking U.S. intelligence assessments of whether Israel planned to permanently displace Palestinians out of northern Gaza. The response reflected a troubling "lack of imagination": Colleagues argued there was no need to probe the possibility since it was so unlikely.

Other State Department players' role in the NSM-20 report also bolstered concerns it would give Israel a pass regardless of the facts. Deborah Lipstadt, Biden's antisemitism envoy, was invited to make a submission on whether Israel was respecting its obligations under U.S. and international law even though she had no experience in the laws of war or aid delivery. Lipstadt often included herself in Gaza discussions seemingly outside her remit, two senior State officials told me, and one said top Blinken aides repeatedly and without explanation pulled her into meetings focused on Palestinians that had nothing to do with antisemitism. Lipstadt believed some criticism of the war was driven by hatred of Jews; she later condemned some antiwar protesters and defended the Trump administration's crackdown on students.[8] At the end of March, Biden's ambassador in Jerusalem, Jack Lew, submitted a rosy cable about Israel's treatment of aid in which he advised Blinken to endorse Israel's assurances that it was respecting international law and its agreements with the United States. I broke the news of Lew's cable; later, a senior U.S. humanitarian official described it to me as "a complete fantasy compared to what our people, our partners, and anyone watching CNN was seeing." It proved, they said, "what we were up against within our own government to speak the truth." Lew visited an IDF military facility amid deliberations about the report and was "awed" by Israeli capabilities, a U.S. official recalled to me. That offical, who had both combat and diplomatic experience, added: "You can put up the guise of a very sophisticated military operation and still be killing civilians left and right." According to one senior Biden aide, Lew regularly aligned with McGurk against skeptics of Israel's conduct in the war; separately, another U.S. official recalled Lew clashing with other U.S. ambassadors who urged Washington to be less deferential to Israel, notably those in Jordan and Egypt. As the report was finalized, administration officials told Van Hollen that the process was being "quarterbacked" by Chollet, the State Department's counselor and a close Blinken advisor, the senator later told me. A senior intelligence official recalled to me that the submission to the report from intelligence agencies was restricted to Chollet and a few other political aides, "cutting out the analytic experts."

Some at the National Security Council went so far as to call the process "the whitewash." The lead team at the White House for the report was the defense directorate, whose remit was arms sales and military operations, and which was close to the IDF, rather than humanitarian or human rights officials, and they organized few meetings to hear how other agencies were approaching the report.

Internal discussions surrounding the development of the memo consistently reflected that a process ostensibly about clear-cut laws and documented suffering was being shaped by deference to Israel and stood little chance of meaningfully helping Palestinians. Though USAID recommended in its memo to Blinken that the United States suspend support for Tel Aviv, that memo noted that Blinken could acknowledge Israeli misconduct but use a waiver to keep weapons and money flowing, the senior humanitarian official said, calling that option "truthful at least." A senior State Department official told me that talks with the Israelis about the report had revealed a stunning detail: The IDF's chief military prosecutor had opened more than 800 investigations into Israeli troops' allegedly illegal actions in Gaza. U.S. officials argued that the number of investigations should be released, because they felt it would bolster Israel's image, and also could have provided a public indication of what Israel knew about its own misconduct, and a yardstick for tracking if accountability occurred. But when they proposed this, their Israeli counterparts panicked, likely fearing fury from right-wing Israelis, and the Biden team never convinced the Israelis to disclose any such figure throughout the war.

By mid-April, many officials doubted the administration even wanted honesty. Talking to government contacts, Van Hollen began suspecting "there were big areas they were not planning to address" and their product would not be "an unvarnished, factual report," the senator later told me.[9] Inevitably, assessments from various offices, most arguing Israel was violating international law and breaching its commitments to the United States, leaked to Reuters and the aid-focused news outlet Devex.

Outraged, Blinken called a meeting of top State Department officials. The discussion showed that months into the war, his deputies were still struggling to square Gaza's dark realities with the administration's preferences on Israel, as they "spouted talking points trying to figure out what he wanted to hear, without saying anything specific," an official present told me. Access to the drafts was restricted to the White House, whose officials removed incidents of Israeli misdeeds, and a team of aides to Blinken led by Suzy George and Tom Sullivan—Jake's brother—tasked with producing a streamlined report out of the various submissions. Significantly, NSM-20's overall conclusion remained unknown, days away from the deadline for finalizing it, recalled the State official. He described contention over including certain details, based on whether the administration wanted to say Israel was breaking the law. The fate of millions of Palestinians and Israelis still depended on the choices and opinions of a handful of men. Right until the draft went to Blinken and Defense Secretary Lloyd Austin (whose agency's NSM-20 submissions largely blamed Hamas for problems in Gaza), "it was written in a way where [they] could make a determination of the Israeli government committing wrongful acts and restricting aid, and at minimum further assistance being conditioned," the same State official said. Another senior State Department official confirmed that the secretary saw enough evidence that he actually considered saying Israel had violated its agreements by blocking U.S.-funded aid. Still, the official continued, Blinken felt that applying consequences by barring weapons would have made the Israelis even more aggressive on Rafah, and increases in aid following American pressure over the WCK killing affected his conclusion that Israel had not triggered the statute[10] (though there was no certainty that improvement would be permanent). Ultimately, even if Blinken had said Israel was in violation, the decision to stop arms or issue a waiver would have been Biden's, the official said—making a waiver the most likely option.

Like Sullivan and Biden himself, Blinken and Austin decided to simply avoid major conclusions: The report would green-light continued and full-throated support for Netanyahu. Close Blinken aides scrambled to water down the section on Israeli aid restrictions, the first State official recalled, referring to the section of the report that could have said Israeli actions had directly triggered Section 620I of the Foreign Assistance Act by preventing the distribution of U.S.-funded aid to the Palestinians, and potentially required the administration to stop military support for Tel Aviv. State Department lawyers had already furnished Blinken with "an extremely restrictive interpretation" of Section 620I, Andrew Miller, the department's top Israel-Palestine official, later told me, which "clearly did not reflect the intent behind it," but rather sought to avoid coming to a clear conclusion that would require action by the administration. Miller recalled that the attorneys had said that the only other time Section 620I had been triggered had been in the 1990s, over a full blockade of aid by Turkey, and that they questioned whether the supplies Israel was blocking were actually U.S.-funded. "The reason it hadn't been applied in other cases is . . . people forgot about this law," Miller explained. In his view, State Department attorneys could have tried to verify that American funding had paid for particular shipments by asking aid groups, "but they didn't do so for fear that they would learn it did implicate U.S.-provided assistance. So basically: If I don't see the red light, I'm not breaking the law." Regardless of those arguments, the Biden administration had agreed the NSM-20 report would cover a broader category of aid than Section 620I: not just U.S.-funded assistance but broadly "United States Government–supported international efforts to provide humanitarian assistance."[11]

As Israeli tanks rolled toward Rafah, the administration released its NSM-20 report. The document said it was "reasonable to assess" Israel had violated its commitments internationally and to the United States in using American weapons and described "serious concerns" about IDF conduct—then embellished Israeli aid policy, focusing on the brief period of improvements after the WCK strike, and called Israel's promises to respect international and American law "credible and reliable." Where Biden's handling of the bombs had shown American will was not strong enough to sustain his red line for Israel, the report signaled American law would not do that either. "What they're trying to do is make clear that they recognize how bad the situation is, but they don't want to have to take any action," Van Hollen told reporters.[12] At the State Department, a humanitarian official with twenty years' experience read the final draft and decided to quit. "We could have AI write the report because it is not informed by reality or context or the informed opinions of subject matter experts," Stacy Gilbert told me in her first post-resignation interview. The Biden administration's resolve and honesty had reached a new low just as it represented the final hope for Palestinians' last refuge in Gaza.

"WE PRETENDED"

The administration abandoned its red line slowly, with officials bringing the fuzzy logic and cynicism they fine-tuned during the NSM-20 process to their approach. When Egypt protested the IDF's capture of the Rafah Crossing and refused to reopen the facility on its side, McGurk discussed threatening Cairo with Section 620I, saying that Egypt was preventing U.S.-provided humanitarian supplies by keeping the crossing closed, two sources told me. "We treat Israel . . . just as we would treat any other country," Blinken told NBC on May 12, defending the NSM-20 report. But this claim was belied by the fact that the administration was considering enforcing against Egypt, after two days, a law that it had declined to enforce against Israel for months. "We don't talk about red lines when it comes to Israel," the secretary continued,[13] providing a more accurate description of U.S. policy. (McGurk's spokesperson denied that he had suggested applying Section 620I to Egypt.)

The low likelihood of Biden applying consequences over Rafah was clear. U.S. officials turned to the question of saving face—downplaying Israel's offensive and effectively working hand-in-glove with Netanyahu. The administration was fueling what it had earlier called unacceptable: a mass betrayal of civilians. The struggle among relatives of Abood Okal, one of the Americans the administration boasted about helping leave Gaza, encapsulated the growing nightmare. One of Okal's sisters was still sheltering in Rafah, hearing air strikes and shelling come closer and wondering whether she should leave—but that likely meant heading to Mawasi, the coastal region with no infrastructure. Another sister who was already there could rarely communicate with the family because Mawasi was farther from the Israeli telecommunications systems on which Palestinians were now relying. When she did, she reported that unsanitary overcrowding was making her children ill. The other so-called safe zone for those fleeing Rafah, near eastern Khan Younis, was strewn with unexploded bombs.[14] Agonizing over how to help, Okal was reminded of the dark beginning of the war, he told me, and it felt worse the second time around: "The negligence and the arrogance and the lack of accountability are manifesting themselves into the last neighborhood of the Gaza Strip."[15]

Washington ensured Israel's advance could continue and withstand criticism by denying cause for alarm. The attack was not a "major ground operation," White House spokesman John Kirby said on May 10, and days later, the administration signaled it did not envision its red line being crossed—or any end to weapons for Israel—by telling Congress it had approved $1.2 billion in new ammunition and equipment for the IDF.[16] Biden aides had designed most arms deals with Tel Aviv to be just under the dollar value requiring an official notification; now they advanced one so large it had to be declared, just as the administration was promoting its pro-Israel bona fides after the pause on bombs. On May 19, Sullivan visited Israel in another surreal demonstration of business as usual. He came in from Saudi Arabia; his statement reiterated enthusiasm for a U.S.-Saudi-Israel deal, and on Rafah, he simply referenced Biden's "long-standing position"—without specifying, as the White House usually had, that U.S. support for a battle there depended on a humane plan for the displaced.[17] With Biden's red line up for reinterpretation, Israeli officials claimed they were helping civilians evacuate and receive aid;[18] another U.S. statement about Sullivan's trip praised Israel for "new alternative approaches . . . to address [Biden's] concerns."[19] The mutual back-patting was pure PR. Fleeing Palestinians—among them up to six hundred thousand children—were heading to worse-off areas, risking death and losing the few supplies they had, the United Nations reported.[20]

Biden's clearest boost for the Israeli line on Rafah came through his biggest publicity stunt of the war: On May 16, U.S. troops completed their floating pier off Gaza's coast, and food, shipped in from Cyprus after Israeli inspections, was transferred to UN staff the next day.[21]

The need was severe, with famine spreading in northern Gaza, but the pier's capacity was nowhere near that of land routes, including the now-closed Rafah Crossing. "The humanitarian environment in Gaza has become a lot more complex in the last two weeks," Sonali Korde, the USAID official who often challenged criticism of Israel from administration colleagues, told the BBC, without acknowledging U.S. responsibility for that trajectory.[22] Another American humanitarian official suspected the pier was vital to creating "an enabling environment" for the U.S.-Israeli Gaza policy to continue, telling me that with the Rafah route closed, "the fear was they would be accused of implementing a full siege, so they needed . . . the narrative of an alternative."

Still, the unfolding catastrophe was obvious. Ireland, Spain, and Norway—U.S. allies—formally recognized Palestinian statehood, long understood as a pressure tactic on Israel, and on May 24, the International Court of Justice issued its first order for Israel to stop attacks in Gaza.[23] Washington aided the pushback: State Department spokesman Matthew Miller nixed drafted statements from colleagues acknowledging the ruling and fear for civilians, while Sullivan's comments on alleged IDF moderation were quoted in an American Jewish Committee statement saying the ICJ ignored "unprecedented Israeli efforts to mitigate civilian harm."[24] The moment underscored how a range of Americans with influence over Israel and wariness of Netanyahu—like Biden, the committee had condemned his far-right allies—were together shielding the Israeli leader during the biggest test of his war plan.

Many knew they were being disingenuous. "Ultimately, Israel did not meet all of [Biden's] criteria, and we pretended as if they had done so," a senior U.S. official later told me. Separately, another senior official said the spirit of Biden's red line—no ground operation in Rafah and winding down, not escalating, the war—was indisputably violated. But the administration was committed to behaving otherwise. On May 26, Hamas launched rockets at Tel Aviv for the first time in months, citing "the massacre of civilians" in Rafah. The assault was intercepted, but the IDF soon bombed a tent camp in Rafah—sparking a huge fire, likely by hitting stored fuel. Palestinians "literally burned alive in their tents," an emergency doctor working nearby reported; the strike killed at least thirty-six and reportedly decapitated some victims; and the bombs, inevitably, came from America.[25] After the IDF promised one of its notoriously ineffective investigations, Kirby indicated that was good enough for Biden, implying those questioning the episode had forgotten about Hamas atrocities; he argued the "devastating" strike actually proved Israeli caution because it did not involve "big" bombs while also claiming it was not his role to speak for Israel or comment on its tactics.[26] Amnesty International later concluded militants in the camp were "knowingly endangering the lives of civilians" but said the attack was still likely disproportionate, noting the IDF could have used more precise missiles and did not kill one of its two senior Hamas targets.[27] Kirby's message was not about specifics, however, but U.S.-Israeli alignment. His remarks ended any remaining sense the United States might reject Israeli behavior in Rafah, as he minimized IDF advances and said, when asked what level of deaths would be excessive, there was no "measuring stick." A tacit Biden-Netanyahu understanding was now overshadowing the toll among Palestinians, one of Kirby's colleagues told CNN: "They are trying to do it in a way that allows the administration to say it's below the line. But the net effect will be the same."[28]

For months, the red line discussion had spurred more American acknowledgments of Israeli misconduct, as U.S. officials said their ally had to do better. By the end of May, Biden's team was back to defending Israeli practices regardless of ground conditions. It echoed the earliest period of the war—suggesting few lessons learned over the past seven months.

BIBI BESTS BIDEN

With the Rafah battle progressing on terms the United States and Israel embraced, both governments wanted to define the moment for their own political and strategic reasons—and though they shared a dim view of Palestinian life, their broader visions still differed. Biden and

Netanyahu posed new public challenges to each other. The latter won, ensuring bloodshed continued, and the president's weakness on his red line defined his broader legacy of failing Gaza and hurting trust in the United States globally.

Biden's advisors pinned their hopes on a speech from the president about ending the war. Officials had since November discussed such an address, aimed at the Israeli public to rally them to sway Netanyahu and describing "two pathways": a prolonged Gaza offensive, with unclear chances of saving hostages or vanquishing Hamas and a risk of broader conflict; or a truce and prisoner swap leading to a permanent Israeli-Palestinian settlement, and Israel growing closer to regional powers wary of its treatment of Palestinians, chiefly Saudi Arabia.

The idea and continued discussions about it partly reflected wishful thinking. Since October 7, surveys in Israel and comments from across its political spectrum showed minimal tolerance for Palestinian autonomy. Serious U.S. pressure would be needed just to begin negotiations, but that was unlikely under Biden; even if applied, it would involve Americans confronting their record on Israel-Palestine. To a degree, discussing the "day after" the war was an avoidance tactic for Biden aides frustrated over Gaza—a way to say they were advancing peace, but effectively a face-saving technique resembling the argument from Sullivan and other ardent backers of Israel's right to defend itself that Israel's daily violence was not their responsibility. One national security expert attended a White House meeting a few weeks before the Rafah invasion that summarized the surreal tendency. Hady Amr, the State Department envoy to Palestinians, and McGurk aide Terry Wolff had gathered outside analysts, who hoped to debate Rafah—yet Amr instead spoke about when fighting had somehow ended, describing private investment and water desalination plants for Gaza. When the looming battle came up, a Biden aide expressed uncertainty about what Israel would do, saying its various officials often gave Washington conflicting messages. "The United States is not a bystander," the expert later fumed to me. (A State Department official told me the Biden administration never discussed private investment in Gaza.)

The "two pathways" idea relied on Biden's popularity among Israelis, which Netanyahu steadily eroded by squabbling with the president and implying he would defend Israel in a way the United States never would. High-level approval for the speech was delayed because of McGurk's claims every few weeks that a ceasefire was in reach—even though there was no indication that either side, but chiefly Netanyahu, would budge enough for a deal—and Biden's aversion to challenging Israel, a White House official told me. By mid-May, when the president was comfortable with the proposal and his advisors saw it as a way to discuss something other than Rafah, Biden had "lost a lot of the altitude he had with the Israeli public," the official said, and the Palestinian Authority, key to the plan as an alternative to Hamas, had been severely weakened by Netanyahu. Still, aides prepared the remarks, scheduled for May 31—and then the plan changed on forty-eight hours' notice. The administration heard Israel's war cabinet had approved ceasefire language resembling what Hamas accepted weeks earlier, and McGurk and Sullivan wanted a rewrite, not posing a challenge to Israel but praising it. When Biden spoke, he said Israel had offered a "comprehensive new proposal" for a three-phase ceasefire and suggested the barrier now was Hamas. Referencing the possible Saudi deal, Biden presented himself in historic—and notably not dovish—terms: "As the only American president who has ever gone to Israel in a time of war, as someone who just sent the U.S. forces to directly defend Israel when it was attacked by Iran, I ask you to take a step back and think what will happen if this moment is lost."

The remarks reflected the Biden administration's priorities and might have convinced its imagined Israeli counterpart. In reality, Netanyahu had his own interests and little to lose from defying the president. He confirmed he had approved a possible ceasefire plan but reiterated his goal of eliminating Hamas, then announced he would soon address Congress, highlighting his reach in Washington beyond 1600 Pennsylvania Avenue. Netanyahu aides undercut Biden's depiction of the proposal; though it was championed by the families of Hamas hostages, they also demanded Netanyahu's resignation and had little impact on his decisions.[29] Rather than forcefully advocating for his ceasefire idea, Biden praised Netanyahu's handling of Rafah and said on June 6: "He's listening to me."[30] The administration was reverting to its bear-hug strategy, proven not to restrain Israel but to prolong war. On June 8, the IDF conducted its biggest hostage rescue raid yet, freeing a group of captives that included one of the best-known, twenty-six-year-old Noa Argamani, whose dying mother begged for her freedom; claiming militants shot at the Israelis, the military then killed more than two hundred Palestinians in the deadliest single day in Gaza since mid-December.[31] Netanyahu treated the moment as a triumph, publicizing a visit to the freed hostages, and though the next day the UN Security Council blessed the ceasefire outline and his war cabinet lost another prominent Israeli politician, Benny Gantz, the prime minister showed no indication of moving toward a ceasefire.

Instead, Netanyahu on June 18 released an English-language video accusing the United States of an "inconceivable" monthslong halt on military supplies while "America's closest ally [was] fighting for its life." Providing no proof, he claimed Blinken had admitted as much and promised to expedite deliveries.[32] Netanyahu was returning public attention to whether Biden was sufficiently pro-Israel—a specious debate largely ignoring overwhelming U.S. support for the IDF and its horrifying impact on Palestinians—and remarkably, the administration was again caught flat-footed. "We genuinely do not know what he's talking about," White House press secretary Karine Jean-Pierre responded at a briefing.[33] Later, a Pentagon official complained to me that the video killed the chance of a private agreement between the United States and Israel against the use of heavy bombs, rooted in months of negotiations that a senior White House official said never resumed after this point. Yet because of their own choices, Biden's team had little ability to challenge Netanyahu's narrative. Since the president's speech, State Department leaders like Jack Lew, the ambassador in Jerusalem, had been promoting the old idea that disagreeing with Israel would prevent a ceasefire by emboldening Hamas, a lawmaker recalled to me. Though agency staff had, to a degree, been increasing red tape and internal deliberations around weapons, per a senior State official, they would not say so. And there was by now no prospect of Biden deploying real pressure on Tel Aviv, even for his ceasefire effort: The White House had demonstrated that, per a former senior American official, it remained "open season with arms sales [which] let the Israeli side off the hook" in negotiations. U.S. officials claimed their cancellation of a summit about Iran was a rebuke, but Netanyahu had canceled a previous iteration, and other high-level U.S.-Israeli meetings remained on the schedule.[34] Meanwhile, with Biden's red line dissipated, others in Washington were defaulting to carte blanche for Israel: Gregory Meeks, the Democratic congressman who had used his position on the House Foreign Affairs Committee to stop $18 billion in weaponry for Israel, withdrew the objection.[35]

The open clash with Israel the Biden team had resisted was now underway, evolving in a direction that suited Netanyahu. White House spokesperson Kirby spoke of "deep disappointment," but the prime minister used U.S. outrage to posture as a martyr, telling the American news outlet Punchbowl News—a favorite in Congress, indicating his audience—he had tried to quietly settle the matter and would "suffer personal attacks as long as Israel receives the ammo it needs."[36] Designed to grab headlines, the spat ended with a public impression Biden was rightfully chastised. Israeli defense minister Yoav Gallant headed to the United States for a previously planned trip, aiding Netanyahu's scheme, though he claimed to doubt it, by declaring the visit was "critical"; at the Pentagon and the White House, Gallant's aides and U.S. officials together went through hundreds of American shipments for Israel, and a Biden aide told reporters they "prioritized things according to Israel's needs."[37] In a week, the administration had shifted from treating the crisis as manufactured to validating it, with officials blaming bureaucrats for "bottlenecks" and misunderstanding Biden's pause on some bombs as requiring greater scrutiny of all arms for Israel.[38] In Gaza, the reason for international scrutiny—IDF attacks—persisted. But the talk in Washington was of a united front: "In every family . . . disagreements may arise," Gallant said.[39] Netanyahu's ruse had successfully shored up both his war and a vision of U.S.-Israel relations in which Palestinian deaths and White House plans were largely irrelevant. Together, he and the administration ensured that the end of the Rafah red line was the end of any limits on the devastation Israel could cause in Gaza on Biden's watch.

A RECKONING

"I can't explain what it feels like living through constant displacement," Mohammed Abu Radwan said a few weeks after Israel invaded Rafah. He had fled the town with his wife, six children, and twelve other relatives; they first lived in the open, then built a tent but still lacked clean water and fuel. "We have nothing," Radwan continued. "All of this destroys us mentally."[40]

Biden's red line for Rafah was not just about the type of bombs the IDF could drop there. It did not involve a particular battle plan or number of acceptable civilian casualties. The administration repeatedly said Israel should not seize the city and leave Palestinian civilians worse off. Yet that is exactly what happened. U.S. officials, recognizing the gravity of the moment, sought absolution long afterward—usually by assuming the person they were talking to was comfortable with some level of death and disruption for innocent Palestinians. One senior Biden aide later told me the administration slowed Israel's attack by probing its plans and offering recommendations, creating time for more Palestinians to leave. Separately, one of his colleagues argued the battle killed fewer civilians than past Israeli advances, saying the experience proved Biden could effectively lean on Israel but remained almost always unwilling to do so. That a lasting, and terrifying, detachment from the significance of individual Palestinian lives had come to define those involved in the war became ever clearer after the Rafah assault. Broadly, many U.S. officials knew they facilitated a tragedy, with a third official telling me the campaign did not just reduce aid but cause "a drop off the cliff, as we had predicted." Yet between abstraction and its collaboration with Israel in twisting the meaning of the red line, the administration after Rafah was more deeply implicated in the brutality Gaza would face in months ahead. "How do you confuse something like a red line? The whole point is supposed to be clarity," a fourth official told me, describing the subsequent Israeli approach to escalating the war and retaining U.S. support as "just a matter of muddying the waters enough."

The episode also proved the bar for creating uncertainty was low. In physical terms, Rafah "looks almost identical to what I've seen in northern Gaza, in central Gaza and in Khan Younis," CNN correspondent Jeremy Diamond reported on an IDF-organized trip to the area after fighting subsided in July.[41] A death toll for the battle remained elusive, because Israel allowed no independent access to the town, and casualties likely included those buried under the rubble and subsequent Israeli bulldozing, as well as an unknown number of Palestinians who moved elsewhere and then died from injuries sustained during the offensive. Gaza health ministry figures from before and after the campaign suggested roughly three thousand died in that period, but a group of health experts wrote in a June 19 letter to the medical journal *The Lancet* that the toll of the war was likely severely underreported, between the ministry's diminished capacity to gather data and indirect deaths; the authors suggested the conflict had actually killed around 186,000 Palestinians so far, compared with the ministry's overall count of 37,396.[42] That would represent a staggering 8 percent of Gaza's population.

For the administration, vagueness about Rafah was invaluable. It reduced public concern and shielded the administration's confidence in its choices, which was already being privately bolstered in this period. Pulling America's Arab partners closer to Tel Aviv, to form a U.S.-directed partnership against Iran and other foes, remained a fixation for the Biden team—and in May, even as Arab states publicly condemned the Rafah assault, top Israeli and Arab military officials held close consultations at an American base in Qatar.[43] The widely shared belief in the administration's top ranks that Palestinian deaths could not hinder U.S. strategic ambitions—which consistently helped prevent consequences for Israel—got a boost thanks to Palestinians' putative allies.

The war was not over: Netanyahu spoke of new missions, and, on June 15, Hamas killed eight Israeli soldiers in its deadliest attack since October 7.[44] Biden had set himself up to have far more symbolic blood on his hands—one more reason to doubt his judgment as skepticism rose of his bid for another term as president.

CHAPTER 8

CAMPAIGN TRAIL

June–August 2024

JUST AS THEY FELT RAFAH WAS SETTLED, THE PRESIDENT and his advisors confronted a dilemma they took far more seriously: reelection. Though Democratic Party officials consistently argued faraway fighting would not decide the presidency, they knew most Democratic and independent voters disapproved of the war, and Biden's position on Gaza alienated core Democratic-leaning constituencies such as young people and nonwhite voters. The president presented his ceasefire push as the core of his policy, but rhetoric could not overshadow footage of families reduced to scattered body parts by American weapons. More broadly, Biden was trailing Donald Trump in swing states on the issues voters said they cared about most, the economy and immigration.[1]

By July, Biden lost the confidence of Democratic leaders and relinquished the Democratic presidential nomination, prompting two questions for the war. Would the president's aspiring successor, Kamala Harris, change course? And would the administration make different choices with Biden now ostensibly free of political considerations around Israel?

The White House and the Harris campaign largely settled that question with a clear "no" in the subsequent weeks, while Netanyahu deployed moves from an assassination to Washington politicking to undermine U.S. attempts at a ceasefire. With continued—and even enhanced—American backing, the IDF squeezed Palestinians further. Biden's pledges of ending the fighting, returning October 7 hostages to their families, and limiting turmoil across the Middle East became more doubtful as Washington, fixating on the election, gave Israel even freer rein.

BECOMING A LAME DUCK

On June 27, Biden and Trump had their first debate of the 2024 election. Biden performed so badly it was also his last. Running as the oldest presidential candidate in American history at eighty-one, Biden looked frail, drifted off midsentence, and failed to land attacks on Trump.[2] The performance boosted attacks from Republicans, tapping public suspicions that the president and his team were hiding his diminished capacity, a belief now gaining ground among Democrats. Still, Biden spokespeople lambasted journalists for questioning his age despite even high-ranking officials seeing him far less frequently and some officials understanding that, as one later told me, "He was a potato—Jake [Sullivan] was the president."

For Palestinians, the episode was a bitter confirmation their depiction in America's national conversation largely ranged from objectionable to irrelevant, while U.S. politicians credulously repeated Israeli talking points. Asked what leverage he would use over both Israel and Hamas, Biden argued only the latter wanted to prolong the war and claimed Netanyahu backed his ceasefire plan.[3] In fact, the Israeli leader had recently confirmed he would only accept a partial deal allowing continued fighting in Gaza.[4] The president also downplayed his hold on some two-thousand-pound bombs, in keeping with the administration's post–red line focus on proving they were, as Biden said, "the biggest producer of support for Israel."[5]

Trump outlined a contradictory policy like Biden's, speaking both of peace and bolstering Israel's war machine, but his message focused on personality, asking voters to trust a seemingly tougher alternative to the consistently unpopular president. "You should let them . . . finish the job," Trump said, echoing Netanyahu's video claiming Biden had hindered Israel and slowed weapons shipments. Then, using "Palestinian" as a slur—an emerging trademark that, like many Trump tactics, was both vile and revealing about American society—he suggested Biden had "become like a Palestinian. But they don't like him, because . . . he's a weak one." Biden never said the word "Palestinian," and neither man acknowledged a basis for doubting Israel's Gaza strategy. The night confirmed that American permissiveness toward Israel would outlast election season, and that one way or another, Biden was nearing the end of his presidency.

As change seemed likely in the United States, Israel's American-backed Gaza offensive seemed stuck in a bloody cycle. Each day brought news of a U.S.-backed strike that might in another time and place have been a major scandal in its own right; together, the dizzying pace of the attacks made it easier for them to be taken for granted. July 10 saw the fourth Israeli attack in four days on a school where Palestinians were sheltering, killing at least twenty-five.[6] On July 13, an attack in the IDF-marked safe zone killed at least ninety, producing what an UNRWA staffer called "the most horrific scenes I have seen in my nine months in Gaza . . . toddlers who are double amputees, children paralyzed and unable to receive treatment."[7] Israel called the bombing precise, saying it killed Mohammed Deif, a planner of the October 7 attack and the commander of Hamas's armed wing, Al-Qassam Brigades.[8]

As experts predicted, the lack of a strategy for replacing Hamas and anguish among Palestinians helped the faction regroup. Rather than reconsider its approach, the IDF returned to the sites of past battles, launching new attacks in northern Gaza that killed dozens and razed neighborhoods, and issuing a fresh displacement order on July 1 for two hundred fifty thousand Palestinians in Khan Younis, the central Gaza city that Israel had pummeled in December and January and the area some Palestinians had fled to just recently from Rafah.[9] Moving again meant heading to neighborhoods where "it was like an earthquake had struck," reported Ruwaida Amer, who brought her elderly parents to her sister's bombed-out apartment.[10] They replaced the decimated walls with nylon sheets and relied on bringing back water from half a mile away, carrying what they could—never as much as they needed—because carts could not traverse the pulverized streets. Humanitarian efforts to mitigate Palestinians' pain continued to be undercut. Israel's obstruction of aid persisted, relief groups said, while supplies that did enter Gaza faced growing looting by criminal gangs, fueled by the breakdown of order amid the war and the IDF's bombing of Gaza's police force.[11] Israeli government statements promoting the number of approved shipments to deny a man-made crisis ignored that distribution problem and included truckloads of commercial goods, which were sold at prices few Palestinians could afford and were often dominated by cigarettes or candy.

Biden administration officials overlooked the causes of the rising looting dilemma and, a U.S. humanitarian official told me, conducted "mental gymnastics" to avoid confirming, even privately, that Israel's displacement orders violated international law. For instance, they fixated on questions such as whether Israel was an occupying power, a contention that was likely irrelevant, since Israel was a warring party with obligations to civilians in a war zone. "This was a daily tactic for them. The fact that no one in the U.S. government could say how we interpret it was astonishing," the official continued, saying: "I can't make suggestions if you can't tell me legally how we view [Israel's obligations]." They also noted the seeming arbitrariness of when American officials identified apparent crimes: Given Biden's order to sanction violent West Bank settlers, internal government messages regularly said ethnic cleansing was occurring in that Palestinian region, the official said, with another official telling me the government standard was met by the summer of 2024, but with no such directive on Gaza, few firm determinations were made about developments there. The resistance to U.S. recognition of near-certain Israeli violations of international law had strengthened after the collapse of the red line; growing proof of Israeli troops using Palestinians as human shields and deploying sniper drones, known as quadcopters, seemingly indiscriminately, drew no response from the administration either.[12]

Meanwhile, there were new portents of another devastating U.S.-backed campaign, in Lebanon. Israeli officials had sought such an offensive for months and in mid-June approved a battle plan they said would batter the whole country, not just the Hamas-aligned Hezbollah militia.[13] While ongoing, the Biden administration's Israel-Hezbollah diplomacy was a long shot. "We have let Israel face zero consequences for crossing all of our red lines in Gaza so they are emboldened and know they will face no consequences for going into Lebanon," a Pentagon official told me at the time. At the Defense Department, skepticism of a Lebanon invasion extended to Defense Secretary Lloyd Austin. But a health scandal withered his influence, and staff turnover at the department further reduced its sway in administration discussions, making it hard to raise concerns such as weapons shipments to Israel and deployments linked to Gaza diminishing U.S. resources and distracting from elsewhere, like the Pacific, a U.S. official told me, while helping the bellicose Brett McGurk concentrate power over Middle East policy.

To the extent the administration sought to avert a war, American envoy Amos Hochstein used his messages to Hezbollah through intermediaries to nudge the group to make unilateral concessions, which would be ideologically difficult and risk its popularity.[14] On July 10, Hezbollah leader Hassan Nasrallah said he could halt firing into Israel in claimed solidarity with Palestinians—which had been intensifying as Israel escalated its own cross-border attacks—if a Hamas-Israel deal was reached. Israeli officials, however, wanted to permanently kneecap Hezbollah, not just find an agreement allowing civilians to return to their homes along the Israel-Lebanon border. Importantly, the prospect of a Lebanon war was a rare point of agreement between Netanyahu and those in his government who doubted his Gaza strategy and were closer to Biden aides, like defense minister Yoav Gallant.

Ceasefire talks continued: On July 6, Hamas largely accepted the phased proposal Biden had outlined, softening its position that Israel must commit to ending the war. But Netanyahu was toughening his own demands, sensitive to his ultranationalist allies' threats to topple his government if it seemed conciliatory.[15] Instead of pushing back, the United States helped him to posture as a hero for his nation and to defy pro-ceasefire demonstrations by Israelis by announcing it would release some of the bombs Biden had withheld. Flip-flopping and diminishing his own ceasefire gambit, ensuring brutality in Gaza kept growing and horrifying Americans, the president was playing right into Trump's narrative that he represented weakness and bloody chaos.

U.S. pressure to save Palestinian lives also became less likely as the summer brought the pro-Israel lobby AIPAC its clearest opportunity since the war began to demonstrate its abiding power in American politics, creating a chilling effect on discussing Gaza and antiwar advocacy. AIPAC and allies, notably Democratic Majority for Israel, had made good on their promise to spend tens of millions of dollars against Democrats who questioned Israel. As results in primary elections rolled in at the end of June, they claimed their first success by unseating New York congressman Jamaal Bowman. The moment validated their playbook of identifying incumbents facing strong rivals and mostly funding attacks on them on issues other than Israel. They already had another target in their sights, Missouri congresswoman Cori Bush—one of the first lawmakers to urge a ceasefire, as Biden was now doing—and Democrats nationally got a clear warning.

And the minimal American efforts to help Gaza that were still underway were confirmed to be severely lacking. On July 17, the United States ended its pier mission, with Vice Admiral Brad Cooper claiming it had, in two months, "achieved its intended effect to surge a very high volume of aid into Gaza."[16] In fact, over the twenty days when it actually functioned, the $230 million pier provided enough assistance to feed only 450,000 Palestinians for 1 month, failing to supply 500,000 or more for 3 months as the U.S. government had promised, a USAID audit soon revealed.[17] Again, the GOP could link Biden to danger and failure: "The only miracle is that this doomed-from-the-start operation did not cost any American lives," Roger Wicker, a Mississippi senator and the ranking Republican on the Senate Armed Services Committee, said in a statement. (A later Pentagon report said one service member was killed and 62 were injured.) Seeking a silver lining, a State Department official later told me the pier's repeated snafus at least spurred Israel to permit American aid through its own Port of Ashdod, north of Gaza. Tel Aviv had permitted shipments through Ashdod earlier, amid blowback to the IDF killing of World Central Kitchen workers, and the port was an unreliable entry point for U.S.-funded aid; by October, goods usually sat there for a month between arrival and being cleared to begin an uncertain journey toward hungry Palestinians.[18] The pier effort did suggest that when the IDF chose to, partly because of expectations from U.S. counterparts, it could help advance humanitarian aid deliveries. But as with the upticks of aid amid the November 2023 truce and after the April 2024 WCK killing, the moment was not treated by Tel Aviv or Washington as a lasting example for how to improve Palestinians' conditions.

In both foreign policy and domestic politics, Biden remained loath to question his choices. Calling the debate a "bad episode," the president insisted he was healthy and the Democrat most likely to beat Trump; he emphasized that he saw his statesmanship as part of his appeal by promoting his candidacy at a press conference after a NATO summit.[19] Aides, used to his stubbornness, began envisioning surreal scenarios: Deputy National Security Advisor Jon Finer, for instance, told a friend the president could digest information but was no longer capable of strong public performances, so the ideal option would be for Biden to win reelection, then leave before finishing his term. (Finer denied this.) Yet beyond the White House, Democrats—crucially including Nancy Pelosi, one of the few party figures of Biden's age and stature—strongly hinted the president should step aside.

On July 13, a would-be assassin shot Trump at a campaign rally in Butler, Pennsylvania. Thomas Matthew Crooks hit Trump's ear, drawing blood, before the candidate ducked and Crooks was shot himself. The arresting footage of the GOP nominee—who emerged with a fist up to the crowd—energized his supporters' view he was both a savior and a near-martyr and turbocharged election anxiety among liberals. Biden and his confidants deliberated. Then on a blazing summer Sunday,

July 21, he became the first president to abandon a reelection bid since Lyndon B. Johnson in 1968. Like his fellow Democrat Johnson, he did so as his handling of a foreign war had divided the party.

Biden quickly said Harris should take up his mantle. She had 107 days to pitch herself as president to a range of constituencies, and when it came to Gaza, she faced a blatant gap between the U.S. embrace of Israel she represented, as the number two in the administration, and views among Democrats, only 23 percent of whom now approved of the Israeli military campaign.[20] Netanyahu had little motivation to make concessions to Harris or her outgoing boss and a greater incentive to prop up a known quantity, Trump. The day after Biden quit, the IDF once again shrank its so-called safe zone for Palestinians, this time by more than 15 percent.[21]

"OUR FIGHT IS YOUR FIGHT"

Harris's young campaign faced an immediate test on Israel-Palestine, with Netanyahu's visit to Washington to address Congress already scheduled for three days after her ascension. Biden's choices meant she was at a disadvantage in trying to project herself as an equal: The Israeli leader knew he could defy the administration with impunity, while Harris had little experience shaping Gaza policy, with one U.S. official telling me her role in decision-making amounted to "no involvement whatsoever." The vice president had aides working on Gaza—Phil Gordon, Nasrina Bargzie, and Ilan Goldenberg—but they had had little sway relative to Biden confidants Sullivan and McGurk.

Some suspected she would differentiate herself from Biden, because of her perspective and the chance to court voters appalled by the war and the impression of U.S. humiliation at Netanyahu's hands. A Black and South Asian woman twenty-two years younger than the president, Harris spoke more extensively about Palestinian suffering, and her advisors, known to be skeptical of military-driven efforts to reshape the Middle East and of Netanyahu, would likely be empowered if she won. One U.S. official told me those around Harris saw information about Gaza "impacting her," noting that she had listened to the recording of Hind Rajab's excruciating death. Additionally, Harris emphasized her career as a prosecutor—and legal probes kept demonstrating Israeli misconduct. The International Court of Justice on July 19 issued an advisory opinion calling Israel's occupation of Palestinian regions illegal and a violation of the global ban on racial segregation and apartheid, saying countries must stop supporting it. Crucially, it also confirmed Israel was the "occupying power" in Gaza, with special obligations to Palestinian civilians there that it was failing to meet; other countries, including the United States, were obligated to enforce Israel's compliance, per the opinion. Harris could be more sincere than Biden in applying international law to America's Israel policy and signaling U.S. government lawyers should let the facts, not politics, guide investigations of whether Tel Aviv broke international and American law, people close to her and some observers believed. As Netanyahu's visit neared, there were mounting signs she had political room to challenge him: Seven major unions—core Democratic supporters—called for ending military aid to Israel, and nearly half the Democrats in Congress said they would skip his speech.[22] (Harris herself had a prior commitment to an event being held by a historic Black sorority.)

The Israeli leader's visit was the first chance since October 7 for most bureaucrats and lawmakers to directly confront the person they were enabling: the unapologetic subject of corruption trials at home and international charges of genocide, crimes against humanity, and enforced starvation, a figure who regularly made a mockery of U.S. government pleas. With bipartisan approval, Washington officialdom was giving Netanyahu an honor the United States' own commander in chief received only once a year.

On the morning of Netanyahu's speech, I followed several dozen antiwar activists as they halted traffic with "Stop Arming Israel" banners and pushed a towering effigy of a handcuffed Netanyahu—clutching a cardboard missile marked "Made in USA" and mounted on a shopping cart—down the National Mall. As we sweated on a gray, humid D.C. morning, they told me their reasons for protesting, which ranged from seeing Palestinian rights as part of a global struggle for justice to viewing the U.S.-Israel relationship as strategically harmful; one of several military veterans present wore a cap reading "Make Israel Palestine Again." They merged into throngs of other demonstrators as we approached the Capitol. Meanwhile, my press pass got me through the security fence erected a mile away from the Capitol, and I filed into the congressional complex alongside dozens of people who were dressed up, giggling in the queue, and exuding a sense of anticipation. As thousands screamed out against mass death a short walk away, others were experiencing a kind of festival day. It was the latter view that received official protection: Mike Johnson, the Republican Speaker of the House of Representatives, announced that any disruption during the address risked prosecution.

Even after years of tracking Netanyahu's hubris and U.S. enabling of him regardless, I was not prepared for how surreal it would feel to watch from the press gallery as he strode into the House grinning, to cheers, whistles, and a prolonged standing ovation. Ironically, the boycott offered him a friendlier audience; many Democratic seats lay empty, but hundreds of Republican lawmakers were visibly excited, some craning across others to shake Netanyahu's hand. Several Democrats greeted him with smiles too; Chuck Schumer, who helped make the speech possible, nodded to him from the front row of the audience. Several rows behind Schumer sat Rashida Tlaib, the sole Palestinian American in Congress, solemn, a keffiyeh over her shoulders, and mostly alone throughout the speech.

Netanyahu thanked the United States but also referenced the old argument that America needed Israel for its own interests—and by treating the countries' actions as intertwined, he weakened Biden officials' claim they bore little responsibility for Israeli choices. "Our fight is your fight! And our victory will be your victory!" he proclaimed. While his speech was ostensibly for Americans of all political views, Netanyahu reiterated Trump's line that the administration was not "fast-tracking" weapons, and if it did so, he could "finish the job faster" in Gaza. And he inserted himself into the domestic argument over the war by calling demonstrators "Iran's useful idiots," providing no evidence but winning applause. Netanyahu tried to drive home the point with a deeply cynical attempt at a laugh line: "Some of these protesters hold up signs proclaiming, 'Gays for Gaza.' They might as well hold up signs saying, 'Chickens for KFC' . . . [for supporting] the Tyrants of Tehran, who hang gays from cranes." Legislators guffawed at his invocation of a common right-wing claim suggesting liberals ignored threats, particularly from the Muslim-majority world, and were both foolish and hypocritical. The trope was rooted in a muddying of specifics: It developed after gay Syrian and Iraqi men described persecution by the Islamic State (ISIS)—itself a product of the U.S. invasion of Iraq and before it American funding for extremists in Afghanistan.[23] Though some governments punished same-sex sexual activity with the death penalty, none pushed gay men off buildings like ISIS did (as Trump had once suggested Saudi Arabia did); nor did Hamas, though Iran had hanged regime critics from cranes.[24]

Yet the argument was not about accuracy but about mocking generally young protesters before members of Congress who are generally older than their constituents and often typecast younger people as naïve and fixated on matters that members view as trivial, like queer identity. Netanyahu was challenging the increasingly common view of Palestinian freedom as inseparable from human rights broadly, including LGBTQ+ rights. Simultaneously, he was implying gay people should fear Palestinians and not align with forces that were themselves homophobic. Conservatives pushing Islamophobia also often attack gay parenthood and transgender rights, and Netanyahu's far-right allies, Itamar Ben-Gvir and Bezalel Smotrich, attended a notorious "Beast Parade" where Ben-Gvir compared LGBTQ+ people to animals while Smotrich called himself "a fascist homophobe"; though they disavowed those positions, their coalition still included a proponent of banning Pride parades.[25]

Netanyahu dismissed criticism of Israel's war strategy, dishonestly claiming civilian casualties in Rafah were "practically none." His guests for the speech included celebrated IDF soldiers and former hostage Noa Argamani, a reminder the war had freed Hamas captives, albeit only a few; she was seated near Netanyahu's wife and the pro-Trump billionaire Elon Musk. More than one hundred hostages remained in captivity, of course, and even the IDF was increasingly doubting Israel's approach in Gaza, with spokesperson Daniel Hagari saying on June 20: "This business of destroying Hamas . . . it's simply throwing sand in the eyes of the public. If we don't bring something else to Gaza, then at the end of the day, we will get Hamas."[26]

Despite lacking an alternative plan for the region, Netanyahu was still requesting unconditional U.S. backing, and the assembled lawmakers—many wearing yellow ribbon pins, symbols of concern for the hostages distributed by the Israeli embassy—repeatedly applauded his pitch. The rough patches in the sea of approval were minimal: Tlaib silently held up a small sign reading "Guilty of Genocide" on one side and "War Criminal" on the other, and separately, six Israeli hostage relatives in the audience stood up and revealed T-shirts reading "Seal the Deal Now"—only to face shouts of "USA!" and "Am Yisrael Chai!" from fellow attendees and be arrested by Capitol Police. Overall, Netanyahu got a show of his stature in America, helping stiffen his resistance to calls for moderation. Just before the speech, his ally Ben-Gvir endorsed Trump, and prior to Netanyahu's departure, Israel's parliament had passed a resolution opposing Palestinian statehood, still the United States' stated goal.[27] Some blasted the address, with Pelosi saying it was "the worst presentation of any foreign dignitary [given that] privilege,"[28] but critics could not turn back time or revoke the boost U.S. officials had given a leader who ignored U.S. exhortations. Chris Van Hollen, the Maryland senator, noted to me that the Biden administration enabled a key line in Netanyahu's speech: In smearing anti-war Americans as "useful idiots" manipulated by Iran, the Israeli leader cited a statement from Avril Haines, the director of national intelligence, on July 9 that said Iran's government was driving activism over Gaza.[29] Van Hollen received a classified briefing from intelligence officials afterward that provided "extremely limited examples" of Iranian involvement, contrary to the depiction from Netanyahu. That prompted him to write to Haines to say that he was "very concerned about the selective and misleading use of official public statements." Van Hollen highlighted that Haines had not issued any similar statement about "much more extensive" Israeli efforts to influence American elected officials. Intelligence personnel had told him they had not issued such a statement because information about the Israeli influence campaign was publicly available, such as in a *New York Times* investigation, but he did not find that reason compelling.[30]

"You are entrusted with objectively analyzing intelligence information and providing the public with balanced assessments. . . . I do not believe the U.S. Intelligence Community's public statements currently meet that standard," Van Hollen wrote. The senator told me he was generally alarmed about "the abuse of intelligence by the president and the White House" that enabled violence by Israel in Gaza, citing as an additional example statements from American officials that Israel used to justify its November 2023 attack on Al-Shifa Hospital, supporting the assertion it was a Hamas hub. Concerns among American officials about the administration's handling of intelligence grew throughout the war: A senior administration official told me that as analysis and briefings were developed, before they flowed up the chain to Haines, they were often shaped by high-ranking officials Brett McGurk and Amos Hochstein, two Biden aides known for trusting Israeli narratives about the war. Some intelligence staff felt pressure to frame material to support the administration's preference of staying close to Israel, two former U.S. officials told me. One described pervasive "self-censorship" among intelligence officials from junior analysts to those who were involved in assembling the President's Daily Brief, while another recalled that McGurk had in prior government roles tried to influence intelligence assessments to cast his policy choices in a more flattering light. Meanwhile, the Office of the Director of National Intelligence (ODNI) indicated to other government bodies that any inquiries about Israeli compliance with international law would have to come from the Cabinet level, a senior intelligence official and a senior State Department official both told me—thereby adopting a higher standard for colleagues' access to intelligence assessments than the ODNI had for other situations and partner countries.

The kerfuffle around the Netanyahu address saw officers arrest several anti-Netanyahu protesters, including some outside Union Station, where people had scrawled "Hamas is coming" graffiti that pro-Israel groups highlighted to cast all the demonstrators as extreme. That evening, I interviewed Zahiro Shahar Mor, one of the family members of hostages who visited for the speech and was detained during it. Mor said he could not abide Netanyahu behaving as "an American statesman" when the freedom of people like his seventy-nine-year-old uncle, Abraham Munder, depended on U.S. pressure on the Israeli leader for a settlement with Hamas. Calling congressional applause "mind-boggling," he continued: "You have to oppose Netanyahu! It's not that you're an antisemite—you're truthful."

The clarity felt refreshing after Netanyahu's sleights of hand. And the next day gave the administration a chance to heed Mor's advice, as the Israeli leader met with both Harris and the president. Afterward, Harris—not Biden—described the meetings, calling the status quo unsustainable. "We cannot allow ourselves to become numb to the suffering. And I will not be silent," she said.[31] Israeli officials quickly leaked that even the hint of a rebuke upset Netanyahu—and tried to undercut her by deploying a line Washington and Tel Aviv used against even mild questioning of the U.S.-Israeli approach, saying "daylight" between the countries aided Hamas and Iran.[32] The next day, Netanyahu and his wife, Sara, flashed huge smiles as they posed with Trump at his Mar-a-Lago resort in Florida.

Netanyahu returned home with proof his critics had not made him a pariah, wariness of Harris without any tangible sign she would restrain him, and a rekindled bond with her rival. Combined with new polling showing his support increasing among Israelis,[33] he was well positioned to be more stubborn about the war. Four days after Netanyahu's speech, Israeli negotiators introduced new conditions for a deal with Hamas, insisting on control of the Gaza-Egypt border and complicating plans for letting displaced Palestinians return home.[34] Then Israel launched a dramatic double whammy escalating tensions over Gaza, Lebanon, and the region at large. On July 30, the IDF again struck a crowded area of Beirut, killing prominent Hezbollah leader Fuad Shukr—and three others, two of them children[35]—in claimed retaliation for a rocket attack that killed twelve children in the Israeli-occupied Golan Heights. (Hezbollah denied responsibility.)[36] Hours later, Israel assassinated Hamas's political chief, Ismail Haniyeh—in Iran's capital of Tehran, where he had traveled for the country's presidential inauguration. It appeared no escalation was off the table now, and the Biden administration's pledge to prevent war beyond Gaza, including with Iran, was as empty as its Rafah red line. Washington had no advance warning of the assassination, Tony Blinken announced, saying he would not speculate on its impact.[37] The prime minister of Qatar, a key facilitator in ceasefire talks, was more direct: "How can mediation succeed when one party assassinates the negotiator on the other side?"[38]

CONVENTION-BOUND

With Netanyahu unlikely to move toward peace on his own, U.S. pressure to shift his calculus still seemed like the likeliest path to a ceasefire—and Harris's rise gave opponents of the war a different dynamic to work with. Her campaign emphasized new excitement among Democrats. Beyond meeting traditional political goals, raising $200 million in fresh donations, and signing up 170,000 new volunteers within a week,[39] the Harris team invested heavily in social media and organic, informal messaging, identifying with the fierce "brat" branding of pop singer Charli xcx and TikTok remixes of Harris's comments (especially about coconuts). The approach suggested interest in making the vice president appear distinctive—strong and au courant compared with Biden—and in rallying younger voters, a constituency especially frustrated with the war. As the party weighed how Gaza could relate to the nascent campaign, one group defined the push for Harris to adopt a new policy, particularly ahead of the Democratic National Convention: the Uncommitted movement.

Uncommitted's campaign for voters in the Democratic presidential primary to withhold support for the party's standard-bearer had, since its initial success in Michigan, won the movement an undeniable but modest slice of official representation from across several states. Thirty-six of the 4,695 delegates heading to the convention were Uncommitted.[40] The group wielded outsized power, however, through a consistent message, aggressive media strategy, and savvy backroom dealing. Uncommitted cast itself as firmly within the Democratic Party tent. Its cofounder Abbas Alawieh, a longtime party operative, felt he would be doing "a disservice" to fellow Democrats if he did not demonstrate how intense the fury over Gaza was among voters, he later told me. The movement collaborated with others, such as student protesters and pro-Palestinian organizations, but uniquely focused on Democratic leaders meeting specific demands—chiefly, halting weapons for Israel—in one election season.

The strategy "created leverage out of thin air," according to Beth Miller of Jewish Voice for Peace (JVP) Action. "The broader Palestinian rights movement is traditionally at odds with both political parties," she told me; JVP, for instance, is anti-Zionist and supports the Boycott, Divestment, and Sanctions movement against Israel, positions shared by few Democratic leaders. And some war critics were battling the party, like the small but vocal "Abandon Biden" movement, which morphed into "Abandon Harris."[41] Uncommitted was saying Democrats could simultaneously save lives and secure votes. When Biden was at the top of the ticket, his aides' dialogue with Uncommitted was mostly a one-way street: Though they would hear it out, they did not credit antiwar organizing with influencing decisions such as the pause on bombs but then, Alawieh told me, asked Uncommitted to praise the president's call for a ceasefire in May, which the group did not do because Biden would not speak of cutting off firepower for Israel.

With Harris, he said, "we felt the shift" among campaign officials. The vice president discussed Gaza with the mayor of the Arab-majority city of Dearborn, Michigan, and meeting with Julie Chávez Rodriguez, still the campaign manager, on August 15, Alawieh gave her draft language to signal a break with Biden's policy that the campaign said it would consider. Antiwar organizers also cheered Harris's August 6 choice of

Minnesota governor Tim Walz as her running mate, over alternatives such as Josh Shapiro, the Pennsylvania governor who had blasted student protests. Nearly 20 percent of Democratic primary voters in Walz's state identified as Uncommitted, and he had told CNN the party must "take them seriously."[42]

But the goodwill started fading when Uncommitted and the campaign began discussing actual policy—an early sign that Democratic elites' sensitivity around the appearance of challenging Israel could keep the two at odds. Harris aides invited Alawieh and another Uncommitted cofounder, Layla Elabed, to greet the candidate ahead of a rally in Detroit on August 8. In brief, separate conversations, each asked Harris for a meeting about halting weapons for Israel. Both told me she agreed, expressing genuine sympathy, per Elabed, and making Uncommitted feel it "secured something after months of being totally ignored by Joe Biden," Alawieh said. The group—which had faced attacks from some antiwar voices saying Democrats would never shift on Gaza and calling Uncommitted naïve or party stooges—announced Harris's "openness" to a meeting about an arms embargo. The campaign panicked. "You don't put words in the vice president's mouth," an aide later argued to me, describing the campaign team as "super fucking pissed" and feeling they had "no choice but to slap them down." Phil Gordon, Harris's national security advisor, announced she did not support an arms embargo on Israel, emphasizing her support for its defense.[43]

Despite initial appearances, Uncommitted and the campaign were not miles apart. Later, another campaign aide told me Gordon's statement was misunderstood as a blanket defense of Israeli policy; it mentioned upholding international law and shielding civilians, and crucially, both aides separately said it did not rule out Harris enforcing conditions on the U.S. supply of weapons for Israel—which Biden had never done. For their part, Alawieh and Elabed later told me they knew halting arms was not Harris's policy while she was in the administration; they asked for immediate change because, Elabed said, "we need to save lives right now, we couldn't wait for November." The way the episode unfolded, however, permanently damaged Harris's prospects of wooing antiwar voters. Uncommitted felt misunderstood and sacrificed for political expediency, Alawieh said, telling me party officials privately expressed remorse; publicly, the campaign had pushed the group away and proved it retained Biden-style paranoia of being seen as abandoning Tel Aviv and emboldening pro-Israel hard-liners. Simultaneously, Harris's team had become even warier of the segment of the Gaza protest movement that was most committed to their election chances. Already, since the vice president's ascension, Gordon had become more risk-averse in arguing for being tougher on Israel in internal policy discussions, a senior Biden aide told me. Come 2026, he continued touting the Biden administration's pro-Israel credentials, ironically bolstering doubts about the team's judgment, writing on X: "Biden resisted enormous pressure to condition aid, as required by U.S. law," Gordon wrote on X, in a comment that was widely circulated by critics of the Gaza policy.[44]

Beyond specific choices, the mood around the young campaign was hardly conducive to introspection or tough conversations among Democrats. Many felt they had an almost-unimaginable second chance in the election and had no choice but unqualified enthusiasm. Israel-Palestine—an issue that was seen as hurting Biden's image and was easy to write off as intractable—especially aggravated loyalists, even when raised by those who agreed that Trump should not regain the White House. When Alawieh mentioned Gaza during a Michigan Democratic Party call two days into Harris's candidacy, another attendee retorted, with no objection from anyone else: "Shut up, asshole." After Harris's interaction with Alawieh and Elabed, pro-Palestinian protesters interrupted her Detroit rally. Attendees booed back, and Harris first smiled and said all voices mattered, then as the chants continued, more firmly proclaimed: "If you want Donald Trump to win, then say that. Otherwise, I'm speaking." Her supporters broke into extended applause as some standing behind her gestured for the demonstrators to leave and brandished their signs higher. The moment went viral. To Harris fans, it was a welcome throwback to a line she used during Democrats' successful 2020 election campaign and a vindication of their new standard-bearer's toughness—but in antiwar circles, it suggested she was no different from Biden in dismissing emotion over Gaza and bolstered apathy toward Democrats. Noura Erakat, a leader in the Palestinian American community, referenced the moment to say she was publicly considering joining the Green Party's presidential campaign.

Professional Democrats helped ensure an environment of inflexibility regarding the war. Lawmakers who had been calling for limiting American support to Netanyahu grew quieter. "Before Biden dropped out, we were so done with him we didn't care if we were going against him or not," a Democratic congressional aide told me, but once Harris took over, the thinking shifted to "let's just win this and then we'll figure it out . . . we might actually win." The aide did not comment on the human life that could be lost in that period. And the campaign itself remained, in the words of one Harris staffer, "98 percent Biden-land," dominated by figures like Jen O'Malley Dillon, who insisted three weeks before the president abandoned the race that he was "probably in better health than most of us."[45] Touchy after being publicly embarrassed and loyal to Biden, campaign leaders resisted recommendations for Harris to deviate from him, on Gaza among other matters, by citing the short span of her campaign and past vice presidents' presidential bids, the staffer recalled to me, saying influential Democratic consultants also argued that Harris, as a woman of color, might not be seen as strong. That left little room for those arguing she should emphasize her different perspective and remember that the last time a president ended his candidacy amid outrage over a war, Vietnam in 1968, his vice president, Hubert Humphrey, was still seen as implicated and lost badly. Someone familiar with the campaign told me they suspected the mismanagement was partly deliberate, arguing that Biden tapped Harris not because of faith in her but to frustrate Pelosi and others seeking his exit, such as Barack Obama and Democratic fundraiser George Clooney, and urging an open nomination process for his successor. Resentment in his circle ran deep: "It was an act of insanity by the Democratic leadership to have forced Biden out," the president's advisor Mike Donilon later said.[46] Saying Biden had been "a dead man walking" and his staff and consultants felt he would lose yet saw the campaign as an opportunity for themselves regardless, the person reflected the deep rifts among Democrats that the euphoria around Harris's ascension only papered over.

Significantly for Gaza, rigidity and caution also defined the campaign's treatment of Jewish Americans. Historically, they overwhelmingly voted Democratic, but Trump was courting them, claiming the party was antisemitic and dominated by unwavering Israel critics like Rashida Tlaib (while himself often describing Jews as loyal to Israel, not America). Between that narrative and aggressive anti-Israel rhetoric in some antiwar demonstrations, some Jewish voters told campaign staff they felt "unseen in progressive spaces," another Harris aide told me. A September poll by the Jewish Democratic Council of America saw American Jews rank Israel as ninth in importance among eleven issues determining their vote.[47] Yet the campaign conflated pro-Israel events with Jewish American events, the aide recalled, calling colleagues "afraid" of organic interactions such as rallies with Harris's husband, Doug Emhoff, who would, if she won, be the first Jewish member of the First Couple.

As the Democratic National Convention approached, Democrats' domestic discussion about Gaza remained unsettled. The administration attempted an international gamble: McGurk and Sullivan—their careers in question in a way they had not been weeks earlier—suddenly began saying indirect negotiations in Qatar could produce an Israel-Hamas deal before the convention's end and organizing urgent calls with reporters to tout their success.[48] "We are closer than we've ever been," Biden proclaimed soon after announcing another $20 billion in weapons for the IDF.[49] The day before the convention, Blinken visited Israel and claimed Netanyahu supported a "bridging proposal" covering remaining disagreements and that Hamas was the obstacle to an agreement.[50] The tactics, from invented urgency to stressing U.S.-Israel friendship, had been unsuccessfully tried before, and the true hurdle—Netanyahu's domestic political imperative to continue the war—was unchanged.[51] One senior administration official identified the moment to me as Biden's best hope of a Gaza ceasefire, but then shifted the focus, arguing that it was near-impossible to get Hamas and Israel to agree to a deal at the same time and that beyond Israel, the United States should have pressured countries close to Hamas, like Qatar and Turkey, by threatening to close the huge American military bases there. Yet another senior official, who similarly described the period as the "sliding doors moment" for a deal, said that in this instance, Israeli and U.S. recalcitrance was the determining factor. The president did not meaningfully press Netanyahu, no deal came, and the antiwar movement, from Uncommitted to Students for Justice in Palestine, remained determined to use the convention to spotlight Democrats' continued failure on Gaza.

CHICAGO

Starting on August 18, a Sunday, the Democratic National Convention was inescapable in Chicago, from merchandise and reunions of far-flung political insiders in airports, restaurants, and hotel lobbies to a persistent buzz of gossip about securing the right invites. Party conventions are not just about a presidential candidate or officialdom. A universe of lobbyists, activists, donors, journalists, and even celebrities surrounds the proceedings—and given Harris's shock ascension and the sense Democrats were revitalized, this convention became an especially hot ticket, with new attractions like a John Legend concert added after the change in candidate.[52] The frenzied vibe combined with a triumphant narrative from the party that was designed to move on from months of fumbles: Beyond promoting Harris, pins and posters thanked Biden for stepping down and declared "Democrats Deliver."

American complicity in violence abroad was not a big focus. On Monday, as the four-day convention officially began, antiwar organizers held a "March on the DNC," where attendees referenced the infamous Vietnam-era Democratic convention, also held in Chicago, and tied concern for Palestinians to justice for the many minorities to whom Democrats have promised equality.[53] Even the rally's leaders conceded it drew fewer demonstrators than expected. Earlier in the day, a health official in Gaza reported that shortages of supplies since the Rafah invasion meant that effectively, its "entire health sector has collapsed,"[54] as U.S.-backed Israeli bombing killed at least thirty-five more Palestinians.

By the time I arrived in Chicago, party leaders were already setting limits on discussions of Gaza at the convention. Democrats had drafted their 2024 platform in July, before Biden quit, and though a possible arms embargo on Israel was the chief sticking point, the platform committee did not consider the question.[55] That Monday, the party adopted a platform showing little evolution in Israel-Palestine thinking, echoing Biden's talk of a ceasefire and a two-state solution without specifying how the United States could make Israel serious about those goals.

While operatives and campaign officials had decided the party's response to the antiwar groundswell would be fully symbolic, they struggled to offer even symbolism that suggested true respect—worsening the intraparty wound over Gaza by the convention's end. The plan began with the first-ever official Democratic National Convention event on Palestinian rights. Uncommitted's Layla Elabed was on the panel, beside Jim Zogby, a longtime Democratic official and Arab American activist who described how past mentions of Palestine at Democratic conventions, in 1984 and 1988, were due to one party leader, Rev. Jesse Jackson, but now a "bottom up" movement questioning Israel had built real heft. "The prize is a change in policy," Zogby said, but he argued the Harris campaign had sent a message by agreeing to the event, and Elabed spoke of "an opportunity to restore the soul of the Democratic Party." Wearing a pin displaying intertwined American and Palestinian flags, Elabed specified Uncommitted's vision: They were inspired not by the chaotic 1968 convention but by 1964, when civil rights activist Fannie Lou Hamer lobbied the Democratic National Convention for fair representation from Mississippi instead of an all-white delegation.[56] Uncommitted had for weeks been asking Democratic officials to allow Gaza-focused remarks from the convention stage. The group was by now seeking two speeches: one from Tanya Haj-Hassan, a doctor who treated patients during the war, and one from a Palestinian American.

Party officials had a different, more upbeat focus, and a sense of finality: After the panel, two approached the Uncommitted representatives, saying they should rush to a private room for an update. "The vibe of the conversation was, 'We did something historic together . . . this is the moment to unify and look at what you guys are doing. Isn't this incredible?'" Abbas Alawieh recalled to me. Elabed responded that they were still waiting for an update about a speaker or a policy speech on Gaza. There was no such news, but the group was invited to head to the United Center, the site of the evening events, in convention-provided SUVs; there, remembered Uncommitted's Waleed Shahid, "they handed us [convention] credentials as if they were $1 million checks." Shahid, a fast-moving spokesperson in constant contact with reporters about the antiwar bloc's concerns, already suspected an ulterior motive: "The goal of their pomp and circumstance was, 'Let up on doing press on us.'"

Convention officials had been quietly planning a speech by the family of a Hamas hostage and believed remarks by Keith Ellison, the Muslim American attorney general of Minnesota, could prevent a sense of imbalance.[57] They were still treating the war as an issue of identities rather than a litmus test of the party's commitment to its stated ideals of humanity and equality; Democratic-aligned pundits relied on that logic to say antiwar voters would inevitably support Harris against Trump, the champion of the Muslim ban, and to dodge questions about the politically sensitive possibility of altering U.S.-Israel relations. Yet Ellison's role had little to do with Gaza—and because the Biden administration and the Harris campaign said a policy change was impossible, pointing war skeptics to her rhetoric about Palestinians, they had themselves dramatically increased the significance of public comments focused on the war. On Monday night, the first major reference to Gaza from the convention stage came from Alexandria Ocasio-Cortez, but the New York congresswoman's speech credited the vice president with "working tirelessly to achieve a ceasefire" without acknowledging the administration's continued shipments of U.S. weapons to Israel, sparking backlash.[58]

Still, for most on the ground, celebrations were in full swing, and a clash over the war did not seem inescapable by Tuesday. Uncommitted won over more convention attendees, who called themselves "ceasefire delegates" and sported keffiyehs, buttons, and T-shirts, subtly raising Gaza throughout the convention. Democratic officials had yet to formalize the speaker lineup. And with Harris advisors still fine-tuning how she would discuss Gaza in her speech, the capstone of the convention, some war skeptics were privately trying to influence the language. "Hope is making a comeback!" Michelle Obama proclaimed from the stage that night, and onlookers to my left and right were visibly overcome, chanting "Yes!" after key lines of her speech. Snuck into a VIP area by a friend, I got a taste of how the establishment was feeling: Terry McAuliffe, the former Virginia governor and a prolific party fundraiser, was smiling wide, and we clinked glasses. Then I mentioned my reporting for this book, and he looked at me quizzically and asked whether, given October 7 and Netanyahu's personality, Biden could really have done better. A speech was not guaranteed to shake top Democrats out of their convenient position—bashing the Israeli leader while absolving the United States, his enabler—but the status quo certainly would not.

The following day brought confirmation the party elite preferred comfortable, willful blindness. On that sunny Wednesday morning, I attended Uncommitted's daily press conference, at a park in view of the convention center but well outside its security barrier. Alawieh, six foot six and with a keffiyeh stamped "Democrats for Palestinian Rights" over his gray suit, led the customary moment of silence for the forty thousand (and probably more) who had been killed in Gaza,[59] before introducing allies entrenched in the party establishment, like sitting congresswomen Ilhan Omar and Cori Bush and Jeremiah Ellison, a Minneapolis council member and Keith's son. "We are all ready to work every single day until November 5 to secure a win against Donald Trump," Omar told reporters, "but it will take not just all of us. . . . It will take for the top of the ticket to have a policy shift to invite every single voter that cares about peace and humanity." Ellison emphasized that Uncommitted supported a speech by relatives of a Hamas hostage and saw remarks from a Palestinian American as providing "equal footing"; the group had already narrowed its demand to just one speech.

That evening, I watched with members of J Street—the liberal Zionist group that had helped Democrats question AIPAC and become a fixture in the party establishment—as the convention stage featured Jon Polin and Rachel Goldberg, whose Israeli American son Hersh was captured at the Nova music festival as he celebrated his twenty-third birthday. With photographs of Hersh projected behind them, Polin decried "a surplus of agony on all sides," crediting Biden and Harris with seeking a ceasefire to free hostages and "stop the despair in Gaza." Support for his family helped them breathe, he said, "in a world without air."

The remarks from the two were gutting. For the question of the convention's approach to the war, the moment underscored that the Biden-Harris Gaza policy had borne little fruit over a period of, per small pieces of tape that Hersh's parents wore on their chests, three hundred twenty days; and that the crowd could handle a discussion of tragedy in Israel-Palestine. Hadar Susskind, another Zionist Democrat, who ran the group Americans for Peace Now, told me he encouraged that speech—and that he had sought a Palestinian American address too, because the convention denying a platform to someone from the anguished community on the other side of the war would be "immensely stupid politics but also just wrong."

Yet that was the choice conveyed to Uncommitted's leaders on Wednesday night, which they shared with reporters at a patch of sidewalk between the brightly lit entrance to the United Center and a CNN-sponsored trailer reserved for political and media elites. Sweating and still in his gray suit, Alawieh said he was convinced Harris knew about the ask. Surrounded by allies—a tableau of Democrats rejected by their own tribe—he began a sit-in, saying she might relent. Throughout the night, multiple lawmakers endorsed the protest, while party operatives visited repeatedly, ensuring the demonstration was not dispersed and offering more meetings yet no speaking slot.[60]

What happened? Uncommitted heard a variety of explanations: that their push might overshadow Harris's big moment and that all the Palestinian Americans they mentioned had accused Israel of genocide, which could upset Jewish Democrats. Party figures repeatedly suggested that proposed speakers such as Ruwa Romman, a Georgia state representative, did not pass vetting, a narrative that Romman told me especially stung because the convention had that night featured a speech from an anti-abortion, Democrat-bashing Republican from her state—one of several staunch conservatives given speaking slots. Later, Alawieh and Shahid told me they heard plausible, revealing explanations from two more senior Democrats. Negotiations with party staff meant little, one said, because on issues as delicate as Israel, decisions were made at a different level—among "the people who paid for that stage," namely donors. Another cited Harris's sensitivity toward Biden, particularly as he struggled to handle Netanyahu, and pointed to the network of uncompromisingly pro-Israel Democrats who could exacerbate "disunity in the ranks," like Pennsylvania senator John Fetterman.

On Wednesday night and beyond, sources suggested to me that the decision was shaped by powerful Democrats reluctant to cede control of the schedule or ideologically, from O'Malley Dillon and convention organizer Stephanie Cutter to the longtime Democratic fundraiser Chris Korge, and months later, some antiwar figures believed the veto must have come from Harris herself. One of her longtime associates, the Palestinian American political operative Hala Hijazi, was among the speaker options too. What's certain is the group at the heart of the Democratic National Convention comprised an opaque team of insiders, facing a challenging campaign but also fundamentally guarded; it was a parallel of the circle running Gaza policy at the Biden White House, and the similarities extended to defensiveness and ultimately sending a message that some lives mattered less.

Defenders of the decision against the speech argued last-minute uncertainty was not an option. The Palestinian American speaker might not fully reflect the DNC's position or, if the speaker did, be "attacked as an Uncle Tom," one Harris staffer later told me, saying Uncommitted could have claimed success by citing the panel on Palestinian rights but "chose to make a Palestinian American speaker the centerpiece . . . they turned it into a loss." Jeremy Ben-Ami, president of J Street, called the choice "a missed opportunity" but suggested the speech should have been planned weeks in advance—the route Uncommitted attempted. With dozens of speakers, concerns about timing were omnipresent, but Uncommitted was flexible, Susskind noted: The speech did not have to be prime time and could be from a Harris-friendly figure. He added that such events have built-in flexibility: "They let Bill Clinton speak—you know that's throwing your schedule!" Fundamentally, most arguments revolved around what Shahid called the defining factor in the decision: "fear of a Palestinian voice."[61] Again, the disconnect between Democrats' foreign policy and their claimed values seemed increasingly untenable.

Throughout the convention's last day, pressure for a Palestinian American speaker grew. The United Auto Workers union, more elected officials, and celebrities such as actor Mandy Patinkin endorsed the demand and Uncommitted released a speech from Romman that emphasized Democratic solidarity and defeating Trump alongside describing anguish among Palestinians. It was never enough. On Thursday evening, I gathered with other reporters as the sun set and Uncommitted held its last press conference of the convention. After the tension of the previous night, it was a moment of release: Some people were crying, others smiling gingerly. Though they had not met their goal, Alawieh said he was "so proud," repeating the phrase several times. The failure was not that of the antiwar movement but of the party, he continued: "I feel bad for them because they are out of step." He urged Harris to meet with relatives of those killed in Gaza and Lebanon well before the election, underscoring the activists' fight was not over while U.S.-backed attacks continued. "No more genocide no matter who is the victim," argued June Rose, a delegate from Rhode Island who repeatedly emphasized that keeping their Jewish community safe did not require killing children. Zogby offered a sense of history and slow but determined success in pushing Democrats to acknowledge

Palestinians. Then, shoulder to shoulder, the Uncommitted delegates walked in to take their place among the party faithful.

Squashed between two cheering Democratic governors, I watched as Harris gave a nomination acceptance speech offering nothing new on Israel-Palestine but a promise to ensure the United States had "the strongest, most lethal fighting force in the world." Beth Miller later called the moment the final proof the party was uninterested in antiwar votes: "I can't imagine a message less appealing to people who are trying to push toward a human rights–focused foreign policy," she told me. Even Ben-Ami, a Democratic stalwart since his work in the Clinton White House, conceded to me that although he felt Harris's rhetoric showed an important shift toward balance compared to Biden, it remained an open question if a Harris presidency would "go beyond rhetoric to actually put the rights of the Palestinian people on the same plane as Israeli security." Tellingly, the campaign felt it covered all necessary bases: "It got almost the entire Democratic Party—except for Arab Americans," a staffer told me of the address months later.

The end of the convention left Uncommitted members fearful and humiliated. After Harris's speech, thrilled Democrats filed out laughing and cheering; several told me they were fired up to help her win. Whether that win could mean anything for Gaza remained unclear.

A CHANCE SQUANDERED

The morning after Harris's speech, I learned Blinken had appointed Mira Resnick—one of the administration's most steadfast supporters of U.S. weapons for Israel whatever its conduct—as the State Department's new top official for Israeli-Palestinian affairs. Breaking the news fourteen hours after covering the decision about the Palestinian American speaker, I spotted a convergence between Washington and Chicago: As Gaza bled, Democrats' rigidity about their policy remained strong enough to keep defining both the Biden administration and the Harris campaign.

Lacking a tangible victory, antiwar organizers at least left the

Democratic National Convention confident they had, as political philosophers Michael Brownstein and Alex Madva later described early anti-Trump activism, "lost loudly . . . a crucial feature of successful political movements."[62] They used the moment to force more attention on choices by Biden and the party and prove Gaza had created a potentially consequential wedge in the anti-Trump coalition.

Democrats, meanwhile, had suggested their capacity for introspection was selective. Ahead of and during the convention, party officials resistant to concessions to Uncommitted suggested its demands were never clear, that the group of self-identified Democrats had few differences with the "Abandon Harris" camp, and that the outreach they made to antiwar groups—on the establishment's terms, so never truly threatening it—should be sufficient. The spin could not obscure daily footage of U.S.-backed killing in Gaza or the evidence that after choosing a new candidate through tough introspection, Democrats were rejecting a similar process regarding the U.S.-Israel relationship, even as they knew it was skewed and harmful morally, strategically, and politically. Privately, administration officials had long tried to distance themselves from Gaza decision-making by saying it was a matter of Biden's old-fashioned thinking and instincts. The president's grip had slipped, however, and those around him were still choosing a policy failing Palestinians. In the months ahead, leading up to the election, that choice would deeply harm Lebanese too—encouraging Netanyahu down a maximalist path and further strengthening Trump's election chances.

CHAPTER 9

ADRIFT

September–November 2024

AS SUMMER TURNED TO FALL, THE COMPREHENSIVE FAILURE of the Biden administration's Gaza policy was encapsulated in two killings, one week apart, of young Americans. At the Democratic National Convention, Rachel Goldberg had closed her heart-rending speech with an appeal to her kidnapped son. A football lover hoping to travel the world, he lost part of his left arm as he lobbed grenades out of the bunker he and his friends crammed into on October 7, and Hamas in April released a disturbing video in which he spoke of needing medical care.[1] "Hersh, Hersh," Goldberg had said during her speech, her voice shaking, "If you can hear us: We love you. Stay strong. Survive." Days later, Hamas fighters shot Hersh Goldberg-Polin twice in the head in a tunnel under Rafah and murdered five other hostages kept with him.[2] Israeli soldiers heading for the tunnel found the bodies; the IDF announced the discovery on August 31, and Hamas later said its militants were under new directives about how to handle captives if the IDF was approaching.[3]

On September 6, an Israeli bullet killed activist Ayşenur Ezgi Eygi in the occupied West Bank, as she protested Israeli settlements that were illegal under international law and, officially at least, opposed by the United States. At twenty-six, Eygi had been an activist for years, challenging Trump's 2016 election and the Dakota Access Pipeline; she was known at the University of Washington, from which she had graduated months earlier, for "a gentle, generous, and powerful spirit."[4] The IDF said it shot at an instigator of stone-throwing, then claimed Eygi was "highly likely hit indirectly and unintentionally," expressing "deepest regret."[5]

Neither loss swayed Washington's faith in its disastrous policy—though the difference in the administration's reactions was telling. Goldberg-Polin got unique attention from the White House. Amos Hochstein, the Lebanon envoy who fellow officials said Biden treated as a surrogate son, was a friend of the family, and Jake Sullivan later described the killing as a personal defeat; by September 3, Attorney General Merrick Garland unveiled federal charges against Hamas leaders, citing their hundreds of victims but naming only Hersh.[6] But while officials knew the ceasefire deal they backed and Hamas had moved toward would have quickly freed Goldberg-Polin and two other executed hostages, the administration remained unwilling to tackle the remaining obstacle: Netanyahu's blank check from Washington to continue the war.[7] As the Israeli leader stuck by his political partner Itamar Ben-Gvir, Ben-Gvir's talk of brutality toward Palestinian prisoners intensified Hamas's violence toward Israeli detainees, one captive said upon being freed.[8] Biden, Sullivan, Tony Blinken, Brett McGurk, and others held a two-hour call to discuss whether they could have done anything differently to save Goldberg-Polin—and reached the comfortable conclusion nobody was to blame except Hamas, assessing, per a report in *The Atlantic*, the house magazine of the D.C. elite, that no "magical act of diplomacy" or "brilliant flourish of creative statecraft" could produce a better trajectory.[9] One straightforward route—consistent, targeted U.S. pressure on Israel—had, of course, never been attempted.

Eygi's case pointed to a pattern of high-profile Israeli violence toward American citizens that predated Biden's presidency and continued because it drew few consequences. She was volunteering with the International Solidarity Movement (ISM), a nonviolent group supporting Palestinian rights; in 2003, an Israeli military bulldozer crushed twenty-three-year-old ISM volunteer Rachel Corrie, a Washington State native like Eygi, as she tried to prevent the demolition of a Palestinian family's home.[10] The IDF cleared its soldiers for Corrie's death, and the United States never investigated the incident.[11] In 2022, when Israeli firing killed the Palestinian American journalist Shireen Abu Akleh, Israel initially denied involvement, then conceded a soldier likely shot her, but, as with Corrie, punished no personnel. Still, after Eygi's killing, the administration said Israel should investigate itself, with the president first hypothesizing the fatal bullet ricocheted off the ground and then, after the IDF statement, saying he was "outraged" but it was "a tragic error."[12] Even after *The Washington Post* undercut Israel's narrative—finding Eygi was hit in the head more than thirty minutes after Palestinians clashed with IDF soldiers and was far from the troops—State Department spokesperson Matt Miller said the United States would not launch its own inquiry until the Israelis completed their probe.[13] Ultimately, Biden never opened a U.S. investigation into Eygi's killing.

A double standard for misdeeds by Israel compared with those by others was clear but not new. What the Goldberg-Polin and Eygi deaths revealed, however, was that the United States was now fueling continued killing without even a plausible reason why; American persuasion was not influencing Israeli decisions on how and whether to keep fighting and neither were American priorities such as hostages. With military and diplomatic support from Washington on autopilot, Netanyahu exacerbated the decimation of Palestinians in Gaza, launched outrageous attacks and then a full-scale war in Lebanon, and worsened tensions with Iran—deepening Americans' complicity in war crimes, crimes against humanity, and future conflict.

IMPUNITY

The Biden administration's war policy seemed in a state of drift by September as it lacked any sense of building toward a goal or evidence the officials responsible for it were even trying to provide direction.

Their choice to be rudderless had tangible ramifications, from human loss to damage in legal, moral, strategic, and political terms.

U.S. officials were once again boosting Tel Aviv's sense of being above U.S. law. Conversations about Israel violating Section 620I of the Foreign Assistance Act, through its restrictions on U.S.-funded humanitarian aid, were new—a product of the war—but Eygi's killing reignited long-running concerns about the Leahy Law, which bars U.S. military support for foreign forces over accusations they commit major human rights violations and do not penalize perpetrators. Though Washington regularly applied Leahy to other partner countries to spur them to improve their behavior, no administration applied it to Israel, never providing a "substantive or credible" reason, Tim Rieser, a congressional staffer who crafted the statute in 1997 alongside then-senator Patrick Leahy, told me. Blinken said Israel was not exempt, but in May and August said minor IDF reprimands were sufficient for the United States to keep arming Israeli units allegedly involved in grave abuses.[14] Effectively, Biden's team offered "lip service," Rieser said, adding: "If the law had been implemented over the years, maybe the IDF would have complied with their obligations." Less than two years after Blinken announced he would not apply Leahy to the ultra-Orthodox Netzah Yehuda unit because Israel had "effectively remediated" its misconduct, some of its soldiers detained a crew of CNN journalists, assaulting one.[15]

Administration officials put the onus on Israel to improve its rules of engagement; the IDF's habits were, however, partly American creations that endangered Americans, while ignoring Leahy undermined U.S. attempts to encourage stability. In July, Chris Van Hollen, the Maryland senator, traveled to Israel and the West Bank. He met relatives of Tawfic Abdel Jabbar and Mohammad Khdour, teenage U.S. citizens who were fatally shot by Israelis earlier in 2024, among the more than 550 Palestinians, including 131 children, killed in the region since October 7.[16] When Van Hollen raised the cases to Jack Lew, Biden's ambassador in Jerusalem, Lew said Israel was investigating and it was "a slow process," the senator recalled to me. No result or discipline ever came, and Van Hollen told me of the administration: "There was never the determination to seek justice."

The United States was instead deepening the man-made humanitarian crisis forced upon Palestinians in Gaza by Israel. Malnutrition among children nearly quadrupled in northern Gaza and increased 150 percent in the south by July, the United Nations reported.[17] The average daily number of truckloads of supplies allowed in by Israeli authorities, the Biden administration's preferred measure for aid in Gaza, reached a record low in August, down to sixty-nine compared with five hundred before the war, and had already been insufficient, humanitarian groups reported, saying more than 1 million Palestinians received no food rations at all that month.

The United Nations stopped distributing supplies that did enter the strip because the IDF kept expanding its no-go areas.[18] Overcrowding of displaced Palestinians combined with Israel's destruction of health and sanitary infrastructure—which resulted in reduced vaccination rates, widespread open sewage, and severe shortages of clean water—to cause an outbreak of polio, the virus eradicated in most of the world, including in Gaza twenty-five years earlier. Aid groups began preparing a polio vaccination campaign to reach hundreds of thousands of children, while knowing at least 289 humanitarian workers had been killed by Israeli air strikes so far.[19] Israeli officials denied that Palestinians faced mass deprivation, promoting a draft paper from Israeli academics that used Israeli defense ministry data to suggest people in Gaza were receiving calories exceeding accepted humanitarian minimums. The paper covered only January to April, overlooked aid distribution problems, and analyzed what entered the strip, not what Palestinian families received, the nonprofit Refugees International noted.[20] Though the Biden administration publicly rejected some Israeli contentions, like the claim Hamas stole aid en masse, its tolerance of Israel's mishandling of supplies tacitly bolstered Tel Aviv's dubious arguments—morally aligning the United States with Netanyahu against Israeli rights organizations and most humanitarian experts, including American officials. Meanwhile, as Biden's spokespeople publicly touted American aid donations and advocacy, U.S. officials' impact was limited as top officials from various domains worked inconsistently and separately on different projects and requests of the Israelis, "in their own orbits," a USAID official told me, recalling that USAID "wouldn't share even the most basic information with" the team of Lise Grande, who had taken over as Biden's humanitarian envoy for Gaza. Like her predecessor Satterfield and other administration leaders, Grande continued "losing the forest for the trees" in negotiations with Israel, a State Department official told me. The administration continously tolerated "sleight of hand," a State lawyer separately argued to me, saying Israeli concessions on one concern, say visas for aid workers, would distract from worsening behavior elsewhere, like closing a crossing point into Gaza.

Brett McGurk—who was understood as a key player because he had Biden's ear—and his team by now had minimal involvement in assistance, the USAID official said, though they occasionally intervened in other U.S. officials' discussions with aid workers about delivering supplies with instructions that were "some combination of not realistic, not principled, but whatever was convenient for the government of Israel." The USAID staffer interpreted the change as an indication that humanitarian improvement was no longer a prime concern for Washington and was now disconnected from the ongoing ceasefire bid.

As the administration continued promising a truce and a two-state solution, officials stuck to orthodoxies that had not delivered those aims while long eroding regional stability. Senior White House officials knew Netanyahu was maximalist in negotiations, but they did not challenge his posturing or overhaul their diplomatic strategy. "No one is more committed to freeing the hostages than me," Netanyahu claimed after Goldberg-Polin's murder. Soon afterward, the German newspaper *Bild* published a document purporting to show Hamas was stymieing the ceasefire talks; Israeli prosecutors later said Netanyahu aides illegally leaked the material to create that impression.[21] Blinken insisted a deal was close even as Netanyahu said otherwise and called on his cabinet to endorse his demand for Israel to control the Gaza-Egypt border, a position other top Israelis felt was not about security but about torpedoing ceasefire talks.[22] Gershon Baskin, an Israeli peace activist and negotiator, told me he brokered an alternative draft truce with Hamas contacts that he repeatedly pushed U.S. officials to consider, only to be told McGurk refused to change course in negotiations. By mid-September, the faction toughened its terms too, demanding a bigger Palestinian prisoner release.[23]

Core to the stasis on a deal and Netanyahu's intransigence was general Israeli skepticism of Palestinian self-actualization, and while the administration said it felt differently, Biden aides were falling back into foreign policy patterns that gave Middle Eastern populations little say in their future. In early September, Blinken, McGurk, and other officials participated in a first-of-its-kind "Middle East–America Dialogue"—an exclusive summit that featured no Palestinian speakers but a mix of Republican and Democratic elites, prominent Israelis, and officials from Arab autocracies. At the State Department, Blinken hosted Tony Blair, the chief British architect of the disastrous 2003 U.S.-led invasion of Iraq. Drafted with input from Israel and the United Arab Emirates but not the Palestinian Authority, their eventual postwar proposal for Gaza minimized Palestinian control of the strip; it resembled the pre–October 7 thinking of offering Palestinians little political independence but better living conditions, which was widely seen as helping to inspire the attack.[24] The secretary was also leaning on Jamie Rubin, a friend from their days in the Clinton administration who became "the only person [Blinken] was listening to," a State Department official told me, fueling frustration among his other advisors that he was becoming steeped in "1992 ideas." Amid the War on Terror, Rubin had argued that "excuse makers" should be admonished for suggesting Zionism, colonialism, or the Iraq invasion drove militancy—a position that dodged U.S. culpability, treated military crackdowns as unavoidable, and cast some people, chiefly Muslims, as intrinsically hateful.[25]

The administration had already proved stasis and fear around U.S.-Israel ties would define its Gaza policy more than domestic dissent, and policy elites were ensuring more U.S.-fueled slaughter was likely regardless of the election result. Now, the political ramifications of those positions were becoming clearer. On September 19, Uncommitted announced it could not endorse Harris, even though Trump would "accelerate the killing," because she would not abandon Biden's "unconditional weapons policy" for Israel.[26] With her campaign meeting none of their demands, the group felt providing its blessing would de-motivate supporters, spokesperson Waleed Shahid later told me. Separately, a Harris campaign official told me it was understood that Uncommitted would not help the campaign to organize, but argued the group riled up voters without planning for how to calm them—once more casting antiwar voters, not decision-makers, as irresponsible. Though Democratic officials argued avoiding a rejection was a success, and Harris could not have risked pro-Israel support, the move confirmed a party-wide rift over Gaza would persist through November. The Trump campaign, meanwhile, continued its double game to whittle away support for Harris. Hours after Uncommitted's announcement, the GOP nominee again called himself Israel's "protector," saying American Jews should abandon Democrats and promoting the antisemitic idea that "the Jewish people would have a lot to do with a loss" for him.[27] Trump allies were simultaneously wooing Arab Americans and Muslim Americans, particularly in Michigan, by citing Biden's Gaza record and liberal social policies, as a conservative political action committee was, in Arab-majority Dearborn, funding ads calling Harris a steadfast Israel supporter.[28] The war might not determine the election, but the intersection of the two reflected a general theme of Democrats playing defense on Biden's record, in which Americans had consistently been disappointed.

WAR, WAR, AND MORE WAR

Many observers, including critics of Israel, called war in Gaza a necessity, self-defense against Hamas. War in Lebanon, on the other hand, was universally understood as a choice. Hezbollah, the Hamas-aligned Lebanese group, had long violated UN Security Council resolution

1701, which said only Lebanese authorities and UN peacekeepers should be armed in southern Lebanon, between the Litani River and the "Blue Line"—the quasi-border established in 2000 when the IDF ended a twenty-two-year occupation of Lebanese territory, which had sought to quash Palestinian militancy but by committing mass atrocities ended up fostering Hezbollah. After October 7, Hezbollah's indiscriminate, ostensibly pro-Palestinian strikes from outposts near the line were violations too, but so were Israeli responses, which intensified the back-and-forth.[29] Biden aides hoped both could be persuaded to resume uneasy coexistence, reassuring tens of thousands living near the border, many of whom had fled their homes; the tit-for-tat had by mid-September already killed at least 137 Lebanese civilians and 26 Israeli civilians. Yet for a year, the administration misread Israel's perspective while influencing it not toward compromise but conflict, exported weapons American officials knew were intended for use in Lebanon, and, particularly in the run-up to Israel's eventual invasion, bolstered pro-war arguments.

The administration assumed the human toll of a Hezbollah-Israel war was intolerable, and that U.S. diplomacy on Gaza could ease tensions generally. Neither prospect meant much in Tel Aviv, however, as Netanyahu scrambled ceasefire efforts and U.S. officials struggled to convince their Israeli counterparts Hezbollah could kill thousands of their citizens; Israel felt Hezbollah's strength meant it was time to kneecap it, with unfettered support from Washington. Other players felt a Lebanon war was too dangerous: France, an ally of Lebanese Christians for centuries, the country's former colonial ruler and still a key economic partner, and the U.S. ally closest to Hezbollah; Arab states, chiefly Saudi Arabia, which might again be asked to fund rebuilding Lebanon after Israeli attacks; and Iran, Hezbollah's patron. But the administration was in no position to develop a united front, despite shared concerns for the 6 million Lebanese, 1.5 million Syrian refugees in their country, and possible ripple effects of another war, including a U.S.-Iran confrontation. Sticking to bellicose American foreign policy and Israeli preferences, Biden had avoided U.S. diplomacy with

Iran, making it difficult to now coordinate on de-escalation; and while France could nudge Hezbollah toward concessions for a deal, which the group wanted, Biden was unlikely to deliver Netanyahu. Offers of closer ties with the Saudis had failed to sway his Gaza calculus, and the red line moment had ended administration discussions of using U.S. leverage. On September 16, Biden's Lebanon envoy Hochstein met with Netanyahu, still promoting diplomacy. The very next day, Israel began a hugely brutal Lebanon war that Hochstein and other U.S. officials soon cheered on.

At 3:30 p.m. on Tuesday, September 17, thousands of pagers began beeping in homes, grocery stores, and streets across Lebanon. People—some of them part of Hezbollah, which had distributed the pagers, some relatives or bystanders—reached for the devices, as the digital age has trained us all to do. Then the pagers exploded. "Everything went dark. . . . I felt I was in a whirlpool," Sarah Jaffal, a twenty-one-year-old who picked up a family member's device, later said; she lost her right eye and four fingers and sustained extensive injuries to her face.[30] Others still had pagers in their pockets, collapsing in sudden pain or being blown off motorcycles.[31] As people panicked and ambulances tried to help the roughly 2,800 wounded, no one knew whether more violence was coming and hospitals were overwhelmed, performing emergency amputations and other chilling surgeries: "In my past twenty-five years of practice, I've never removed as many eyes," an ophthalmologist at Beirut's Mount Lebanon University Hospital said.[32] Among the twelve casualties were two children and two health workers; the injured included Hezbollah personnel in Syria.

Understood as Israeli even before journalists confirmed the Mossad spy agency had intercepted the pagers, and captured in videos that went viral, the assault petrified the Lebanese. It affirmed Israel's growing campaign would extend beyond Hezbollah fighters, discounting international safeguards for civilians much like the IDF's Gaza operation. Among those carrying pagers were staff of the group's nonmilitary institutions—and those triggering the explosions likely did not know where the devices were at the time of detonation—while legal experts noted booby traps violated a global protocol to which Israel had agreed.[33] Simultaneously, the pager attack showed Israel had infiltrated everyday life in Lebanon, a nation already scarred by repeated Israeli interventions, to a dystopian degree. One witness to blood running down a street in Tyre spoke of "panic in every sense of the word . . . it's as if we are watching an episode of 'Black Mirror'—these things aren't supposed to happen." Traumatized, another society of millions now felt as Gaza had for nearly a year: that nowhere was safe.

The anxiety swelled when, around 5:00 p.m. the next day, another set of larger explosives went off in walkie-talkies, setting apartments ablaze and sparking chaos at crowded sites such as the funerals for a child and a medic killed by the pagers.[34] As emergency personnel struggled to get through the pandemonium, those blasts killed 20 and injured 450. Subsequently, messages circulated telling people to turn off their wi-fi routers and fear "normal items you have at home" ahead of another attack, *Los Angeles Times* correspondent Nabih Bulos reported.[35] A sense of grim anticipation and Lebanese vulnerability grew as Israeli defense minister Yoav Gallant tacitly took credit for the attacks, praising Israeli intelligence and military operatives and speaking of being at "the beginning of a new era in this war."[36] That he was comfortable endorsing tactics that twenty-two UN experts condemned as possible war crimes underscored how the harrowing pager attack had not, over twenty-four hours, drawn any meaningful rebuke for Israel, particularly from the United States; instead, there was a fascination bordering on enthusiasm about the Israeli spycraft and technical skill behind the operation.[37] Some of Israel's supporters treated the deadly incident as a rallying cry—a basis for pride and for mocking Tel Aviv's critics, hinting they could face death by pager, as a September 19 cartoon in the right-wing magazine *National Review* did about Rashida Tlaib. Netanyahu eventually began gifting shiny commemorative pagers to ardent Israel backers like Senator John Fetterman of Pennsylvania and Trump as symbols of Israel's prowess.[38] It was another moment that crystallized the dichotomy in experiences of Israel's post–October 7 choices between pro-Israel voices internationally, mainly Americans and Europeans, and those directly affected by its U.S.-backed decisions.

Obscured by Israel's triumphalism was the reality that the brazen attacks did not constitute a strategy: There was still no sign of either a plan for entering and then leaving Lebanon or concluding its campaign in Gaza. As Hezbollah continued striking Israel, CNN and *Axios* reported that Tel Aviv activated the pagers because it felt the Lebanese group was about to uncover the plot; months later, Netanyahu publicly confirmed as much.[39] The risks of a Lebanon war remained high, and an Israeli political official told Mossad representatives: "We cannot make [such] a strategic decision . . . while counting on a toy," indicating both wariness and how policy discussions were minimizing civilian deaths.[40] The Biden administration, however, was still dodging scrutiny of Israel's choices; while White House spokesman John Kirby tried to distance the United States from the attacks and other officials clarified Washington had no specific warning of them, Blinken blamed sudden events for repeatedly derailing Gaza ceasefire talks without specifying the Israeli-caused devastation.[41] Still drifting, the Biden team was bringing millions to a darker place. In the days following the walkie-talkie attack, Israel drastically increased air strikes into Lebanon, leveling buildings, striking far north of the Israel-Lebanon border, and, on September 23, killing at least 558 people, in the deadliest day for the Lebanese since the last Israel-Hezbollah war nearly twenty years earlier.[42] Though the IDF said it was targeting Hezbollah weaponry and fighters, local health officials reported many civilian deaths. The stage was set for a shocking redux: The conflict monitor Airwars reported that by October 2, Israel's attacks on Lebanon represented "aside from Gaza . . . the most intense aerial campaign that we know of in the last twenty years."[43]

DELUSIONS OF DIPLOMACY

Bombing notwithstanding, Israeli officials still maintained that they might not invade Lebanon—an impression the Biden administration promoted, helping Netanyahu expand his new war step-by-step as U.S. suggestions of imminent peace staved off pushback that might restrain him. Israeli officials spoke of a surreal concept of "de-escalation through escalation": Under more pressure, including from Lebanese terrified of collective punishment, Hezbollah might agree to decouple its strategy from the Gaza war and stop attacking Israel, the logic went. U.S. officials endorsed that rationale, noting Israel was targeting shared enemies like militants involved in killing Americans in 1983, even though they knew many Israeli decision-makers sought not a deal with Hezbollah but to erode the group, which would entail far broader fighting.[44] The dynamic made it easy for both Washington and Tel Aviv to quickly ditch diplomacy. At the end of September, the United States pivoted from encouraging calm to echoing Israeli bravado. Largely occurring during the annual UN gathering of world leaders in New York, the shift underscored that Biden's presidency, which began by pledging judicious American policies abroad compared with the prior Trump era, was closing by facilitating international havoc and mammoth violations of globally agreed-upon standards.

The United States and Israel often sought support for their policies by calling Iran the root of Middle Eastern violence for threatening them and backing vicious forces like Syrian dictator Bashar Assad, Hamas, and Hezbollah. But as the UN high-level week began on September 24, Iran was projecting moderation and, unlike its foes, bombing no one. That morning, I was at a long U-shaped table with other reporters invited to meet the new Iranian president, Masoud Pezeshkian, whose July inauguration had been immediately followed by an Israeli strike on Tehran. He praised Hezbollah's rockets into Israel and said regional carnage was driven by U.S. support for Israel—while also emphasizing interest in another international agreement over the Iranian nuclear program, a step toward less enmity between Tehran and Washington. Flanked by Iranians who negotiated the last nuclear deal, which he noted the United States abandoned under Trump despite Iran's compliance, Pezeshkian repeatedly asked: "In what language do we need to tell the world we do not seek instability?" (A canny politician whose rise was inseparable from Iran's hard-line leadership, he dodged questions about Iranian repression by pointing to Gaza, demonstrating how impunity for human rights violations enables abuses worldwide.)

Several hours later, at a gathering of journalists and officials on a midtown Manhattan rooftop, I spotted Amos Hochstein, the Biden aide at the heart of ongoing talks to avert a Lebanon war. The United States was working on Israel and the Lebanese government—which Hezbollah opponents hoped would limit the group's power—while France managed discussions with Hezbollah and its allies, a French official later told me. Yet when I got Hochstein alone, he gave little impression the United States was seriously challenging Israel's pro-war arguments. An IDF veteran himself, the American peace emissary enthusiastically spoke of Israeli success in infiltrating Hezbollah and claimed nearly every home in southern Lebanon housed military equipment for the group, a depiction suggesting a sweeping assault was justified. Other sources described Hochstein to me as usually effective in handling the Israelis and Lebanese and wary of an invasion, but also sometimes credulous of Israeli counterparts and keen to suggest he and the United States were shaping events, so he would shift positions to create that impression. "Amos is very Washington-smart . . . he knows where power is blowing and he gets there," Ben Rhodes, who worked with Hochstein in the Obama administration, later told me. That evening, as other reporters mobbed Hochstein, he mostly smiled and batted away questions about whether a Lebanon deal was imminent. I felt I'd gotten an answer.

The next day, September 25, Biden and French president Emmanuel Macron issued a joint statement urging an immediate Israel-Lebanon deal. Privately, a twenty-one-day truce to buy time for crafting a final agreement, as well as for possible success in Gaza negotiations, had been blessed by Hezbollah, and U.S. officials said it had Israel's support, a French official later recalled to me. Lebanese prime minister Najib Mikati, who was using UN appearances to highlight how Israel's bombardment had killed hundreds of his people, was ready to endorse an accord, and U.S. officials expected a public green light from Netanyahu too.[45] But the administration seemed to have again relied on its own rosy vision of Israeli preferences and politics rather than acknowledging the country's reality, producing what the French official called "a fake ceasefire." The official said Israel was always clear it sought full-blown war without a Hezbollah settlement in its favor; that was hard to square with the Biden administration's belief that Tel Aviv could embrace an accord also tolerable to the Lebanese group. After the Franco-American statement, Netanyahu's ultranationalist political allies Itamar Ben-Gvir and Bezalel Smotrich threatened to topple his government—reprising the spoiler role they had played amid other peace efforts in a way officials could have foreseen and which, once more, gave Netanyahu cover to revert to talk of war. His office soon denied a Lebanon truce was close, and upon reaching New York, Netanyahu said Israel would "continue to hit Hezbollah with all our might."[46] The United States was not only in the backseat but humiliated, and Lebanon seemed even more vulnerable as Biden's dealmaking on its behalf appeared as hollow as his Rafah red line.

White House spokesperson John Kirby accused Israel of flip-flopping, and privately, Hochstein and Brett McGurk harangued Israeli minister Ron Dermer, while Biden told confidants he was angry with Netanyahu.[47] The truth of the administration's position, however, came in an announcement from Israel's defense ministry, saying it had received another package of U.S. military aid worth almost $9 billion.[48] "That was amazing to us—it was just, what?" the French official sputtered to me; Netanyahu still had free rein. Two Biden aides later told me they felt manipulated by Israel. Yet after countless instances of Netanyahu stymieing the administration with the same playbook, much of the blame for the mounting crisis rested with Washington for failing to adapt. Even as Hochstein seemed sincere about his diplomacy, some senior U.S. officials believed Israel was stringing him along, but space in the administration for opposing views and policy changes—like threatening to halt weapons—had shrunk, creating an environment like the one in which, a year earlier, Biden blessed the onset of the Gaza offensive.

As momentum toward war sped up, the administration did little to slow it. On September 27, Netanyahu addressed the UN's General

Assembly, calling it a "swamp of antisemitic bile" and saying Israel wanted peace while its critics spread "lies and slanders." Shortly afterward, the IDF dropped at least eighty bombs on Beirut—fifteen or more of them U.S.-made "bunker busters" that are especially damaging—and leveled four high-rise buildings. Netanyahu published a photograph of himself approving the strike between UN meetings in New York, underscoring how international discussions seemed irrelevant to Lebanon's darkening fate. The bombing killed Hassan Nasrallah, the longtime Hezbollah leader, and several others. Riling up Israelis—who saw an archvillain eliminated and an opportunity to debilitate Hezbollah while it was reeling—as well as Hezbollah's supporters in Lebanon and beyond, the assassination also eliminated the possibility of compromise.

The United States and France continued to promote their truce, but a French official told me it was clear "it was too late." Israel began carpet bombing Dahiyeh, the southern suburb of Beirut where Hezbollah dominated but where hundreds of thousands of civilians lived too. As in Gaza, the IDF issued orders for people to flee that provided little notice—thirty to forty-five minutes on average, and mostly coming between 10:00 p.m. and 4:00 a.m., according to a later report from Oxfam and ActionAid[49]—and were often inaccurate. Still, nine hundred thousand Lebanese fled their homes in just the last week of September.[50]

By September 30, Biden aides were privately telling me and other reporters an Israeli invasion of Lebanon—the sixth in fifty years—was beginning but saying it would be limited. The claim was doubtful: "Everyone who says it's going to be 'limited' is a white man who thinks a million dead brown people is 'limited,'" a U.S. official told me for an article I published at the time.[51] Israeli strikes had killed more than one thousand people, a quarter of them women and children, over the previous two weeks, and Hezbollah had an extensive arsenal and tens of thousands of fighters.[52] The IDF confirmed its incursion early on October 1, describing narrow raids in an echo of the United States' message, but it had readied thousands of additional troops in northern Israel.[53] A week later, the administration was fully aboard with a war it once called unacceptable: Officials told CNN they no longer sought an Israel-Hezbollah deal, and when Biden and Kamala Harris held their first call with Netanyahu since August, on October 9, a White House readout did not mention a Lebanon ceasefire. Biden's team felt Hezbollah should have ended its Gaza-linked attacks sooner and heeded Hochstein's messages to the group that without shift, he could not hold off an Israeli offensive, a senior Biden aide later told me.[54] "It was better . . . to buy the Israeli narrative because they wouldn't get anything else," the French official concluded of the United States. They pointed me to a French saying: "Make of what is imposed on you a virtue."

The new offensive, however, looked far from virtuous, as Israel deployed brutal tactics that had been normalized in Gaza. Attacks on health-care workers became a theme; while some were associated with Hezbollah's civilian arm, that did not erase the special protections medical infrastructure holds under international law. Israeli strikes killed seven at a medical center in Beirut on October 3 and the following day hit two hospitals, forcing one, where seven paramedics were killed, to shut down. A Human Rights Watch investigation soon found no evidence for the Israeli allegation that militants used ambulances and hospitals to hide fighters and weaponry (a line the IDF also used to justify decimating Gaza's health sector); one of the paramedics the group interviewed was soon killed in a separate Israeli strike.[55] Meanwhile, Israel's dozens of orders telling people to abandon villages and neighborhoods or risk death eventually displaced 1.4 million Lebanese and put new pressure on hundreds of thousands of Syrian refugees who were already impoverished. The latter were excluded from some shelters and evicted from others; facing an impossible choice, roughly 375,000 returned to Syria, where resources were even more scarce and they risked persecution, with some almost immediately arrested by the Assad regime.[56] They trudged along crowded roads reduced to rubble by Israeli strikes: "We almost died getting here," Issa Hilal, one Syrian refugee, told the Associated Press at a border crossing.[57] The IDF also bombed areas home to Palestinian refugees, saying it was pursuing Hamas. As parts of south Lebanon emptied and Israel took full control, Israeli troops bulldozed and blew up homes, cemeteries, mosques, and agricultural infrastructure, leaving some areas with more than 70 percent of structures destroyed. Israel's argument—building on the thinking shared by U.S. officials like Hochstein—was that such damage was necessary to incapacitate Hezbollah. Visual evidence showed soldiers removing weapons and filling in tunnels, however, proving they could pursue alternatives, Amnesty International reported.[58] More sinister motivations seemed plausible: sheer ruthlessness or a deliberate plan to retain land—as Israel often did after invading its neighbors—by effectively ethnically cleansing the region; some far-right Israelis were already talking about establishing settlements in Lebanese territory.[59]

The journey into another U.S.-backed Israeli war was a microcosm of how fecklessness and callousness had come to define the Biden administration. For the long run, it ensured American policy and weapons had exacerbated hatred in the region, potentially for generations. The Star of David was carved into the earth of one Lebanese town, satellite imagery showed. Adiba Finsh, age sixty-six, who had left her village six months before the invasion, eventually found a video of the IDF blowing up her home. "They shouted: 'Wow! Yay!'" Finsh told Amnesty. "I watch this video every day."

A HOLLOW ANNIVERSARY

At the one-year anniversary of Hamas's onslaught and Israel's ever-expanding retaliation, Washington focused on solidarity with Tel Aviv. Marking a horrifying past, the moment lacked any meaningful sense of success, lessons learned, or progress toward a better future.

The Biden administration's commemorations pledged never to forget Israel's losses while only gesturing to those of others. The president mentioned Palestinian suffering but repeatedly blamed Hamas without acknowledging Israeli killing; he condemned "hate in all its forms" but twice mentioned antisemitism without acknowledging animus toward Muslims or Arabs, despite the killing of six-year-old Wadea al-Fayoume, the attack on Palestinian students in Vermont, an attack in May on a three-year-old Palestinian American girl in Texas, and a severe uptick in complaints of anti-Muslim bias, many at work and school, received by the Council on American-Islamic Relations.[60] America "mourns the death of every innocent who died on October 7 and in the year since," Blinken's statement read, but neither he nor the president offered new ideas for how Washington might stem the bleeding and rage nurturing further violence.[61] The day before, an Israeli attack in the packed Gaza town of Deir al-Balah hit a mosque that was so close to a morgue, the nineteen Palestinians killed were simply carried over.[62] Witnessed by NPR producer Anas Baba, Hakima Al Jamal cried out as she watched her dying father be moved: "Enough, world. . . . We're so tired." In Israel that same day, an Arab citizen killed a young police officer and wounded nine others.[63]

Within Gaza-focused chat groups among government officials, members that morning said they refused to even read Blinken's statement and were questioning their careers. Higher-ranking Biden administration personnel still, however, sought a positive sheen for their policy. At Israel's embassy in Washington, Jake Sullivan gave a speech, choking up as he described a reading of a Hebrew prayer in the White House that morning. Calling the past year a "crucible," Sullivan suggested it had silver linings, arguing Israel's "remarkable capacity" and "ironclad" American backing could produce "enduring strategic gains." The word salad reflected Sullivan's thinking and the inclinations of the U.S. national security establishment he embodied: Regardless of the gut-wrenching cost and their mutual disdain, Netanyahu and Biden might still take credit for a new Middle East in which Israel held more sway.

A deeper reflection on the anniversary benefited few policymakers. Both U.S. and Israeli statements said Hamas-led attackers had killed twelve hundred people; the IDF, its American backers, and Netanyahu had disagreements, but all could face tough questions if they acknowledged the growing signs Israel's response to the invasion caused some of the deaths that day. People such as Efrat Katz, a sixty-eight-year-old remembered as the "perfect, most indulgent grandmother," were killed as the IDF shot at vehicles heading back to Gaza, with officers later saying that troops followed the Israeli military's "Hannibal directive" by attacking vehicles suspected of carrying abducted Israeli soldiers to prevent their being captured and forcing concessions from their government.[64] (The IDF neither confirms nor denies following such a directive, but an Israeli air force probe reportedly confirmed it was in use on October 7.)[65]

Netanyahu marked the date by dodging protests or scrutiny through a prerecorded address to the government's official commemoration that echoed Sullivan, trumpeting U.S.-Israeli battlefield success. He framed Hamas's attack as "the price of our revival" and rejected "prematurely" ending the U.S.-backed wars.

In their amorphous talk of strategy and state power, officials were helping obscure human agony. The Biden administration was once again dovetailing with Netanyahu more than the group it called its priority and saw him as neglecting: hostage families, who overwhelmingly supported an immediate deal with Hamas. Some, as well as some relatives of those killed on October 7, held an alternative to the prime minister's memorial. Speakers demanded that Netanyahu be held accountable for permitting the attack and still not freeing the 101 remaining hostages—half still alive, facing torture, threats, and other mistreatment from their Palestinian captors while Hamas still denied visits from the International Committee of the Red Cross despite months of appeals for humanitarian monitoring.[66] (Israel had also barred the Red Cross from visiting its Palestinian prisoners, including at least one thousand taken from Gaza,[67] for the past year.)[68] In Washington, activists lined up thousands of pairs of empty shoes before the White House to represent slaughtered Palestinian children and, that evening, gathered in Malcolm X Park for a somber memorial before a banner with a phrase from Jewish theology that had become a pro-peace slogan across religious and ethnic lines: "Every life, a universe."

A week later, Tel Aviv and Washington redoubled their claims of being vindicated when Israel announced its killing of Yahya Sinwar. Eliminating the Hamas chief and October 7 planner was perhaps the biggest symbolic victory of the entire Gaza campaign. Israeli soldiers on a routine patrol in Rafah on October 16 had killed three Palestinian fighters, the IDF said, then left their corpses and only suspected and eventually confirmed one was Sinwar during another patrol the next morning.[69] It was at once incredibly dramatic and shockingly bland: Israel had exacted vengeance upon the man it had treated as Public Enemy Number One for a year, but the way it did so underscored the seeming randomness of the ongoing killing.

Netanyahu and his allies in Israel treated the unplanned moment as a masterstroke that should silence their critics.[70] In Hebrew, he argued: "It is now clear to everyone, in Israel and in the world, why we insisted on not ending the war."[71] In a subsequent English statement on video, Netanyahu spoke of the "beginning of the end" of the war—while making no mention of Palestinians' future and hinting at pursuing other conflicts by pledging to eliminate Hamas allies in Iraq and Yemen.[72] He was buoyed and pugnacious.

Biden validated Netanyahu's presentation, congratulating him and saying the development increased the chances for his ceasefire proposal; he even sought to make the killing part of his own legacy, noting the United States gave Israel intelligence on Hamas leaders.[73] As ever, the soft touch was futile. Netanyahu could now be more obstinate about matters like freeing Palestinian prisoners in exchange for hostages, and, knowing both Trump and Harris were calling to end the war, he would likely hold back concessions in the Hamas negotiations so he could deploy them to please Biden's successor.[74] Saying the IDF "bumped into the guy accidentally," a senior U.S. official later complained to me that Israelis and their hard-line American supporters began arguing that if Biden had provided more aggressive American military support, Sinwar would have been killed sooner. For Israel, the lame-duck administration was at most a mix of arsenal and punching bag.

CARVING UP GAZA

The irrelevance by now of the Biden administration's stated goals of ending the war and upholding international law became clearest in October, as the IDF took its most brazen steps toward ethnic cleansing and annexing Gaza—violations of U.S. and UN edicts that no one was likely to punish.

Northern Gaza had particular importance throughout Israel's offensive. Home to 1.2 million Palestinians before the war—largely in urban neighborhoods in the strip's eponymous largest city, the vast Jabalia refugee camp and the village of the same name, and the towns of Beit Hanoun and Beit Lahiya—the area still had four hundred thousand residents, two hundred thousand of them children, mostly under the age of ten.[75] Israeli officials and analysts argued the lingering population made it impossible to root out Hamas; Palestinians there, many descended from people who had been forced out of areas that became Israel during the 1948 Nakba, said they would not leave for fear of permanent displacement.[76] Significantly, the region faced the tightest IDF siege: Its northern and eastern land borders were with Israel, and Israeli forces controlled its southern frontier and blockaded its coastline. Far from the main entry points for aid along Egypt's border with Gaza, the north was hardest hit as Israeli restrictions on the few approved shipments limited their flow northward, adding hours to journeys across the strip and often canceling them altogether. Famine set in, U.S. officials, the United Nations, and the humanitarian group Refugees International said, in April, May, and September, respectively.[77] For some, falling chances of Palestinian survival in the north represented an opportunity: Far-right Israelis had spoken of ejecting Gaza's population throughout the war, and the north was the section both most desperate and most contiguous with Israel.

On October 6, after nearly a week of allowing no aid into the north, the IDF told civilians to leave Jabalia and the two towns, then initiated heavy bombing and ground attacks.[78] Doctors without Borders highlighted that the so-called humanitarian zone in southern Gaza was already overwhelmed, and among those directed to move were at least eighty patients at three hospitals Israel was ordering closed who could not be safely transported.[79] "The Israeli military appears to be cutting off North Gaza completely," the UN's human rights office reported on October 14, noting near-daily attacks on schools-turned-shelters, reports of the IDF blocking the route south and repeatedly shooting at fleeing Palestinians, and the destruction of one of two remaining stations for emergency workers, who, like everyone else, lacked fuel.[80] Tens of thousands were trapped as bodies piled up on the roads and relief was out of reach. Salma Altaweel, a local aid worker for the Norwegian Refugee Council, described dehydration as widespread and prices for a couple of pounds of potatoes hitting $80 while a box of thirty eggs cost $107.[81] Beyond bombings, the IDF was bulldozing thousands of structures and roads; saying it sought military gains, not harm to civilians, it was replacing neighborhoods with zones for military operations, toppling whole buildings if militants used them once, and blowing up tunnels with explosions that decimated anything above.[82] Comparing Jabalia to hell, resident Khaled al-Ayla reported: "All you see is destruction."[83]

The developments suggested Tel Aviv was embracing a proposal known as the Generals' Plan, championed by retired Israeli commander Giora Eiland. He had from early in the war encouraged Israel to create a humanitarian crisis as a military tactic, saying the spread of disease among Palestinians would hasten victory; the remarks won praise from Bezalel Smotrich, the far-right minister.[84] By September, arguing Netanyahu mismanaged the war, Eiland pitched Israeli lawmakers on a more detailed strategy of treating North Gaza as a military zone, saying after a brief evacuation period, "every figure is a target and, most importantly, no supplies enter," to force Palestinians to surrender or starve; targeting both "land and dignity" was key, he argued.[85] The vision was in direct contravention of international law, under which civilians retain protected status even if they do not follow orders to move, and Israel had particular responsibility for ensuring the welfare of Palestinians because it was the occupying power governing their homeland.

Netanyahu confirmed he was considering the plan in late September. Once it appeared to be underway, he denied implementing Eiland's proposal—but on October 23, his government conceded at Israel's Supreme Court that it halted aid to northern Gaza for weeks because of military operations.[86] (Israel maintained Palestinians there still had sufficient supplies.) Eiland, meanwhile, claimed to *The Washington Post*: "It is illegal to cause the starvation of civilians . . . but it is legal if they are offered a way and time to leave." Suggesting the IDF could facilitate mass displacement, he said if Palestinians "choose to stay and die, that is their choice."

The Biden administration publicly rejected the Generals' Plan. Theoretically, the U.S. position could help the proposal's naysayers within Israel's government, such as the administration's preferred counterpart, defense minister Yoav Gallant. But Netanyahu had experience outplaying both Gallant, a domestic political rival he personally disliked, and Biden, and little basis to fear their opposition would involve substantial pressure. On October 13, Blinken and Defense Secretary Lloyd Austin sent Tel Aviv a letter suggesting continued U.S. support for Israel could be in question if it did not allow more aid throughout Gaza, noting levels were at their lowest since the war began, and asking the Israeli government to confirm there was "no Israeli government policy of forced evacuation of civilians from northern to southern Gaza." U.S. officials and Harris campaign aides described the message to me as a signal, to Israel and to Americans, that Netanyahu did not enjoy carte blanche—yet the letter confirmed Washington's continued political fear of questioning Israel, because it suggested that implications for Israeli noncompliance would not come until thirty days later, after the election. State Department figures could have used their positions to begin the process of triggering consequences by saying that months after the NSM-20 report in May, with conditions worsening, Israel's assurances of respecting international law should be re-evaluated. But assistant secretaries with relevant portfolios, like Middle East czar Barbara Leaf and humanitarian chief Julieta Noyes, had privately indicated to colleagues that they were still unwilling to do so. And publicly, Biden's spokespeople bolstered Israeli denials of heeding Eiland's advice. Though long-standing, Washington's pattern of suggesting extreme Israeli commentary was simply hyperbole and pleading ignorance about the IDF's operations was especially cynical in this instance. "It was too easy to dismiss it as an options paper, but the minute you start seeing elements implemented—this feels like it's a lot of the Generals' Plan," a senior State Department official later told me. "And the plan was ethnic cleansing."

Simultaneously, other IDF operations hinted at long-term Israeli control of Gaza, quashing hopes of Palestinian autonomy and likely signing up the United States for prolonged entanglement against an insurgency. Israeli troops had demolished Palestinian villages and agriculture to develop a road running horizontally across the strip, from the Mediterranean to the Israeli border, and used that corridor—named Netzarim after a former Israeli settlement in the strip—to control Palestinian movement. Starting in September, they accelerated their entrenchment there, building dozens of bases and extending the zone to cover 13 percent of Gaza's territory.[87] Israeli military officials told journalists the area was militarily vital and their infrastructure could be quickly removed, but they were creating similar buffer zones—leveling Palestinian homes and farms—along the Gaza-Egypt border and in a kilometer-wide area along the Gaza-Israel border. The return of Palestinian infrastructure seemed unlikely. On October 25, Israelis held a pro-settlement rally near the frontier with northern Gaza in which two senior Netanyahu ministers and several leaders in his party participated.[88]

Accounting for the damage in the north only became possible several months later, after the January 2025 ceasefire. Palestinians who returned saw little hope of restoring their communities. Arwa Al-Masri, from Beit Hanoun, told CNN her brother found no water in their town and had to travel to Gaza City just to be able to call relatives and tell them not to go back.[89] A Palestine TV reporter interviewed people journeying back to shelters in the south after seeing what had been their homes in Gaza City; witnessing them reduced to piles of sand left some feeling dead, they said.[90] The triumph Eiland visualized never materialized—eleven months after aspects of his plan went into effect, Israel launched yet another northern Gaza offensive against Hamas—but the added trauma he envisioned for Palestinians did.

NEXT STOP, TEHRAN?

Iran was still wary of a full-fledged Middle East war with Israel and, by extension, the United States, but the confrontation between the two sides had by now crossed many of its past limits, entering more dangerous territory, largely because of Israeli escalation. In October, Tehran, Tel Aviv, and Washington moved closer to all-out conflict that could be catastrophic in the region and destabilizing globally—further evidence that decision-making rooted in failed Gaza policy was precluding future stability.

On October 1, Iran launched more than 180 ballistic missiles at Israel—a much larger barrage than its attack in April, with far less notice—in stated revenge for the assassinations of Hezbollah's Nasrallah, Ismail Haniyeh of Hamas, and the Iranian commander Abbas Nilforoushan. The assault was a beacon for Iran's allies, as they had watched Israel pummel Lebanon in a way many assumed Tehran and Hezbollah would not permit, and a demonstration of Iranian capacity, striking several Israeli bases even as it caused limited damage. In a reminder that Palestinians were uniquely vulnerable in the neighborhood's worsening contest of egos and power players, including Iranian officials who claimed to be their champions, the sole casualty was Sameh Al-Assali, a Palestinian laborer hit by shrapnel in the West Bank, which despite being under Israeli control for fifty-seven years had not received air raid sirens like the country's formal territory. Al-Assali was originally from Gaza.[91]

U.S. military support had amplified Israeli missile defense, likely saving many lives. The Biden administration now turned to Israeli decision-making, aiming to prevent a big retaliation that risked a spiral into a major conflagration. The United States promoted Israeli confidence, with Jake Sullivan calling the Iranians "defeated and ineffective" and Biden saying Israel might even strike oil fields that were key to the Iranian economy, while privately encouraging a measured response.[92] Washington wanted to avoid Iran's most sensitive infrastructure, its nuclear and oil sites; trying to manage Tel Aviv's desire for vengeance, the United States imposed new sanctions on Iran and deployed an additional U.S. air defense system and one hundred soldiers to operate it to Israel.[93] On October 26, Israel launched air strikes against Iran that reflected Biden's hopes: While hitting military facilities and killing four Iranian soldiers, their impact was limited enough that Iran could downplay the moment.

Netanyahu denied being guided by "American dictates," but U.S. officials claimed credit for a rare instance of his choices matching their advice. Realistically, other factors he felt less able to manage than Biden mattered too: Arab states close to Tel Aviv, notably the United Arab Emirates and Saudi Arabia, had urged de-escalation despite their own skepticism of Iran, fearing being caught in a crossfire; and mobilizing Israelis for a third, potentially far more costly offensive was challenging.

Overall, the likelihood of eventual war had grown. The two sides had set another, higher precedent in their tit-for-tat. Soon, U.S. intelligence analysts privately concluded the attack was probably a prelude to an Israeli strike on Iran's nuclear facilities, with Netanyahu focusing on weakening Iran's air defenses in advance.[94] Biden's maneuvers in this period, meanwhile, bolstered the prospect of American forces ultimately becoming involved in a show of force against Iran. Washington launched its most advanced strikes yet on the Iran-backed Houthi militia in Yemen amid the uncertainty over the shape of Israel's retaliation, more closely tying the United States' own signaling toward Tehran to Israeli decision-making.[95] A senior U.S. official told me the administration also gave Tel Aviv "a yellow light" to begin joint planning for U.S.-Israeli bombing of Iran—a longtime goal for Netanyahu that was shared by General Michael Erik Kurilla, the top U.S. military commander for the Middle East. The official emphasized that Biden never approved executing such a plan.[96] The Israeli prime minister was playing a long game anyway. When he eventually got his wish in the summer of 2025, it was partly possible because of the post–October 7 surge of U.S. military forces across the Middle East that Biden green-lit and the ties Israeli officials established with Kurilla during the Biden era.[97] Amid the administration's struggles in policymaking and handling Tel Aviv, the hawkish Army general "had better information about what [Israel was] up to and what they were seeing in their intelligence before we got it than anyone else in [the U.S.] government," per the senior official. Eight months later, though Kurilla too had left office by then, Netanyahu and the dynamics honed in the Biden era were key to an ever broader U.S.-Israeli assault on Iran.

FOREVER WAR

As soon as the pagers exploded in Lebanon, one senior State Department official told me they quickly thought of an ancillary benefit to Netanyahu besides targeting an Israeli foe: hurting the election hopes of Kamala Harris. The view of the Lebanon war as a political move spread across Washington ahead of the presidential election, and despite that and ever-greater U.S.-backed Israeli violence in both Lebanon and Gaza throughout October, the administration was still deferential toward the Israeli leader. By the end of the month—as UNICEF reported that since Israel's invasion began, at least one Lebanese child was killed and ten injured daily, and the overall Lebanese death toll since October 2023 approached 2,900—Biden advisors McGurk and Hochstein were inching toward a Israel-Hezbollah deal involving American support for "active enforcement" by the IDF, which essentially meant tolerance for attacks inside Lebanon.[98] Another month of bloodshed would pass before their diplomacy bore fruit.

When he stepped down as the Democratic presidential nominee, Biden called himself "the first president in this century to report to the American people that the United States is not at war anywhere in the world."[99] Factually untrue, with the United States bombing the Houthis six weeks before his speech and again two weeks after it, his comment also reflected a philosophical failure: The president and many around him knew there was exhaustion with War on Terror–style "forever wars" but still refused to acknowledge U.S. complicity in conflicts taking forms other than ground invasions.[100] In November, as Americans voted on the status quo that Biden and, by extension, Harris represented, his administration's handling of the American relationship with Israel ensured part of that story was interminable war.

CHAPTER 10

CRAVING A HERO'S DEPARTURE

October 2024–January 2025

THE 2024 ELECTION BROUGHT DEMOCRATS A DIRE REBUKE OF the relationship between their party apparatus and the voters they needed. Biden and his aides spent their final months in office smarting from Americans' broad repudiation of their party and their obvious shortcomings on Gaza and other matters, including the pledge to move the country on from Trump. They responded by trying to burnish their legacy. They had limited time to confirm they deserved positions of public trust, for posterity in the president's case and for future career prospects in the case of his advisors. Once election results were announced, officials had options for addressing a dysfunctional U.S.-Israel dynamic and getting the Gaza ceasefire for which they wanted credit. They might pressure Netanyahu unlike ever before. They could even confirm Israel broke various U.S. laws, mandating a halt to some American military aid; this period saw them come closer than ever to that course of action. Or they could trust in Trump, hoping he would change Netanyahu's calculus and saying he was vital to sustaining plans for the region—notwithstanding his disregard for Palestinian life and U.S. and international law, and his fickle attention span. Biden's team picked the Trump track, rejecting a new course on policy and some restoration of faith in America's commitment to human rights, though they had received new intelligence about Israeli misconduct and had reason to suspect any deal Trump oversaw would collapse.[1] The president and his aides celebrated working with the incoming administration to secure an Israel-Hamas agreement that was essentially the plan Biden proposed seven months and at least eleven thousand deaths earlier. Israel unilaterally broke the truce within two months, with its initial strikes killing more than four hundred Palestinians, many of them children.[2] Taking his predecessor's Gaza policy to its logical conclusion, Trump confirmed Netanyahu would face no consequences, fantasized about an economic miracle rooted in fully voiding Palestinians' claims to their land, and allowed Israel to quash what remained of independent humanitarian operations.

The administration's final moves on Gaza dealt lasting damage to Biden's promises of sage global leadership, of upholding values like the law of war, and of encouraging Israeli-Palestinian amity. Almost always, that was because of deliberate choices by officials, still following a leader many now doubted. Saying Biden had political cover to challenge Israel both before the election and after it, one State Department official later told me, "The president made a decision that he didn't want his legacy to be anything other than a fully faithful defender of Israel to the very end." Biden's defense made many unsafe for years to come.

AMERICA VOTES

For the wars in Lebanon and Gaza, the period around the vote turbocharged some of the most alarming trends in American and Israeli politics.

Abbas Alawieh, the Democratic operative who cofounded the Uncommitted movement, saw his antiwar advocacy and political organizing collide with new personal anguish: Like many other Arab Americans in Michigan, Alawieh was of Lebanese descent, and he later told me his days began to be defined by family text chains about "what it feels like when eighty tons of bombs are dropped" and where his ninety-year-old grandmother could sleep without worrying she might never wake up. Many in his community had decried U.S.-backed Israeli massacres in Gaza; now they were attending funerals for those killed in similar ways in Lebanon, in part because of the sense of impunity created by that other war. In September, at the Uncommitted press conference denying Harris their endorsement, Alawieh had been the only one of the group's leaders to say he would vote for her, "not as a love letter but a chess move" given Republicans' total antipathy toward Palestinians. Weeks later, he felt "the people who currently control the Democratic Party would prefer that people like my family, maybe even me, didn't exist." Still, party officials spoke of antiwar discontent as separate from other strands of public frustration, not a bellwether.

As the party wooed voters, it associated itself with a vision of global affairs that assumed a U.S. embrace of Israel and largely ignored that union's victims. Harris repeatedly campaigned with Liz Cheney, the former Republican congresswoman known for aggressive foreign policy preferences—including support for Israel's annexation of the occupied West Bank[3]—and a daughter of Iraq War architect Dick Cheney, whose endorsement Harris also touted. To court Jewish voters, she dispatched Democratic congressman Ritchie Torres, whose resistance to questioning Israel was out of step with both most Democrats and most American Jews.[4] (Like many ardent Israel boosters, Torres is not Jewish.) And days before the election, the Harris campaign sent former president Bill Clinton to Michigan, where he said Israel was "forced" to kill civilians, sparking outrage.[5] Cumulatively, the Democratic approach made campaigning hard for the Harris backers who did court antiwar voters, particularly in Michigan, where Trump used one of his closing campaign rallies to declare: "Kamala is campaigning with Muslim-hating warmonger Liz Cheney."[6] An AI-produced graphic placing Harris's face and wreckage in Gaza beside Alawieh's face and those of other Arab and Muslim Democrats, calling them "faces of genocide," spread widely in his community, Alawieh later told me, saying: "We carried water for the party in a community where it really hurt to do that." (Arab American and Muslim American officials in the Biden administration had long received similar attacks.)

As the November 5 vote neared, Netanyahu repeatedly demonstrated disdain for the sitting administration and the idea any outcome could cost Israel unconditional U.S. support. Rather than Biden's ceasefire proposal, Israeli officials began pushing a temporary truce in exchange for the release of some Hamas captives, which Hamas called a non-starter.[7] On October 28, Netanyahu took a step the United States had explicitly warned him against in a letter two weeks earlier, calling Washington's bluff. His Likud Party led Israel's parliament—including lawmakers from opposition parties whom the Biden administration treated as friendlier alternatives—in overwhelmingly passing legislation to torpedo UNRWA by preventing the agency supporting more than 5 million Palestinians from working in territory claimed by Israel (including Palestinian-heavy East Jerusalem) or even communicating with Israeli officials who controlled its ability to enter, work, pay salaries, or provide supplies in Gaza and the West Bank.[8] The following day, the IDF killed 132 people—members of one extended family, including dozens of children—by leveling a building in northern Gaza. Mass graves were dug the following morning, but a relative, Ola Abu Naser, spent months afterward documenting each of her dead loved ones, as many Palestinians had to because their civic infrastructure was in tatters.[9] The United States demanded but never received answers; Israel's military never released evidence for its claim a militant was on the roof of the structure.[10]

Just before American polls opened on Election Day, Netanyahu fired Yoav Gallant, his defense minister. Global attention was on voting machines in the Pennsylvania suburbs rather than his consolidation of power. Within Israeli politics, the move provided a useful, distracting new topic of conversation just after a Netanyahu aide had been arrested in the "BibiLeaks" case for allegedly sharing sensitive information with reporters to hurt the ceasefire negotiations. The arrest bolstered the impression the prime minister was deliberately prolonging the conflict.[11] From Netanyahu's standpoint, the moment suggested he felt well positioned regardless: Eliminating Gallant meant removing a rival whom U.S. officials had tapped to influence internal Israeli policy discussions, leaving Netanyahu more empowered to push back against the

White House, whoever its occupant. Gallant had before the war blasted Netanyahu's effort to weaken Israel's judiciary; in a statement about his dismissal, he noted the two men now disagreed about concessions for a deal over Gaza.[12]

TRUMP'S AMERICA

By the morning of November 8, 2025, America's rejection of the Biden era was clear. Democrats lost every swing state, both chambers of Congress, and more than 55 percent of seats in state legislatures. Party operatives highlighted Harris's brief campaign, her close margins in battleground states, and how incumbent governments globally had faced voter rage over inflation caused by the pandemic, but later analysis of voter files showed many who backed Biden in 2020 switched to preferring the GOP, and Democrats lost ground among groups who traditionally supported them, including voters of color and younger voters, while turnout dropped in Democratic areas.[13] Harris's bid for conservative votes flopped, as 94 percent of self-identified Republicans supported Trump, and the particular unpopularity of the Biden administration was further reflected in some down-ballot Democratic candidates outperforming her.[14] Trump failed to win mass support—though he beat Harris in the popular vote, he lacked a majority and his margin was the smallest of any popular vote winner in twenty-four years—but the United States was entering a period of right-wing dominance, and the president-elect was clear he would govern as though he had what he called an "unprecedented and powerful mandate."[15]

While Trump's rise suggested some complications, Netanyahu correctly assessed they were mostly surface-level, and both men quickly indicated Washington would draw even closer to Tel Aviv. "I'm going to stop wars," Trump said in his victory speech, and his circle increasingly included members of the GOP's New Right movement who held some anti-interventionist views. Still, he remained close to pro-Israel hard-liners like mega-donor Miriam Adelson, and as Trump aides discussed slashing and overhauling government agencies, they showed no interest in a similar systematic challenge to the entrenched ideas, individuals, and institutions behind American support for Israel. Israel's leader and his incoming counterpart underscored their stylistic and ideological affinity—particularly for extreme steps seemingly designed to madden critics—through their appointment of ambassadors. On November 8, Netanyahu tapped far-right settler Yechiel Leiter as Israel's new emissary to the United States, and a few days later, Trump nominated Mike Huckabee, a Christian Zionist who rejected the existence of a Palestinian identity or any Israeli occupation, as his representative in Israel.[16]

Gaza and Lebanon remained under U.S.-provided Israeli fire, with the vote offering no clear directive about Americans' preferences on the Middle East. Pledging peace, Trump had become the first GOP candidate in twenty-four years to win Arab-majority Dearborn, Michigan, and notched record support from Arab Americans in that state as well as from foreign-born citizens nationally, a group including many Arab and Muslim Americans. Later, polling from the Institute for Middle East Understanding, a pro-Palestinian group, said Gaza was the top voting issue for 29 percent of voters who backed Biden in 2020 and did not vote for Harris.[17] But in the moment, Biden administration personnel working on the wars described themselves as shell-shocked, and the chances of ceasefires, as well as changes in the U.S. approach that might encourage them, still depended on choices by a few top officials, who soon demonstrated that their aversion to altering Israeli-American relations outlasted campaign season. No longer able to say political sensitivities or an all-out focus on stopping Trump justified their policy, the Biden administration kept fueling preventable, likely illegal killing.

THE COMFORT OF THE STATUS QUO

Days after the election, a State Department official told me it was unclear what priorities Biden's team would abandon.[18] Officials had for months prior been quietly discussing a raft of new ways to use American leverage to change Israel's behavior. After the vote, with famine once again confirmed in Gaza on November 8, the case for doing so seemed stronger and a meaningful way to use Biden's waning power to have a lasting positive impact.[19] As the administration began quashing those hopes, it publicly confirmed—including to Trump and Netanyahu—its limited ambition and fundamental cowardice in managing U.S.-Israel relations.

Blinken was key to deciding whether Tel Aviv would face consequences and pressure to reform. In late September, the secretary told aides at a high-level meeting that the United States should be more assertive, an official present told me, adding that they suspected that was partly because ceasefire talks had stalled. Such a signal mattered in the State Department hierarchy. Though the secretary had repeatedly declined to sanction Israel under the Leahy Law, which bars U.S. military aid for foreign forces credibly involved in human rights abuses, officials had begun fresh Leahy investigations in the middle of 2024. They homed in on Unit 504 and Force 100, two IDF units accused of abusing captive Palestinians from Gaza and held at the Sde Teiman base in a facility that subjected inmates to permanent restraints, beatings, and medical malpractice.[20] Israel itself began investigating Force 100 in July, spurring right-wing protests while strengthening suspicions of serious misdeeds. (Israel established a humanitarian hub at Sde Teiman the same month, summoning U.S. aid officials to meet there, spurring complaints and a sense it was, per one, "trolling.")[21] Patterns that had stymied other administration investigations persisted: A State Department lawyer recalled to me that some colleagues focused on questioning the testimony of specific detainees, stalling the process of confirming there were at least some credible allegations of torture. Still, between the evidence, the fact that detainee mistreatment was hard to blame on Hamas or the fog of war, and the sense the administration should do something about U.S.-backed Israeli abuses in the Gaza war before leaving office, the idea of sanctioning the two units gained ground in deliberations. And astonishingly, even the department's arms-sales office, Middle East bureau, and embassy in Jerusalem did not object. Applying Leahy to Israel would be staggering:

a first-of-its-kind reprimand subjecting the country to the same standards as other U.S. partners (even if Washington would likely lift the suspension of military support quickly, and the lack of Leahy enforcement thus far was its own depressing indicator). By the end of October, Blinken had a unanimous State Department memo endorsing sanctions on Israeli personnel on his desk. Additionally, a State official told me he submitted a recommendation that month for the secretary to acknowledge that Israel's policies triggered Section 620I of the Foreign Assistance Act, the U.S. law banning support for countries that block American-funded aid.

Separately, Blinken and Defense Secretary Lloyd Austin had given Israel a thirty-day window to improve its approach to aid for Gaza or face a reevaluation of U.S. military support through their October 13 letter. The message was taken seriously by Israeli officials, and for U.S. government aid experts, the deadline felt like a watershed moment after months of midwifing a crisis.[22] "Stuff would happen every single day that anywhere else in the world we'd be losing our minds over," a USAID official later told me, pointing to Israeli troops' mishandling of carefully planned aid convoys. "The idea that the UN and Red Cross emblems were meant to be respected was not understood by the IDF" even after months of fighting.

But Biden aides' legal obfuscation and vacillation about Israeli actions meant the administration eventually neutered its own pressure tactic. Two weeks after the Blinken-Austin letter was sent, before it was clear whether Israel was meeting U.S. demands, deputy national security advisor Jon Finer told a meeting of external experts that there would be no suspension of weapons for Tel Aviv, a person present at the meeting told me. When an outside contact raised Israeli violations of its agreements with the United States as a reason to suspend military support, Finer responded that the administration had huge discretion in reaching legal conclusions. Similarly, he deflected a question about an FBI inquiry into the Israeli killing of Turkish American Ayşenur Eygi, getting angry when an interlocutor said the United States was not valuing all lives equally, a witness told me. Overwhelmingly, it appeared clear that White House officials had internalized the belief that applying the law to Israel was an option, not a responsibility, and an undesirable one at that.[23]

Prior to the election, the impossibility of "a tough decision on arms sales was taken for granted," the USAID official recalled. Some hoped that subsequently, facts and analysis would guide policy. By November 12, the end of Blinken's thirty-day window for Tel Aviv, many State Department experts and independent humanitarian groups said Israel had not implemented most American directives to boost aid—with the latter saying Israel had in some ways backtracked and "dramatically worsened" conditions and highlighting Section 620I.[24] Looting by gangs, which had become a major problem for humanitarian access, was linked to IDF tolerance of the activity in an internal UN memo and by aid workers.[25]

The White House and the secretary's political advisors argued for a fuzzy interpretation of the facts, giving Israel credit for partially easing aid flows.[26] Blinken chose that course. His spokesperson Vedant Patel publicly said the administration still had no assessment that Israel broke the law but would "continue to assess their compliance." (Within months, Patel joined the public relations firm SKDK, soon after it was hired by the Israeli government.) A gray area of avoiding hard, potentially self-incriminating conclusions was a convenient place for Biden's team. For fellow Democrats, the administration's decision was an embodiment of failure and cynicism that would haunt the party for years to come. Officials issued the letter when they were politically "worried," setting a postelection deadline for a decision and "reading the riot act [about] the same problems we have seen the entire time," then used minimal improvements to return to a position of "it's okay, we won't press them hard," Jeff Merkley, the Oregon senator, told me.

On November 18, the administration unveiled fresh sanctions on settlers for violence in the West Bank, notably targeting Amana, a major pro-settlement group already sanctioned by Britain and Canada. The step suggested Washington still saw value in some challenges to Israel even if Trump would reverse them, and a senior U.S. official later described the settler policy to me as a legacy achievement: "This is a tool that will come back if there's a Democratic administration again, and that Joe Biden did it, who is probably the most pro-Israel Democrat remaining in the establishment, will give cover." The way the official depicted the policy, however, was revealing about how the administration's thinking—dominated by fear of being called anti-Israel—may have guaranteed its failure. "We were not sanctioning settlers for settlements: We were sanctioning people tied to violence," the official told me, saying the administration avoided individuals and organizations "too deeply intertwined with the United States." The settlement enterprise inherently violates international law and was unlikely to be truly weakened while it kept receiving millions of dollars from U.S. citizens. The administration's simulacrum of action could then even be counterproductive, the way some analysts believe U.S. officials' talk of Israeli-Palestinian negotiations has distracted policymakers from Israel's creeping suppression of Palestinian aspirations. Democrats might keep issuing sanctions, but paired with ever-expanding settlements, general U.S. tolerance for settlers, and the precedent of exceptions that Biden established, they could prove irrelevant other than for American consciences, making his presidency a key moment in killing chances for a Palestinian state rooted in the West Bank. Already, between November 2023—when Biden began moving to sanction settlers—and November 2024, nine new settlements and forty-nine additional settler outposts, illegal even under Israeli law, were established, per the United Nations.[27]

Still confident they were uniquely capable of managing U.S-Israel ties, administration officials continued fighting to stop even their allies from influencing policy. Bernie Sanders had long wanted to force Congress to hold its first-ever votes on blocking U.S. weapons for Israel—a reckoning for the relationship. Knowing most Democrats dreaded intraparty dissent before the election, the Vermont senator introduced legislation the Senate would consider afterward. With Republicans unified in a no-questions-asked approach toward Netanyahu that some Democrats shared, the bills could not pass, but the number of Democratic votes for them could send a strong message, particularly if the proposal won more support than past legislation over the Gaza war. For the Biden administration, which sought ceasefires in Lebanon and Gaza as closing achievements, the moment presented a chance to unite U.S. calls for Netanyahu to reach deals and ease civilian suffering. The White House and senators critical of the Israeli leader were ostensibly on the same side, and the former could use discontent on Capitol Hill as a negotiating tool, as U.S. presidents often do with foreign leaders; though unlikely to disparage its own arms deals, the administration could eschew lobbying lawmakers either way or even whisper they should amplify the signal to Tel Aviv, knowing the weapons would be sent in any case. Biden aides instead worked to minimize the message. Before the November 20 vote, the White House sent Democrats a set of talking points whose contents ranged from the stunning, George W. Bush–style claim that supporting the Sanders bills meant helping Hamas and Hezbollah to a blessing of Israel's brutal "escalate to de-escalate" logic in Lebanon. I obtained and published the document, then also revealed that Senate Democratic leader Chuck Schumer was privately urging colleagues to oppose the legislation.[28] In the final hours before voting, Blinken made a similar plea in person.

Ultimately, nineteen senators voted for the bills, including several Democrats who rarely challenged Israel.[29] It remained jarring that there was never any question of the chamber denying Israel equipment like tank rounds the IDF used against children, and that most senators (including all Republicans) would not question U.S. weapons tied to widespread savagery even through a symbolic vote—but the antiwar camp won more support than when Sanders had forced a vote on Israeli conduct in January, including the backing of nearly half of Senate Democrats. A sliver of hope for Palestinians and Lebanese had grown.[30]

The Biden team, meanwhile, had tied themselves to a view their party was increasingly abandoning, siding with forces who often tried to hurt Democrats politically while bolstering Republicans. AIPAC later funded a six-figure ad blitz against legislators who supported such bills—yet in July 2025, another Sanders bill to block some weapons for Israel was backed by twenty-eight senators, and a similar bid in April 2026 was supported by forty: nearly all Democrats and almost half the Senate.[31] Seeking to define their place in history during their final months, Biden's aides suggested it was beside Netanyahu, AIPAC, and Trump.

IF YOU CAN'T BEAT THEM . . .

Continuity with Trump defined Biden's Israel-Palestine policy before October 7; after Hamas's onslaught, the administration instituted Trump-style policymaking, led by a stubborn, often angry boss convinced of his own wisdom and the loyalists around him. Following Trump's second election victory, the Biden team echoed him further, then began a full-fledged collaboration with him and his movement, whom they had cast as an intolerable threat to American democracy and the U.S.'s global standing. Officials such as Jake Sullivan presented the partnership as proof that the Biden administration was wisely and patriotically defying partisanship, in descriptions to the press and at a January 14, 2025, event at the U.S. Institute of Peace—ironically one of the institutions of American foreign policy that the Trump administration assaulted within weeks of taking office.[32] A more honest portrayal would acknowledge that in dealing with Palestinians and many other non-Americans, U.S. elites across party lines had long agreed on dehumanizing and destabilizing ideas and practices.

On November 21, the International Criminal Court issued arrest warrants for three individuals accused of war crimes and crimes against humanity amid the Gaza war: Netanyahu, Gallant, and Hamas military chief Mohammed Deif.[33] The judges of the ICC identified "reasonable grounds" to charge Netanyahu and Gallant with intentionally enforcing starvation, blocking essential fuel and medicine, and murdering civilians; in targeting Deif, the ICC noted evidence he was responsible for rape, murder, and torture on October 7 and in Hamas's treatment of hostages. (Proposed warrants for other Hamas leaders were canceled after Israel assassinated them.)

It was a thunderbolt. One hundred twenty-four countries that were members of the court were now legally bound to arrest the men if they touched their soil; many were close to Israel, and Netanyahu and Gallant regularly traveled internationally. (Unlike most states, the United States and Israel were not ICC members; the United Kingdom and Israel both challenged the court's jurisdiction over Israelis, but the judges rejected their bids, noting Palestine's membership was their basis for assessing the war.) Additionally, the court's statement hinted at U.S. culpability in alleged crimes: When Israel boosted aid for Gaza, it was "often conditional . . . a response to the pressure of the international community or requests by the United States of America"—suggesting Washington could prevent illegal man-made hunger, and rebutting the Biden administration's view that Israel and the United States had wiggle room in complying with international law. An independent group of respected jurists from various countries was indicting not just individuals but a whole system of choices.

The process was contentious, a reality pro-Israel voices highlighted. When ICC prosecutor Karim Khan announced he would seek the warrants in May, he had not conducted interviews in Gaza or with high-ranking Israelis beyond a December 2023 visit, and he "shot for the moon" in pursuing Netanyahu and Gallant rather than mid-level figures, a senior State Department official later argued to me; another U.S. official said his "precipitous" action frustrated sympathetic Biden aides. Some believed Khan's timing was about his own reputation: Also in May, he faced accusations of sexual misconduct toward a female employee that evolved into a probe of alleged retaliation against ICC staff who brought the complaints and saw another woman present similar claims.[34] (Khan denied wrongdoing but eventually took a leave of absence; his fate was unclear as of this writing after UN investigators and independent judges reportedly concluded there was insufficient evidence he committed misconduct but the facts remained disputed. Khan's bid to be cleared largely hinged on choices by ICC member countries.)[35]

Still, factors beyond Khan's control, including Israeli and American actions, affected the ICC's work too. The devastation in Gaza and potential for further injury likely weighed on the prosecutor, while the court, based in The Hague in the Netherlands, endured increasing intimidation. The institution had been harassed for nearly a decade by Israel, and that spring, then–British foreign secretary David Cameron and Republican senator Lindsey Graham privately threatened the court, per Khan.[36] Court personnel also began receiving anonymous threatening calls as well as warnings from local police. The interference grew so serious Khan issued a statement saying threats of retaliation against the court risked prosecution, and ninety-three countries, including U.S. allies France, Germany, and, ironically, Britain, issued a joint defense of the court's independence.[37]

The Biden administration opposed an effort in Congress to codify U.S. sanctions on the court but by the time the Gaza warrants came, the administration had embraced the anti-ICC position of far-right leaders globally, from Netanyahu to Trump and their mutual friend Viktor Orbán of Hungary, who announced plans to host the Israeli leader.[38] Previously, some administration officials had attempted to cast an ICC case as inappropriate by the court's own standard of complementarity, which bars addressing situations that national authorities were tackling themselves, the senior State Department official told me. Between Netanyahu blocking independent Israeli inquiries into his choices and American officials speaking of sanctioning ICC investigators rather than encouraging Israel to pursue prosecutions, that argument shriveled. Now, Biden was condemning and misrepresenting a court the United States had helped craft to uphold liberal international values and accountability. "Biden wanted to be stronger than Trump was going to be," the senior State official told me, so he ceded a chance for a more measured response and established a U.S. precedent of condemnation that made it easier for his successor to crack down on the ICC. The president's decision simultaneously undermined one of the few routes to make Israeli officials answer for heinous apparent excesses, from engineering starvation that analyst Alex de Waal soon suggested had killed at least ten thousand to eradicating dozens of Palestinian families at a time.[39] Biden was aiding skeptics of global standards who called the United States inconsistent and self-interested in its talk of morality, emboldening others to feel they could dodge consequences for barbarity. And he was again demonstrating the bipartisan nature of unpopular, pugnacious, and often ineffective American foreign policy: His position mirrored that of Graham, the Trump ally who now called the court "rogue" and said defying it was key to ensuring it did not target Americans—but who had, like Biden, cheered the ICC warrant for Russian president Vladimir Putin over his full-scale invasion of Ukraine.[40]

The ICC episode marked the rough start of the Biden administration operating as a junior partner for the Trump team on Middle East policy. Between their own shortcomings and concern for their legacy and Trump's bluster, they ushered in an era of greater pain for civilians, peril across the region, and moral bankruptcy for the United States.

A ceasefire in Lebanon set the tone for the union between Biden and Trump aides. Both Netanyahu and Hezbollah were readying for another Trump era; the unpredictable president-elect might be more willing than Biden to break with Tel Aviv to fulfill his campaign promise of ending wars, but could also eventually fulfill Republican and Israeli hopes of a bigger clash with Iran's regional network, for which the Lebanese group wanted to preserve its remaining capabilities. The two agreed to a sixty-day peace deal starting on November 27. Though it was announced by Biden, after being negotiated by his envoy Amos Hochstein, Trump's aides quickly claimed credit for the accord and outside experts agreed: "We see the Trump factor at work," Dennis Ross, the former State Department official who served as an informal advisor to the Biden administration, wrote, noting that Netanyahu had taken the rare move of defying his ultranationalist political base.[41]

Cooperating between the teams was arguably necessary for Biden to secure any progress because his administration's days were numbered. "In that and perhaps only in that I give Brett [McGurk] and Jake [Sullivan] credit: understanding they would not get anywhere in the negotiations without embracing Trump's people," a State Department official unhappy with the Gaza policy broadly told me. But Biden's aides went farther in seeking recognition and attempting to justify their policy, defending the entire ruinous course of the war. One senior official later told me the administration had not wanted a ground invasion but noted Hezbollah chose to launch pro-Hamas attacks and was significantly debilitated, benefiting Israel strategically and Netanyahu politically. He "took a risk and I think in their view it paid off massively," the official said. The depiction suggested a low bar for justifying violence involving enormous air strikes, the flattening of residential areas and centuries-old monuments, and the traumatic displacement of 1.3 million people.[42] Administration officials had, however, become comfortable with a nightmarish style of warfare, as the Biden administration had—despite its rhetoric—allowed Israel to degrade standards for fighting wars that experts saw as vital to shielding innocents and limiting future conflict. "As devastating as Lebanon was, it was more surgical than Gaza," a senior Biden humanitarian official argued to me months later, quickly adding, "But it was still way beyond what I would say are acceptable civilian casualties." Even in the moment, claims of success were questionable: The terms of the truce offered little recourse for ceasefire violations by the IDF that began almost immediately and became endemic, including further attacks, killing at least 127 Lebanese civilians and repeatedly hitting UN peacekeepers and civilian structures, and Israeli occupation of Lebanese territory. Hezbollah, meanwhile, continued refusing to disarm. It was alarmingly simple to slip into another no-holds-barred war in Lebanon in 2026.

Amid the Lebanon diplomacy, Sullivan began speaking regularly with Mike Waltz, the Florida congressman whom Trump tapped as his national security advisor. It was easy for the two to bond. They were both well-credentialed white men of roughly the same age, serving two other white men from the same generation; both were favorites of Washington's national security establishment and had worked in government for decades. It was also strategically understandable for them to work together, because other nations might seek advantage in playing the Biden and Trump teams off each other. But there was reason for alarm when the two operated as what Waltz called "hand in glove . . . one team."[43] Many disastrous U.S. national security choices, most famously the Iraq invasion, have drawn Democratic and Republican support; bad ideas can overcome seeming ideological divides, especially when—as in the case of unchecked U.S. support for Israel—both parties have incentives to maintain the status quo.

Still, for the Biden administration, playing into Washington's fetish for bipartisanship was beneficial. Sullivan pled ignorance of political affairs to deflect when he was later asked about whether Biden was fit to run for president.[44] McGurk had long worked for GOP presidents and was unlikely, in cooperating with Trump aides, to face pushback rooted in progressive values, as he did when Desirée Cormier Smith, the Biden State Department's envoy for racial justice, argued to him at an internal meeting that the administration valued Palestinian lives less than those of Israelis. When McGurk became angry, saying he rejected the notion the policy was racist, Cormier Smith quoted back James Baldwin: "I can't believe what you say, because I see what you do."[45] Figures like Waltz—a foreign policy hawk close to AIPAC who opposed even minor criticism of Netanyahu, said a Gaza ceasefire helped Hamas, and argued the United States had to spend money on Israel because Biden was feeble—made sense to Biden national security aides who felt less progressive and extremely defensive relative to many Democrats.[46] And in areas where they differed, like whether the IDF should do more to spare civilians, the outgoing team had had little success anyway. Praise was the cherry on top: *Politico* cheered the Waltz-Sullivan dialogue as "sealed off from politics . . . no small feat given the hyper-partisan cloud of acrimony descending on Washington."[47] Political differences, of course, translate to life and death; the Trump-Biden symbiosis treated Palestinian survival as a secondary concern at best.

CASTLES IN THE AIR

By early December, Biden aides were growing confident they could sell their destructive Israel policy as an overall achievement and even purport to be delivering on long-standing plans. They had a Lebanon narrative; now they were focused on Gaza, Saudi Arabia, and Syria.

Both Trump and Biden sought a pre-inauguration ceasefire freeing American and Israeli hostages and ceasing the drumbeat of stomach-churning reports of Palestinian deaths. The United States could deploy several new factors in negotiations: Trump's warning there would be "hell to pay" for Hamas, which some felt could force it to make deep concessions like Hezbollah; his unconventional advisors, like his confidant and new Middle East envoy, businessman Steve Witkoff; and the incoming president's open longing for a Nobel Peace Prize. "Momentum is coming back" to talks, Qatari prime minister Mohammed bin Abdulrahman Al Thani, a mediator between Israel and Hamas, said on December 7.[48] Like Trump, Witkoff had financial interests across the region and close ties with the Qataris.

For Gaza, where UNRWA said a "sickening normalization" had now set in about chilling records such as the territory seeing the world's biggest number of child amputees per capita, any respite would be welcome.[49] Keen for a quick agreement, the negotiators began discussing a sixty-day deal that dodged important long-term questions, such as how Netanyahu would handle Hamas's abiding power, the group's demand that Israel leave Gaza, its ability to regroup fighting forces, and the importance of its thousands of civil employees for any rebuilding of the strip. A future for Palestine beyond cycles of violence still looked uncertain as the U.S.-backed Palestinian Authority in early December began an offensive against Hamas and other militants in the Jenin refugee camp in the West Bank, displacing residents and increasing tensions, after the IDF had already conducted a punishing operation there in August and September that killed twenty-one.[50] The region was additionally reeling from growing evidence of deaths and worsening treatment among West Bank Palestinians jailed by Israel.

The Palestinian territories remained a small but essential part of what Biden aides wanted to be known for in the region: a U.S.–Israel–Saudi Arabia agreement as a bulwark against Iran, China, and Russia. Many in Washington across political identities still saw themselves in a strategic contest in which human rights concerns were an irritant and partners' appalling, often deadly decision-making was tolerable or easily overlooked.

For years, Sullivan, McGurk, and Hochstein privately worked to clinch a deal alongside Lindsey Graham, the Republican senator close to Trump, who felt Democrats in Congress would approve the price the Saudis demanded—a treaty compelling U.S. troops to defend the kingdom—only under a Democratic president. The men now felt they had their last shot, tapping both the outgoing and incoming administrations. Their continued talks about the possible deal "went into hyperdrive" in spring 2024 and the deal was "98 percent done" by the summer, a senior Biden aide claimed to me, noting the huge remaining hurdle: Israel agreeing to a ceasefire and a Palestinian state developing along a specific timeline. That was a tremendous and, many believed, unlikely outcome, but the senior official noted to me, "Sometimes Bibi did things people thought he didn't want to do." Washington tried to convince Israeli officials to pursue the deal, arguing that even if they felt they were ending the Gaza war prematurely, they would gain in terms of regional security. Some in Israel's security establishment agreed but Israeli political officials—consistently keen to present the Biden administration as a bad ally—pushed the idea that the United States was exaggerating what the Saudis wanted for the Palestinians, seeking a concession that was actually the goal of U.S. officials. Netanyahu's chief advisor, Ron Dermer, visited Washington in early December and met with Waltz and Sullivan. At the White House, Sullivan told his Israeli counterpart he had spoken with the Saudi ambassador to the United States and the pact could be finalized that very night, a person familiar with the discussions told me, saying that hours later, Graham planned to host the two and McGurk for a celebratory dinner.[51] (Sullivan denied this account through his spokeswoman.)

The gambit showed that Biden's advisors were still loath to alter their thinking. Sullivan told Dermer that Palestinian statehood could be addressed in the distant future, and Israel could quickly assuage the Saudis by easing up on Gaza and the West Bank, the source familiar with the discussion said. It was a rehashing of U.S. thinking that had helped drive the war and a portrayal that—in D.C. style—discounted other players' agency and evolution: The Saudis had toughened their stance, calling an irreversible path to a Palestinian state nonnegotiable, and Netanyahu had made preventing such a state the core of his political identity. Bringing them to a middle ground would require enormous, muscular American diplomacy, yet the administration still did not want to get tough with Israel. Dermer was at the White House as reports were mounting of Israel violating the ceasefire in Lebanon. During the visit, McGurk and Michael Herzog, the Israeli ambassador in Washington, suggested the allegations were laughable, the source said. (McGurk denied this.)[52] A senior Biden aide who criticized the effort of colleagues as "all model UN" told me so-called normalization with Saudi Arabia was consistently treated as the chief incentive the United States could give Israel "to dial down things in Gaza"; use of other American leverage by Biden was almost always inconceivable. By the end of December, the Israelis made clear they would not budge on accepting a Palestinian state, and the possibility of achieving the deal under Biden died, another senior official told me.

Obstinate about its Middle East policy, the administration was shameless about claiming it yielded benefits. On December 8, rebels in Syria captured the capital, Damascus, and Bashar Assad, the reigning tyrant, fled, in a moment that felt cathartic for many of his victims and in geostrategic terms benefited the United States and Israel, because Assad was close to Russia and Iran. "Developments in Syria very much prove the case of President Biden's assertive foreign policy," John Kirby soon declared at a White House press briefing, an argument his boss then echoed.[53] In truth, the administration's approach to both military action and diplomacy had been helpful for Assad. Washington cautioned Israel against bombing pro-Iran forces in Syria, on whom the regime depended, a congressional aide told me, while another said the Biden team hindered efforts to isolate Assad for his rights abuses, letting American partners—notably the United Arab Emirates—rekindle ties with him and, according to the French newspaper *Le Figaro*, attempting

U.S. outreach to Damascus through McGurk. Basically, the administration made "a terrible assessment of the fragility" of Assad's rule, a senior official later conceded to me. While publicly claiming a win, Biden's staff privately knew their record was contested: When McGurk sought a triumphant White House event with Syrian Americans, officials quashed the idea because, an administration official told me, they knew he was widely seen as "an architect of UAE-led normalization and rehabilitation of Assad."

Top officials' lack of reflection on their strategy, and the mismanagement of Israel that defined it, complicated the suggestion the Biden team was serious about strengthening Syria. IDF forces moved into parts of the country near the Golan Heights, a Syrian region Israel had already been occupying since 1973; bombed Syrian military equipment, saying the rebels could not be trusted with the weapons; and set up a new post in an internationally administered buffer zone intended to prevent Syria-Israel conflict, shooting at locals who protested.[54] Months later, the IDF was organizing hiking trips in Syria for tourists.[55]

Notwithstanding signs that U.S. policies were sowing the seeds of future Middle East conflict, Sullivan continued projecting Biden—and himself—as perceptive beyond others' comprehension. "The president has been operating on a time horizon measured in decades, while the political cycle is measured in four years," he told *The Washington Post*.[56] It was widely understood in the foreign policy community that Sullivan intended to keep shaping policy throughout those coming decades.

"KNOWINGLY COMMITTING WAR CRIMES"

Fourteen months into the war, hunger in Gaza was entrenched, inescapable, and corrosive to Palestinian society. "I feel humiliated and degraded, begging every day to secure food," Ghada al-Kafarna, a mother of ten in central Gaza, told Al Jazeera.[57] Overwhelmed, she raged at her children: She had hit her eight-year-old son when he cried for food, then "he cried himself to sleep, and I spent the night in tears."

Flour shortages and mounting anarchy meant not a single bakery in the strip was operating as of December 2, a UN-led network of humanitarian groups reported.[58] Its members were, in still-besieged northern Gaza, receiving calls from Palestinians trapped in homes and shelters who were out of food and water, and in southern Gaza—where Israel forced much of the strip's population into its "safe zone"—the groups observed young Palestinians' futures swapped for hopes of immediate relief, through forced marriages and child labor. The few supplies available were phenomenally expensive. An update from Oxfam described how an employee had sought an egg to provide calcium to a wounded relative and could only find one selling for $6. "Adults tell their kids not to play so they don't get dizzy" from lack of nutrition, a displaced man told the aid group.[59]

Starting in mid-November 2024, the Biden administration came closer than ever to concluding that the starvation reflected a deliberate Israeli plan, as I revealed in a news story a year later. Some U.S. officials up to Blinken began privately using the kind of language that they had suggested war skeptics were hysterical and unfair for using to describe Israel's actions in Gaza—terms like "ethnic cleansing."[60] (Blinken neither confirmed nor denied using that term.)

The shift in their thinking was rooted in new American intelligence assessments that suggested that Israel was knowingly committing war crimes, multiple then-serving officials later told me. Two officials described the basis for those assessments as signals intelligence that had captured discussions among Israeli officials in which they seemingly acknowledged the possibility that Israel had violated international law. My sources were extremely careful about characterizing the information, sharing nothing classified, but one specified that it included discussions of military operations and mass forced population movement among Palestinians. The findings were so serious that they spurred an urgent meeting where Biden personally considered whether American and Israeli officials might be liable for violations of international and U.S. law in Gaza, and a high-ranking intelligence official urged him—unsuccessfully—to end some American support for the Israeli campaign so as to shield U.S. personnel.

Administration leaders were already familiar with charges that Israel was violating its obligations to let aid flow to civilians under the Fourth Geneva Convention and Section 620I of the U.S. Foreign Assistance Act, as well as conducting disproportionate attacks. They were used to deflecting blame to Hamas and repeating Israeli promises to respect the law. Now they were confronting the very real possibility that they themselves might be deemed culpable: Given the new knowledge about the Israelis' thinking, continuing the U.S. policy of providing weapons and intelligence to Tel Aviv would involve "very likely legal exposure," a senior American humanitarian official told me.

The White House faced a decision. Biden could acknowledge Israel's violations and limit support to Israel; if he simply acknowledged that Israel's actions had triggered Section 620I, he could even, per his own preferences, issue a waiver to keep support flowing regardless. Either choice would demonstrate respect for facts, or at least credible allegations, and for the law, and might spur Israeli restraint. Or the president and his advisors could call the findings vague, absolve themselves of possible blame, and once again, in effect, treat legal standards as optional for Israel, while claiming that a firm determination of wrongdoing would hurt ceasefire talks by angering Netanyahu, and would hurt advocacy for aid by sparking backlash from pro-Israel voices in the United States. Notably, the second route would help stymie broader efforts at accountability over Gaza: U.S. acknowledgment of illegal behavior could, one official told me, "make the ICC prosecutor's case for him."

Biden and his advisors had by now seen the results both of applying consequences for Israeli behavior, by forcing more aid after the World Central Kitchen killings, and of suggesting Tel Aviv could steamroll American standards, by abandoning their red line over Rafah and so driving a collapse in Palestinians' conditions. Their choice over the new intelligence findings represented their final chance to show they had learned from their experience and to even partially redeem America's role.

Up to this point, the administration had generally avoided acknowledging its complicity by avoiding firm U.S. conclusions about Israeli misdeeds. In December 2023, State Department lawyers had told Blinken that Israel had likely broken international law. Separately, two officials told me, multiple attorneys at State's Office of the Legal Adviser had expressed alarm about Israeli behavior throughout the war, with one saying many of them were certain Section 620I had been triggered.[61] But the office never formally advised Blinken to enforce that law by stopping arms shipments to Israel.

Broadly, talk of U.S. officials being liable for actions in Gaza escalated in 2024, a senior State Department official told me, because the NSM-20 process had begun and because—in part due to post–October 7 misgivings about Israeli intelligence—the United States had strengthened its own intelligence capabilities for "independent reporting" on Israel-Palestine. By early April 2024, State's human rights office had circulated an internal memo across the department recommending that Blinken find Israel's actions had triggered Section 620I, a State Department official told me. Yet almost immediately, the office of Blinken aide Uzra Zeya demanded the document be withheld, on the ground that Biden had asked Netanyahu just that day to allow in more aid after the WCK strike and was hopeful that Israel would comply.

Persistent ambiguity among government lawyers helped limit the impact of more officials concluding that the Gaza policy had to change, as they acknowledged colleagues' objections over 620I and other laws but crafted ways to sustain Biden's arms shipments and other support. That posture had an effect: When it comes to supporting Israel, "if you don't have lawyers definitively say, 'You can't,' the people who want to move are going to win every time," a State Department lawyer told me. A different State Department official assigned responsibility for the situation to the White House, saying Sullivan "deliberately refused" to initiate discussions among legal experts that would have made him and the president confront questions of Israeli war crimes. (Sullivan's spokesperson told me he "did not opine on legal matters—he left that to the lawyers," urging them to "reach their judgments without any pressure or influence from policymakers.") The same State Department official said that talks led by Joshua Geltzer, the National Security Council

Legal Advisor, did not challenge the evident default preference in the administration to continue supporting Israel. Geltzer discussed possible Israeli violations of the law of war in meetings with lawyers from the State Department, Defense Department, Justice Department and intelligence agencies, a senior official recalled to me, but, he added, "Interagency lawyers were reluctant to reach firm conclusions." (Through a spokesperson, McGurk said that he never "received reports of U.S. legal violations.")

The same senior official shed light on dynamics that made a yes or no answer on Israeli misconduct extremely unlikely—shielding the administration's decision-makers from making uncomfortable choices in response, either to ignore confirmed crimes or to anger pro-Israel forces. He recalled government attorneys arguing that it took years for international tribunals and judges to prove violations of international law and reiterated to me the view among Biden's advisors that proving intent was necessary in confirming most law of war violations, which would have required substantial cooperation from the Israelis (and which contradicts the view of many international law experts).[62]

However, the Biden administration itself had said it would uphold a standard of not transferring weapons simply if it was "more likely than not" that they would be used in serious violations of international law. In their October 13 letter to the Israelis, Blinken and Austin noted that U.S.-Israeli discussions about shielding civilians over the last year of war "to date have not produced the necessary outcomes." They urged a meeting of a new "channel" to discuss attacks on civilians. It never happened. A State Department official told me that the meeting was scheduled for mid-November but the Israelis canceled it the day after Trump won the election.[63]

The administration could have become more willing to reach definite answers based on its observation of Israeli patterns, such as launching strikes that appeared disproportionate and rarely giving U.S. officials exculpatory material or evidence that Israeli troops were being held accountable. It could even have pushed specifically for decisions about incidents that seemed almost certainly illegal, like the indiscriminate pager attack in Lebanon. When I raised those points to the senior official, his defense of the administration's record was both startling and unconvincing. He acknowledged that "the information that came back from the Israelis ranged in how explanatory or not it was—often not," but said that, in response to both the Israelis' continued shallow explanations and the growing U.S. concern about Palestinian deaths, Biden aides' "lawyer-written talking points for engaging with the Israelis . . . got sharper." With no tangible consequences for the Israelis, their behavior predictably never significantly improved. Regarding the pagers—which wounded more than 3,000 and killed 12, including 2 children—the official said that Washington "spent less time on that" because the United States was surprised by the tactic and it did not appear to involve U.S.-provided equipment, but he also said that discussions were occurring about whether military and intelligence support for Tel Aviv was legal. Yet such discussions would have been incomplete if they did not fully consider Israel's willingness to use audacious tactics.

Factors beyond data from Gaza and the degree of American involvement helped drive the failure to be conclusive, like the United States' own propensity for staggering violence and possible violations of international law: A different senior official told me that Pentagon lawyers suggested findings of Israeli war crimes could set precedents that would limit America's future military operations. Separately, a State Department lawyer described a disheartening culture of Washington insularity and coziness. As attorneys from across the administration regularly met to discuss apparent wrongdoing by Israel, that lawyer summed up the common attitude as: "We've all worked together so long, and will continue to work together in future administrations, so everyone should play nice." Even when discussions included deep distress about U.S.-backed Israeli actions and the possibility of illegal actions, summaries of them that were circulated within the administration simply stated that the conversations mentioned concerns without reaching conclusions, which "really wasn't an accurate representation," this lawyer told me. The product of the discussions was, consistently, plausible deniability for Biden's senior staff: "At the top, people are saying, 'Our lawyers have never asked us to find that something is a war crime.' But you have lawyers saying: 'You never asked me to find a war crime, and if you asked me to, I could, pretty easily.'"

Still, by the fall of 2024, intelligence agencies had briefly suspended some cooperation with the Israelis based on their own suspicions that Tel Aviv was violating the law of war.[64] Then came the new American intelligence suggesting intentional Israeli wrongdoing, which was "really explicit, unlike anything we'd seen before," an official told me. Even with that proof, administration staff treated the matter as "a hot potato—no one wanted to touch it," a senior humanitarian official told me, saying his colleagues were concerned about the potential harm to their careers of attaching their names to serious allegations against Israel. That such a consideration would drive them was, he said, "in itself appalling." Yet the evidence of what that official called "specific motivations" among Israelis to breach international law and U.S. standards by, for example, using food as a weapon of war and indiscriminately bombing civilians, was strong enough that it soon reached the most senior officials. At several meetings in late 2024, high-ranking administration personnel considered whether intelligence sharing with the IDF could even continue, one official told me. That official and another senior official said conversations at the time addressed their suspicion of mens rea: knowledge of wrongdoing by Israeli officials.

A change in how frank the administration was willing to be about Gaza, at least privately, was clear beyond the White House: Many State Department officials were by this point regularly using the term "ethnic cleansing" to describe Israeli actions, two officials told me, and a third said they observed Blinken himself asking if it applied.[65]

"The leadership was assessing whether or not there was an appetite to go harder [in acknowledging Israeli misconduct]," that State Department official told me, saying the final weeks of Biden's presidency were the first time high-ranking officials had asked Israel direct questions about its tactics.

Yet the administration settled its dilemma by repeating a routine among officials that had, throughout the war, precluded introspection, evolution, or full public understanding of the Biden team's blundering: declining to find a clear answer and, therefore, doing nothing. Top officials never conclusively confirmed that ethnic cleansing was occurring, the State Department official said, and when other State Department staff who were focused on international law requested an intelligence briefing on the question, intelligence officials denied the request. In the White House discussions about the new intelligence findings, McGurk and Jack Lew, Biden's ambassador in Jerusalem, strongly opposed the idea of accusing Israel of criminal behavior. A handful of counterparts who were convinced that Israel was violating the law and that U.S. officials might be aiding and abetting it pushed to suspend the provision of arms and intelligence to demonstrate the United States' commitment to international and American law. Avril Haines, who as director of national intelligence oversaw the assessments that prompted the discussions, was reportedly affected by evidence of Palestinian pain, but a U.S. official working on Middle East policy told me she had kept her distance from staff who questioned Israeli narratives about the war. Multiple officials told me they had, before this period, directly told Haines that evidence from Gaza suggested intelligence-sharing with Israel should be reviewed.

Without a high-level green light for a recommendation that could have been drastic, leading government lawyers opined that the United States lacked enough evidence to conclude definitively that continued U.S. support for Israel would be illegal—"something you can always say," the senior humanitarian official noted. The convenient vagueness was shared across the board, from Geltzer to the legal office at the State Department, traditionally seen as an elite and independent-minded custodian of international law. A senior official told me of how the interagency lawyers' group handled the moment: "No one in that group of sophisticated international and domestic law experts said, 'I think we're at the point where we are legally obliged to make this shift in policy.'" The U.S. would remain implicated in mass killing.

THE HAND-OFF

Turning a blind eye to corroboration of their role in some of the most egregious crimes possible helped administration staffers avoid discomfort. The preferred justification among officials for that selective view of law and fact was that a Gaza ceasefire was close, and upsetting Israel or emboldening Hamas would derail it. They deployed that line repeatedly without delivering a truce. By the end of 2024, however, Trump's greater assertiveness toward Israel meant a ceasefire truly was more likely, so the old excuse for inaction strengthened—covering officials until they reached the safety of jobs involving less scrutiny, with little risk of consequences for their Gaza choices.

A senior Biden aide later argued to me that the vacillation by government lawyers confirmed that the United States could not prove "systemic" impropriety by Israel. While this person acknowledged individual "indefensible" Israeli actions, he reiterated Israel's talking points by saying that such actions also occurred in American wars, meaning, presumably, that Israel should not be punished for them. The same official, however, told me that Tel Aviv centralized decisions over aid for Palestinians, denying flexibility to commanders at checkpoints, requiring cabinet votes about details like how much fuel would reach Gaza's hospitals, and needing major persuasion from Washington to make even minor improvements. "That's not our dysfunction or their deliberate dysfunction," they said, without clarifying who, if anyone, might be held responsible for devising and enabling that system.

Even those who nitpicked about the case for Israeli accountability, such as that official, said the administration was frozen on possible policy shifts not because of their merits but because the president and senior officials often embraced the narrative that a ceasefire was around the corner. The most enthusiastic proponent of that line was McGurk, who, a State Department colleague told me, saw ad hoc deals as the only appropriate option for the region, characterizing McGurk's thinking as: "The Middle East [is] a jungle, and therefore the law of the jungle applies."

The joint Biden-Trump push for a ceasefire before the inauguration gave McGurk even greater sway as the Biden confidant closest to the Israel-Hamas negotiations, which shrank the chances for any last-ditch pleas to rein in Israel. Though Chris Van Hollen, the crusading Maryland senator, published an op-ed urging sanctions on far-right Israeli ministers, American recognition of a Palestinian state, a red line against more settlements, and an acknowledgment of Israel breaking U.S. law, the administration was treating Trump as its prime ally, not fellow Democrats. In the closing days of the administration, Blinken received both another extensive memo from USAID documenting Israeli violations of international law and another recommendation from a senior State Department official to apply the Leahy Law to Israeli forces, two senior officials told me, but he did not act on those recommendations.[66] The Leahy recommendations left on Blinken's desk included those to sanction the units who allegedly tortured Palestinians at the Sde Teiman prison; by 2026, after experiencing impunity for human rights abuses under both Biden and Trump, Israel ended its own case over the claims and freed the accused soldiers. (Meanwhile, the government tried to prosecute the Israeli army's former top lawyer for her work on the case, including an alleged leak.)

Any of the administration's proposed steps to prod Israel might be reversed, but presidents often use their lame-duck period to challenge contested policies and prove they are not immutable. The Biden administration itself in January revoked Cuba's status as a state sponsor of terror "just to be on the record saying we do not agree with this," a senior aide told me, noting that was possible years earlier, but the administration was now thinking about its legacy. Trump canceled the step six days later.

Though better policymaking in the future would involve admitting shortcomings, most around Biden were getting even more stubborn. A senior official told me that "with Trump showing up in two weeks," the thinking among colleagues was startling: "Let's just focus on the good we've done and forget the rest." On December 24, Lew publicly attacked the Famine Early Warning Systems Network (FEWS NET), a USAID program, for issuing another warning of famine in northern

Gaza, and U.S. officials forced the group to retract its analysis; it did not issue another comment on Gaza for eight months amid Trump's decimation of the U.S. government's humanitarian apparatus.[67] Two weeks later, Biden told *USA Today* he believed he could have won the 2024 election.[68] Democratic Party operatives continued battling those who questioned their campaign choices, rather than reflecting on why America resoundingly rejected them, with Ammar Moussa—one of many campaign staffers who attacked journalists for saying Biden's age alarmed voters—repeatedly targeting the Uncommitted movement on social media, saying it hurt both Harris and Palestinians. Toward the end of 2025, Democratic National Committee chief Ken Martin said he would not publish a review of why the party lost the 2024 election.

The parting vindication Biden and his aides most coveted—a Gaza ceasefire—still depended on Netanyahu embracing the draft deal with Hamas that he had rebuffed since May. Israel's leader was cautious about the president-elect; Trump had fumed over Netanyahu acknowledging Biden's 2020 election win, telling journalist Barak Ravid he had "done more for [Netanyahu] than any other person," then adding: "Fuck him."[69] Biden's aides "used the incoming administration as somewhat of a bogeyman," a U.S. official close to the Trump team told me, arguing they did so "because they had squandered every other tool; they weren't taken seriously but people took Trump seriously." Unlike Biden, Trump was not only bashing one side of the talks for complicating them: When, on January 7, he again threatened "all hell" without a deal, a former senior Israeli official said Trump's comment "sounded like it was directed as much toward us as to Palestinians."[70] The following day, Trump posted a video of an academic accusing Netanyahu of fomenting "endless wars."[71]

Hamas's remaining objections to an agreement, about identifying living hostages, were ironed out by January 11, the group told Qatari and Egyptian mediators. Witkoff, Trump's negotiator, headed from Doha to Jerusalem the same day.[72] Seeing Netanyahu on Shabbat—the Jewish holiday when his right-wing government rarely held meetings—Witkoff emphasized his boss's desire for a deal so fervently Netanyahu "had no choice but to say yes very quickly," the former senior Israeli official told *The Washington Post*.[73] Samantha Sutton, a Biden White House aide involved in high-level discussions at the time, said members of Trump's team "were able to speak to the Israelis in a way that if my boss ever spoke to the Israelis, it would have closed things entirely." Speaking on a podcast in October 2025, Sutton did not address how Biden and his advisors' own choices—constantly showing Netanyahu he could outplay them—made that so.

For the Israeli leader, the pill of a deal was easier to swallow given the accurate expectation Trump would, after claiming a triumph, allow renewed Israeli ruthlessness in Gaza and other goals of Netanyahu's ultranationalist coalition, like attacking Iran and annexing the West Bank. Two U.S. officials told me Biden's chief White House advisors dismissed suggestions to codify the ceasefire through a UN Security Council resolution, which could rally international pressure for Trump and Netanyahu to respect the truce. They wanted to finalize the agreement and proclaim a triumph before surrendering power, and they remained hypersensitive about Israel, arguing that UN action would upset Tel Aviv, the officials said. (An aide to Sullivan pinned the blame on Biden, telling me that Sullivan unsuccessfully recommended a UN resolution to the president.)

Relief for families in Gaza and Israel again hinged on America's political calendar, with the ceasefire set for four days later, the last full day of Biden's presidency and before Trump's inauguration, as he had pledged.[74] Such delays were costly: Israeli air strikes immediately after the announcement killed at least seventy-three Palestinians, and in late December, when negotiations floundered,[75] IDF bombing and raids around northern Gaza's last major medical facility, Kamal Adwan Hospital, killed health workers, shuttered the hospital as part of what the United Nations called "the systematic dismantling" of the strip's health system, and led to the arrest of its director, Hussam Abu Safiya, who then lost nearly half his body weight in brutal Israeli detention.[76] Still, Biden cast Israel's battering of Gaza and Lebanon as boons that "changed the equation" in the Middle East—and he and his team wanted immediate praise for their involvement.[77]

Asked whether Trump sealed the deal, the president laughed. His aides highlighted McGurk's work before Witkoff's appointment, crowed to reporters about "the amount of history [Biden and Netanyahu] have seen together," and promoted an impression summarized in *The New York Times*: "what can be accomplished when political differences are set aside."[78] The presentation ignored McGurk's Republican background, long-running Biden-Trump continuity on Israel, and, most critically, that a deal could have come sooner, and lives saved, if Biden and Netanyahu had a different relationship. The Israeli leader was more forthright: His statement extensively "commended" Trump and only in the last line "thanked [Biden] as well for his assistance."

The Biden team's victory lap had a surreal aspect. McGurk and Witkoff were feted as improbable partners. Yet it was rumored that McGurk was hoping to be hired by Trump, although McGurk denied to me that this was the case. One Trump administration official told me he was familiar with McGurk's push, adding: "Nobody cared." Just before the announcement, Sullivan and Waltz held an amicable joint event. The administration was projecting nonpartisan grace—blessing successors who were preparing a literal chainsaw for the U.S. foreign policy apparatus—while still hoping observers would conclude the war went better than it might have under Trump's team or any other administration. Deep doubts persisted about both messages. In internal meetings throughout the war, officials all the way up to Blinken would list American aid and say Gaza could be bloodier, a senior State Department official later recalled to me. This person's response: "Someone's got shot. You're offering a Band-Aid. But also, you're the one who provided the gun. It doesn't make sense!"

For the administration, the war closed as it started—not with logic but with vivid drama. On January 19, after another hours-long delay during which U.S.-backed Israeli bombing killed an additional thirteen Palestinians, the ceasefire began.[79] Gaza celebrated and, finally, exhaled, as more aid trucks rolled in; three Israeli women violently kidnapped by Hamas-led militants were reunited with their loved ones; and ninety jailed Palestinian women and children—the youngest just twelve—walked free.[80]

A TROUBLING LEGACY

The settlement in Gaza was shared by the two administrations, but its aftermath confirmed it was Biden's decisions that ensured ongoing bloodshed—genocide, many increasingly said—even as he and his aides denied being answerable.

After claiming mastery in policymaking, the outgoing president looked confused and alienated at Trump's inauguration. The following day, Israel launched its biggest operation in the West Bank in decades, targeting refugee camps, killing dozens, and displacing forty thousand, the most Palestinians pushed out of their homes in the territory since Israeli began its occupation there in 1967.[81] With continued U.S. military aid, including the bombs Biden had paused and Trump quickly green-lit, Israel was deploying its Gaza playbook, Human Rights Watch said.[82] By March, that script was in play in the strip again too, after Israel unilaterally broke the ceasefire. And June saw Israel spur the U.S.-Iran war that Biden saw as his chief fear, foreshadowing the even more calamitous U.S.-Israeli campaign against Iran in 2026.

Biden and his aides concluded their Gaza policy with a veneer of stability—one that helped hundreds, perhaps thousands, of people, but masked a rot those officials had helped intensify, ensuring eminently predictable damage on their watch and beyond. For much of the war, Biden's inner circle had often described a sense of powerlessness, deflecting blame to Netanyahu, the president himself, Hamas, or others. Now, Biden's career was over. But it was hard to imagine that any of those officials could be trusted again with power either.

EPILOGUE

TRUMP'S FIRST YEAR BACK IN OFFICE SAW U.S.-BACKED Israeli policies kill another 25,000 Palestinians, including at least 238 in the occupied West Bank, where Israel had made no declaration of war and there was no Hamas rule. As 2026 began, most Palestinians in Gaza entered another year in tents amid persistent Israeli strikes and Israeli-imposed shortages of supplies. The new president imbued policy with his trademark flashiness and insensitivity: Early in his term, Trump used conversations with reporters and social media to suggest ejecting Gaza's residents and establishing a "Riviera of the Middle East," complete with a gold statue of him. But chiefly, Trump fueled deeper devastation in the region because he followed the Biden administration's playbook: impunity for Israel as it defied legal and humanitarian experts and undercut U.S. goals; refusal to treat Palestinian pain and aspirations as important; and deep hubris among U.S. officials. The combination of Biden-era patterns with Trump's disdain for human rights and affinity for Netanyahu made peace even more elusive.

The similarities between the two administrations in mismanaging Gaza soon became clear through the United States' approach to humanitarian aid. In March, when Netanyahu abandoned the ceasefire, he halted all shipments to Palestinians, claiming most were stolen by

Hamas though Israeli officials lacked proof for that assertion.[1] A full Israeli blockade continued for nearly three months with American support, hinging on a vital precedent: the tolerance for unprecedented man-made deprivation among Palestinians that grew in Washington under Biden. Prices for remaining products shot up more than 1,400 percent, and relief organizations ended or slashed support for a population that had only briefly begun to recover.[2] "We just wish we could cook a normal meal, but there's nothing," Suad, a mother, told Oxfam, saying her sickly son kept pleading for a single potato.[3] Writing for *The Guardian* after thirty hours without eating, Aya Al-Hattab said Palestinians felt "as though . . . we're living in some distant, forgotten galaxy. Our lives are marked by suffering and strangeness, while the rest of the world carries on."[4] Mike Huckabee, Trump's ambassador to Israel, responded to concerns from the United Nations by echoing the chilling—and potentially illegal—logic that Brett McGurk endorsed at the start of the war, saying access to essential goods hinged on Hamas freeing hostages.[5]

When international condemnation grew so strong that Israel began reconsidering its aid freeze, the Trump administration deployed a Biden-style response. Washington helped Tel Aviv jerry-rig a controversial new humanitarian system to replace the UN-led model trusted by relief workers. With American and Israeli backing, the so-called Gaza Humanitarian Foundation (GHF) began operating in late May. As critics had warned, relying on Israeli troops and American military contractors to operate aid hubs proved deeply dangerous; at least 2,256 Palestinians were killed while seeking aid in the following months, most of them near GHF sites and due to Israeli firing, per the United Nations.[6] (The foundation denied any role in the deaths and disputed allegations of war crimes by a former staffer.)[7] Among the handful of medical personnel Israel permitted into Gaza that summer was an American emergency doctor named Mark Brauner. Speaking with me after his return, in July 2025, Brauner described bloodshed "like clockwork": Within forty minutes of a GHF distribution, a flood of patients and bodies would arrive at Nasser Hospital, where he was volunteering.

The toll of dead and injured he witnessed reflected both the desperation of hungry Palestinians and the viciousness of the methods the U.S.-backed Israeli forces had become accustomed to using, particularly as the Israelis seemingly treated most males as combatants. Many victims were boys trying to help their families, Brauner said; a countless number were shot directly between their eyes, in their foreheads, or in their temples. Sometimes, "it was almost like they were changing the game.... We'd get all head injuries, then we'd have several hours or a day of all neck injuries, or all chest or all groin," he told me.[8] By August, widespread starvation was so clear that the Integrated Food Security Phase Classification initiative, a cautious multiparty UN-backed monitor, issued its first confirmation of famine in Gaza.[9] Other experts, including U.S. government analysts and the humanitarian group Refugees International, had already reached that conclusion in 2024.

Facing failure in Gaza, Trump, like Biden, doubled down on War on Terror–style militarism and quixotic attempts to shape regional affairs. In June, he let U.S. diplomacy with Iran wither by joining an Israeli bombing campaign that left open the prospects of follow-up fighting, because it failed to eliminate Iran's nuclear and missile capacities. As in the Biden era, a U.S. president was helping Netanyahu posture as a major world figure with unparalleled sway in Washington, while upsetting his own base, in this case anti-intervention Trump supporters.

By mid-September, Trump moved to rein in Israel, after the IDF's pursuit of Hamas leaders extended to bombing them in Qatar. Tel Aviv was imperiling his personal interests: Qatar had business ties to Trump's family and gifted him a luxury jet to use as Air Force One, and continuous U.S.-linked escalations endangered Trump's dreams of a Nobel Peace Prize. The president made Netanyahu apologize to Qatar and clinched another Israel-Hamas ceasefire agreement in early October. But like Biden's plans, his twenty-point framework avoided pressing Israel or prioritizing Palestinian concerns for autonomy and accountability—instead outlining a quasi-colonial vision of Gaza's future featuring heavy American influence. The Trump administration established another new effort to control aid and sustain a ceasefire through a center staffed with hundreds of U.S. troops but including no Palestinians, and in November, Trump secured a UN Security Council endorsement of his proposal for an unelected board to rule the strip, featuring no timeline for Palestinian statehood or Israel's withdrawal from the more than half of Gaza it still controlled. Unsurprisingly, the truce became increasingly meaningless for Palestinians. Israeli bombs, shelling, and shooting intensified again, particularly after Hamas released more captives, and killed at least 738 Palestinians by the time of this writing, while Israel further restricted aid flows and humanitarian groups' operations, as it had, step by step, through both the Biden and Trump eras.[10]

In its hollowness, Trump's treatment of Gaza resembled the ongoing bipartisan mess of U.S. policy in Lebanon, where he and Biden contended they had paved a path to Israeli-Lebanese peace with their November 2024 ceasefire. The professed aim of Tel Aviv and Washington, disarming Hezbollah, remained out of reach, while Israeli intervention, from bombing runs to military deployments in southern Lebanon, persisted. Effectively, the outcome was a lasting wound, without reconstruction or a path to recovery for more than sixty-four thousand still-displaced Lebanese. "The war will end when . . . there's no drone in the sky, when [Israel] doesn't hit a house every day," Mounifa Aidibeh, in the city of Tyre, told Reuters in October 2025.[11]

Trump's similarity to Biden on Gaza meant his administration took U.S. policies to their logical and disturbing next steps—boosting tensions and weakening Washington's commitment to its highest ideals, whether of free speech and sustaining international institutions or justice for civilians. Domestically, Trump adopted and intensified the suggestion from the Biden White House that antiwar protests often defended Hamas and threatened Jews, citing that portrayal as an excuse to crack down on academia and to try deporting foreign students who questioned American policy toward Israel. Internationally, Trump built on Biden's bid to limit critique of Israel with an overt assault on the International Criminal Court, slapping sanctions on court personnel and those helping them, such as Palestinian rights groups. In July, I broke the news the administration was even targeting a UN official, special rapporteur Francesca Albanese.[12] It soon appeared the Trump administration was willing to torpedo the court altogether rather than let it examine the plain reality that Israeli policies allegedly amounting to war crimes were continuing and worsening. Gaza's erosion of global order was growing faster than many had predicted.

At the end of 2025, the Trump White House released its National Security Strategy, a traditional statement of each administration's worldview. The depiction of the Middle East was a surreal repetition of Jake Sullivan's analysis in *Foreign Affairs* just before the slaughter on October 7: Trump's aides wrote that the region was "no longer the constant irritant, and potential source of imminent catastrophe, that it once was."[13] With similar brashness and myopia about conditions the United States itself fosters, Washington seemed once again to be courting bloodcurdling surprises and misadventures rooted in arrogance.

On February 28, 2026, Trump initiated a broad U.S.-Israeli war on Iran—fulfilling a decades-long goal for Netanyahu which might have remained elusive if Biden had not emboldened the Israeli leader, helping him rebuild his political heft after October 7 and gain an unprecedented sense of license from Washington. Spurring mass bloodshed among civilians and economic damage globally as Iran retaliated, the war quickly resembled the Gaza campaign, with strikes repeatedly killing schoolchildren and U.S. officials denying any need to show restraint. The ghastly similarities grew as Israel then launched yet another offensive in Lebanon, and Israeli officials said they would treat the country like the Palestinian strip, demolishing hundreds of thousands of homes. As of this writing, the death toll from those wars is in the thousands and continues to climb, including among Israelis and Americans. Gaza itself is increasingly ignored, still facing deadly, U.S.-backed Israeli strikes and acute aid restrictions, with little progress toward rebuilding, accountability, or a future in which Israel, Hamas, the United States, or anyone else offers dignity to millions of Palestinians who have persevered through the inconceivable.

Biden and his top aides oversaw disaster and then lost power, but few were humbled by the experience. Many still sought to be treated as respected and powerful officials, to continue shaping global affairs, and to reject responsibility for Gaza.

I met Brett McGurk for the first time in April 2025, on the night of my thirty-third birthday and just after I finished my first draft of this book. We had spoken before by phone, but it was still jarring when I spotted him at a crowded reception at the Smithsonian. After I approached him with a mutual friend, reiterating my requests for an interview, McGurk quickly killed the small talk with a finger in my face and a sharp "I just want to say . . . " Clutching a champagne flute so tightly I thought it might break, he raised his voice to claim I was obsessed with him and had made up things about him, seeming to base the latter accusation just on the fact that most of my sources of information about him were anonymous—even as his tirade demonstrated why many of his colleagues asked to remain nameless. Specifically, he referenced my article about his early 2024 plan to end the war, reconstruct Gaza, and reshape the region, the road map whose existence the White House had first denied and then attacked me for revealing.[14] McGurk said he was not naïve enough to think the United States could halt the war then. That was a remarkable admission. Multiple high-ranking officials had told me that McGurk's constant claims he was close to securing a truce, including in late 2023 and early 2024, had bolstered Biden's refusal to pressure Israel to end its offensive. If true, that meant he was now conveniently disavowing a narrative that helped ensure U.S.-backed attacks persisted and Palestinians continued to starve. Standing beside McGurk, his wife, journalist Gina Chon, said that my reporting lacked credibility because I had never once approached him for comment. I could only assume that was what he had told her. She appeared genuinely surprised when I responded that I had always sought comment from him when writing about him and that we had in fact spoken off the record extensively twice.

To me, McGurk's behavior is an extreme example of the defensiveness among many Biden-era officials over Gaza. Many people singled out McGurk as the villain of the piece. As he was in the administration, however, McGurk is less an outlier than a forthright representation of the mindset among his colleagues that enabled atrocities for sixteen months. In discussing the war, former Biden aides have avoided acknowledging their complicity and instead relied on diversion, to the easy targets of unpopular Netanyahu, openly barbarous Trump, and their old-fashioned boss, or to rosy misrepresentations of their record.[15] Nearly all the officials I interviewed for this book sought anonymity. While I understood their sensitivity about discussing coworkers and internal debates, I often sensed in those requests the tendencies that created Biden's horrific policy, from a hesitancy to challenge Washington power players—above all, the president—to a sense that forthright assessments of U.S. foreign policy, particularly on Israel-Palestine, are professionally detrimental, even if strategically valuable.

Simultaneously, some senior officials have sought to obscure their roles. "If I'm mentioned in this book, how will I be portrayed?" asked one of the staffers closest to Biden, who regularly defended the president's approach to the media. When I asked Tony Blinken's spokeswoman, Erin Pelton, for comment for a story mentioning Blinken's internal inquiries about whether he was enabling ethnic cleansing, Pelton berated me.[16] The implication from Biden's circle—a big part of the Democratic brain trust that hopes to regain positions of power in post-Trump politics—has consistently been that the greater offense is not in the horror of the war but in questioning those who shaped it.

Some of America's most powerful institutions have helped Biden-era officials perpetuate that impression. After leaving office, former administration members have gained positions at Harvard and Columbia; on the boards of the Council on Foreign Relations, the Carnegie

Corporation, and the Center for American Progress; and in wealthy private firms. Biden and Blinken signed book deals, and McGurk became a CNN pundit. Jake Sullivan was appointed Harvard's first-ever Kissinger Professor of the Practice of Statecraft and World Order—a title presumably envisioned as a compliment, yet one that felt painfully accurate to those who accused Sullivan of moral vacuity.

In perhaps the most unsettling twist of all, some Biden personnel have actually sought kudos for their handling of Israel. Writing in *The New York Times*, Blinken argued the Biden administration "set the table" for Trump to use force against Iran and then pursue nuclear negotiations.[17] But predictably, Trump-led diplomacy has repeatedly failed. Arguably, the Biden-era amassing of U.S. military resources in the Middle East bolstered Israel's confidence that the United States would support its military gambits—in addition to America largely paying for its defense—and so paved the way for policies like war with Iran and Trump's futile more than $1 billion U.S. bombing campaign in Yemen. Sullivan has repeatedly defended Biden's unfettered supply of weapons for Israel by saying Tel Aviv faced threats from multiple fronts.[18] Yet the animosity Israel faces in its neighborhood has intensified, even if its foes are temporarily weaker. In early 2026, Biden advisor Amos Hochstein responded furiously to Netanyahu suggesting that the Biden administration had slowed the delivery of military equipment and so caused casualties among Israeli soldiers, with Hochstein posting on X a list of actions he said Israel should be thankful for, including "more than $20 billion" in military support, sending U.S. aircraft carriers to the Middle East, and "SAVING countless lives of Israelis."[19] Sustaining Netanyahu's continued grip on power—opposed by many Israelis—and immeasurable anguish among Palestinians went unmentioned.

As this book documents, Biden administration officials repeatedly chose to uphold a ghastly and self-defeating Gaza policy. They ignored off-ramps and alternatives, contributing to hundreds of thousands of deaths of innocent Palestinians, Lebanese, and Israelis, and creating a more dangerous world. Their attempts to rewrite history disrespect us all.

In less than two years, Joe Biden irreversibly changed America's role in Israel-Palestine and may have permanently altered Americans' approach to foreign affairs.

He and fellow Zionists often highlight that he was the first U.S. president to visit Israel at a time of war. The choice encapsulates how Biden developed an approach that weakened both his own goal of U.S.-Israel intimacy and public trust in policymaking. More than any predecessor, the Biden administration treated an Israeli-Palestinian war as an American war—making Israeli choices a matter of U.S. officials' credibility, while defying their own constituents, allies, and staff, as well as blatant evidence of agony and failure, with the stubbornness Washington usually reserves for its own misadventures. They did so when faith in elite decision-makers was already shaky—hurt by a pandemic and challenges to the status quo of American politics from the right and left—and after claiming that Biden would restore competence and concern for international law to policymaking after Trump's first presidency. American hypocrisy on Israel-Palestine was a constant throughout Biden's life that he perpetuated, but his administration took it to lengths that made it unsustainable.

For the Democratic Party, as it looks to regain power, Biden's Gaza record is glaring proof that its talk of inclusion, professionalism, and championing American ideals has been at odds with its policies abroad. Where such evidence was easier to muddy in the past, live streaming, digital archives, and greater diversity within the United States—tying more Americans to foreign nations and brown and Black communities—make it harder to cite remoteness to downplay U.S.-linked foreign horrors. Gaza became a personal issue for many Americans that heightened broader Biden-era dissatisfaction; the administration came to represent both floundering and inauthenticity. Democratic candidates and activists have told me that honesty about Gaza has become a gut test for voters that demonstrates that a figure means what he or she says and can be trusted, as was the case for New York City mayor Zohran Mamdani, who drew attacks for his criticism of Israel but triumphed while standing by it. For decades, political and policy figures have sustained what Palestine Legal founder Dima Khalidi calls a "Palestine exception," particularly to the equal application of U.S. values like free speech, but also in how laws shape decision-making. The Biden era saw more Americans reject that selective thinking. Subsequently, Democrats have increasingly abandoned unchecked support for Israel, with more heeding calls to, for instance, reject donations from AIPAC, and even establishment figures challenging weapons for Tel Aviv, as most Democratic senators did in striking votes in July 2025 and April 2026. (Some Biden aides have changed their tune amid the shifting winds: In August 2025, Jake Sullivan said senators voting against arms for Israel was "credible" because conditions had changed from when he was in government and in 2026, Sullivan said the Biden administration "should have done more" to pressure Netanyahu.)[20]

A reenergized Democratic Party pitching itself as the answer to Trump-era damage will face questions about its role in his choices—and the noxious continuity between the Biden administration enabling bloodshed in Gaza and its successor doing so is clear. The way the policy has exacerbated rage and danger in the United States itself has become clearer too, through incidents targeting Muslims, Jews, and Arabs, including the appalling 2025 killing of Israeli embassy staffers in downtown Washington. Few are likely to buy Biden aides' assertions that they could do no better because they lacked sufficient influence over Israel, or their exaggerations of their support of Palestinian civilians. Sullivan and Jack Lew, for example, have said their aid policy was a success since an official famine declaration in the strip did not occur until after they left office, but Jeremy Konyndyk, an aid expert who served in the Biden administration before the war, emphasized the cynicism of that claim. "What the Israeli government has been doing to Gaza for the last two-plus years is basically holding Gaza's head underwater and each time as Gaza is about to fully drown, briefly letting it up for air before pushing it under again," Konyndyk told me in the fall of 2025. "The Biden people never allowed Israel to quite get to the point of fully drowning [Gaza], and Trump did, but they still allowed Israel to hold [it] underwater. Do they deserve credit for that? I don't think so."

Because both Biden and Trump sustained and expanded the Gaza war, pushback to the U.S.-Israel relationship and its ramifications has grown across the political spectrum. It's inappropriate that the smaller country dominates Washington's approach, some conservative commentators argue; they say Trump's handling of Tel Aviv is a barometer of his commitment to being "America First," and they have loudly complained when they feel he has failed, notably by joining Netanyahu's assaults on Iran. Given the uncertainty about the Republican Party's future after the mishmash of Trump-era positions on domestic and foreign policy, Israel skeptics in its ranks—some who focus on anti-interventionism, others who veer into far-right and antisemitic dog whistles—see a chance to shift GOP positions. Polling showing far lower support for Tel Aviv among younger conservatives helps them make their case. As they do so, their arguments often draw attention to policies pushed by Biden, citing the U.S. role in mass killings or permitting assaults on Palestinian Christian communities and highlighting efforts to limit speech on Israel (albeit with little sympathy for the immigrants targeted over it). Israel-Palestine has become a chief focus of those saying the U.S. approach to global affairs needs an overhaul, and the Biden era has given them a clear, lasting example to cite.

Globally, the administration's Gaza record will influence the prospect of any standards for how governments should act and the concerns of U.S.-aligned countries, from the viability of their ties with Washington to the stability of their own societies. To resolve conflicts and manage flashpoints—from Ukraine to Taiwan—some faith among states in shared international law is crucial. Restoring such confidence will be impossible if the innumerable violations of global principles in the Gaza war are overlooked. A year after the 2024 election, Biden's former White House director for strategic planning, Thomas Wright, published an essay saying Democrats must argue for the United States to be a "team captain" for like-minded countries. He accused Trump and the leaders of China and Russia of ending the rules-based international order but made no mention of Gaza.[21] I wondered what trust in American leadership could mean after many of the figures presenting themselves as stewards of U.S. ideals and rationality have discredited themselves, and whether the compromises usually inherent in being "like-minded" with Washington—like heavy support for Israel—are still acceptable to many governments, given their own populations' shifting views.

The Biden administration began its tenure by unveiling a new phrase to suggest it had adopted a more equitable position on Israel-Palestine: Officials spoke of wanting "equal measures of freedom, prosperity, and democracy" for both Israelis and Palestinians.[22] The position ignored the Democrats' resistance, during intraparty discussions months earlier, to endorse policies that might upset pro-Israel hard-liners, and it now looks almost laughable given the administration's record. In the aftermath of Biden's Gaza policy, with the International Court of Justice likely to rule by 2027 on whether Israel's campaign—impossible without U.S. support—constituted genocide, and with the war firmly entrenched in millions of minds, future policymakers will need to address harder questions than whether they believe in Israeli-Palestinian equality, like what they will do to ensure it and whether Tel Aviv still deserves unparalleled economic, military, and diplomatic aid. No answer will be complete without an understanding of the period between October 7, 2023, and January 20, 2025.

ACKNOWLEDGMENTS

The sensation of being in Gaza amid Israeli bombardment, Israeli restrictions on all escape routes, and anxious discussions of whether America would use its leverage to save lives lodged itself in my psyche long before I ever imagined this book. My deepest gratitude goes to people who endured and saw far, far worse over the period I have written about and who documented the toll of one of the darkest man-made catastrophes in our lifetimes, making it possible to try to make sense of it. They are Palestinians, Lebanese, and Israelis. Their torments included losing loved ones, communities, and basic dignity, and the oppressive feeling there was no accountability for the handful of people shaping their excruciating circumstances. And their ranks include heroic humanitarian personnel and journalists from further afield, many of whom faced attacks—overwhelmingly U.S.-backed Israeli assaults—despite American promises to protect their work. May we do justice to their commitment to truth and humanity.

Dan Gerstle at W. W. Norton approached me about writing a book after he read my profile of Brett McGurk in December 2023. His initiative, curiosity, and kindness convinced me to embark on this project, and tremendous support from Norton brought it to completion. That backing chiefly came from my remarkable editor, Huneeya Siddiqui. Huneeya helped this reporter find his voice as an author; she sharpened my arguments and narrative and, crucially, understood the importance of producing not a "Washington book" of drama and gossip among power players but a record of why tens of thousands of people lost their lives that emphasizes non-American lives are not statistics. She did so with an aspirational blend of calm and purpose. I am additionally thankful to many other talented members of the Norton universe, including Bob Byrne, Emmy Wenstrup, Meredith Dowling, Devon Zahn, and Derek Thornton.

Amanda Annis and Audrey Crooks, my agents at Trident, are the fairy godmothers of this book. Their faith in me, their work to fine-tune my proposal, and their commitment to meaningful work and advocacy for their authors made the seemingly insurmountable feel doable. I've been humbled by their constantly evolving support and their pitch-perfect understanding of when I need either space and downtime or a sharp nudge.

A staggering number of people have trusted me with their insights and recollections. Most faced professional and personal risks; as national security professionals, many have little or zero experience communicating frankly with journalists, and their willingness to do so offered another measure of how morally and strategically abhorrent the Biden administration's Gaza policy became. I hope those who cannot be named here know I am deeply grateful to them. Some, however, can be, like members of the group of more than a dozen resignees over the war; in particular, Josh Paul, Annelle Sheline, Lily Greenberg Call, Stacy Gilbert, Harrison Mann, Mike Casey, Hala Rharrit, and Steve Gabavics have been hugely helpful to my understanding of the administration's dynamics and U.S. government operations broadly. I am also grateful to many Palestinians and Israelis who have informed my thinking through the years, particularly Yehuda Shaul, George Zeidan, Ghada Alhaddad, and Elad Strohmayer. And I know my career would not be possible without help from professionals in the foreign policy and journalism communities; among those who have been especially supportive, many of them helping move this project along, are Matt Duss, Mehdi Hasan, Lara Friedman, Thanassis Cambanis, Joy Reid, Waleed Shahid, Loren Voss,

Azmat Khan, Scott Paul, Lauren Hartnett, Joyce Karam, Brian Finucane, Lydia Polgreen, Sarah Harrison, John Hudson, Veronica Pedrosa, Nermeen Shaikh, Andrew Leber, Khaled Elgindy, Jeremy Konyndyk, Ed Wong, Maryum Saifee, Maya Garg, Nida Khan, and many who cannot be named here. I am sure I am forgetting kind, wise people who have helped me grow. I apologize in advance, and also: Thank you.

I came to America to study at Yale. I met mentors and friends who had a lasting, important impact on my thinking and development; I'm especially thankful to professors Mark Schoofs, Thomas Graham, John Negroponte, Michele Malvesti, and Scott Boorman, and to the incredible community at the *Yale Daily News*.

Inspired by my grandmother, I wanted to be a journalist at thirteen. Several brilliant editors in Pakistan took a chance on my writing and have tirelessly rooted for me ever since: Kamal Majidulla, Rehana Hakim, Samina Ibrahim, and Sairah Irshad Khan. Working at *HuffPost*, I've learned from some of the most talented, thoughtful, and moral people in American media. George Zornick has been an editor beyond compare, immeasurably kind and adept at quickly grasping the implications of exclusives, complex source relationships, and intricate foreign policy maneuvers. Fellow editors, notably Whitney Snyder, Ani Vrabel, Lilli Petersen, Nick Baumann, Amanda Terkel, Eline Gordts, Kate Palmer, Elise Foley, Kevin Robillard, and Ryan Grim, were integral to my work too, as were whip-smart colleagues who became cherished friends, like Jessica Schulberg, Chris Mathias, Sanjana Karanth, Sabrina Siddiqui, Alexander Kaufman, and many others. The inimitable Arianna Huffington made those relationships and, to a degree, this book possible.

I am thankful to Andy Young for bringing a veteran researcher's eye and an astonishing font of stories to the process of completing this book; to Anika Arora Seth for diligent, creative support; and to Jessica Friedman, who went beyond the call of duty.

No one is lucky enough to deserve the people in my personal life. Aisha, my Hayx, knows this book basically as well as me, having shepherded and cheered it on through pitches, drafts, and bullet points; I can never praise her extraordinary mind and heart enough. Dear friends have kept me sane and loved and tolerated me when I have been far from it: Shaha, Sara, Anushae, Emily, David, Swati, Ali, Lauren, Allie, Isabella, Adela, Amanda (Shaddy!), Isaac, Julia, Abbas, Azam, Hiba, Aaminah, Aisha (Tom!), and many others. I am thankful to so many in my family, particularly my inspiring khala, Nicky; my cousins Iman, Nemah, Maryam, and Aalya; Ali and Co. in Britain; Amer and Matt for nearly fifteen years of shepherding me through American adulthood; and to the Nolans. My mother, Yasmine, is a legend in her own time on several continents, and she has championed a child she never anticipated, poking bears she wishes he could leave alone, with aplomb, compassion, and sharp intelligence. Finally, to Zack: Thank you for letting this book take over our life before it could settle into an appropriate shape, for suggestions in the middle of the night and when the start of your day coincides with the end of mine, and for sharing with me your unique blend of love, patience, commitment, savvy, and adventure. You're a find that outshines any scoop.

NOTES

INTRODUCTION

1. Michael Spagat et al., "Violent and Nonviolent Death Tolls for the Gaza War: New Primary Evidence," medRxiv, June 20, 2025; Michael Spagat et al., "Violent and Nonviolent Death Tolls for the Gaza Conflict: New Primary Evidence from a Population-Representative Field Survey," *The Lancet Global Health*, April 2026; Joel Gunter, "'In Every Street There Are Dead': Gaza Rescuers Reckon with Scale of Destruction," BBC, January 20, 2025. In January 2026, Israel's military said roughly 70,000 Palestinians had been killed by its attacks, accepting the then–death toll compiled by authorities in Gaza after years of Tel Aviv claiming it was exaggerated.
2. "Just 1.5 Per Cent of Gaza's Agricultural Land Remains Accessible and Undamaged," UN News, August 6, 2025.
3. Seham Tantesh and Julian Borger, "'It's Like a Nuclear Bomb Has Hit': Shocked Palestinians Return Home to Devastation," *The Guardian*, October 18, 2025.
4. Jake Sullivan, "What Donald Trump and Dick Cheney Got Wrong about America," *The Atlantic*, January/February 2019; Gerhard Peters and John T. Woolley, comps., "Press Briefing by Press Secretary Jen Psaki and National Security Advisor Jake Sullivan," American Presidency Project, University of California, Santa Barbara, February 4, 2021.

CHAPTER 1: FROM SHOCK TO SHOCK AND AWE

1. James Jacoby, "Brett McGurk," *Frontline*, PBS, December 8, 2023.
2. Gerhard Peters and John T. Woolley, comps., "Pool Reports of October 7, 2023," American Presidency Project, University of California, Santa Barbara, October 7, 2023. Pool reports authored by Laura Figueroa Hernandez of *Newsday*; compiled and uploaded by the American Presidency Project.
3. Gerhard Peters and John T. Woolley, comps., "Background Press Call by a Senior Administration Official Regarding Hamas Terrorist Attacks in Israel," American Presidency Project, University of California, Santa Barbara, October 7, 2023.
4. Benjamin Netanyahu, "Statement by Prime Minister Benjamin Netanyahu," Ministry of Foreign Affairs, gov.il, October 7, 2023; Ibrahim Dahman et al., "Netanyahu Says Israel

Is 'at War' after Hamas Launches Surprise Air and Ground Attack from Gaza," CNN, October 7, 2023.

5. "October 7 Crimes against Humanity, War Crimes by Hamas-Led Groups," Human Rights Watch, July 17, 2024. The definition of "civilian" is extremely contested in this context. The figure 815 is cited by Agence France-Presse, citing several sources, and subsequently cited by Human Rights Watch (which suggested the number of civilians may be higher according to the definition under the law of war). Israel's government also suggests the October 7 attack killed more than 800 civilians. But many politicians (even some critics of Israel like Senator Bernie Sanders) and some press reports refer to all 1,200 casualties as noncombatants. Israel initially said the death toll was 1,400 but revised it down.
6. Finer denied this portrayal to me.
7. Gabavics first revealed the finding anonymously in a May 2025 documentary by the media company Zeteo, then went public in an interview with *The New York Times* in October.
8. "Israel/OPT: Investigate Possible War Crimes during Israel's Military Offensive on Gaza in May 2023," Amnesty International, June 13, 2023.
9. Jacob Magid, "The Day after That Never Came: How Time Ran Out on Blinken's Plan for Postwar Gaza," *Times of Israel*, December 5, 2025.
10. Katie Rogers, "Jake Sullivan's 'Quieter' Middle East Comments Did Not Age Well," *New York Times*, October 26, 2023.
11. Ronen Bergman and Adam Goldman, "Israel Knew Hamas's Attack Plan More Than a Year Ago," *New York Times*, November 30, 2023.
12. Renee Rigdon and Amy O'Kruk, "Maps Show the Extreme Population Density in Gaza," CNN, October 11, 2023.
13. "Israel Retaliation Kills 230 Palestinians after Hamas Operation," Al Jazeera, October 7, 2023.
14. "Situation Report #2 on the Situation in the Gaza Strip," United Nations Relief and Works Agency for Palestine Refugees in the Near East (UNRWA), October 8, 2023.
15. Akbar Shahid Ahmed and Rowaida Abdelaziz, "Gaza Prepares to Once Again Become One of the World's Bleakest Battlefields," *HuffPost*, October 10, 2023.
16. "Situation Report #3 on the Situation in the Gaza Strip," United Nations Relief and Works Agency for Palestine Refugees in the Near East (UNRWA), October 9, 2023; "Extermination and Acts of Genocide: Israel Deliberately Depriving Palestinians in Gaza of Water," Human Rights Watch, December 19, 2024.
17. Humeyra Pamuk, "Special Report: Emails Show Early US Concerns over Gaza Offensive, Risk of Israeli War Crimes," Reuters, October 4, 2024.
18. Ahmed and Abdelaziz, "Gaza Prepares."
19. "'You Feel Like You Are Subhuman': Israel's Genocide against Palestinians in Gaza," Amnesty International, December 5, 2024.
20. Carrie Keller-Lynn, "Gallant Vows to 'Wipe Hamas from Earth,' after 'the Worst Terror Attack' in History," *Times of Israel*, October 12, 2023.
21. *Times of Israel* Staff, "Bennett: 'This Is 100x Worse Than Yom Kippur War. We're Facing Equivalent of Nazis,'" *Times of Israel*, October 9, 2023. Post within a live blog of news updates for this date.
22. Mark Lander, "'Erase Gaza': War Unleashes Incendiary Rhetoric in Israel," *New York Times*, November 15, 2023.
23. Peter Baker, "Biden's Israel Ties Rooted in Long Career: 'From His Gut to His Heart to His Head,'" *New York Times*, October 28, 2023.
24. Ashley Killough, "Joe Biden: Bibi and I Are 'Still Buddies,'" CNN, November 10, 2014.
25. Yaniv Kubovich, "The IDF Took Away Weapons from Gaza Border Communities in Recent Years, and Armed West Bank Settlers in the Thousands," *Haaretz*, October 20, 2023.
26. Barak Ravid, "Scoop: Israel Assures U.S. New M16s Won't Go to West Bank Settlers," *Axios*, November 6, 2023.

27. Joseph R. Biden, "Remarks by President Biden on the Terrorist Attacks in Israel," White House, October 10, 2023. Archived on the official White House website as part of the Biden administration records.
28. Yasmeen Abutaleb and John Hudson, "White House Grapples with Internal Divisions on Israel-Gaza," *Washington Post*, November 26, 2023.
29. Notably, Biden criticized Netanyahu for his judicial overhaul plan before October 7 alongside many of these organizations.
30. Gerhard Peters and John T. Woolley, comps., "What They Are Saying: President Biden Makes Powerful, Heartfelt Statements of Support for Israel, Condemns Terrorist Attacks," American Presidency Project, University of California, Santa Barbara, October 12, 2023. This is a press release issued by Biden's office in October 2023.
31. Antony J. Blinken, "Press Conference on the Israel-Hamas War," American Rhetoric Online Speech Bank, October 12, 2023.
32. Helene Cooper and Eric Schmitt, "Austin Returns to Israel with a Tougher Message and Lessons Learned," *New York Times*, December 18, 2023.
33. Karen DeYoung and Missy Ryan, "How Joe Biden Lost His Grip on Israel's War for 'Total Victory' in Gaza," *Washington Post*, October 3, 2024.
34. Associated Press, "Blinken Calls for Protecting Civilians as Israel Prepares an Expected Assault on Gaza," CBS News, October 14, 2023.
35. Michael D. Shear, David E. Sanger, and Edward Wong, "Biden's Support for Israel Now Comes with Words of Caution," *New York Times*, October 30, 2023.
36. John Hudson, "Blinken Invokes Jewish Ancestry in Address to Grieving Israeli Public," *Washington Post*, October 12, 2023.
37. António Guterres, "Why Israel Must Reconsider Its Gaza Evacuation Order," *New York Times*, October 13, 2023.
38. Pamuk, "Special Report."
39. Emanuel Fabian and Amy Spiro, "90-Minute Panic over Mass Drone Invasion in Northern Israel Proves to Be False Alarm," *Times of Israel*, October 11, 2023.
40. Franklin Foer, "The War That Would Not End," *The Atlantic*, September 25, 2024.
41. Abutaleb and Hudson, "White House Grapples with Internal Divisions."
42. Karine Jean-Pierre and Jake Sullivan, "Press Briefing by Press Secretary Karine Jean-Pierre and National Security Advisor Jake Sullivan," White House, October 10, 2023.
43. Liv Martin, Clothilde Goujard, and Hailey Fuchs, "Israel Floods Social Media to Shape Opinion around the War," *Politico*, October 17, 2023.
44. Oren Liebermann, Natasha Bertrand, and Brad Lendon, "US Sending Second Carrier Strike Group, Fighter Jets to Region as Israel Prepares to Expand Gaza Operations," CNN, October 15, 2023; "Security Council Rejects Russian Resolution on Gaza," UN News, October 16, 2023.
45. Gabe Gutierrez et al., "How President Joe Biden's Israel Trip Came Together," NBC News, October 17, 2023.
46. Jacoby, "Brett McGurk."
47. Eyal Weizman et al., "'When It Stopped Being a War': The Situated Testimony of Dr Ghassan Abu-Sittah," *Forensic Architecture*, October 17, 2024.
48. Peter Baker et al., "The U.S. and Israel: An Embrace Shows Signs of Strain after Oct. 7," *New York Times*, December 31, 2023.
49. David Remnick, "The Price of Netanyahu's Ambition," *New Yorker*, January 14, 2024.

CHAPTER 2: DISSENT, THEN DEFLECTION

1. Akbar Shahid Ahmed, "'On Thin Ice': Some Biden Administration Staffers Feel Stifled Discussing Horrors in Gaza," *HuffPost*, October 18, 2023.
2. Ahmed, "'On Thin Ice.'"

3. Meredith Deliso, "Man Convicted of Hate Crime in Fatal Stabbing of 6-Year-Old Palestinian-American Boy," ABC News, February 28, 2025.
4. Ahmed, "'On Thin Ice.'"
5. Office of Congresswoman Pramila Jayapal, "Jayapal, Casar, Lee, McGovern, Castro, Escobar, García Release Statement Calling for Ceasefire," October 17, 2023; Akbar Shahid Ahmed, "Biden's Israel-Gaza Approach Sidelines State Department, and Officials Fear the Worst," *HuffPost*, November 2, 2023.
6. Akbar Shahid Ahmed and Rowaida Abdelaziz, "'Who Would Accept Such a Life?' Gaza Conditions Worsen as U.S. Aid Comes Up Short," *HuffPost*, November 10, 2023; Julian Borger, "Aid Convoy Set to Enter Gaza a 'Drop in the Ocean of Need' Says WHO," *The Guardian*, October 19, 2023.
7. Yuval Abraham, "Expel All Palestinians from Gaza, Recommends Israeli Gov't Ministry," *+972 Magazine*, October 30, 2023.
8. Adam Taylor and Manuel Canales, "Visualizing Gaza's Aid Shortage as 'Man-Made' Famine Looms," *Washington Post*, March 28, 2024; Tom Fletcher, X, October 22, 2023. Under the username @UNReliefChief; "Israel: Unlawful Gaza Blockade Deadly for Children," Human Rights Watch, October 18, 2023.
9. "Damning Evidence of War Crimes as Israeli Attacks Wipe Out Entire Families in Gaza," Amnesty International, October 20, 2023.
10. "Israel / OPT: 'Nowhere Safe in Gaza': Unlawful Israeli Strikes Illustrate Callous Disregard for Palestinian Lives," Amnesty International, November 20, 2023.
11. Yuval Abraham, "'Lavender': The AI Machine Directing Israel's Bombing Spree in Gaza," *+972 Magazine*, April 3, 2024.
12. Bethan McKernan and Harry Davies, "'The Machine Did It Coldly': Israel Used AI to Identify 37,000 Hamas Targets," *The Guardian*, April 3, 2024.
13. McKernan and Davies, "'The Machine Did It Coldly.'"
14. Abraham, "'Lavender.'"
15. Dan Williams and Nidal Al-Mughrabi, "Israel Shows Images of Tanks in Gaza as War on Hamas Militants Deepens," Reuters, October 29, 2023.
16. Becky Sullivan and Daniel Estrin, "Israel Says It's 'Expanding' Ground Activities in Gaza as Internet Blackout Takes Hold," NPR, October 27, 2023.
17. IDF Personnel Directorate, "Swords of Iron: IDF Casualties," Ministry of Foreign Affairs, gov.il, November 3, 2023.
18. James Elder, "Gaza Has Become a Graveyard for Thousands of Children," UNICEF, October 31, 2023. Comments from UNICEF spokesperson James Elder at a press briefing at the Palais des Nations in Geneva.
19. Ryan Geitner et al., "Patterns of Harm Analysis: Gaza, October 2023," Airwars, December 2024.
20. Akbar Shahid Ahmed, "Emails Show Biden Staffers' Confusion Trying to Help Desperate Americans in Gaza," *HuffPost*, October 23, 2023.
21. Akbar Shahid Ahmed, "Israel's Strike on Iran Prolongs an Excruciating Limbo for Palestinians," *HuffPost*, April 19, 2024.
22. Gordon F. Sander, "How a U.S. President Known to Disparage Jews Became Godfather of Israel," *Washington Post*, May 13, 2023.
23. "$26,000,000 U.S. Aid to Israel Resumed as She Halts Canal; Eisenhower Announces Action after Decision to Stop Work on Jordan River Project," *New York Times*, October 29, 1953.
24. "Eisenhower Reveals His 1957 Aims to Penalize Israel on Sinai Issue," Jewish Telegraphic Agency, September 22, 1965.
25. David Ben-Gurion, "Statement to the Knesset by PM Ben-Gurion," Ministry of Foreign Affairs, gov.il, March 5, 1957.
26. Dennis Ross, Nicholas Rostow, and Michael Mandelbaum, "LBJ and the June 1967 War: Lessons from the American Role," Washington Institute for Near East Policy, June 9, 2017.
27. John Judis, "Apocalypse Now: Bush's Failed Israel Strategy," Carnegie Endowment

for International Peace, August 2, 2006. This piece was initially published by the *New Republic Online*. Ron Kampeas, "Gerald Ford: Backing Soviet Jews, and Pressuring Israel to Give Back the Sinai," Jewish Telegraphic Agency, May 7, 2018.

28. Bernard Gwertzman, "U.S. Decides to Sell Some Arms to Israel That It Blocked in Past," *New York Times*, October 12, 1976.
29. Steven R. Weisman, "Reagan Ends Ban on Sending Israel 16 Jet Warplanes," *New York Times*, August 18, 1981.
30. Don Oberdorfer and John M. Goshko, "Gesture of Cooperation," *Washington Post*, May 20, 1983.
31. Crispian Balmer, "Despite Clashes with US Presidents, Israel's Netanyahu Usually Gets His Way," Reuters, June 22, 2025; Robert Malley and Hussein Agha, "Camp David: The Tragedy of Errors," *New York Review of Books*, August 9, 2001.
32. Judis, "Apocalypse Now."
33. "Israel Pushed Gaza to 'Brink of Collapse': WikiLeaks," NBC News, January 5, 2011. NBC News does not list an author for this article in the byline but credits "msnbc.com staff and news service reports" as its source.
34. Chris Megerian, "'A Zionist in My Heart': Biden's Devotion to Israel Faces a New Test," Associated Press, October 12, 2023.
35. "The First Intifada," Al Jazeera, December 9, 2003; Ishaan Tharoor, "How Israel Helped Create Hamas," *Washington Post*, July 30, 2014.
36. Andrew Higgins, "How Israel Helped to Spawn Hamas," *Wall Street Journal*, January 24, 2009.
37. Ezra Klein and Tareq Baconi, "Transcript: Ezra Klein Interviews Tareq Baconi," *New York Times*, December 5, 2023. Transcript of an episode of the *Ezra Klein Show*.
38. Suzanne Goldenberg, "US Plotted to Overthrow Hamas after Election Victory," *The Guardian*, March 4, 2008.
39. Klein and Baconi, "Transcript."
40. Akbar Shahid Ahmed, "Hamas' Political Headquarters in Qatar Is on Shaky Ground," *HuffPost*, April 22, 2024.
41. "Our Narrative . . . Operation Al-Aqsa Flood," *Palestine Chronicle*, January 2024.
42. Peter Baker, "Terrible Choices and Deep Distrust: The Path to the Hostage Deal," *New York Times*, November 22, 2023.
43. Benjamin Netanyahu, X, August 29, 2018. Under the username @IsraeliPM.
44. Zohreen Shah and Ayesha Ali, "New Details on Biden's Private Apology to Muslim Americans for Rhetoric on Palestinian Civilians," ABC News, November 29, 2023.
45. Yasmeen Abutaleb and John Hudson, "How Biden Became Embroiled in a Gaza Conflict with No End in Sight," *Washington Post*, March 18, 2024.
46. Warren P. Strobel and Nancy A. Youssef, "U.S. and Israel's 'Unprecedented' Intelligence Sharing Draws Criticism," *Wall Street Journal*, March 31, 2024.
47. Arab American Institute, "Arab Americans Special Poll: Domestic Implications of the Most Recent Outbreak of Violence in Palestine/Israel," Arab American Institute, October 2023.
48. Benjamin Netanyahu, "Statement by PM Netanyahu," Ministry of Foreign Affairs, gov.il, October 28, 2023.
49. Chris Walker, "Rabbi Interrupts Biden Speech to Demand He Forcefully Call for Ceasefire in Gaza," *Truthout*, November 2, 2023.
50. Abutaleb and Hudson, "How Biden Became Embroiled."
51. Ben Rhodes, *The World as It Is: A Memoir of the Obama White House* (New York: Random House, 2018), 251.
52. "Statement on the Release of Amnesty International's Report," Gisha, February 1, 2022; Kayla Guo, "House Censures Rashida Tlaib, Citing 'River to the Sea' Slogan," *New York Times*, November 7, 2023.
53. Alexander Ward and Erin Banco, "Democrats in Senate, House Discuss Conditioning Military Aid to Israel," *Politico*, November 18, 2023.

54. Charles O. Blaha, "Israel and the Leahy Law," *Just Security*, June 10, 2024.
55. Shannon K. Kingston, "Blinken's Increased Pressure on Israel over 'Pauses' Signals Shifting U.S. Strategy: Analysis," ABC News, November 3, 2023.
56. Barak Ravid, "Scoop: Blinken Tells Israelis Humanitarian Pause Will Buy Israel Time for Gaza Operation," *Axios*, November 3, 2023.
57. Ahmed Asmar, "'Bomb the Food Stores in Gaza': Israeli Minister Calls for Starvation of Palestinians," Anadolu Ajansi, May 6, 2025.
58. "Netanyahu Says Not Seeking to 'Occupy' Gaza but 'Demilitarise' It," Al Jazeera, November 10, 2023.
59. Tia Humphries and Justin Gomez, "Biden Expresses Frustration with Israeli Prime Minister Netanyahu, Confirms 3-Day Pause Request," ABC News, November 9, 2023; "Israeli Forces Close In on al-Shifa Hospital, Trapping Thousands," Al Jazeera, November 11, 2023.
60. Emine Sinmaz, "Gaza's Largest Hospital Being Bombarded, WHO Says," *The Guardian*, November 10, 2023; Billy Briggs et al., "The Israel Defense Forces Used a Scottish Museum's 3D Models in Propaganda Videos," *The Ferret*, October 8, 2024.
61. "A Voice from Gaza's Al-Shifa Hospital: 'We Are Alone Now. No One Hears Us,'" Médecins Sans Frontières (Doctors Without Borders), November 11, 2023.
62. Kevin Liptak, "White House Says Intelligence Shows Hamas Using al-Shifa Hospital for Command Node, Storing Weapons," CNN, November 14, 2023.
63. Louisa Loveluck et al., "The Case of al-Shifa: Investigating the Assault on Gaza's Largest Hospital," *Washington Post*, December 21, 2023.
64. Medical Aid for Palestinians (MAP) et al., "Israeli Attacks Put Healthcare on Death Row in Gaza," Islamic Relief, May 29, 2025; Office of the High Commissioner for Human Rights, "UN Commission Finds War Crimes and Crimes against Humanity in Israeli Attacks on Gaza Health Facilities and Treatment of Detainees, Hostages," United Nations, October 10, 2024.
65. Liz Skalka, Daniel Marans, and Akbar Shahid Ahmed, "Over 50 DNC Employees Sign Letter Urging Biden to Call for Israeli Cease-Fire in Gaza," *HuffPost*, November 3, 2023.
66. Maria Abi-Habib, Michael Crowley, and Edward Wong, "More Than 500 U.S. Officials Sign Letter Protesting Biden's Israel Policy," *New York Times*, November 14, 2023; Mark Murray, "Poll: Biden's Standing Hits New Lows amid Israel-Hamas War," NBC News, November 19, 2023.
67. TOI Staff, "Released: Ditza Heiman, 84, Beloved 'Savta' Returned in a Wheelchair," *Times of Israel*, October 18, 2023.
68. Netanyahu, "Statement," October 28, 2023.
69. Akbar Shahid Ahmed, "Families of Hamas Hostages Urge U.S. to Use Its 'Highest Leverage' to Bring Captives Home," *HuffPost*, November 8, 2023.
70. Ahmed, "Families of Hamas Hostages."
71. Ilan Goldenberg, "ICYMI: Can Trump's Peace Plan Survive Reality?," J Street Substack, October 22, 2025.
72. Franklin Foer, "The War That Would Not End," *The Atlantic*, September 25, 2024.
73. Peter Baker, "Terrible Choices and Deep Distrust: The Path to the Hostage Deal," *New York Times*, November 22, 2023.
74. "Top Legal Experts on Why Aid to Gaza Can't Be Conditioned on Hostage Release, in Response to Remarks by US Official," Just Security, November 20, 2023.
75. Al Jazeera Staff, "Gaza Truce Deal: What Have Hamas, Israel and Qatar Said?," Al Jazeera, November 22, 2023.
76. Alexander Ward, Adam Cancryn, and Jonathan Lemire, "Biden Admin Officials See Proof Their Strategy Is Working in Hostage Deal," *Politico*, November 21, 2023.
77. TaRhonda Thomas, "Pennsylvania Family Relieved as Hamas Releases 84-Year-Old Grandmother," 6ABC, November 29, 2023.
78. Meron Rapoport, "Netanyahu Is Prolonging the War to Save His Life's Mission," *+972 Magazine*, November 17, 2023.

79. Michael Birnbaum, "Israel Agrees to Protect Civilians When Gaza War Resumes, Blinken Says," *Washington Post*, November 30, 2023.
80. Lauren Leatherby, "Gaza Civilians, under Israeli Barrage, Are Being Killed at Historic Pace," *New York Times*, November 30, 2023.
81. "IRC: As a Humanitarian Organization, We Cannot Countenance a Restart to the Fighting in Gaza," International Rescue Committee, November 30, 2023.
82. Paul Adams, "When This Truce Ends, the Decisive Next Phase of War Begins," BBC News, November 24, 2023.
83. Office for the Coordination of Humanitarian Affairs, "Statement by Principals of the Inter-Agency Standing Committee, Humanitarian Chiefs Will Not Take Part in Unilateral Proposals to Create 'Safe Zones' in Gaza," United Nations, November 16, 2023.
84. John Hudson, "CIA Director Pushes Big Hostage Deal in Secret Meeting with Mossad Chief," *Washington Post*, November 28, 2023.
85. Finer told me he did not recall this.
86. Julia Ioffe, "What Is Hamas Hiding?," *Puck*, December 6, 2023.
87. Barak Ravid, "Hamas May Not Want to Release Women to Keep Them from Talking, U.S. Official Says," *Axios*, December 4, 2023.
88. "IDF Appears to Push Back on 'Irresponsible' US Claim Hamas Refusing to Release Raped Hostages," *Times of Israel*, December 5, 2023.
89. Office of the Special Representative of the Secretary-General on Sexual Violence in Conflict, "Mission Report: Official Visit of the Office of the SRSG-SVC to Israel and the Occupied West Bank," United Nations, March 4, 2024.
90. Office of the High Commissioner for Human Rights, "Israel's Escalating Use of Torture against Palestinians in Custody a Preventable Crime against Humanity: UN Experts," United Nations, August 5, 2024.
91. Office of the High Commissioner for Human Rights, "UN Report: Israeli Use of Heavy Bombs in Gaza Raises Serious Concerns under the Laws of War," United Nations, June 19, 2024.
92. Eugene Daniels and Holly Otterbein, "Kamala Harris Pushes White House to Be More Sympathetic Toward Palestinians," *Politico*, December 14, 2023.
93. Karine Jean-Pierre and John Kirby, "Press Briefing by Press Secretary Karine Jean-Pierre and NSC Coordinator for Strategic Communications John Kirby, December 7, 2023," White House, December 8, 2023.
94. Patsy Widakuswara, "White House Downplays Biden's Remarks on Israel's 'Indiscriminate Bombing,'" Voice of America, December 13, 2023.
95. Erin Banco, Jonathan Landay, and Humeyra Pamuk, "Exclusive: US Intel Found Israeli Military Lawyers Warned There Was Evidence of Gaza War Crimes, Former US Officials Say," Reuters, November 7, 2025; Warren P. Strobel and Nancy A. Youssef, "U.S. and Israel's 'Unprecedented Intelligence Sharing Draws Criticism," *Wall Street Journal*, March 31, 2024.
96. "Death Toll Across Palestine Surges to 18,897, over 55,000 Wounded," WAFA News Agency, December 15, 2023.
97. Monica Alba, "How the White House Persuaded Israel to Open the Kerem Shalom Crossing into Gaza," NBC News, December 22, 2023.

CHAPTER 3: ENABLING MAN-MADE MISERY

1. See, e.g., Gerhard Peters and John T. Woolley, comps., "Remarks and Q&A by National Security Advisor Jake Sullivan at the 2024 World Economic Forum in Davos, Switzerland," American Presidency Project, University of California, Santa Barbara, January 16, 2024.

2. Jonathan Guyer, "US Insists It's Trying to Get Aid into Gaza as UN Warns Millions 'at Risk of Famine,'" *The Guardian*, January 19, 2024.
3. Antony J. Blinken, "Secretary Antony J. Blinken with David Remnick of *The New Yorker* Radio Hour," U.S. Department of State, January 17, 2025.
4. Al Jazeera Staff, "How Has the UNSC Voted since the Beginning of Israel's War on Gaza?," Al Jazeera, November 21, 2024.
5. Farnaz Fassihi, Cassandra Vinograd, and Thomas Fuller, "U.S. Vetoes Security Council Cease-Fire Resolution," *New York Times*, February 20, 2024.
6. Damilola Banjo, "Linda Thomas-Greenfield, US Envoy, Can Stop Holding Her Breath," PassBlue, December 11, 2024.
7. Linda Thomas-Greenfield, "Remarks by Ambassador Linda Thomas-Greenfield at a U.N. General Assembly Commemorative Meeting for International Day for the Elimination of Racial Discrimination," U.S. Mission to the United Nations, March 21, 2024.
8. "UN Security Council Adopts Resolution Calling for 'Humanitarian Pauses' in Gaza," Al Jazeera, November 15, 2023.
9. António Guterres, Letter dated 6 December 2023 from the Secretary-General addressed to the President of the Security Council, United Nations, December 6, 2023.
10. Akbar Shahid Ahmed, "The U.S. Is About to Make a Decision at the U.N. That Could Change Gaza's Fate," *HuffPost*, December 18, 2023.
11. "UN General Assembly Votes by Large Majority for Immediate Humanitarian Ceasefire during Emergency Session," UN News, December 12, 2023.
12. "Israel Is Starving Gaza," B'Tselem, January 8, 2024.
13. IPC Global Initiative, "The Gaza Strip—IPC Special Brief," January 2024.
14. Office for the Coordination of Humanitarian Affairs, "Humanitarian Situation Update #257 | Gaza Strip," United Nations, January 22, 2025.
15. Kaag did not respond to my request for comment.
16. Yasmine Salam, Rima Abdelkader, and Matthew Mulligan, "Abandoned Babies Found Decomposing in Gaza Hospital Weeks after It Was Evacuated," NBC News, December 2, 2023.
17. Hajar Harb, Miriam Berger, and Niha Masih, "Journalist Who Broke Story on Decomposing Babies in Gaza Is Shot, Injured," *Washington Post*, December 18, 2023; Committee to Protect Journalists, "Mohammed Balousha," December 14, 2024.
18. Natasha Bertrand and Katie Bo Lillis, "Exclusive: Nearly Half of the Israeli Munitions Dropped on Gaza Are Imprecise 'Dumb Bombs,' US Intelligence Assessment Finds," CNN, December 14, 2023.
19. Jason Crow et al., Letter to President Biden regarding Israel and Gaza, December 20, 2023.
20. Abigail Hauslohner, "Democratic Lawmakers Demand Oversight on U.S. Assistance to Israel," *Washington Post*, December 20, 2023; Elizabeth Warren et al., Letter to President Biden re: civilian harm from Israel's use of U.S. weapons in Gaza, December 5, 2023.
21. Josh Paul, LinkedIn post, December 29, 2023.
22. Jacob Magid, "Saudi Normalization Still Possible Post-War, but Price for Israel Is Higher—Officials," *Times of Israel*, January 11, 2024; Barak Ravid, "Sullivan: U.S. Post-War Strategy Links Saudi-Israel Peace Deal with Two-State Solution," *Axios*, January 16, 2024.
23. Akbar Shahid Ahmed, "A Top Biden Official Is Pushing an Urgent Post-Gaza Plan That's Alarming Some Insiders," *HuffPost*, January 12, 2024. McGurk did not object to the article when it was published.
24. Julia Ioffe, "Who's Afraid of Brett McGurk?," *Puck*, February 7, 2024.
25. Nahal Toosi, "The Saudi Crown Prince Is Talking about an Assassination. His Own," *Politico*, August 14, 2024.
26. Ahmed, "A Top Biden Official Is Pushing an Urgent Post-Gaza Plan."

27. Catherine Cleveland and David Pollock, "New Poll Sheds Light on Saudi Views of Israel-Hamas War," Fikra Forum, Washington Institute for Near East Policy, December 21, 2023.
28. Akbar Shahid Ahmed, "The U.S. and U.K. Launch Airstrikes on Yemen," *HuffPost*, January 11, 2024.
29. Ben Smith, "Semafor Media," *Semafor*, January 15, 2024; Laura Wagner, "HuffPost Presses White House over 'Smear' of Gaza Story," *Washington Post*, January 19, 2024. (That was not the end of the story; see the epilogue.)
30. Peters and Woolley, "Remarks and Q&A by National Security Advisor Jake Sullivan at the 2024 World Economic Forum in Davos, Switzerland"; Jamey Keaten, "Blinken Calls a Pathway to a Palestinian State a Necessity for Israeli Security," Associated Press, January 17, 2024; Barak Ravid, "Blinken Meets MBS in Saudi Arabia as U.S. Pushes for Post-War Deal," *Axios*, February 5, 2024.
31. Paul Wood, "Brett McGurk: A Hero of Our Time," *New Lines Magazine*, April 19, 2021; Ioffe, "Who's Afraid of Brett McGurk?"
32. Mark Lowen, "Netanyahu Publicly Rejects US Push for Palestinian State," BBC News, January 19, 2024.
33. AP and TOI Staff, "Saudi Arabia's Top Envoy: No Recognizing Israel without Path to Palestinian State," *Times of Israel*, January 22, 2024.
34. David Horovitz, "The Ambassador's Farewell Warning: You Can't Ignore the Impact of This War on Future US Policymakers," *Times of Israel*, January 12, 2025.
35. Korde did not dispute this, telling me: "It was the responsibility of all Bureau and office heads (or designees) to review and clear fact sheets and documents."
36. John Hudson, "Israel-Hamas Ceasefire Deal Brings Hope for Devastated Northern Gaza," *Washington Post*, January 16, 2025.
37. Office for the Coordination of Humanitarian Affairs, "UN Humanitarian Chief Martin Griffiths Calls for Immediate Ceasefire and Humanitarian Access in Gaza Crisis—Briefing to the Security Council on the Situation in the Middle East, Including the Palestinian Question—31 January 2024," United Nations, January 31, 2024.
38. Asked about this depiction of the system, Satterfield told me: "The entire senior administration foreign policy/national security leadership was focused on gaining the most accurate information possible regarding reported attacks on civilians. We drew at the mission in Israel upon all possible sources of information in our effort both to determine facts and to work to prevent reoccurrence."
39. "The Ceasefire Is Not the End of the Extreme Suffering in Gaza," Doctors Without Borders, October 21, 2025.
40. News Agencies, "UNRWA Probes Employees over Suspected Involvement in October 7 Attack," Al Jazeera, January 26, 2024.
41. Guardian Staff, "US Intelligence Casts Doubt on Israeli Claims of UNRWA-Hamas Links, Report Says," *The Guardian*, February 22, 2024.
42. Jacob Magid and TOI Staff, "Israel Lauds US Ban on UNRWA Financing until 2025 under New Government Funding Bill," *Times of Israel*, March 23, 2024.
43. Jo Becker and Adam Rasgon, "Records Seized by Israel Show Hamas Presence In U.N. Schools," *New York Times*, December 8, 2024.
44. Jane Arraf, "Israel Takes Steps to Shut Down International Aid Groups in Gaza and the West Bank," NPR, October 22, 2025.
45. Akbar Shahid Ahmed, X, January 16, 2024. Under the username @AkbarSAhmed.
46. "Van Hollen, Durbin, Kaine, Schatz Announce Growing Momentum for Amendment Requiring the Use of U.S. Supplemental Aid Comply with U.S., International Law," Office of Senator Tim Kaine, January 19, 2024.
47. Yasmeen Abutaleb and Liz Goodwin, "Biden Says Countries Receiving U.S. Weapons Must Adhere to International Law," *Washington Post*, February 8, 2024.

48. Akbar Shahid Ahmed, "The Biden Administration Is Investigating Israel's Possible War Crimes—Despite Public Claims to the Contrary," *HuffPost*, February 13, 2024.
49. Karine Jean-Pierre and John Kirby, "Press Briefing by Press Secretary Karine Jean-Pierre and White House National Security Communications Advisor John Kirby," White House, February 15, 2024.
50. Barbara Matusow, "Can Nice Guy Chris Van Hollen Finish First?," *Washingtonian*, June 1, 2008.
51. Akbar Shahid Ahmed, "These Injured Palestinians Made It Out of Gaza. Their Loved Ones Did Not—and the Distance Is Agony," *HuffPost*, March 5, 2024.
52. Barak Ravid, "Biden 'Running Out' of Patience with Bibi as Gaza War Hits 100 Days," *Axios*, January 14, 2024; Carol E. Lee et al., "Biden Disparages Netanyahu in Private but Hasn't Significantly Changed U.S. Policy toward Israel and Gaza," NBC News, February 12, 2024.
53. Michelle Nunn et al., "We Are No Strangers to Human Suffering, but We've Seen Nothing Like the Siege of Gaza," *New York Times*, December 11, 2023.
54. Reuters and Jacob Magid, "US Envoy: Israel Hasn't Provided 'Specific Evidence' Hamas Is Stealing Aid Shipments," *Times of Israel*, February 17, 2024.
55. Katie Polglase et al., "Dying for a Bag of Flour: Videos and Eyewitness Accounts Cast Doubt on Israel's Timeline of Deadly Gaza Aid Delivery," CNN, April 10, 2024.
56. Polglase et al., "Dying for a Bag of Flour."

CHAPTER 4: SOMETHING HAS TO GIVE

1. Peter Baker, "White House Disavows U.S. Islamic Group after Leader's Oct. 7 Remarks," *New York Times*, December 8, 2023.
2. Christian Piekos, "CAIR Executive Director Nihad Awad Pushes Back on Criticism for October 7 Comment," ABC7, December 8, 2023.
3. TOI Staff and AFP, "Bagging Iowa, Trump Vows to Solve Israel and Ukraine Wars 'Very Fast' if Reelected," *Times of Israel*, January 16, 2024.
4. Maya King, "Black Pastors Pressure Biden to Call for a Ceasefire in Gaza," *New York Times*, January 28, 2024.
5. Reid J. Epstein and Erica L. Green, "In Private Remarks to Arab Americans, Biden Aide Expresses Regrets on Gaza," *New York Times*, February 9, 2024.
6. Tyler Pager, "Biden Visits Michigan amid Arab Community's Anger over Israel-Gaza War," *Washington Post*, February 1, 2024; Matt Flegenheimer and Katie Glueck, "Young Joe Biden and His Non-Radical 1960s," *New York Times*, October 18, 2020.
7. Abdullah Hammoud, X, January 26, 2024. Under the username @AHammoudMI.
8. Zoe Magee and Ruwaida Amer, "Some Gazans Say They're Forced to Use Bird Feed in Place of Flour," ABC News, February 1, 2024.
9. Jihan Abdalla, "'It Was a Hot Conversation': White House Team Meets Arab-American Leaders," *The National*, February 8, 2024.
10. Epstein and Green, "Private Remarks to Arab Americans."
11. Epstein and Green, "Private Remarks to Arab Americans."
12. James Jacoby, "Brett McGurk," *Frontline*, PBS, December 8, 2023.
13. Brett Murphy, "Blinken Is Sitting on Staff Recommendations to Sanction Israeli Military Units Linked to Killings or Rapes," ProPublica, April 17, 2024.
14. Delaney Simon, "The Lessons of the Biden Administration's Efforts to Sanction Israeli Settlers," Century Foundation, June 25, 2025.
15. Nan Levinson, "Aaron Bushnell Told Us Why He Self-Immolated—Why Didn't We Believe Him?," *The Nation*, July 18, 2024.
16. Niha Masih, "Crutches and Chocolate Croissants: Gaza Aid Items Israel Has Rejected," *Washington Post*, April 11, 2024; Tamara Qiblawi et al., "Anesthetics, Crutches, Dates.

Inside Israel's Ghost List of Items Arbitrarily Denied Entry into Gaza," CNN, March 2, 2024.

17. Wafaa Shurafa and Samy Magdy, "Food Deliveries into Northern Gaza Are Halted because of the War's Chaos, Increasing Famine Risk," Associated Press, February 20, 2024.
18. Loveday Morris, Hazem Balousha, and Karen DeYoung, "Gaza Aid Delivery Hampered by Israeli Attacks on Police, Rising Chaos," *Washington Post*, February 22, 2024.
19. "Gaza: Families Forced to Forage for Food Left by Rats as 1.1 Million Children Face Starvation," Save the Children, February 22, 2024.
20. John Hudson, "USAID's Samantha Power, Genocide Scholar, Confronted by Staff on Gaza," *Washington Post*, January 31, 2024.
21. News Agencies, "Palestinians Rush to Shore as Aircraft Drop Aid into Gaza amid Israel War," Al Jazeera, February 28, 2024.
22. Aamer Madhani, Zeke Miller, and Matthew Lee, "Biden Approves Military Airdrops of Aid into Gaza after Chaotic Encounter Left More Than 100 Dead," Associated Press, March 1, 2024.
23. Scott Paul, X, February 29, 2024. Under the username @ScottTPaul.
24. Ari Shapiro, Linah Mohammad, and Elena Burnett, "Airdropping Aid Is Inefficient—So Why Is the U.S. Doing It in Gaza Anyway?," NPR, March 6, 2024.
25. "U.S. Central Command Conducts 11th Humanitarian Airdrop into Gaza," U.S. Central Command, March 15, 2024.
26. Chris Panella, "60 Bundles of Food Fell into the Sea as a US Military C-130 Aircraft Attempted to Drop Aid into War-Torn Gaza," *Business Insider*, April 2, 2024.
27. AbdelQadder Sabbah et al., "At Least 12 Palestinians Drown Trying to Retrieve Aid Parcels Dropped into the Sea," CNN, March 27, 2024. The U.S. denied responsibility for airdrop deaths; Britain, France, Egypt, and the UAE also carried out such drops.
28. "2018: Plight of Gaza Fishermen after Israel's Gradual Destruction of Their Sector," B'Tselem, February 11, 2019.
29. Office of Inspector General, "USAID's Gaza Response: External Factors Impaired Distribution of Humanitarian Assistance through the JLOTS Maritime Corridor," U.S. Agency for International Development, August 27, 2024.
30. Yonah Jeremy Bob, "IDF to Produce Interim Reports on War Crimes Probes," *Jerusalem Post*, February 12, 2024; Jeremy Sharon and Agencies, "Israel Reports to ICJ in The Hague on Actions Taken to Comply with Court Orders on Gaza," *Times of Israel*, February 26, 2024.
31. Carol E. Lee et al., "Biden Disparages Netanyahu in Private but Hasn't Significantly Changed U.S. Policy toward Israel and Gaza," NBC News, February 12, 2024.
32. ALEPH et al., PIN Cease-Fire Letter, Progressive Israel Network, March 5, 2024.
33. Linda Gradstein, "Israel Welcomes Biden Plan to Increase Gaza Aid," Voice of America English News, March 8, 2024; Tia Goldenberg and Wafaa Shurafa, "Pressure Grows on Israel to Open More Aid Routes into Gaza by Land and Sea as Hunger Worsens," Associated Press, March 6, 2024; "A Timeline of Our Humanitarian Aid Efforts," Israel Defense Forces, idf.il, November 12, 2024.
34. Akbar Shahid Ahmed, "Israel's Limits on Aid for Gaza Make U.S. Military Support Illegal, Activists Argue," *HuffPost*, March 12, 2024.
35. Yamiche Alcindor et al., "Administration Officials Watered Down Kamala Harris' Gaza Speech before Delivery," NBC News, March 4, 2024.
36. "Netanyahu Rival Benny Gantz to Meet US Leaders," Al Jazeera, March 4, 2024.
37. Stephen Collinson, "A Speech That Sent Shockwaves from Washington to Jerusalem," CNN, March 15, 2024.
38. David E. Sanger and Peter Baker, "Biden Embraces Schumer's Speech Castigating Netanyahu," *New York Times*, March 15, 2024.
39. Annie Karni, "'Part of My Core': How Schumer Decided to Speak Out against Netanyahu," *New York Times*, March 19, 2024; Morgan Rimmer, Ted Barrett, and Manu

Raju, "Schumer Slams Trump Criticism of His Israel Speech as 'Unadulterated Antisemitism,'" CNN, March 19, 2024.

40. Barak Ravid, "Scoop: U.S. Creates Special Representative Post Focused Solely on Palestinian Affairs," *Axios*, November 22, 2022.
41. "Wednesday, January 10, 2024," Chronology of the Palestinian-Israeli Conflict, Institute for Palestine Studies, January 2024.
42. Moien Odeh, "Without Free Palestinian Elections, There Can Be No Lasting Peace," Century Foundation, April 22, 2024.
43. Public Opinion Poll No (90), Palestinian Center for Policy and Survey Research, November 22–December 2, 2023.
44. Adrienne Watson, "Statement by NSC Spokesperson Adrienne Watson on the Appointment Today of Dr. Mohammed Mustafa as Prime Minister of the Palestinian Authority," White House, March 14, 2024.
45. Amjad Iraqi, "Why Benny Gantz Is One of Israel's Most Dangerous Leaders," *+972 Magazine*, August 23, 2022; Omar M. Dajani and Limor Yehuda, "A Two-State Solution That Can Work," *Foreign Affairs*, September 19, 2024.
46. Steve Hendrix and Hajar Harb, "16 Children Have Died of Malnutrition in Aid-Starved Gaza, Health Officials Say," *Washington Post*, March 6, 2024.
47. Sana Noor Haq et al., "Newborns Die of Hunger and Mothers Struggle to Feed Their Children as Israel's Siege Condemns Gazans to Starvation," CNN, March 7, 2024.
48. Antony J. Blinken, "Secretary Antony J. Blinken Remarks to the Press," U.S. Department of State, March 22, 2024.
49. Abeer Salman et al., "Israeli Troops End Al-Shifa Hospital Raid, Leaving Behind Bodies and Trail of Destruction," CNN, April 1, 2024.
50. Nadeen Ebrahim et al., "Why Israeli Forces Are Raiding Gaza's Al-Shifa Hospital—Again," CNN, March 28, 2024.

CHAPTER 5: WHAT MIGHT HAVE BEEN

1. Karen DeYoung and Missy Ryan, "How Joe Biden Lost His Grip on Israel's War for 'Total Victory' in Gaza," *Washington Post*, October 3, 2024.
2. "7 WCK Team Members Killed in Gaza," World Central Kitchen, April 1, 2024.
3. Camilla Alcini, "7 Aid Workers Killed in Gaza during IDF Attack That Israeli Official Calls 'Grave Mistake,'" ABC News, April 2, 2024.
4. António Guterres, X, April 2, 2024. Under the username @antonioguterres. "Gaza: Israeli Strike on NGO Aid Team Condemned as Humanitarians Renew Access Call," United Nations Türkiye, April 3, 2024.
5. Matthew Miller, "Department Press Briefing—March 27, 2024," U.S. Department of State, March 27, 2024.
6. U.S. Embassy Jakarta, "Statement from President Joe Biden on the Death of World Central Kitchen Workers in Gaza," U.S. Embassy and Consulates in Indonesia, April 4, 2024.
7. Zachary Basu, "Tide Turns Sharply against Israel's War in Gaza," *Axios*, April 4, 2024.
8. Yasmeen Abutaleb and Matt Viser, "Biden Rebukes Israel over Aid Workers, but His Gaza Policy Is Unchanged," *Washington Post*, April 3, 2024.
9. James Hider, "World Central Kitchen Pauses Gaza Aid, as Netanyahu Acknowledges an 'Unintended Hit,'" NPR, April 2, 2024.
10. Jeff Mason, "Chef Jose Andres Says Israel Targeted His Aid Workers 'Systematically, Car by Car,'" Reuters, April 3, 2024; Jess Bidgood, "When Food, War and Politics Collide," *New York Times*, April 5, 2024; "Chef José Andrés: Israel Conflict 'a War against Humanity Itself' after Death of Aid Workers in Gaza," ABC News, YouTube video, April 3, 2024.

11. Hans Nichols and Barak Ravid, "Scoop: Inside José Andrés' Risky Mission to Get Food to Gaza," *Axios*, March 8, 2024.
12. David E. Sanger and Peter Baker, "Biden Is 'Outraged.' But Is He Willing to Use America's Leverage with Israel?," *New York Times*, April 3, 2024.
13. Akbar Shahid Ahmed, "'Unprecedented in Modern History': U.S. Aid Experts Warn Gaza Likely Already Experiencing Famine," *HuffPost*, April 2, 2024.
14. Akbar Shahid Ahmed, "U.S. Government Believes Famine Is Occurring in Gaza, Samantha Power Says," *HuffPost*, April 11, 2024.
15. Katie Rogers and Erica L. Green, "'Stop It Now': Jill Biden Privately Urges an End to Conflict in Gaza," *New York Times*, April 3, 2024.
16. Kevin Liptak and Sam Fossum, "Biden Criticizes Netanyahu's Approach to War with Hamas as Mistake," CNN, April 9, 2024.
17. Abutaleb and Viser, "Biden Rebukes Israel."
18. Rebecca Shabad, "Israel to Open More Aid Routes to Gaza and Increase Deliveries after Pressure from Biden," NBC News, April 4, 2024.
19. Alon Pinkas, "The World Central Kitchen Debacle Happened in a World Already Suffering from 'Israel Fatigue,'" *Haaretz*, April 5, 2024.
20. Sullivan did not respond to a request for comment on this point.
21. Vince Chadwick, "How 'Deconfliction' Is Getting Aid Workers Killed in Gaza," Devex Newswire, April 11, 2024.
22. "Conclusion of the Investigation into the Incident in Which 7 WCK Employees Were Killed during a Humanitarian Operation in Gaza," Israel Defense Forces, idf.il, April 5, 2024.
23. "WCK's Statement about the IDF Preliminary Investigation," World Central Kitchen, April 5, 2024.
24. Mark Pocan et al., Letter to President Biden and Secretary Blinken regarding WCK air strike and U.S. arms transfers, April 5, 2024.
25. CNN, X, April 9, 2024. Under the username @NewsCentralCNN.
26. Jeffrey M. Jones, "Majority in U.S. Now Disapprove of Israeli Action in Gaza," Gallup, March 27, 2024.
27. Padmananda Rama and Chuck Quirmbach, "Wisconsin's 'Uninstructed' Voters Send Biden a Strong Message on the War in Gaza," NPR, April 3, 2024.
28. Robert Jimison, "Outrage over Slain Aid Workers Deepens Democratic Resistance to Arming Israel," *New York Times*, April 5, 2024.
29. Isabel Kershner et al., "Aid Flows to Gaza Are Rising, U.N. Says, but More Is Needed," *New York Times*, April 27, 2024.
30. Nicholas Kristof, "What Happened to the Joe Biden I Knew?," *New York Times*, April 19, 2024.
31. Yaniv Kubovich, "IDF Legal Chief Avoided Probes into Gaza War Crimes, Citing Right-Wing Backlash, Sources Say," *Haaretz*, November 2, 2025.
32. Alia Chughtai and Marium Ali, "How Much Aid Has Entered Gaza?," Al Jazeera, August 5, 2025.

CHAPTER 6: THE ROAD TO RAFAH

1. Karen DeYoung and Missy Ryan, "How Joe Biden Lost His Grip on Israel's War for 'Total Victory' in Gaza," *Washington Post*, October 3, 2024.
2. Franklin Foer, "The War That Would Not End," *The Atlantic*, September 25, 2024.
3. Kareem Fahim, Susannah George, Shane Harris, and Suzan Haidamous, "Israel Braces for Tehran's Response after Deadly Damascus Strike," *Washington Post*, April 4, 2024.
4. Matt Bradley, "An Uneasy Alliance of Arab States Helped Defend Israel from Iran. Their Resolve May Soon Be Tested," NBC News, April 16, 2024.

5. Islamic Republic of Iran Mission to UN, NY, X, April 13, 2024. Under the username @Iran_UN; Susannah George, "Iran Crosses Old Red Lines and Sets 'New Equation' with Attack on Israel," *Washington Post*, April 14, 2024.
6. TOI Staff, "In Recording, Shin Bet Chief Vows to Kill Hamas Chiefs 'in Lebanon, Turkey, Qatar,'" *Times of Israel*, December 4, 2023.
7. The explosion was not caused by Israel, Hezbollah, or any other actor, though Hezbollah has stymied independent investigations of it.
8. Matthew Miller, "Department Press Briefing—January 3, 2024," U.S. Department of State, January 3, 2024; Akbar Shahid Ahmed, "Joe Biden Risks a Major Middle East War if He Makes the Wrong Choices," *HuffPost*, January 6, 2024.
9. Yonah Jeremy Bob and Jerusalem Post Staff, "Gallant Warns Hezbollah: Israel Can Do in Beirut What It Is Doing in Gaza," *Jerusalem Post*, December 17, 2023; William Christou, Alex Horton, and Meg Kelly, "Israel Used U.S.-Supplied White Phosphorus in Lebanon Attack," *Washington Post*, December 11, 2023.
10. Joseph R. Biden, "Statement from President Joe Biden Marking 100 Days of Captivity for Hostages in Gaza," White House, January 14, 2024.
11. Barnett Rubin, X, January 14, 2024. Under the username @BRRubin.
12. Yasmeen Abutaleb and John Hudson, "How Biden Became Embroiled in a Gaza Conflict with No End in Sight," *Washington Post*, March 18, 2024.
13. Max Tani, "Pro-Israel Group Targets Post Reporter," *Semafor*, February 18, 2024.
14. Jacob Magid and Jeremy Sharon, "US Lambasts 'Meritless' South African Request for ICJ to Charge Israel with Genocide," *Times of Israel*, January 4, 2024.
15. "Order of 26 January 2024: Application of the Convention on the Prevention and Punishment of the Crime of Genocide in the Gaza Strip (South Africa v. Israel)" (No. 192), International Court of Justice, January 26, 2024.
16. "Kirby Says U.S. Has 'Not Seen' Israel's Plan for Rafah, Praises IDF Efforts to Protect Civilians," *Times of Israel*, February 13, 2024; Jacob Magid and TOI staff, "Biden Aide: Israel Taking Steps to Protect Civilians That Even U.S. Might Not Have," *Times of Israel*, December 14, 2023.
17. Jake Sullivan, "Remarks and Q&A by National Security Advisor Jake Sullivan at the 2024 World Economic Forum, Davos, Switzerland," White House, January 16, 2024.
18. Oona A. Hathaway and Azmat Khan, "'Mistakes' In War," *University of Pennsylvania Law Review* 173: 1, 2024.
19. Joseph R. Biden, Jr., "Memorandum on United States Conventional Arms Transfer Policy," White House, February 23, 2023.
20. Reuters reported that White House officials including McGurk expressed skepticism in this vein: Erin Banco, Jonathan Landay, and Humeyra Pamuk, "US Envoys Blocked Early Warning of 'Apocalyptic Wasteland' in Gaza," Reuters, January 30, 2026.
21. Harrison Mann, "Why Should US Troops Pay the Price for Biden's Failure to Rein In Netanyahu?," *The Guardian*, August 13, 2024.
22. Ivana Kottasová and Adi Koplewitz, "Israel's Repudiation of a Deal with Hamas Draws Fury from Hostage Families," CNN, February 9, 2024.
23. Jennifer Hansler, "Blinken Says Hamas Response on Hostages and Ceasefire Deal 'Creates Space for Agreement to Be Reached,'" CNN, February 7, 2024; "Israel Escalates Rafah Bombardment as US Warns of a 'Disaster,'" Al Jazeera, February 8, 2024.
24. Benjamin Netanyahu, "Statement by Prime Minister Benjamin Netanyahu," IsraeliPM, YouTube video, February 7, 2024.
25. Amir Tal et al., "Netanyahu Directs Israeli Military to Draw Up Plan to Evacuate More Than One Million People from Rafah as Offensive Looms," CNN, February 9, 2024.
26. Meredith Deliso, "Netanyahu Ahead of Rafah Ground Invasion: 'Victory Is within Reach,'" ABC News, February 10, 2024.
27. Helen Regan and Abeer Salman, "Israeli Airstrikes Kill More Than 100 in Rafah as International Alarm Mounts over Anticipated Ground Offensive," CNN, February 12, 2024.

28. Jerusalem Post Staff, "Netanyahu Is Slowly Regaining Support; Gantz Is Losing Momentum," *Jerusalem Post*, February 14, 2024; Ksenia Svetlova, "Netanyahu Might Be Losing Ground, but His Politics Still Resonate with Most Israelis," Atlantic Council, March 6, 2024.
29. Steve Hendrix, Claire Parker, and Miriam Berger, "Standoff over Rafah Assault Tests Israel's Most Important Alliances," *Washington Post*, February 15, 2024.
30. Foer, "The War That Would Not End."
31. Bret Stephens, "No, Israel Is Not Committing Genocide in Gaza," *New York Times*, July 22, 2025.
32. Thomas D. Arnold and Nicolas Fiore, "Five Operational Lessons from the Battle for Mosul," *Military Review*, January–February 2019.
33. Joseph R. Biden, "Remarks by President Biden on the October 7th Terrorist Attacks and the Resilience of the State of Israel and Its People," White House, October 18, 2023.
34. Banco et al., "US Envoys to Israel Blocked."
35. VOA News, "Netanyahu Orders Military to Plan for Civilian Evacuations of Rafah," Voice of America English News, February 9, 2024.
36. Office for the Coordination of Humanitarian Affairs, "UN Relief Chief Warns Military Operations in Rafah Could Lead to a Slaughter in Gaza and Put a Fragile Humanitarian Operation at Death's Door," United Nations, February 13, 2024.
37. Kevin Liptak, "How Joe Biden's Red Line on Israel Went from a 'Parlor Game' to a Murky Millstone," CNN, May 30, 2024.
38. "What Defines Us," Axel Springer, 2025.
39. Aya Batrawy, Itay Stern, and Alon Avital, "A Timeline of Events Leading Up to Israel's Rafah Offensive," NPR, May 8, 2024.
40. Bilal Shbair and Ben Hubbard, "'Everything Is Difficult': The Struggle for Life's Basics in Rafah," *New York Times*, March 14, 2024.
41. Barak Ravid, "Blinken Unloads on Bibi: 'You Need a Coherent Plan' or Face Disaster in Gaza," *Axios*, March 22, 2024.
42. "Israel's Netanyahu Says He Told Blinken We Will Go into Rafah Alone if Needed," Reuters, March 22, 2024.
43. Robert Wood, "Explanation of Vote Delivered at the UN General Assembly Emergency Special Session on the Palestinian UN Membership Resolution," United States Mission to the United Nations, May 10, 2024.
44. International Court of Justice, "Order of 28 March 2024."
45. "Gaza's Children: Trapped in a Cycle of Suffering," UNICEF, March 26, 2024.
46. Chimène Keitner, "The ICJ's Modified Provisional Measures Order in South Africa v. Israel," *Lawfare*, April 2, 2024.
47. Linda Thomas-Greenfield, "Explanation of Vote Delivered by Ambassador Linda Thomas-Greenfield following the Adoption of a UNSC Resolution on the Situation in the Middle East," United States Mission to the United Nations, March 25, 2024.
48. Hannah Birkenkötter, "Why Today's UN Security Council Resolution Demanding an Immediate Ceasefire Is Legally Binding," *Verfassungsblog*, March 25, 2024; Eric Bazail-Eimil and Mona Zhang, "US Allows Passage of UN Resolution Calling for Cease-Fire in Gaza, Prompting Retaliation from Israel," *Politico*, March 25, 2024; María Antonia Sánchez-Vallejo, "US Sparks Controversy at the UN with Claim That Gaza Ceasefire Resolution Is 'Non-Binding,'" *El País*, March 29, 2024.
49. "Israeli Banks to Unfreeze Accounts of Sanctioned 'Settlers,'" Jewish News Syndicate, March 31, 2024.
50. Barak Ravid, X, March 29, 2024. Under the username @BarakRavid. Delaney Simon, "The Lessons of the Biden Administration's Efforts to Sanction Israeli Settlers," Century Foundation, June 25, 2025.
51. Jeremy Sharon, "Court Refuses to Extend House Arrest for Settler Suspected of Killing Palestinian Activist," *Times of Israel*, August 1, 2025.

52. Catie Edmondson et al., "How the House Voted on Foreign Aid to Ukraine, Israel and Taiwan," *New York Times*, April 20, 2024; Blaise Malley, "The Democrats Who Flipped on Israel Aid, and Why," *Responsible Statecraft*, April 23, 2024.
53. Mira Resnick, LinkedIn post, December 2024.
54. Bobby Allyn, "President Biden Signs Law to Ban TikTok Nationwide Unless It Is Sold," NPR, April 24, 2024.
55. Abigail Hauslohner, "Evangelicals Are Fed Up with the House GOP's Israel Aid Holdouts," *Washington Post*, April 13, 2024; Jacob Kornbluh, "'God Wants Us to Do the Right Thing': How Schumer Persuaded House Speaker Johnson to Pass Foreign Aid Bill," *The Forward*, April 28, 2024.
56. UN News, "Mass Graves in Gaza Show Victims' Hands Were Tied, Says UN Rights Office," United Nations, April 23, 2024.
57. Executive Committee of the University of Pennsylvania Chapter of the American Association of University Professors, "Statement on Threats to Academic Freedom, University Governance, and Safety at the University of Pennsylvania," AAUP-Penn, October 28, 2023.
58. Emily Tamkin, "Elise Stefanik's Fight against Antisemitism Is Quite the Exercise in Chutzpah," *Slate*, June 11, 2024.
59. Lauren Gambino, "US University Presidents Face Firestorm over 'Evasive' Answers on Antisemitism," *The Guardian*, December 8, 2023.
60. Anemona Hartocollis, "Jewish Students Describe Facing Antisemitism on Campus to Members of Congress," *New York Times*, March 1, 2024; Jordana Horn, "In DC, Jewish Students Tell House Committee: 'It's Open Season on Jews on Our Campus,'" *Times of Israel*, March 1, 2024.
61. Alex Isenstadt, "Stefanik Raised More Than $7 Million in First Quarter, after Grilling Colleges on Antisemitism," *Politico*, April 4, 2024; "Rep. Elise Stefanik Accepts 'Dr. Miriam & Sheldon G. Adelson Defender of Israel Award' at ZOA Florida Sold-Out Packed Gala," Zionist Organization of America, March 19, 2024.
62. Nicholas Fandos and Sharon Otterman, "Inside the Week That Shook Columbia University," *New York Times*, April 23, 2024.
63. Kiara Alfonseca, "As Columbia University Protests on Israel-Hamas War Come to a Head, What to Know," ABC News, April 30, 2024.
64. Irie Sentner, "I Was a Columbia Student Journalist. Here's What to Know about Mahmoud Khalil," *Politico*, March 13, 2025.
65. Eugene Daniels and Elena Schneider, "Biden Camp Not Sweating Political Fallout from Latest Round of Campus Protests," *Politico*, April 23, 2024.
66. Eli Stokols, "White House Condemns Columbia Student Protest Leader Who Called for Zionists to Die," *Politico*, April 26, 2024; Emily Forgash, "CUAD Member Issues Apology for January Video in Which They Said 'Zionists Don't Deserve to Live,'" *Columbia Daily Spectator*, April 26, 2024. Columbia University Apartheid and Divest later retracted its apology. Bates told me in 2026: "My public statements explicitly defended the right of demonstrators to peacefully protest and . . . stressed the need for empathy toward protesters and for every community harmed by the war. I denounced specific violent, hateful, antisemitic statements made by individual demonstrators." He expressed regret about Biden's handling of the war.
67. Gregory Krieg, "College Campus Protests Highlight Tensions in Biden's Coalition," CNN, April 30, 2024.
68. Debra Messing, Instagram, April 21, 2024. Under the username @therealdebramessing.
69. Christina Fan, Marcia Kramer, and Natalie Duddridge, "Columbia, City College Protests Lead to Nearly 300 Arrests. NYC Mayor Blames 'Movement to Radicalize Young People,'" CBS News, May 2, 2024.
70. Isha Banerjee, "White House, Trump Comment on NYPD Sweep of Hamilton Hall and 'Gaza Solidarity Encampment,'" *Columbia Daily Spectator*, May 1, 2024.

CHAPTER 7: THE RED LINE IS CROSSED

1. Kat Lonsdorf, "Fact Checking Netanyahu's Claim That Rafah Civilian Casualties Are 'Practically None,'" *All Things Considered*, NPR, July 25, 2024.
2. "Situation in Southern Gaza 'Horrific and Apocalyptic': WFP," UN News, May 31, 2024; "UNRWA Situation Report #125 on the Situation in the Gaza Strip and the West Bank, Including East Jerusalem," United Nations Relief and Works Agency for Palestine Refugees in the Near East, July 31, 2024.
3. "Press Release: New Study Shows Israel Air-Dropped 2000lb Bombs within Lethal and Damage Ranges of Hospitals in Gaza," FXB Center for Health and Human Rights, Harvard University, October 10, 2024; Robin Stein et al., "A Times Investigation Tracked Israel's Use of One of Its Most Destructive Bombs in South Gaza," *New York Times*, December 21, 2023.
4. Barak Ravid, "Scoop: U.S. Put a Hold on an Ammunition Shipment to Israel," *Axios*, May 5, 2024.
5. Barak Ravid, X, March 26, 2023. Under the username @BarakRavid.
6. Peter Baker, "Turning Point or Breaking Point? Biden's Pause on Weapons Tests Ties to Israel," *New York Times*, May 8, 2024; Ravid, "Scoop: U.S. Put a Hold."
7. "Maggie Goodlander," Open Secrets, December 31, 2024.
8. Lauren Markoe, "Deborah Lipstadt, Exiting as US Antisemitism Envoy, Is Hoping for the Best Under Trump," *Times of Israel*, January 17, 2025.
9. Akbar Shahid Ahmed, "Joe Biden Is Days Away from a Key Statement on Israel and Gaza. Here's What to Expect," *HuffPost*, May 3, 2024.
10. Blinken's view is he needed all the time available to take account of and reconcile conflicting views on Israel's conduct.
11. Joseph R. Biden, Jr., "National Security Memorandum on Safeguards and Accountability with Respect to Transferred Defense Articles and Defense Services," White House, February 8, 2024.
12. Akbar Shahid Ahmed, "Biden Administration: 'Reasonable' to Say Israel Is Violating International Law, but U.S. Aid Can Continue," *HuffPost*, May 10, 2024.
13. Meet the Press, X, May 12, 2024. Under the username @MeetThePress.
14. Lauren Frayer and Anas Baba, "In Gaza, a Hidden Threat Could Kill Palestinians Even after a Cease-Fire," NPR, May 13, 2024.
15. Akbar Shahid Ahmed, "Palestinians Ordered by Israel to Flee Rafah Have Nowhere Better to Go," *HuffPost*, May 7, 2024.
16. Nancy A. Youssef and Jacob Malsin, "Biden Moves Forward on $1 Billion in New Arms for Israel," *Wall Street Journal*, May 14, 2024.
17. "Readout of National Security Advisor Jake Sullivan's Meetings in Saudi Arabia and Israel," U.S. Embassy Jerusalem, Department of State, May 19, 2024.
18. "Gallant Tells Sullivan: 'We Are Committed to Expanding Rafah Operation,'" i24News, May 20, 2024.
19. "Readout of National Security Advisor Jake Sullivan's Meetings in Israel," White House, May 20, 2024.
20. Philippe Lazzarini, X, May 18, 2024. Under the username @UNLazzarini.
21. Lolita C. Baldor and Jon Gambrell, "Trucks Are Rolling across a New US Pier into Gaza. But Challenges Remain to Getting Enough Aid In," Associated Press, May 17, 2024.
22. Paul Adams, "Can US Floating Pier Improve Gaza's Critical Aid Pipeline?," BBC, May 16, 2024.
23. "Order of 24 May 2024: Application of the Convention on the Prevention and Punishment of the Crime of Genocide in the Gaza Strip (South Africa v. Israel)" (No. 192), International Court of Justice, May 24, 2024.

24. Brett Murphy, "A Year of Empty Threats and a 'Smokescreen' Policy: How the State Department Let Israel Get Away with Horrors in Gaza," ProPublica, January 15, 2025; "What You Need to Know about the Latest International Court of Justice Action in the Case against Israel," American Jewish Committee, n.d.
25. Hadeel Al-Shalchi and Anas Baba, "An Israeli Airstrike Killed 45 Palestinians in an Encampment for Displaced People," NPR, May 27, 2024; Miriam Berger and Hajar Harb, "Eyewitnesses Describe Horrific Scenes after Israeli Strike on Rafah Camp," *Washington Post*, May 30, 2024.
26. Gerhard Peters and John T. Woolley, comps., "Press Briefing by Press Secretary Karine Jean-Pierre and National Security Communications Advisor John Kirby," American Presidency Project, University of California, Santa Barbara, May 28, 2024.
27. "Israel/OPT: Israeli Attacks Targeting Hamas and Other Armed Group Fighters That Killed Scores of Displaced Civilians in Rafah Should Be Investigated as War Crimes," Amnesty International, August 27, 2024.
28. Kevin Liptak, "How Joe Biden's Red Line on Israel Went from a 'Parlor Game' to a Murky Millstone," CNN, May 30, 2024.
29. TOI Staff, "Smotrich Said to Consult Rabbis on Leaving Coalition over Proposed Hostage-Ceasefire Deal," *Times of Israel*, June 3, 2024; Benjamin Brown and Sophie Tanno, "Netanyahu Says No Gaza Ceasefire until Israel's War Aims Are Achieved, Raising Questions over Biden Peace Proposal," CNN, June 1, 2024.
30. Jessie Yeung et al., "June 6, 2024 Israel-Hamas War," CNN, June 7, 2024.
31. Raffi Berg, "Mother of Rescued Israeli Hostage Noa Argamani Dies," BBC, July 2, 2024.
32. Benjamin Netanyahu, "Statement by Prime Minister Benjamin Netanyahu," Prime Minister's Office, gov.il, June 18, 2024.
33. Ron Kampeas, "Netanyahu Accuses Biden of Withholding Weapons. White House: We 'Do Not Know What He's Talking About,'" Jewish Telegraphic Agency, June 18, 2024.
34. Barak Ravid, "Scoop: White House Cancels Meeting, Scolds Netanyahu in Protest over Video," *Axios*, June 18, 2024.
35. John Hudson, "Key Democrats Approve Major Arms Sale to Israel, Including F-15s," *Washington Post*, June 17, 2024.
36. Jake Sherman, "Jake Sherman Interviews Benjamin Netanyahu: Full Transcript," Punchbowl News, June 21, 2024; Jacob Magid, "US Vexed, Disappointed by Netanyahu Claim of Arms Holdup: 'No One Has Done More for Him,'" *Times of Israel*, June 20, 2024.
37. Barak Ravid, "U.S. and Israel Resolve Weapons Supply Problems, but 2,000-lb. Bombs Still on Hold," *Axios*, June 26, 2024.
38. Ravid, "U.S. and Israel Resolve Weapons Supply Problems."
39. "Gallant Underscores U.S.-Israel Bond during Multi-Day Trip to Washington," Foundation for Defense of Democracies, June 26, 2024.
40. Wafaa Shurafa, Samy Magdy, and Lee Keath, "'We Have Nothing.' As Israel Attacks Rafah, Palestinians Are Living in Tents and Searching for Food," Associated Press, May 28, 2024.
41. Jeremy Diamond, "Israel Says Its Operation in Rafah Is 'Limited.' Fighting There Has Left Parts of It Unrecognizable," CNN, July 7, 2024.
42. Rasha Khatib, Martin McKee, and Salim Yusuf, "Counting the Dead in Gaza: Difficult but Essential," *The Lancet* 404, no. 10449, July 20, 2024.
43. David Kenner, "Arab States Deepened Military Ties with Israel while Denouncing Gaza War, Leak Reveals," International Consortium of Investigative Journalists, October 11, 2025.
44. Emanuel Fabian, "Eight Troops Killed in Rafah Explosion, in Deadliest Incident for IDF in 6 Months," *Times of Israel*, June 15, 2024.

CHAPTER 8: CAMPAIGN TRAIL

1. "Ipsos 2024 U.S. Swing State Election Survey—June 2024," Ipsos, June 20, 2024.
2. G. Elliott Morris and Kaleigh Rogers, "Biden's Biggest Weakness—His Age—on Full Display at Debate: Analysis," ABC News, June 27, 2024.
3. CNN Staff, "Read: Biden-Trump Debate Transcript," CNN, June 28, 2024.
4. "The Latest | Netanyahu Says He Will Only Accept a Partial Cease-Fire Deal That Would Not End the War," Associated Press, June 24, 2024.
5. CNN Staff, "Read: Biden-Trump Debate Transcript."
6. Chantal Da Silva, "Dozens Killed as '4 Schools in the Last 4 Days' Struck in Gaza," NBC News, July 10, 2024.
7. Abeer Salman et al., "At Least 90 Palestinians Reported Killed in Israeli Strike Targeting Hamas Military Chief," CNN, July 14, 2024.
8. Dana Karni, Sophie Tanno, and Mostafa Salem, "Israeli Military Says It Killed Hamas Chief Mohammed Deif in Gaza Last Month," CNN, August 1, 2024.
9. Kareem Khadder et al., "Israeli Military Retreats from Northern Gaza, Leaving Dozens of Palestinians Killed and Razing Neighborhoods to the Ground," CNN, July 12, 2024; Mohammad Jahjouh, Samy Magdy, and Julia Frankel, "Israel Orders Palestinians to Flee Khan Younis, Signaling Likely New Assault on Southern Gaza City," Associated Press, July 1, 2024.
10. Ruwaida Amer, "In July Came the Evacuation Orders. We Had One Option—a Bombed Gaza Flat," Al Jazeera, July 20, 2024.
11. Greg Myre and Aya Batrawy, "Food Aid Is Piling Up Inside Gaza. Here's Why It's Not Reaching Those in Need," NPR, July 15, 2024.
12. "Eyewitnesses in Gaza Say Israel Is Using Sniper Drones to Shoot Palestinians," NPR, November 26, 2024. The IDF denied indiscriminate shooting by its drones.
13. Emanuel Fabian, "Top Israeli Generals Approve Lebanon Offensive Battle Plans, Army Says," *Times of Israel*, June 19, 2024.
14. Nahal Toosi, Erin Banco, and Lara Seligman, "US to Hezbollah: Don't Count on Us to Stop an Israeli Attack," *Politico*, June 24, 2024.
15. News Wires, "Hamas Drops Key Demand to Accept Phased US Deal on Ceasefire, Hostages," France 24, July 6, 2024; Jonathan Lis, "Netanyahu Hardens Demands, May Derail Talks, Gaza Hostage Deal Sources Say," *Haaretz*, July 13, 2024.
16. Haley Britzky and Natasha Bertrand, "US Military Ends Troubled Temporary Pier Mission Off Gaza Coast," CNN, July 17, 2024.
17. Office of Inspector General, "USAID's Gaza Response: External Factors Impaired Distribution of Humanitarian Assistance through the JLOTS Maritime Corridor," U.S. Agency for International Development, August 27, 2024.
18. "WFP Sounds Alarm: Urgent Action Needed as Food Insecurity in Gaza Reaches Critical Levels," World Food Program USA, October 29, 2024.
19. Alexandra Hutzler, "Biden Dismisses Concerns about Mental Fitness, Says He'd Drop Out if the 'Lord Almighty' Told Him To," ABC News, July 5, 2024; Washington Post Staff, "Read Biden's Letter Telling Democratic Lawmakers He Won't Drop Out of 2024 Race," *Washington Post*, July 8, 2024.
20. Megan Brenan, "Disapproval of Israeli Action in Gaza Eases Slightly in U.S.," Gallup, July 10, 2024.
21. Wafaa Shurafa and Melanie Lidman, "Israel Orders Evacuation of Part of Gaza Humanitarian Zone as War's Toll Passes 39,000 Palestinians," Associated Press, July 22, 2024.
22. Michael Sainato, "Seven Major US Labor Unions Call on Biden to 'Shut Off Military Aid to Israel,'" *The Guardian*, July 23, 2024.
23. Michelle Nichols, "Gay Men Tell U.N. Security Council of Being Islamic State Targets," Reuters, August 24, 2015.

24. Jon Gambrell, "Iran Execution: Man Publicly Hanged from Crane amid Protests," Associated Press, December 12, 2022.
25. "Israel's Far-Right Finance Minister Says He's 'A Fascist Homophobe' but 'Won't Stone Gays,'" *Haaretz*, January 16, 2023.
26. Nick Schifrin and Dan Sagalyn, "Netanyahu Faces Doubts from Israeli Military Leaders over War in Gaza," *NewsHour*, PBS, June 20, 2024.
27. Noa Shpigel, "With Gantz's Backing, Israel's Parliament Passes Resolution Opposing Palestinian Statehood," *Haaretz*, July 18, 2024.
28. Nancy Pelosi, X, July 24, 2024. Under the username @SpeakerPelosi.
29. Office of the Director of National Intelligence, "Statement from Director of National Intelligence Avril Haines on Recent Iranian Influence Efforts," July 9, 2024.
30. I obtained a copy of Van Hollen's letter to Haines. See also Sheera Frenkel, "Israel Secretly Targets U.S. Lawmakers with Influence Campaign on Gaza War," *New York Times*, June 5, 2024.
31. Chris Megerian, "Harris Tries to Thread the Needle on Gaza after Meeting with Netanyahu," Associated Press, July 25, 2024.
32. Barak Ravid, "Netanyahu Irked by 'Critical' Harris Comments," *Axios*, July 26, 2024.
33. TOI Staff, "Poll: Israelis Prefer Netanyahu as PM to Lapid, Bennett and Gantz," *Times of Israel*, July 27, 2024.
34. Ronen Bergman, Patrick Kingsley, and Adam Rasgon, "Israel Was Less Flexible in Recent Gaza Cease-Fire Talks, Documents Show," *New York Times*, August 13, 2024.
35. "Hezbollah Says Top Commander Fuad Shukr Killed in Israeli Strike on Beirut," Al Jazeera, July 31, 2024.
36. "Israel/Lebanon: Hezbollah Attacks Endangered Civilians," Human Rights Watch, March 7, 2025.
37. Al Jazeera Staff, "Blinken Says US Not Involved in Killing of Hamas Political Chief Haniyeh," Al Jazeera, July 31, 2024.
38. Mohammed bin Abdulrahman bin Jassim Al Thani, X, July 31, 2024. Under the username @MBA_AlThani_.
39. Tom Foreman, "American Battleground: How 'Brat Summer' Set Up Kamala Harris' Remarkable Run," CNN, October 30, 2024.
40. Joey Cappelletti, "The Pro-Palestinian 'Uncommitted' Movement Is at a Standstill with Top Democrats as the DNC Begins," Associated Press, August 17, 2024.
41. Abandon Harris campaign, X, August 23, 2024. Under the username @Abandonbiden24.
42. CNN Transcripts, "CNN Monitors Super Tuesday Turnout," CNN, March 5, 2024.
43. Erica L. Green, "Harris Doesn't Support Arms Embargo on Israel, a Top Adviser Says," *New York Times*, August 8, 2024.
44. Philip Gordon, X, January 31, 2026. Under the username @PhilGordonDC.
45. Jeff Zeleny and MJ Lee, "Biden Campaign Chair Gives a Staunch Defense of the President's Health to Donors, Says Campaign Is Clear-Eyed about Debate," CNN, July 1, 2024.
46. Josh Dawsey, Tyler Pager, and Isaac Arnsdorf, *2024: How Trump Retook the White House and the Democrats Lost America* (New York: Random House, 2024).
47. "September 2024 National Poll of Jewish Voters," Jewish Democratic Council of America, September 2024.
48. Barak Ravid, "Biden's Goal: Gaza Deal by the End of Next Week," *Axios*, August 17, 2024.
49. Tara Copp, "US Approves $20 Billion in Weapons Sales to Israel amid Threat of Wider Middle East War," Associated Press, August 13, 2024.
50. Jennifer Hansler, Alex Marquardt, and Michael Conte, "Blinken Says Israel Has Agreed to US Proposal to Close Remaining Gaps on Ceasefire Deal and Calls on Hamas to Do the Same," CNN, August 19, 2024.
51. Alon Pinkas, "Duped Again: The U.S. Somehow Heard Netanyahu Say 'Yes' to a Gaza Deal. He Didn't," *Haaretz*, August 20, 2024.

52. Lauren Egan, Eli Stokols, and Ben Johansen, "Your Unofficial DNC Party Checklist," *Politico*, August 12, 2024.
53. Sanjana Karanth, "The March on the DNC Is a Modern-Day Rainbow Coalition," *HuffPost*, August 19, 2024.
54. "Israeli Strikes Kill 35 in One Day as Gaza Hospitals Warn of Collapse," Al Jazeera, August 19, 2024.
55. Mariana Alfaro and Michael Scherer, "Democrats' Party Platform Doesn't Call for Arms Embargo on Israel," *Washington Post*, August 18, 2024.
56. Akbar Shahid Ahmed, "Gaza War Critics Are Inspired by the 1964 DNC—and They're Playing the Long Game," *HuffPost*, August 23, 2024.
57. Jonathan Weisman, "Worried about a Convention Clash, Democrats Woo Uncommitted Delegates," *New York Times*, August 12, 2024.
58. Alexandria Ocasio-Cortez, "Remarks at the 2024 Democratic National Convention—Aug. 19, 2024," Carrie Chapman Catt Center for Women and Politics, Iowa State University, August 19, 2024.
59. Office for the Coordination of Humanitarian Affairs, "Humanitarian Situation Update #206 | Gaza Strip," United Nations, August 19, 2024.
60. Waleed Shahid, "Inside Uncommitted: The 1-Year Anniversary of a Missed Turn at the DNC," Waleed's Substack, Substack, August 19, 2024.
61. Shahid, "Inside Uncommitted."
62. Michael Brownstein and Alex Madva, "Why the Texas Democrats' Walkout Worked," *New York Times*, August 29, 2024.

CHAPTER 9: ADRIFT

1. "Hamas Releases Video of Injured Israeli American Hostage," *New York Times*, April 24, 2024.
2. Rachel Goldberg-Polin, "My Son Hersh Was Killed in Gaza. I Won't Stop Speaking Out until All Hostages Are Home," *Time*, January 16, 2025.
3. Chantal Da Silva, "Final Hamas Video of Slain Hostage Hersh Goldberg-Polin Should Be a 'Wake-Up Call,' Parents Say," NBC News, September 6, 2024.
4. Rick Aguilar, "Remembering Ayşenur Ezgi Eygi," Middle Eastern Languages and Cultures, University of Washington, September 16, 2024.
5. Frances Mao, "Israel Says 'Highly Likely' Its Troops Killed US-Turkish Protester in West Bank," BBC, September 10, 2024.
6. Franklin Foer, "The War That Would Not End," *The Atlantic*, September 25, 2024; Office of Public Affairs, "Justice Department Announces Terrorism Charges against Senior Leaders of Hamas," U.S. Department of Justice, September 3, 2024.
7. Lazar Berman, "'Hamas List' Is Israel's Original 40-Name July List of Hostages for Release, Minus 4 Murdered in Tunnel, Elderly Man Killed in Captivity, 1 Rescued," *Times of Israel*, January 6, 2025.
8. TOI Staff, "Ex-Hostage Says Ben-Gvir's Comments on Prisoners Led Captors to Beat Him Unconscious," *Times of Israel*, October 17, 2025.
9. Foer, "The War That Would Not End."
10. Alice Speri, "No Path to Justice: Israeli Forces Kept Killing Americans while U.S. Officials Gave Them a Pass," *The Intercept*, July 13, 2022.
11. Jane Arraf, "21 Years after Her Death in Gaza, Palestinians Remember U.S. Activist Rachel Corrie," NPR, March 30, 2024.
12. Betsy Klein, Nikki Carvajal, and Michael Williams, "Biden Condemns 'Totally Unacceptable' Death of American Activist Killed by IDF in the West Bank," CNN, September 11, 2024.

13. Miriam Berger et al., "New Video, Witnesses Challenge Israel's Account of U.S. Activist's Killing," *Washington Post*, September 11, 2024; Hannah Sarisohn, "State Dept. Defends Not Launching Investigation into Aysenur Eygi's Death," *Jerusalem Post*, September 16, 2024.
14. Charles O. Blaha, "The State Department's Wrong Decision to Exempt IDF Unit from Leahy Law Ineligibility," Just Security, August 9, 2024.
15. The IDF suspended the battalion amid an international outcry. Tal Shalev and Jeremy Diamond, "Israeli Military Suspends Battalion Involved in Assaulting, Detaining CNN Crew in West Bank," CNN, March 29, 2026.
16. Ryan Lucas, "DOJ Silent as Families of Americans Killed in West Bank, Gaza Demand It Investigate," *All Things Considered*, NPR, October 13, 2024; "UNRWA Situation Report #121 on the Situation in the Gaza Strip and the West Bank, Including East Jerusalem," United Nations Relief and Works Agency for Palestine Refugees in the Near Middle East, July 16, 2024; "West Bank: Israel Responsible for Rising Settler Violence," Human Rights Watch, April 17, 2024.
17. Office for the Coordination of Humanitarian Affairs, "Humanitarian Situation Update #208 | Gaza Strip [EN/AR/HE]," United Nations, August 23, 2024.
18. "Israel's Siege Now Blocks 83% of Food Aid Reaching Gaza, New Data Reveals," Norwegian Refugee Council, September 16, 2024; "UN Aid Operations Halt in Gaza after Israeli Evacuation Orders: Official," Al Jazeera, August 26, 2024.
19. "Gaza: One Year On," Oxfam International, October 3, 2024.
20. Jeremy Konyndyk and Jesse Marks, "Untangling the Reality of Famine in Gaza," Refugees International, September 12, 2024.
21. Bar Peleg and Chen Maanit, "Two Leaks, Two Tales: Why the Prisoner Abuse Video Leak and the Bild Hamas Document Are Different," *Haaretz*, November 2, 2025.
22. Da Silva, "Final Hamas Video"; Peter Beaumont, "What Is the Philadelphi Corridor, and Why Is It so Important to Israel?," *The Guardian*, September 3, 2024.
23. "Gaza Ceasefire Talks Stall on Fundamental Differences," Soufan Center, September 19, 2024.
24. James M. Dorsey, "Blinken Touts Problematic UAE Plan for Post-War Gaza," *Times of Israel*, October 25, 2024.
25. Thomas L. Friedman, "Giving the Hatemongers No Place to Hide," *Spiegel International*, July 22, 2005.
26. Akbar Shahid Ahmed, "Major Critics of Gaza War Will Not Endorse Harris—but Say Trump Will 'Accelerate the Killing,'" *HuffPost*, September 19, 2024.
27. Amy Spitalnick, X, September 19, 2024. Under the username @amyspitalnick.
28. Charles Homans, "Trump's In-Law Is Trying to Exploit Democrats' Weakness with Arab American Voters," *New York Times*, October 17, 2024.
29. Eileen Travers, "Explainer: What Is Security Council Resolution 1701?," UN News, October 1, 2024.
30. Bassem Mroue and Sarah El Deeb, "Survivors of Israel's Pager Attack on Hezbollah Struggle to Recover," Associated Press, August 6, 2025.
31. Sheera Frenkel, Ronen Bergman, and Hwaida Saad, "How Israel Built a Modern-Day Trojan Horse: Exploding Pagers," *New York Times*, September 18, 2024.
32. "Lebanon: Pager Attacks 'Bear the Hallmarks of a Sinister Dystopian Nightmare'—Witness Testimonies," Amnesty International, September 20, 2024.
33. William Marx, "Did Exploding Pagers Attack on Hezbollah in Lebanon Violate International Law?," NPR, September 20, 2024.
34. "Lebanon: Pager Attacks," Amnesty International.
35. Kathleen Magramo et al., "Walkie-Talkies Explode in Lebanon Day after Deadly Pager Attack," CNN, September 19, 2024.
36. Rob Picheta et al., "'New Era' of War Beginning, Israel Says, as More Hezbollah Devices Explode across Lebanon," CNN, September 19, 2024.

37. Office of the High Commissioner for Human Rights, "Exploding Pagers and Radios: A Terrifying Violation of International Law, Say UN Experts," United Nations, September 19, 2024.
38. Jacob N. Kornbluh, X, March 19, 2025. Under username @jacobkornbluh.
39. Magramo et al., "Walkie-Talkies Explode"; Barak Ravid, "Israel Conducted Lebanon Pager Attack Fearing Hezbollah Was onto the Operation," *Axios*, September 18, 2024; Lazar Berman, "Security Establishment Shocked Netanyahu Spilled Secret Details of Pager Op—Report," *Times of Israel*, April 29, 2025.
40. Souad Mekhennet and Joby Warrick, "Mossad's Pager Operation: Inside Israel's Penetration of Hezbollah," *Washington Post*, October 5, 2024.
41. Bradford Betz, "John Kirby Denies US Involvement in Lebanon Device Attacks: 'We Want to See the War End,'" Fox News, September 18, 2024; Imtiaz Tyab and Haley Ott, "Israel Conducts 'Targeted Strike' in Beirut Despite U.S. Warning against Escalation after Pager Explosions," CBS News, September 20, 2024; Mekhennet and Warrick, "Mossad's Pager Operation."
42. "Lebanon Says 558 Killed as Israel Bombs Hezbollah, Fueling a Chaotic Exodus and Flight Cancellations," CBS News, September 24, 2024.
43. Cate Brown, "Israeli Strikes in Lebanon Have Been Most Intense and Deadly in Decades," *Washington Post*, October 2, 2024.
44. Barak Ravid, "U.S. Fears War in Lebanon but Hopes Israeli Attacks Push Hezbollah to a Deal," *Axios*, September 21, 2024.
45. "Israel 'Spreading Terror,' Lebanon's PM Tells UN Security Council," Al Jazeera, September 26, 2024; Jonathan Lemire et al., "Biden Told Allies That Netanyahu Doesn't Want to End Fighting in Lebanon," *Politico*, September 27, 2024.
46. Barak Ravid, "Netanyahu Distances Himself from U.S.-Led Proposal for Ceasefire in Lebanon," *Axios*, September 26, 2024.
47. Lazar Berman and Jacob Magid, "Netanyahu Says Israel 'Shares the Aims' of US Truce Proposal, after Rejecting It," *Times of Israel*, September 27, 2024; Lemire et al., "Biden Told Allies."
48. "Israel Says It Has Secured $8.7 Billion In US Military Aid," France 24, September 26, 2024.
49. "Israel's Forced Displacement Orders in Lebanon May Constitute Grave Breaches of International Humanitarian Law, Say Aid Agencies," Oxfam International, December 19, 2024.
50. Daniel Johnson, "Lebanon Crisis: Over One Million People Flee Strikes amid Invasion Fears," UN News, September 30, 2024.
51. Akbar Shahid Ahmed, "Israel Is Preparing a Risky Incursion into Lebanon—as Biden Stands By," *HuffPost*, September 30, 2024.
52. Josef Federman, Matthew Lee, and Abby Sewell, "Israel Begins Ground Offensive against Hezbollah in Southern Lebanon," Associated Press, September 30, 2024.
53. Patrick Kingsley et al., "Israeli Military Announces Ground Invasion of Southern Lebanon," *New York Times*, September 30, 2024.
54. Natasha Bertrand, Kayla Tausche, and Oren Liebermann, "US Is Not Currently Pushing to Revive Israel-Hezbollah Ceasefire Deal, Officials Say," CNN, October 7, 2024.
55. "Lebanon: Israeli Attacks on Medics Apparent War Crimes," Human Rights Watch, October 30, 2024.
56. "Syrian Refugees in Lebanon Face a Crisis within a Crisis," Tahrir Institute for Middle East Policy, October 10, 2024; "Regime Arrests Nine Syrians Returning from Lebanon," *Enab Baladi*, October 2, 2024.
57. Melanie Lidman, Bassam Hatoum, and Bassem Mroue, "Israel Expands Its Bombardment in Lebanon as Thousands Flee Widening War," Associated Press, October 5, 2024.
58. "Nowhere to Return," Amnesty International, August 26, 2025.
59. Maya Rosen, "Inside the Movement to Settle Southern Lebanon," *Jewish Currents*, August 19, 2024.

60. Jason DeRose, "Anti-Muslim Bias Reports Skyrocket after Oct. 7 Hamas Attack on Israel," NPR, April 2, 2024.
61. Antony J. Blinken, "Anniversary of October 7th Attack," U.S. Embassy Cairo, October 7, 2024.
62. Daniel Estrin et al., "Israeli Strike on Gaza Mosque Kills 19 as Conflict Widens in Lebanon," NPR, October 6, 2024.
63. Yuval Barnea, "Israel Border Police Officer Killed in Beersheba Terror Attack, Nine Wounded," *Jerusalem Post*, October 6, 2024.
64. Yaniv Kubovich, "IDF Ordered Hannibal Directive on October 7 to Prevent Hamas Taking Soldiers Captive," *Haaretz*, July 7, 2024; Emanuel Fabian, "Efrat Katz Likely Killed by IAF Helicopter Fire during Oct. 7 Abduction Attempt—Probe," *Times of Israel*, April 5, 2024; Yoav Zeiton and Ronen Bergman, "The First Hours of Black Sabbath," *Ynet News*, January 12, 2024. Originally in Hebrew.
65. Aaron Reich, "All Means Are Kosher: A Look at the IDF's Controversial Hannibal Directive—Explainer," *Jerusalem Post*, February 27, 2025.
66. Sam Stokol and Jessica Steinberg, "At Separate Memorials, Families Demand Accountability as PM Touts Israeli 'Strength,'" *Times of Israel*, October 8, 2024; Nadav Gavrielov, "'Now You're Dead': Freed Hostage Recounts Captivity in Gaza," *New York Times*, April 16, 2025; Office for the Coordination of Humanitarian Affairs, "One Year of Unimaginable Suffering since the 7 October Attack," United Nations, October 7, 2024.
67. "Repeal the Ban on Red Cross Visits to Palestinian Prisoners," Association for Civil Rights in Israel, August 24, 2024.
68. Jeremy Sharon, "High Court Orders Gov't to Justify Ban on Red Cross Visits for Palestinian Prisoners," *Times of Israel*, August 27, 2024.
69. Graeme Baker, "How Israel Killed Hamas Leader Sinwar in a Chance Encounter," BBC, October 17, 2024.
70. Yossi Verter, "End the War? Netanyahu Is Set to Use Sinwar's Death to Keep Himself in Power," *Haaretz*, October 18, 2024.
71. Lazar Berman, "After Sinwar Killing, Netanyahu Sees Vindication in His Rafah Approach," *Times of Israel*, October 18, 2024.
72. Benjamin Netanyahu, X, October 17, 2024. Under the username @netanyahu.
73. "Joe Biden Calls Death of Yahya Sinwar an 'Opportunity to Seek Peace' in Gaza," France 24, October 18, 2024.
74. Jason Burke, "Death of Yahya Sinwar Is Boost for Netanyahu but May Not End War," *The Guardian*, October 17, 2024.
75. Steve Hendrix and Hazem Balousha, "Israeli Siege Plan for Gaza under Scrutiny as U.S. Demands Urgent Change," *Washington Post*, October 16, 2024; "Northern Gaza: 130,000 Children under 10 Deprived of Food and Medicine during 50 Days of Siege," Save the Children, November 25, 2024.
76. Mark Landler, "'Erase Gaza': War Unleashes Incendiary Rhetoric in Israel," *New York Times*, November 15, 2023.
77. Akbar Shahid Ahmed, "'Unprecedented in Modern History': U.S. Aid Experts Warn Gaza Likely Already Experiencing Famine," *HuffPost*, April 2, 2024; Ellen Knickmeyer and Russ Bynum, "A Senior UN Official Says Northern Gaza Is Now in 'Full-Blown Famine,'" Associated Press, May 3, 2024; Konyndyk and Marks, "Untangling the Reality of Famine in Gaza."
78. "New Evacuation Orders Worsen the Humanitarian Catastrophe in Gaza," Doctors Without Borders, October 8, 2024.
79. "New Evacuation Orders," Doctors Without Borders.
80. Office of the High Commissioner of Human Rights, "OHCHR Is Appalled at the Desperate Situation in the North Gaza," United Nations, October 14, 2024.
81. Salma Altaweel, "Life in Northern Gaza: A Voice from the Ground," Norwegian Refugee Council, October 11, 2024.

82. Abdel Kareem Hana and Tia Goldenberg, "Palestinians Confront a Landscape of Destruction in Gaza's 'Ghost Towns,'" Associated Press, January 21, 2025.
83. Peter Beaumont, "'Everything Is Gone': How Israeli Forces Destroyed Jabaliya Refugee Camp," *The Guardian*, December 18, 2024.
84. Omer Bartov, "The Hamas Attack and Israel's War in Gaza," Council for Global Cooperation, November 24, 2023; Bezalel Smotrich, X, November 19, 2023. Under the username @bezalelsm.
85. Sam Sokol, "Netanyahu Tells Lawmakers He's Considering 'Generals' Plan' to Lay Siege to Northern Gaza," *Times of Israel*, September 22, 2024.
86. Government of Israel et al., "Respondents' Response to Request for Interim Order Dated October 14, 2024," Gisha, October 14, 2024. Unofficial translation by Gisha.
87. Aaron Boxerman et al., "Israel Builds Bases in Central Gaza, a Sign It May Be There to Stay," *New York Times*, December 2, 2024; Emanuel Fabian, "In Gaza's Netzarim Corridor, IDF Establishes Temporary Bases for an Indefinite Stay," *Times of Israel*, December 28, 2024.
88. Daniel Estrin, "Israeli Settlers in Gaza? Netanyahu's Allies Lay Out a Strategy," NPR, October 25, 2024.
89. Ivana Kottasová, Kareem Khadder, and Mohammad Al-Sawalh, "'We Came Back for Nothing': Returning Home to Northern Gaza, Palestinians Find Death and Destruction," CNN, January 31, 2025.
90. "The Atmosphere Among Palestinians Who Returned to the Northern Gaza Strip," Meir Amit Intelligence and Terrorism Information Center, Israeli Intelligence Heritage and Commemoration Center, February 9, 2025.
91. Adam Rasgon, "Laborer from Gaza Is First Reported Fatality of Iran's Missile Attack," *New York Times*, October 1, 2024; "Iran Says Missiles Fired at Israel in Response to Assassinations," Al Jazeera, October 1, 2024.
92. Al Jazeera Staff, "US Says Helped Israel Thwart Iranian Attack, Reasserts 'Ironclad' Support," Al Jazeera, October 1, 2024; Nandita Bose and Kanishka Singh, "Biden Says He Would Weigh Alternatives to Striking Iranian Oil if He Were in Israel's Shoes," Reuters, October 4, 2024.
93. TOI Staff, "How Biden Pushed Israel to Limit Its Retaliatory Strike on Iran," *Times of Israel*, October 28, 2024.
94. John Hudson, Michael Birnbaum, and Ellen Nakashima, "Israel Likely to Strike Iran in Coming Months, Warns U.S. Intelligence," *Washington Post*, February 12, 2025.
95. Bethan McKernan, "US Attacks Houthi Targets in Yemen with B-2 Stealth Bombers for First Time," *The Guardian*, October 17, 2024.
96. Alon Strimling, "The U.S. General Israel Doesn't Want to Strike Iran Without," *Ynet Global*, April 19, 2025.
97. Safia K. Southey, "Deterrence or Creep? US Forces Quietly Surge Back to Middle East," *Responsible Statecraft*, April 24, 2025.
98. Léonie Chao-Fong, Daniel Lavelle, and Amy Sedghi, "At Least One Child Killed and 10 Injured Each Day in Lebanon, Says Unicef," *The Guardian*, October 31, 2024; Barak Ravid, "Biden Advisers to Visit Israel to Try to Seal a Deal to End War in Lebanon," *Axios*, October 29, 2024.
99. Benjamin Giltner and Jonathan Ellis Allen, "Fact-Checking Biden's Speech about US Conflicts," Cato Institute, July 26, 2024.
100. Renee Maltezou and Yomna Ehab, "U.S. Strikes at Houthi Targets in Yemen after Claim of Attack on Destroyers," Reuters, August 8, 2024.

CHAPTER 10: CRAVING A HERO'S DEPARTURE

1. See discussion below.
2. Al Jazeera Staff, "At Least 404 Killed as Israel Unleashes Strikes on Gaza, Breaking Ceasefire," Al Jazeera, March 18, 2025.

3. Ron Kampeas, "Republicans Sign Letter Backing Israel's Right to Set Its Own Borders," *Times of Israel*, June 23, 2020.
4. Andrew Lapin, "In Twin Events for Michigan Jewish Voters, Doug Emhoff and Ritchie Torres Stress Kamala Harris' Pro-Israel Bona Fides," Jewish Telegraphic Agency, October 21, 2024.
5. Al Jazeera Staff, "Bill Clinton Criticised for Saying Israel 'Forced' to Kill Gaza Civilians," Al Jazeera, October 31, 2024.
6. Caroline Vakil, "Trump Lashes Out at Cheney, Calls Her a 'Muslim-Hating Warmonger,'" *The Hill*, October 26, 2024.
7. Barak Ravid, "Gaza Ceasefire and Hostage Deal Gets Renewed Push after Two-Month Deadlock," *Axios*, October 24, 2024.
8. Aaron Boxerman and Matthew Mpoke Bigg, "Israel's Parliament Passes Bills Banning Agency That Aids Palestinians," *New York Times*, October 28, 2024.
9. Daniel Estrin, "A Recent Strike in Gaza Was Among the War's Deadliest, a List of the Victims Shows," *All Things Considered*, NPR, December 23, 2024.
10. Daniel Estrin et al., "One Family. One Attack. 132 Names," NPR, April 27, 2025.
11. Lazar Berman, "PM Spokesman Eli Feldstein Suspected of Leaking Intel That May Have Hurt Hostage Efforts," *Times of Israel*, November 4, 2024.
12. Jon Donnison and George Wright, "Protests Erupt in Israel after Netanyahu Fires Defence Minister," BBC, November 5, 2024.
13. Hillary Anderson et al., "What Happened in 2024," Catalist, May 2025.
14. "Analyzing the 2024 Presidential Vote: PRRI's Post-Election Survey," Public Religion Research Institute, December 13, 2024; Stephen Fowler, "After Major 2024 Defeats, the Democratic Party Searches for a New Direction," NPR, January 18, 2025.
15. Domenico Montanaro, "Trump Falls Just Below 50% in Popular Vote, but Gets More Than in Past Elections," NPR, December 3, 2024.
16. Akbar Shahid Ahmed, "Looming Trump Presidency Set to Embolden Netanyahu and Hurt Palestinians," *HuffPost*, November 9, 2024; Jason DeRose and A Martínez, "What Trump Team's Christian Zionism Beliefs Mean for Gaza War, West Bank Settlements," NPR, December 2, 2024; Andrew Kaczynski, "Mike Huckabee Once Said That 'There's Really No Such Thing as a Palestinian,'" CNN, November 12, 2024.
17. "New Poll Shows Gaza Was a Top Issue for Biden 2020 Voters Who Cast a Ballot for Someone Besides Harris," Institute for Middle East Understanding Policy Project, January 2025.
18. Ahmed, "Looming Trump Presidency."
19. Cindy McCain, X, November 8, 2024. Under the username @WFPChief.
20. Missy Ryan, "U.S. Declined to Sanction Israeli Military Units over Abuse Finding," *Washington Post*, February 28, 2025; Israel Defense Forces, "Reservist Soldier Verdict for Abuse against Prisoners at 'Sde Teiman,'" February 6, 2025; International Investigations and Visuals Teams, "Strapped Down, Blindfolded, Held in Diapers: Israeli Whistleblowers Detail Abuse of Palestinians in Shadowy Detention Center," CNN, May 11, 2024.
21. Jonathan Guyer, "US Officials Attend Gaza Aid Meetings on Site of Israeli Prison Accused of 'Horrific' Torture," *The Guardian*, October 14, 2024.
22. David Hodari and Erin McLaughlin, "Stern U.S. Letter Prompts Israel to Allow First Aid into Northern Gaza This Month. Will It Last?," NBC News, October 16, 2024.
23. Finer declined to address this account.
24. Mercy Corps et al., "The Gaza Scorecard," November 2024.
25. Claire Parker et al., "Gangs Looting Gaza Aid Operate in Areas under Israeli Control, Aid Groups Say," *Washington Post*, November 18, 2024.
26. Barak Ravid, "U.S. Won't Suspend Military Aid to Israel as Gaza Deadline Expires," *Axios*, November 12, 2024.
27. Office of the High Commissioner for Human Rights, "Violence Continues to Intensify in the Occupied West Bank," United Nations, December 6, 2024.

28. Akbar Shahid Ahmed, "Exclusive: White House Says Democrats Who Oppose Weapons to Israel Are Aiding Hamas," *HuffPost*, November 20, 2024.
29. "19 Senators Vote against More U.S. Weapons for Israel in Rebuke to Biden," *HuffPost*, November 20, 2024.
30. "Israel/OPT: Israeli Attacks Targeting Hamas and Other Armed Group Fighters That Killed Scores of Displaced Civilians in Rafah Should Be Investigated as War Crimes," Amnesty International, August 27, 2024.
31. Jacob Kornbluh, "AIPAC Attacks Democrats Who Voted to Stop Arms Sales to Israel," *The Forward*, April 8, 2025; Akbar Shahid Ahmed, "Democrats Wrote Off Anti-War Activists in 2024. Now Concern for Gaza Is Unavoidable," *HuffPost*, August 26, 2025.
32. Robbie Gramer, "The Sullivan-Waltz channel," *Politico*, January 8, 2025; U.S. Institute of Peace, "Passing the Baton 2025: Securing America's Future in an Era of Strategic Competition," January 14, 2025.
33. "Situation in the State of Palestine: ICC Pre-Trial Chamber I Rejects the State of Israel's Challenges to Jurisdiction and Issues Warrants of Arrest for Benjamin Netanyahu and Yoav Gallant," International Criminal Court, November 21, 2024.
34. Harry Davies and Robert Flummerfelt, "Second Woman Accuses ICC Chief Prosecutor Karim Khan of Sexual Misconduct," *The Guardian*, August 28, 2025; Harry Davies, "Sexual Abuse Claims Have Dragged the International Criminal Court into Crisis—but What Happens Now?" *The Guardian*, April 11, 2026
35. Stéphanie Maupas, "ICC Member States Divided over Prosecutor Karim Khan's fate," *Le Monde*, March 27, 2026.
36. Harry Davies et al., "Spying, Hacking and Intimidation: Israel's Nine-Year 'War' on the ICC Exposed," *The Guardian*, May 28, 2024; Harry Davies, "Revealed: Israeli Spy Chief 'Threatened' ICC Prosecutor over War Crimes Inquiry," *The Guardian*, May 28, 2024; David Hearst and Imran Mulla, "Exclusive: How Karim Khan's Israel War Crimes Probe Was Derailed by Threats, Leaks and Sex Claims," *Middle East Eye*, June 9, 2025; Mehdi Hasan, "World Exclusive: Mehdi Interviews ICC Chief Prosecutor on Israel Arrest Warrants, Backlash from the US and UK, and Sexual Misconduct Allegations," Zeteo, Substack, April 29, 2026.
37. Chloe Hadjimatheou, "Threat of US Sanctions over Gaza Forced Me Out, Says ICC Lawyer," *The Observer*, June 29, 2025; International Criminal Court, X, May 3, 2024. Under the username @IntlCrimCourt; Belgium UN New York, X, June 14, 2024. Under the username @BelgiumUN.
38. Krisztina Than and Friederike Heine, "Orban Invites Netanyahu to Hungary as ICC Warrant Divides Europeans," Reuters, November 22, 2024; Mike Lillis and Mychael Schnell, "Biden Opposition Leaves House Bill Hitting ICC in Limbo," *The Hill*, May 30, 2024.
39. Alex de Waal, "How Many People Have Died of Starvation in Gaza?," World Peace Foundation, December 17, 2024.
40. Lindsey Graham, X, November 21, 2024. Under the username @LindseyGrahamSC.
41. Dennis Ross, "How the Trump Factor Pushed Israel Towards Lebanon Ceasefire," Washington Institute for Near East Policy, December 1, 2024.
42. Office of the High Commissioner for Refugees, "What Is Happening in Lebanon?," United Nations, December 2, 2024.
43. Mia McCarthy, "Trump's National Security Pick: I'm on Same Page as Jake Sullivan about 'Our Adversaries,'" *Politico*, November 24, 2024.
44. Ali Bianco, "Biden's Former Natsec Adviser Says Ex-President's Debate Performance Was 'a Shock to Me,'" *Politico*, May 15, 2025.
45. McGurk denied this occurred; a third official present at the meeting told me that it did.
46. Ben Samuels, "Trump Reportedly Taps Michael Waltz, Pro-Israel Green Beret, as National Security Advisor," *Haaretz*, November 12, 2024.
47. Gramer, "The Sullivan-Waltz Channel."
48. Adam Rasgon, Aaron Boxerman, and Ronen Bergman, "Cease-Fire Talks between Israel and Hamas Gain Momentum, Officials Say," *New York Times*, December 9, 2024.

49. "Gaza: 'Sickening Normalisation' of Suffering, amid Attacks on People and Aid Convoys," UN News, December 13, 2024.
50. Matthew Mpoke Bigg and Aaron Boxerman, "Israeli Forces Kill 2 Palestinian Militants Wanted in Deadly Attack," *New York Times*, January 23, 2025.
51. Avery Lotz, "Sen. Graham Calls on White House to Normalize Relations between Saudi Arabia and Israel," CNN, April 28, 2024.
52. Herzog did not respond to a request for comment.
53. John Kirby, "On-the-Record Press Gaggle by White House National Security Communications Advisor John Kirby," White House, December 10, 2024; Ayman Mohyeldin and Rajaa Elidrissi, "U.S. Officials Say They Want Peace for Syrians. Their Actions Tell a Much Different Story," MSNBC, December 16, 2024.
54. Hadeel Al-Shalchi, "In Syria's Golan Heights Buffer Zone, Residents Fear Israel Is Making a Land Grab," NPR, January 23, 2025.
55. Bethan McKernan, "Israeli Military Organises Tourist Tours of Newly Occupied Syrian Territory," *The Guardian*, April 11, 2025.
56. Tyler Pager, "Joe Biden's Lonely Battle to Sell His Vision of American Democracy," *Washington Post*, December 28, 2024.
57. Maram Humaid, "'Entire Days without Food': Six Palestinians in Gaza Describe How They Struggle to Feed Their Families amid the War," Al Jazeera, December 11, 2024.
58. "Food Shortages in Gaza: A Protection Nightmare," ReliefWeb, December 2, 2024.
59. "Just Twelve Aid Trucks of Food and Water into the North Gaza Governorate in 2.5 Months," Oxfam International, December 22, 2024.
60. Akbar Shahid Ahmed, "Biden Discussed Potential Israeli War Crimes in Gaza. He Kicked the Can to Trump," *HuffPost*, November 7, 2025.
61. Erin Banco, Jonathan Landay, and Humeyra Pamuk, "Exclusive: US Intel Found Israeli Military Lawyers Warned There Was Evidence of Gaza War Crimes, Former US Officials Say," Reuters, November 7, 2025.
62. See, e.g., International Committee of the Red Cross, "What Is International Humanitarian Law?," May 7, 2022; Ryan Goodman, Michael W. Meier, and Tess Bridgeman, "Expert Guidance: Law of Armed Conflict in the Israel-Hamas War," *Just Security*, October 17, 2023.
63. Joseph R. Biden, Jr., "Memorandum on United States Conventional Arms Transfer Policy," White House, February 23, 2023. Two State Department officials told me another U.S.-Israeli discussion about the channel occurred before Biden left the presidency; the channel was never established, however.
64. Erin Banco and Jonathan Landay, "Exclusive: US Briefly Withheld Some Intelligence from Israel during Biden Era," Reuters, December 12, 2025.
65. Blinken declined to comment on his use of the term.
66. Blinken declined to comment on his treatment of these recommendations.
67. Al Jazeera Staff, "Retraction of US-Backed Gaza Famine Report Draws Anger, Scrutiny," Al Jazeera, December 26, 2024.
68. Susan Page, "Read What Joe Biden Said during His Exclusive Interview with USA TODAY: Transcript," *USA Today*, January 8, 2025.
69. Barak Ravid, "Trump Blasts Netanyahu for Disloyalty: 'F**k Him,'" *Axios*, December 10, 2021.
70. Karen DeYoung, Shira Rubin, and Gerry Shih, "An Unlikely Team of U.S. Negotiators Wrestled Israel and Hamas to a Ceasefire," *Washington Post*, January 18, 2025.
71. Joseph Gedeon, "Trump Shares Inflammatory Video with Crude Reference to Netanyahu," *The Guardian*, January 9, 2025.
72. DeYoung et al., "An Unlikely Team."
73. DeYoung et al., "An Unlikely Team."
74. Lucas Lilieholm et al., "January 15, 2025 Gaza Ceasefire Deal News," CNN, January 15, 2025.
75. "Gaza Ceasefire Negotiations on 'Verge of Collapse,'" *Middle East Monitor*, December 30, 2024.

76. "Kamal Adwan Hospital Out of Service following a Raid Yesterday and Repeated Attacks since October," World Health Organization, December 28, 2024; Shatha Yaish, "Israel Brutally Detaining Gaza Hospital Director as 'Bargaining Chip,' Says Lawyer," *+972 Magazine*, July 22, 2025.
77. Joe Biden, "Remarks by President Biden on Reaching a Ceasefire and Hostage Deal," White House, January 19, 2025.
78. Molly Nagle and Kelsey Walsh, "Administration Official Shares Inside Story of How Hamas-Israel Deal Came About," ABC News, January 15, 2025; David E. Sanger and Michael D. Shear, "How the Cease-Fire Push Brought Together Biden and Trump's Teams," *New York Times*, January 15, 2025.
79. Lorenzo Tondo, Bethan McKernan, and Peter Beaumont, "Gaza Ceasefire Begins with Release of Three Israeli Hostages," *The Guardian*, January 19, 2025.
80. "Tears, Hugs Greet 90 Palestinian Women, Children Freed from Israeli Prisons," Al Jazeera, January 20, 2025.
81. Bar Peleg and Hagar Shezaf, "Israel Says 40,000 Palestinians 'Evacuated' West Bank Refugee Camps, Vows to Stay for a Year," *Haaretz*, February 23, 2025.
82. Steve Holland, Nandita Bose, and Kanishka Singh, "Trump Makes 2,000-Pound Bombs Available to Israel, Undoing Biden Pause," Reuters, January 25, 2025; Omar Shakir, "Israel Imports Gaza Abuses into the West Bank," Human Rights Watch, February 26, 2025.

EPILOGUE

1. Natan Odenheimer, "No Proof Hamas Routinely Stole U.N. Aid, Israeli Military Officials Say," *New York Times*, July 26, 2025.
2. "WFP Runs Out of Food Stocks in Gaza," UN News, April 25, 2025; Inger Ashing et al., "'Let Us Do Our Jobs'—Major Aid Groups in Gaza Warn Aid System Is Collapsing," Oxfam, Oxfam America, April 17, 2025.
3. Oxfam, Instagram, May 8, 2025. Under the username @oxfamamerica.
4. Aya Al-Hattab, "Israel Is Starving Us in Gaza. This Is What That Feels Like," *The Guardian*, May 6, 2025.
5. Mike Huckabee, X, April 21, 2025. Under the username @USAmbIsrael.
6. Office for the Coordination of Humanitarian Affairs, "Palestinians across Gaza Unsafe Six Months On from Ceasefire Announcement, Says Türk," United Nations, April 10, 2026.
7. "'I Witnessed War Crimes in Gaza,' Former Worker at GHF Aid Site Tells BBC," BBC News, 25 July, 2025.
8. Akbar Shahid Ahmed, "Past 'The Point of No Return': Doctor Gives On-the-Ground Insight into Starvation in Gaza," *HuffPost*, July 28, 2025.
9. "Famine Confirmed for First Time in Gaza," World Health Organization, August 22, 2025.
10. Office for the Coordination of Humanitarian Affairs, "Humanitarian Situation Update #355 | Gaza Strip," United Nations, January 29, 2026.
11. Emilie Madi and Maya Gebeily, "Nearly a Year after Truce, Women in South Lebanon Say War Never Ended," Reuters, October 23, 2025.
12. Akbar Shahid Ahmed, "Trump Administration Slaps Sanctions on Prominent U.N. Official Critical of Israel," *HuffPost*, July 9, 2025.
13. Rishi Iyengar and Christina Lu, "Trump's New National Security Strategy Goes Full 'America First,'" *Foreign Policy*, December 10, 2025.
14. Akbar Shahid Ahmed, "A Top Biden Official Is Pushing an Urgent Post-Gaza Plan That's Alarming Some Insiders," *HuffPost*, January 12, 2024.
15. See, e.g., Jacob Lew and David Satterfield, "How to Stop a Humanitarian Catastrophe in

Gaza," *Foreign Affairs*, August 14, 2025; Kat Lonsdorf, Tom Bowman, and Fatma Tanis, "'We Didn't Do Enough': How U.S. Policy Failed Palestinians in Gaza," NPR, August 28, 2025.

16. Akbar Shahid Ahmed, "Biden Discussed Potential Israeli War Crimes in Gaza. He Kicked the Can to Trump," *HuffPost*, November 7, 2025.
17. Antony Blinken, "Trump's Iran Strike Was a Mistake. I Hope It Succeeds," *New York Times*, June 24, 2025.
18. Aaron David Miller, "'That Is a Five-Alarm Fire': Jake Sullivan on the Past and Future of U.S. Foreign Policy," Carnegie Endowment for International Peace, March 13, 2025.
19. Amos Hochstein, X, January 27, 2026. Under the username @AmosHochstein.
20. Jacob Magid, "Former Top Biden Aide Says He Now Backs Withholding Weapons from Israel," *Times of Israel*, August 28, 2025; "Is America Losing the High Ground? A Conversation with Jake Sullivan," *Foreign Affairs*, April 23, 2026.
21. Thomas Wright, "What If 'America First' Appears to Work?," *The Atlantic*, November 18, 2025.
22. Yasmeen Serhan, "A New Word Is Defining the Israeli-Palestinian Conflict in Washington," *The Atlantic*, May 21, 2021.

INDEX